Tammy,

Here's a small gift to help you along the way as you embark on your career as a Neuropsychologist.

It has been a great year working with you and I genuinely enjoyed being your supervisor.

Remember, the door is always open —.

Best

10-25-2013

CLINICAL PRACTICE
OF FORENSIC NEUROPSYCHOLOGY

Also from Kyle Brauer Boone

Assessment of Feigned Cognitive Impairment:
A Neuropsychological Perspective

Edited by Kyle Brauer Boone

Clinical Practice of Forensic Neuropsychology

An Evidence-Based Approach

KYLE BRAUER BOONE

THE GUILFORD PRESS
New York   London

© 2013 The Guilford Press
A Division of Guilford Publications, Inc.
72 Spring Street, New York, NY 10012
www.guilford.com

Printed in the United States of America

This book is printed on acid-free paper.

Last digit is print number: 9 8 7 6 5 4 3 2 1

The author has checked with sources believed to be reliable in her efforts to provide
information that is complete and generally in accord with the standards of practice that
are accepted at the time of publication. However, in view of the possibility of human error
or changes in behavioral, mental health, or medical sciences, neither the author, nor the
editor and publisher, nor any other party who has been involved in the preparation or
publication of this work warrants that the information contained herein is in every respect
accurate or complete, and they are not responsible for any errors or omissions or the
results obtained from the use of such information. Readers are encouraged to confirm the
information contained in this book with other sources.

Library of Congress Cataloging-in-Publication Data

Boone, K. B. (Kyle Brauer)
  Clinical practice of forensic neuropsychology : an evidence-based approach /
by Kyle Brauer Boone.
    p. cm. — (Evidence-based practice in neuropsychology)
  Includes bibliographical references and index.
  ISBN 978-1-4625-0717-7 (hard cover : alk. paper)
  1. Forensic neuropsychology.   I. Title.
  RA1147.5.B66 2013
  614′.15—dc23
                                         2012023450

To Beverly Jane Canine Brauer

As a teenager, my mother was identified as intellectually gifted, and she set as her goal a career in medicine. Unfortunately, in her generation women were rarely helped or encouraged to earn advanced degrees, and she was not able to pursue this career. However, she did have a vision for me: When I was a teenager, and a friend of hers asked when I was going to marry, my mother announced, "She is going to graduate school and not getting married until she is 24." Both predictions came true. I have the career she was meant to have, and I dedicate this book to her.

About the Author

Kyle Brauer Boone, PhD, ABPP, ABCN, is Professor in the California School of Forensic Studies at Alliant International University in Los Angeles and Clinical Professor in the Department of Psychiatry and Biobehavioral Sciences at the University of California, Los Angeles. She is the author of over 100 peer-reviewed research articles, including many on the development and validation of tests to detect feigned cognitive symptoms; the editor of the book *Assessment of Feigned Cognitive Impairment: A Neuropsychological Perspective*; and the author of two tests to detect noncredible cognitive performance, the Dot Counting Test and the b Test. Dr. Boone served on the committee that developed practice guidelines for clinical neuropsychology, which were published by the American Academy of Clinical Neuropsychology (AACN) in 2007; she was also an invited attendee of the 25-member consensus conference that developed practice guidelines for the identification of feigned cognitive symptoms, subsequently published by AACN in 2009. Dr. Boone is board-certified in clinical neuropsychology and is a Fellow of the American Psychological Association and the National Academy of Neuropsychology.

About the Author

Preface

Within the field of psychology, there has been an emerging interest in and emphasis on *evidence-based* practice—that is, on interventions and assessment strategies with an empirical basis. When I was in graduate training, conclusions regarding psychological test results frequently were based on professional folklore and "cookbook" guidelines that often had no supporting documentation. The findings detailed in psychodiagnostic reports were frequently poetic, but one was left wondering, "Where did this come from?," with the suspicion that interpretations were idiosyncratic and probably illuminated more about the psychologist than the patient.

Psychological assessment reports have huge impacts on the lives of those who undergo the exams, and errors in interpretations can have major ramifications. The results of psychological testing are relied upon in determinations of whether individuals should receive disability compensation, lawsuit damages, classroom accommodations, and medications, as well as whether they are competent to stand trial or manage their own affairs (including independent living, parenting, handling finances, and driving). Therefore, it is critical that test interpretations be reliable and accurate, and this can only occur if they are grounded in the empirical literature. The purpose of this book is to challenge and assist neuropsychologists to pursue evidence-based clinical forensic practice.

Chapter 1 covers topics related to conducting a neuropsychological exam, with a focus on issues specific to forensic practice. These include requests for observers, treater–expert relationships, and demands that test names be provided to the test taker and counsel prior to the exam. Critical areas to be covered within the pretest interview are also outlined, as well as the problems associated with interviewing collateral informants. The chapter proceeds with a discussion of neuropsychological test selection in a forensic context, as well as concerns and recommendations regarding the testing of patients who do not speak or are not fluent in English, the use of technicians, and documentation of the exam. The chapter concludes with tips regarding the types of behavioral observations that are particularly informative in a forensic context.

Chapter 2 systematically addresses the incorporation of symptom validity tests (SVTs) in the forensic neurocognitive exam, as well as additional techniques for identifying negative response bias. The individual SVTs have been cataloged and critiqued elsewhere (Boone, 2007a; Larrabee, 2007; Victor, Kulick, & Boone, in press-a, in press-b), and this chapter instead focuses on considerations in the selection and interpretation of these measures.

Chapter 3 provides a comprehensive summary and critique of the literature on the effectiveness of tests specifically developed to identify psychological symptom overreport: the M Test, the original Structured Interview of Reported Symptoms (SIRS) and its revision (SIRS-2), the Miller Forensic Assessment of Symptoms Test (M-FAST), the Structured Inventory of Malingered Symptomatology (SIMS), and the Morel Emotional Numbing Test (MENT). In the companion chapter, Chapter 4, literature on the ability of standard psychological tests to detect overreport of psychological symptoms is analyzed. Commonly used personality inventories are covered, including the Minnesota Multiphasic Personality Inventory–2 (MMPI-2) instruments (but with a focus on the MMPI-2–Restructured Form [MMPI-2–RF]), the Millon Clinical Multiaxial Inventory–III (MCMI-III), and the Personality Assessment Inventory (PAI), as well as projective techniques (e.g., Rorschach Inkblot Test, Draw-a-Person Test). In addition, measures specific to posttraumatic stress disorder (PTSD) are covered: the original and revised Trauma Symptom Inventory (TSI and TSI-2) and the Detailed Assessment of Posttraumatic Stress (DAPS). Special emphasis is placed on research examining whether the various tests are also able to identify noncredible cognitive/somatic symptom overreport. An attempt has been made to provide detailed information on the various studies to allow careful scrutiny of the underlying methodology, because in many cases irregularities in research design have limited the usefulness of the resulting data.

Chapter 5 addresses the next step in the forensic neuropsychological examination process—namely, test scoring and interpretation—and the memorializing of the findings within the neuropsychological report. Again, the focus is on issues particularly pertinent within the forensic context. These include the limitations of methods used to describe premorbid cognitive functioning; effects of "practice" (repeated exposure) on test results;

the importance of viewing test results within the context of medical and academic records; and caveats in interpreting lowered scores, particularly the need to consider normal variability and alternative etiologies aside from the claimed injury. Regarding this last issue, I summarize findings from review articles (primarily meta-analyses) to provide "thumbnail" sketches of the cognitive profiles associated with various medical, psychiatric, and academic conditions, so that clinicians are alerted to variables requiring further consideration and investigation. Suggestions are also provided regarding the documentation of SVT and personality test data, and the chapter concludes with a sample report of a noncredible patient to illustrate one approach to the construction of such reports.

Chapter 6 outlines major flaws commonly observed in forensic neuropsychological reports. These entail failure to assess adequately for symptom invalidity; use of inappropriate tests and/or norms; conclusions that are inconsistent with published research; failure to consider all possible causes for lowered cognitive scores; overinterpretation of lowered scores; incorrect use of test scores to document brain injury; and misinterpretation of the MMPI-2 and MMPI-2-RF.

Chapter 7 discusses common misperceptions regarding mild traumatic brain injury, describes what the empirical literature tells us about this disorder, and (as a corollary) indicates what we can and cannot conclude about this condition in our expert witness roles.

The book concludes with Chapter 8, involving testimony. In particular, this chapter describes how to protect a report and its conclusions from attack and outlines many of the common methods used in attempts to override and discredit neuropsychologists and their data.

Rochelle Serwator, Senior Editor of The Guilford Press, provided the impetus for this book, and I am appreciative of the reviewers who forwarded carefully considered suggestions as to its content. Finally, I am grateful to my husband, Rodney Boone, who cheered me on when the end was not in sight.

Contents

1

The Neuropsychological Exam

This chapter covers critical issues to be carefully considered before and while conducting a forensic neuropsychological evaluation.

DISCLOSURE OF TEST NAMES PRIOR TO EXAM

It is preferable not to disclose the exact names of tests that you plan to administer prior to the exam. Neuropsychological tests can only assess what they were designed to measure if the test taker is naïve to the tests' content and purpose. Unfortunately, some court decisions have ruled that exact test names arc to be disclosed to plaintiff attorneys if requested. For example, in *Carpenter v. Superior Court of Alameda County* (*Yamaha Motor Corporation*, 2006), the court argued:

> In correspondence Yamaha submits to us from publishers of the MMPI and of the written psychological tests, it is contended only that disclosure of the test materials themselves before the examination could affect the integrity of the test. It is not asserted that identification of the names of the proposed tests would pose the same risk. Indeed, we find the prospect unlikely, since the actual test questions are a carefully guarded secret among the publishers and examiners: identification of just the names of the tests—while meaningful to the plaintiff's psychologist for purposes of determining their relevance— would not likely lead to the plaintiff gaining access to the actual questions.

The court apparently did not anticipate that the Internet would give potential examinees and their counsel access to considerable information regarding test content if test names were provided. In fact, research has shown that information accessed on the Internet via test names is a threat to test security, particularly for symptom validity tests (SVTs; Bauer & McCaffrey, 2006; Ruiz, Drake, Glass, Marcotte, & van Gorp, 2002). Specifically, some Internet sites show test stimuli and reproduce test cutoffs, allowing test takers to "try to keep track of and count how many questions they get right or wrong in order to 'pass'" (Bauer & McCaffrey, 2006, p. 125). In a study of undergraduates who were asked to feign brain injury and who were encouraged to prepare for their role, 36% reported searching the Internet—a higher percentage than for any other strategy (Tan, Slick, Strauss, & Hultsch, 2002). Several Internet sites in fact help test takers prepare for independent medical examinations (Horwitz & McCaffrey, 2006).

Regardless of whether disclosing test names in advance allows access to test content, test batteries are typically adjusted in response to patient characteristics; thus neuropsychologists will not necessarily know exactly what tests should be administered prior to the exam. It can reasonably be argued that specifying in advance of the exam the exact battery of tests to be given might constitute malpractice, just as it would be malpractice to list in advance the laboratory tests to be ordered for a patient during a medical evaluation without first obtaining a history and examining the patient.

Figure 1.1 illustrates the type of letter that can be provided if a plaintiff's counsel requests and is entitled to a list of test names before a defense-retained neuropsychological exam.

PAYMENT

Although the American Psychological Association (APA) ethics code (APA, 2010) is silent regarding the practice of working on a lien, the Specialty Guidelines for Forensic Psychology (American Psychology–Law Society, 2011) warn against providing services on a contingent basis, due to potential threats to impartiality. The primary concern in this situation, voiced earlier by other authors (Essig, Mittenberg, Petersen, Strauman, & Cooper, 2001; Mittenberg, Patton, Canyock, & Conlit, 2002; van Gorp & Kalechstein, 2005) is that the examiner is not an unbiased reporter of psychological test data, because he/she is invested in the outcome.

DUAL RELATIONSHIPS: EXPERT AND TREATER

At times a neuropsychologist will conduct a medical–legal evaluation in which it is determined that the patient needs treatment, which the psychologist then provides. Or the psychologist may have initially been the treater,

Given that the plaintiff has reported that cognitive difficulties have interfered with his/her ability to perform at school and work, the purpose of the neuropsychological exam will be to objectively document the level of his/her cognitive function.

Unfortunately, I do not know which tests I will give until I start testing the patient. For example, if during preliminary testing I detect a pattern that suggests learning disability, then I will administer tests to assess the patient's academic skills (e.g., sight reading, spelling, arithmetic). However, if there are no signs of learning disability, then the administration of academic tests may not be necessary. Similarly, if the patient is noted to have considerable difficulty in copying a complex design with paper and pencil, then I will administer a simpler test. If the patient has no difficulty on the complex figure, then there will be no point in administering the simpler designs.

Although I cannot specify at this point exactly which tests will be indicated for the exam of _____, the tests that I will give will be drawn from the following list of commonly used and well-accepted cognitive and psychological tests:

Wechsler Adult Intelligence Scale–III or IV (WAIS-III or IV)
California Verbal Learning Test–II (CVLT-II)
Mini-Mental State Examination (MMSE)
Boston Naming Test
Tactual Performance Test
Finger Tapping Test
Finger Agnosia/Localization Test
Seashore Rhythm Test
Speech Sounds Perception Test
Grip Strength Test
Wide Range Achievement Test–4 (WRAT4)
Grooved Pegboard Test
Rey Auditory Verbal Learning Test (RAVLT)
Wechsler Memory Scale–III or IV (WMS-III or IV)
Rey–Osterrieth (RO) Complex Figure
Beery–Buktenica Developmental Test of Visual–Motor Integration–6th Edition
Memory Assessment Scales (MAS)
Neuropsychological Assessment Battery (NAB)
Minnesota Multiphasic Personality Inventory–2 or 2–RF (MMPI-2 or 2–RF)
Modified Somatic Perception Questionnaire (MSPQ)
Millon Clinical Multiaxial Inventory–III (MCMI-III)
Stroop Test
Color Trails
Trail Making Test
Delis–Kaplan Executive Function System (DKEFS)
Wisconsin Card Sorting Test (WCST)
Category Test
Verbal Fluency Test(FAS)
Ruff Figural Fluency Test
Symptom validity tests

FIGURE 1.1. Example of a letter to be sent to a plaintiff's attorney in response to a request for a list of tests to be used in a neuropsychological exam.

and then steps into the role of expert witness, providing a medical–legal evaluation of the patient.

This practice is strongly discouraged, as laid out by the APA (2010) ethics code (Standard 3.05) and in the Specialty Guidelines for Forensic Psychology (American Psychology–Law Society, 2011), in that the multiple relationships "may impair objectivity and/or cause exploitation or other harm" (2011, p. 7). As Strasberger, Gutheil, and Brodsky (1997) point out, the empathic treatment relationship "has no place in, and is unlikely to survive, the questioning and public reporting of a forensic evaluation" (p. 449), and they caution that "involvement in litigation inevitably affects the empathy, neutrality, and anonymity of the clinician" (p. 451). Specifically, they note conflicting agendas between psychotherapeutic treatment and the forensic process, with the former promoting growth and normalization, but with the latter focusing on and even provoking psychopathology and "developmental arrest or regression" (p. 452) in the service of procuring damage awards. The outcome is that the treater cannot serve both to foster health and to focus on redress. The authors conclude that "the proper role of a treating therapist is not to encourage a lawsuit or to be the patient's legal advocate. Rather it is to assist the patient in deciding whether or not to bring suit and to provide support in going through the legal process if that be the decision. The therapist ought to stand at the same distance from the lawsuit as from any other significant event in the patient's life" (p. 452).

THIRD-PARTY OBSERVERS

States have differing rules in regard to allowing the presence of observers and/or the recording of neuropsychological exams conducted in the context of a lawsuit. The rationale for observers/recording is to ensure that patients are not subjected to an abusive examination and that their legal rights are protected (e.g., to ensure that they are not interrogated regarding liability in subject accidents), as well as to promote fairness and accurate reporting in general. However, allowing observers and/or recording of exams is in direct conflict with the APA's ethical guidelines, which stress the importance of maintaining test security (APA. 2010, Standard 9.11). The development and validation of psychological tests require considerable effort and capital, and to the extent that the general public can gain access to test content, the tests' ability to measure accurately what they were intended to measure is significantly compromised. Allowing attorneys or family members to be present in a neuropsychological exam exposes these individuals to test content that they are under no ethical guidelines to protect. Similarly, video or audio recording of the exam, or having a court reporter transcribe the exam, has the potential to allow test content to be distributed in the general public.

In addition, the presence of observers or the recording of the evaluation renders the exam nonstandard; the APA's ethical standards specifically instruct practitioners to follow standardized administration procedures (APA, 2010, Standard 9.02a). Neuropsychological tests were not normed with observers or recording devices present, and anecdotal reports and empirical studies have documented poorer performance on neuropsychological tests—including SVTs and especially memory tasks—in the presence of attorneys and related third-party observers (Lynch, 2005), family members and close friends/significant others (Binder & Johnson-Greene, 1995; Kehrer, Sanchez, Habif, Rosenbaum, & Townes, 2000), testing supervisors (Yantz & McCaffrey, 2005), video recording (Constantinou, Ashendorf, & McCaffrey, 2005; Reese, Suhr, Larrabee, & Rasmussen, 2011), and audiorecording (Constantinou, Ashendorf, & McCaffrey, 2002). A recent meta-analysis (62 cases, n = 4,405; Eastvold, Belanger, & Vanderploeg, 2012) of the effects of third-party observers on cognitive task performance showed a negative impact (d = −0.24), with most pronounced effects documented for attention and memory. Earlier, Gaven, Lynch, and McCaffrey (2005) computed effect sizes for the impact of third-party observers on neuropsychological scores; they reported medium effect sizes for memory scores, and small effect sizes for attention/executive and motor tasks.

Some have argued that testimony based on test data obtained in the presence of a third-party observer is inadmissible because of unreliability (McCaffrey, 2005). Hypothetically, plaintiff counsel could demand to observe the neuropsychological exam, and then could subsequently claim that the resulting data are invalid, due to the impact of his/her presence on the data collected.

In light of all these issues, the American Academy of Clinical Neuropsychology (AACN, 2001) and the National Academy of Neuropsychology (NAN, 2000a, 2000b) have both issued position statements strongly discouraging the presence of third-party observers during neuropsychological exams, particularly "involved" observers (i.e., persons with a vested interest in the outcome of the evaluation), for reasons of test security and data integrity.

Unfortunately, a neuropsychologist is often caught between contradictory requirements of professional ethics and the legal system, and has to attempt to reconcile the two. For example, in California audio recording of neuropsychological exams is allowed, but observers, video recording, and court reporters are not (*Golfland Entertainment Centers, Inc., v. Superior Court of San Joaquin County*, 2003). The best solution appears to be for the neuropsychologist to handle audio-recording the exam him-/herself, so as to cause the least disruption to the session (i.e., so that the patient is not stopping timed tests to replace tapes, if tapes are being used). The tapes or other recordings (CDs, USB drives, etc.) are then delivered directly to the opposing licensed psychologist via messenger or mail. The receiving professional has the same ethical obligation to protect the tests as the examiner, and has the expertise to determine whether the exam was conducted in an appropriate manner, thus allowing protection of the plaintiff's rights. If the plaintiff's counsel does insist on audio recording of the exam, it would be reasonable for the defense neuropsychologist to point out in his/her report that any low cognitive scores documented on testing could to some degree be related to the fact that the exam was recorded, given evidence that audio recording is associated with lowered psychometric test results. The APA's ethical standards in fact indicate that such factors should be considered in the interpretation of test results (APA, 2010, Standards 9.02a, 9.06).

Some neuropsychologists take the position that they will not conduct exams with audio recording, even if test security is maintained by transfer of the recordings from one licensed psychologist to another. However, as McCaffrey, Fisher, Gold, and Lynch (1996) and Duff and Fisher (2005) have pointed out, this has ramifications for the field of clinical neuropsychology: If qualified, ethical neuropsychologists refuse to conduct exams under conditions mandated by state law, evaluations will become the domain of less qualified and/or less ethical practitioners. Furthermore, plaintiffs' attorneys will soon learn that all they have to do to preclude knowledgeable, ethical neuropsychologists from being retained by defense counsel is to demand audio recording of exams. McCaffrey (2005) and McCaffrey et al. (1996) suggest that this in fact may be the "covert agenda" of opposing counsel, and McCaffrey (2005) warns that "if a subset of the legal community can control who does and who does not perform forensic neuropsychological evaluations, then the entire legal process may not be well-served" (pp. 89–90).

Duff and Fisher (2005) provide an interesting hypothetical case regarding how the presence of observers might subtly, and not so subtly, affect the quality of the examination. As these authors note, the presence of observers even during the interview is problematic, in that it may compromise rapport and interfere with the completeness of the information obtained (e.g., patients may be concerned about what their attorneys think of their answers). Observers of the interview should sit out of the test taker's line of sight (preferably behind him/her), and the presence of such observers, and any audio recording or other method of recording the exam, should be documented in the report (APA, 2010, Standards 6.01 and 6.06). McCaffrey (2005; see also McCaffrey et al., 1996) also suggests that if an observer is present during actual testing, the "Behavioral Observations" section of the report should also contain a description of the observer's behavior, including interactions between the test taker and observer.

Additional discussion of these issues is provided by McSweeny et al. (1998), McCaffrey et al. (1996), McCaffrey, Lynch, and Yantz (2005), and Cramer and Brodsky (2007).

CONSENT FORMS

The APA's ethical guidelines (APA, 2010, Standard 9.03) indicate that patients are to provide informed consent before any psychological procedures, including psychological testing. However, in the forensic arena, when a person contracts with an attorney to represent him/her, decisions about participating in psychological testing are made by that attorney. Defense counsel has the right and obligation to seek information that could be useful in the defense of his/her client(s), including testing conducted by the defense's own expert. Thus, if a plaintiff declines to participate in testing at the request of defense counsel, defense counsel could reasonably request dismissal of the case. Even though a defense-retained psychological testing expert does not need the plaintiff's permission to proceed with testing in many states, it is important to explain the parameters of the exam, so that the plaintiff is fully informed as to the purpose and general procedures. The examiner should also explain that best effort and cooperation is necessary, who will have access to the report, what the examiner's mandated reporting responsibilities are, and so forth. The consent form in Figure 1.2 lays out the relevant issues.

The consent form includes a space for the plaintiff to sign to affirm that all of the issues listed in the form have been discussed. In my experience, approximately 10% of plaintiffs decline to sign the form, usually reporting that their attorneys have instructed them not to sign any documents at the exam. I assure these individuals that I will not interfere with their attorney's instructions and simply note in the margin that all issues were explained to the plaintiff and that he/she declined to sign. However, in some states a signed consent form is required even if testing is conducted at the request of a third party.

Because of the potential for conflict when test takers are asked to sign consent forms in contradiction to their attorney's instructions, some practitioner's opt for an "assent" process to document that the test taker understands the parameters of the exam.

An important issue is whether test takers should be informed about the presence of specific tests of response bias in the exam. I have outlined some of the concerns with this practice (Boone, 2007b): (1) These instructions were not a part of the test validation and standardization process, and thus represent a deviation from standardized test instructions; and (2) measures of response bias are only effective when test takers are naïve as to their

This authorization signifies that Dr. _____ has provided the following information:

1. Has reviewed the purpose of the examination (i.e., objective measurement of my thinking skills, psychological symptoms, and personality traits).
2. Has reviewed the nature of the procedures to be used (i.e., paper-and-pencil testing).
3. Has explained the intended use of the evaluation (i.e., evidence in a legal proceeding, at the request of a disability insurance company, or other: _____).
4. Has revealed the identity of the parties who retained him/her and who are requesting the examination (_____), and has explained that the test report will be released to the referral source; the report cannot be released to me. To maintain test security, requests for information will be limited to provision of a report and scores, with the exception that copies of raw test data sheets can be released to another licensed psychologist.
5. Has explained the limitations on confidentiality regarding data gathered during the evaluation, including the legal obligation to report information regarding child abuse, elder abuse, and threats of assault and/or homicide to the appropriate authorities.
6. Has informed me that no treating relationship exists between myself and Dr. _____ (i.e., there is no doctor–patient relationship).
7. Has explained the importance of performing with my best effort on the testing. Although some patients might be disposed to exaggerate problems on testing as a way of making sure their problems are well documented, I have been informed that this, rather than helping my case, may actually make my test profile more problematic to interpret.

By signing below, I am affirming that I fully understand and agree to the above-described terms and conditions. I give my consent to Dr. _____ to conduct the neuropsychological evaluation of me.

Name _____ Date _____
            (signature)

Name _____
            (printed)

FIGURE 1.2. Authorization to conduct a neuropsychological evaluation.

existence. Research shows that when malingering test takers are informed that specific measures of response bias are included in the battery, they still feign on the tasks, although in a more careful and savvy manner, and, as a result, it is more difficult to document the symptom feigning (Gervais, Green, Allen, & Iverson, 2001; Youngjohn, Lees-Haley, & Binder, 1999). Thus, if the intent in providing this information to the test taker is to prevent feigning, it is not effective (Greiffenstein, 2009). Furthermore, some research shows that when test takers are told about the presence of SVTs in a battery, they are able to identify which are the SVTs and navigate around them (Suhr & Gunstad, 2000).

The impetus on the part of some practitioners to inform test takers about the presence of SVTs in the battery probably stems from two factors: a desire to stop attempts at symptom feigning, and discomfort that the administration of such tests may reflect lack of transparency toward the test taker. As discussed above, informing test takers regarding the presence of SVTs does not stop attempts at feigning; it simply makes the test takers more careful, and thus makes feigning harder to detect. Some examiners may perceive that it is not "above board" to measure response bias when a patient has only been informed that the neuropsychological battery is designed to measure various thinking and motor/sensory skills. However, personality inventories have historically incorporated "embedded" validity scales of which patients are not informed, and psychologists have not expressed concern with this practice. Perhaps the discomfort with administering dedicated SVTs without informing test takers of their presence has to do with their single purpose in measuring response bias; as the field moves to primary use of embedded cognitive SVTs, this concern may recede. As examiners, we need to keep in mind that we have an obligation to the field of neuropsychology to ensure that test results are not manipulated by individuals intent on inaccurately documenting neuropsychological abnormalities. Furthermore, when we serve as expert witnesses, our allegiance is to the courts and to making sure that accurate information is provided to the trier of fact. The only way we can do this is by administering response bias measures of which patients are unaware.

In addition to providing information about effort in the consent form, I tell patients that it is important to give their best performance because I will be looking for "clear-cut" patterns, and that when patients do not perform to their true capability, it becomes harder to interpret the scores. What I do not want is for credible patients to exaggerate their symptoms in a bid to make sure that I accurately document their problems; I want to warn them that, rather than helping, this will backfire. When I provide such a statement, and then a patient in fact fails measures of response bias, I can reasonably conclude that he/she did not wish me to obtain a truly accurate measure of cognitive ability.

THE INTERVIEW

Because neuropsychologists are typically requested to provide opinions about the etiology of any detected neurocognitive abnormalities, in addition to current symptoms, a patient's medical/psychiatric history, educational/occupational background, and language/culture need to be carefully investigated. Various aspects of family history should also be covered, as should any previous neuropsychological testing, recent major stressors, and the patient's "typical day." Suggestions and cautions about interviewing collaterals are provided.

Current Symptoms

Patients should be asked about current physical, cognitive, and psychiatric symptoms that they believe are related to the claimed condition for which they are being referred.

It is strongly recommended that patients be asked regarding current symptomatology in an "open-ended" question format, instead of being provided with checklists of symptoms that they then can endorse. Checklists educate patients as to what symptoms might be expected for their condition, and thereby are likely to prime them for reporting symptoms that might not otherwise occur. At times opposing neuropsychological experts will opine that plaintiffs' presentations were credible because they reported symptoms consistent with their claimed condition, but this only occurred because patients were given a template of likely symptoms via a checklist.

The genesis of the b Test (Boone, Lu, & Herzberg, 2002a) stemmed from the observation that some noncredible patients, when asked what chronic cognitive symptoms they were attributing to their concussion, informed the examiner that they had become "dyslexic" (i.e., they now saw letters upside down and backwards)—symptoms I have never heard a patient with a serious traumatic brain injury (TBI) report. Other patients, when asked, "What problems in your thinking skills are you experiencing now that you think are related to the accident 3 years ago?" respond with "Like what?" Except for those patients with severe brain injury and associated anosagnosia, if an individual has to ask for examples of cognitive difficulties he/she might be experiencing, it can be deduced that any actual cognitive symptoms are not serious or significant; otherwise the patient would be well aware of, and ready to recount, them.

Medical and Psychiatric History

Empirical research shows that the following conditions can all be associated with neuropsychological abnormalities (see pp. 178–188 for literature summaries on some of these conditions). Thus patients should be specifically queried as to any history of the following:

- Head injury with loss of consciousness
  - Patients should be questioned about how long they were unconscious, and if so, what was the last clear memory prior to the

injury (this is used to gauge the length of retrograde amnesia) and first clear memory following the injury (this is used to measure anterograde or posttraumatic amnesia). All this information is used to estimate overall severity of brain injury (see p. 227)
- Brain infections (e.g., encephalitis, meningitis)
- Stroke
- Seizures (including type, frequency, and age at onset, because these factors determine whether the seizures are likely to be associated with cognitive dysfunction)
- Brain tumor (including location and treatment modalities)
- Chronic medical diseases such as hypertension, diabetes, thyroid disorder, respiratory illnesses (sleep apnea, chronic obstructive pulmonary disease, severe asthma requiring hospitalization), and cardiac abnormalities (including bypass surgery)
- Risk for human immunodeficiency virus (HIV) infection
- Previous headache disorder
- Birth complications
- Developmental abnormalities
- Alcohol or drug abuse
- Use of substances or medications by the patient's mother while pregnant with the patient
- Exposure to toxins
- Chromosomal abnormalities (such as Klinefelter, fragile X, and Turner syndromes)
- Psychiatric symptoms and treatment
- Current prescribed medications and dosages, as well as most recent use of pain medications
- Any injury to hands or arms (these can account for poor scores on motor testing)

Educational History

It is important to determine how many years of education the test taker completed, including how many in the United States versus in other countries. As discussed on pages 190–191, educational level is significantly correlated with most neurocognitive scores, even nonverbal tasks that do not have obvious correlates with academic skills; thus is it is critical to know how much formal schooling the patient has completed. In addition, it is important to gather information regarding how much schooling was obtained domestically versus abroad, because years of education completed inside and outside the United States cannot necessarily be equated. Research shows that in general, the greater the percentage of education completed outside the United States, the poorer the performance on neuro-cognitive measures obtained in the United States. More difficult to measure is the quality of education, but preliminary research suggests that this too may have a significant impact on cognitive scores.

If the test taker did not graduate from high school, it is useful to ask why this occurred. Such information can provide insight into whether schooling was discontinued for nonacademic reasons (e.g., pregnancy, need to earn money to support the family) versus inability to perform. In addition, it is essential to obtain, if possible, data regarding performance in school (e.g., grades in high school and college, grade point averages, standardized test scores). These data provide a rough gauge of preinjury cognitive function, with high grades and test scores implying higher premorbid function. If the person did not perform well in school, it is again useful to ask why; specifi-cally, it is important to ascertain whether the person was diagnosed with learning disabilities or attention-deficit/hyperactivity disorder (ADHD), or whether it was suspected that he/she might have these conditions. Learn-ing disabilities and ADHD are typically associated with abnormalities on neurocognitive testing, even in adulthood (see pp. 180–181).

Language and Culture

Regarding language and culture, it is important to obtain information regarding how many languages the person speaks fluently—and, if more than one, which was the first language learned, when subsequent languages were learned, what percentage of time the patient is currently speaking English versus the other languages, and what percentage of time the patient spoke English versus the other languages while growing up. In addition, information regarding cultural factors (such as ethnic background and in which country the person was born and educated) are relevant in inter-preting neuropsychological test scores. Pages 189–190 provide a further discussion of the impact of language and culture on neuropsychological test scores.

Occupation

The type of preinjury occupation held by a plaintiff provides information regarding premorbid level of function. Furthermore, some patients involved in lawsuits may still be employed, and the types of job duties in which they are engaged can be compared against scores obtained during the neuropsy-chological exam for consistency. In a recent evaluation, a phlebotomist who was continuing to work full-time after a claimed mild TBI (mTBI), whose job required that she routinely insert needles into equipment used to gather blood specimens and then use the equipment to draw blood from patients,

obtained Finger Tapping Test scores that were less than half those expecrted
for her age group—a rather implausible finding, given her job duties.

Family Medical, Psychiatric, Educational, and Occupational History

It is valuable to obtain information regarding family background, for obvious reasons (but always query as to whether the patient is adopted; if so,
family history may be less relevant). If an older patient is claiming cognitive changes secondary to a brain injury, but has a strong family history
of Alzheimer's disease, the possibility that he/she has a primary progressive dementia needs to be ruled out. If a patient is claiming that epilepsy,
bipolar illness, major depression, learning disability, ADHD, or the like
is the effect of a TBI, but has a family history strongly positive for these
disorders, it needs to be weighed whether the patient would have developed
these conditions (or in fact already had them) absent the accident. In some
patients with somatoform conditions, one will discover that family members had similar symptoms, suggesting that the relatives provided a model
for illness behavior.

Previous Neuropsychological Testing

As discussed on page 192, previous exposure to neuropsychological tests
can alter subsequent scores. Therefore, it is critical to know whether the
patient has undergone prior neuropsychological testing, and if so when it
occurred. It is always disconcerting to have a patient comment (typically
during administration of the Block Design subtest), "I couldn't do this one
the last time I took this test."

Major Stressors within the Past 5 Years

When one is assessing for emotional damages in the context of a lawsuit, it
is important to gather information regarding possible stressors the plaintiff
has experienced that are unrelated to the subject incident. I ask, "During
the past 5 years, have you experienced any other major stressors aside from
[subject of lawsuit], such as deaths in the family, major illnesses in family members, breakups of relationships, or major financial problems?" I
have frequently been surprised by the reporting of significant stressors (a
child killed in a shooting, deaths of parents, arrests, marital separations,
etc.) that have occurred shortly before or after the incident at issue in the
lawsuit, yet are not referenced in available medical records. The impact
of such events should be considered when one is attributing psychological
symptoms to the subject accident.

Alternatively, if patients fail to report such stressors, but they come to light in records, this might be interpreted as a deliberate attempt to maximize damages in the lawsuit. On one occasion I tested someone who arrived for testing accompanied by his wife, and he denied any marital difficulties on interview. However, I later discovered that at the time of the testing there had been a recent domestic violence incident, and the couple were in fact separated and in the process of filing for divorce.

Many patients with somatoform conditions fail to see connections between often marked psychological stressors in their lives (e.g., a son recently diagnosed with autism, a good friend who recently died of breast cancer) and current psychological symptoms, and attribute all of their current problems to the often minor environmental incident at issue in the lawsuit (e.g., mold in the home).

"Typical Day"

Finally, it is important to obtain a general description of activities of daily living (ADLs) by querying about a "typical day." Ask the patient at what time he/she generally arises, and then ask about specific activities engaged in during a typical day. This information provides data as to how functional he/she is (e.g., driving, working, parenting, handling finances); it also indicates whether test scores match independence in ADLs, and whether there is adoption of the sick role (e.g., whether daily life activities overly focus on illness).

Interviewing Collaterals

Practice recommendations within the field of neuropsychology suggest that interviewing family members and others with knowledge of the patient can be a useful source of information (AACN, 2007). However, the problem with this recommendation in the forensic arena is that the neuropsychologist has no method of verifying that the information obtained is accurate. Family members clearly have a vested interest in the outcome of litigation, and friends may feel an obligation to provide information helpful to the patient's legal case. Neuropsychological test scores should be treated as independent sources of data uncontaminated by the reports of family members or friends. For example, if a patient scores at the 75th percentile on a memory measure, but friends and/or family describe the patient as exhibiting poor memory, what is to be done with the latter information? It does not modify the objective test scores and percentiles.

Relatedly, some neuropsychologists have family members complete behavioral ratings scales on patients (e.g., the Frontal Systems Behavior Scale) and dutifully list the obtained scores along with standard neuropsychological testing results. This gives the illusion that such data are objective measures of the patient's behavior, but there are no validity indices to verify that family reports are in fact accurate.

Arguably, information from collateral sources should be presented to juries, but in a separate forum from the results of objective testing (and preferably under oath). Also, the two data sources should not be viewed as interchangeable.

THE TESTING PROCESS

Selection of Tests

Tests should be chosen that adequately measure the pertinent neurocognitive domains, which typically include memory (verbal and nonverbal/visual), attention, processing speed, executive skills, visual–perceptual/visual–spatial abilities, language skills, motor function, and overall intelligence. Inventories used to measure psychiatric symptoms should also be incorporated.

Conducting a Comprehensive Exam

A comprehensive neuropsychological exam should generally be administered in a litigated case; critical decisions are being based on neuropsychological test results, and the psychologist should err on the side of thoroughness. Some reports show that abbreviated test versions have been employed, but it is difficult to make a case for use of markedly shortened versions in a forensic context, especially since available data suggest that some formally published abbreviated test versions are inaccurate (e.g., the Wechsler Abbreviated Scale of Intelligence [WASI]; Axelrod, 2002).

However, overtesting should be avoided. Various cognitive domains should be adequately sampled, but as discussed on pages 174–177, the more tests administered, the more likely it is that scattered low scores will appear that are associated with normal variability.

Fixed versus Flexible Battery

Historically, research and clinical practice in neuropsychology were dominated by the Halstead–Reitan battery (Reitan & Wolfson, 1985)—a lengthy series of cognitive and sensory-perceptual tasks that, in its original form, does not provide any verbal or visual memory assessment, incompletely measures language and visual-perceptual/visual–spatial skills, and includes several tasks whose "real-world" ecological applications are unclear (e.g., Speech Sounds Perception Test, Seashore Rhythm Test,

Tactual Performance Test). A recent survey of practicing neuropsychologists (Sweet, Nelson, & Moberg, 2006) found that only 7% still employed a fixed battery such as the Halstead–Reitan; the remainder used some version of a flexible battery of individually normed tests targeted to assess critical neurocognitive domains of memory, language, sensory–motor function, problem solving, and attention. Some have argued that in "forensic situations, the expert witness using a standardized battery is the only psychologist who can provide dependable testimony interpreting psychometric test data as a whole to the court" (Russell, Russell, & Hill, 2005, p. 792), because tasks in a fixed battery are co-normed and validated as a group for the detection of brain dysfunction. However, research comparing ability-focused flexible batteries to a Halstead–Reitan battery (even one supplemented with memory testing) has shown no superiority of the latter in sensitivity to brain injury severity (Rohling, Meyers, & Millis, 2003). Similarly, Larrabee, Millis, and Meyers (2008) found equal effectiveness for a flexible versus a fixed battery in discriminating patients of varying types of brain dysfunction from medical controls; the four single tests that best discriminated the groups were a verbal fluency task (written *H* words), two motor tasks (Finger Tapping Test, Grooved Pegboard Test), and a processing speed/executive measure (Trails B)—all types of tests commonly included in a flexible battery. Furthermore, fixed batteries such as the Halstead–Reitan have viewed brain injury as a generic entity to be "detected," whereas more sophisticated thinking in the field has come to appreciate that differing types of brain injury produce differing patterns of cognitive impairment that need to be quantified.

Further discussion of this issue can be found in Larrabee (2008b) and Greiffenstein (2009).

Newer versus Older Versions of Tests

New versions of cognitive tests are frequently pumped out at regular intervals by test publishers; clinicians are encouraged to purchase and use the new versions under the admonition that the APA ethics code warns against use of "obsolete tests and outdated test results" (APA, 2010, Standard 9.08).

However, as noted by Russell (2010), "validated tests do not lose their validity due to the creation of newer versions. . . . In science, no method, theory, or information, once validated, loses that validation merely due to time or the creation of another test or procedure. Once validated, a procedure is only disproved or replaced by means of new research" (p. 60). He also observes that the use of newer versions represents an "extensive nullification" of data collected on 10,000 earlier Wechsler studies—a tremendous waste of effort and resources.

Similarly, Bush (2010) argues that

there is no consensus regarding when tests should no longer be considered acceptable, and there may be sound reasons for delaying or foregoing the purchase and use of new versions of assessment measures. Determining whether or when to transition to a new version of a test can be particularly difficult for clinicians in psychological specialties because it can take years after publication of a revised test for research with special patient populations to be performed and published. As a result, different clinicians may adopt newer versions of tests at different times or elect not to use the newest version, depending on the specific patient population and referral questions. Decisions regarding transitioning to new test versions should be based on the scientific merits of the tests, not on an arbitrarily defined time frame. Clinicians must ultimately use their judgment regarding which test version is best for a given patient at a given point in time. (p. 7)

Loring and Bauer (2010) raise major questions regarding the newest incarnations of the Wechsler Adult Intelligence Scale (WAIS) and the Wechsler Memory Scale (WMS), the WAIS-IV and the WMS-IV. Specifically, they question the need for the newer IQ test, given that the WAIS-III Full Scale IQ (FSIQ) is only 2.9 points higher than the WAIS-IV—hardly a compelling demonstration of the "Flynn effect" (increase in IQ test scores in successive age cohorts). Furthermore, they warn that given the deemphasis on time bonus points in the WAIS-IV, the WAIS-IV should yield fewer low IQ scores, theoretically decreasing the number of individuals eligible for special education services and disability compensation. In addition, the WAIS-IV FSIQ is based on somewhat different skill sets than the WAIS-III FSIQ, and subtest items have been substantially changed, raising concerns that data on WAIS-III sensitivity to brain impairment will not apply to the WAIS-IV.

Regarding the WMS-IV, Loring and Bauer (2010) note that with each new WMS version,

> many of the previously "new" subtests have been discarded due to their failure to adequately assess their intended memory constructs, and replaced with another set of "improved" memory measures. Thus, each subsequent WMS revision fails to provide an accumulated corpus of subtests, and instead represents frequent midstream changes in test development. (p. 687)

The authors caution that "changing the structure of neuropsychological tests with each revision impedes the accumulated development of a clinical knowledge base and adversely affects long-term research/database implementation" (p. 688).

Finally, Loring and Bauer (2010) point out that whereas new drugs cannot be approved and placed into use without research documenting effectiveness, unfortunately no such requirement is in place for psychological tests, and that data on "how well test results predict a certain diagnosis or functional outcome . . . which is of central importance to neuropsychological applications of the Wechsler scales, is absent" (p. 688) for the WAIS-IV/WMS-IV.

These three publications provide support for clinicians' opting to use older versions of the Wechsler scales and other instruments, particularly in those situations when older instruments have more research data relevant to particular clinical issues at hand. At this writing (November 2011), 3 years after publication of the WAIS-IV, a search in PubMed under the terms "WAIS-III" and "WAIS-IV" revealed 304 citations for the former and 17 for the latter. A search in Google Scholar showed 10,700 citations for "WAIS-III" and 478 for "WAIS-IV." Certainly, therefore, the WAIS-III has substantially more empirical research at this time than the WAIS-IV; this would argue for continued use of the WAIS-III.

Preference for Commonly Administered Tests with Adequate Normative Data

It is usually preferable to administer tests that are in common use by neuropsychologists and that have adequate normative data. I have seen medical–legal reports on adult plaintiffs that refer to use of the "Bicycle Drawing Test." If you have never attempted this task, I strongly recommend that you discontinue reading at this point and actually try to draw a bicycle without looking at one. I use this exercise in my assessment courses, and it provides ample entertainment as the students share their reproductions. Conclusions regarding damages in forensic cases must be based on reliable and valid data. The only publication on the Bicycle Drawing Test available in PubMed and Google Scholar at this writing was published in 1994 and relates to its use in children (Greenberg, Rodriguez, & Sesta, 1994).

Similarly, I have seen the Street Visual Gestalt Test (Street, 1931) used in forensic examinations. This is an obsolete visual-perceptual task in which the test taker is to report the identity of degraded pictures. Some of the items are common objects, but of such ancient vintage that it would be doubtful whether anyone under age 75 would know what they were (e.g., an oven/stove with "legs"). Furthermore, there are no appropriate current normative data available for this measure.

Testing of Patients Who Do Not Speak/Are Not Fluent in English

In the case of patients who do not speak or are not fluent in English, the best practice is to refer them to a neuropsychologist who is fluent in their language, if one is available. If a solely English-speaking neuropsychologist evaluates such a patient, and there is in fact a neuropsychologist available locally who speaks the patient's language, the former neuropsychologist opens him-/herself up to justifiable attack. For example, when providing test instructions through an interpreter, the neuropsychologist does not know what is actually being said to the patient (See Artiola I Fortuny and Mullaney [1998] for further discussion). However, for some patients who require neuropsychological testing and do not speak/are not fluent in English but speak a language not known by local neuropsychologists, the only recourse may be to attempt an exam through an interpreter. This may lead to the experience of stating rather succinct test instructions, which, when translated, seem to be much lengthier than warranted for the original verbalization. On one occasion when I tested a patient through a translator, the translator appeared to be arguing with the patient about the appropriateness of the patient's responses to test questions. These types of situations present clear problems for interpretation of the obtained neuropsychological test scores.

Use of Technicians

Survey results published in 2002 indicated that approximately half of neuropsychologists conducted their own testing, with the remainder using technicians (Sweet, Peck, Abramowitz, & Etzweiler, 2002). Position papers in the field indicate that the use of psychometrists to administer tests under the supervision of a licensed psychologist is acceptable (NAN, 2006). I prefer to do my own testing because a wealth of rich qualitative data can be accessed throughout the exam, from histrionic behaviors (e.g., requests to turn off fluorescent lighting and limit light to that from windows because of extreme light sensitivity) to noncredible symptoms (e.g., "stuttering" symptoms that "come and go" during the exam; report of posttraumatic stress disorder [PTSD] symptoms, including exaggerated startle response, but failure to show startle when a cabinet door behind the patient closes loudly). Furthermore, by being present for hundreds of evaluations, a neuropsychologist develops a rich database of expected test-taking behaviors, and then can readily note when patients show atypical response patterns (e.g., copying visual stimuli *upside down*).

A skilled and experienced psychometrist can also develop finely honed clinical observational skills. Some neuropsychologists adopt a "middle ground," conducting some of the testing themselves as well as the interview, with the remaining testing administered by a psychometrist. However, a practice that would be less acceptable is the use of students in training to conduct medical–legal exams. I have read many reports in which students administered the testing and missed obvious signs of noncredible performance—data that were not captured in the test scores subsequently shown to the supervisor (e.g., nonphysiological rhythmic "fast–slow" tapping patterns, lengthy pauses on forward Digit Span). It would be reasonable that in these situations both the supervisor and the student should be deposed, and the student should be asked how many medical–legal evaluations he/she has conducted. I suspect that the field of neuropsychology was slow to identify the issue of noncredible performance precisely because many supervisors had completely "retired" from the business of testing, resulting in a situation in which neither supervisors nor students had adequate direct clinical experience in noncredible presentations.

Documentation of Test Responses and Order of Test Administration

Photocopying of Test Forms

Photocopying of test forms is now understood to be illegal and unethical, and current training programs are vigilant against the practice. For many of us who were trained 25+ years ago, however, copying of forms was ubiquitous at that time and was not given a second thought. Through personal experience (thankfully many years ago), I can assure readers that it is uncomfortable to be in the midst of testifying and to have opposing counsel ask about the copyright symbol clearly visible on photocopied test pages.

Patient Identifiers on Test Data Sheets

I also once learned the hard way that an easy method for an opposing attorney to discredit one's testimony is to ask whether unlabeled raw test data sheets actually pertain to the patient in question. Therefore, I highly recommend that patient identifiers be placed on every raw test data sheet.

Test Administration Order

The clinician should also consider documenting the order in which tests were administered. In at least two depositions I have been asked for the order of test administration, and opposing counsel appeared disconcerted that I actually had written notations as to test sequence. I am not sure exactly what type of attack was in store for me if I had not known this information, but perhaps questions could have been raised about whether test results could have been attributed to time of day or to the patient's being hungry or tired before lunch, or whether administration of particular tests interfered with the validity of subsequent tests. Or perhaps it would just appear "sloppy" to a jury if a neuropsychologist could not report the sequence of the tests administered.

Documentation of Behavioral Observations

The examiner should note important behavioral observations, including keeping track of any requests to take breaks or to get up to stretch (which can be compared against patient reports of debilitating pain); spontaneous use of fingers (which can be compared against results of motor dexterity testing); and evidence (or lack thereof) of significant memory or other cognitive problems (which can be compared against memory and other cognitive tests). An important question for the examiner to continually ask him-/herself is this: "Am I receiving consistent information from all sources of data?"

It can be particularly useful to document dramatic symptoms and atypical reactions to test stimuli (e.g., claims that the test stimuli are giving the patient a headache; frequent sighs when the patient is presented with test instructions; bursting into tears and spontaneous comments about performing poorly when in fact test performances are within normal limits), as well as other signs that the patient views him-/herself as "fragile" (e.g., bringing a cooler of food and drinks to snack on during testing, requesting that lights be dimmed in the office, asking for some test stimuli to be covered so as not to overload his/her eyes) because they can signal the presence of somatoform conditions.

2

Assessment of Neurocognitive Symptom Validity

The viability of psychological/neuropsychological assessment hinges on the ability to verify that test scores are true and accurate. If feigned performance cannot be detected, then our assessments are worthless.

The purpose of a neuropsychological exam is to obtain objective data regarding cognitive and personality function. However, if a test taker engages in *response bias* (i.e., either under- or overreporting of symptoms), then the examiner can no longer achieve, or at least is substantially hampered in achieving, the stated objective of the testing. In this situation, the primary goal of testing changes from documenting cognitive and psychiatric function to documenting the response bias. Thus the first step in a forensic neuropsychological exam is to address the issue of response bias. Specifically, the question that needs to be answered is this: "What do objective data show about the extent and nature of any response bias the test taker is applying to the tests?"

TERMINOLOGY

An understanding of terms relevant to response bias is essential, and the interested reader is referred to the consensus practice recommendations on assessment of effort, response bias, and malingering published by the AACN (Heilbronner et al., 2009) for a thorough discussion of this issue. A brief overview of the terminology is presented here.

Malingering refers to conscious, deliberate feigning of symptoms for an obvious, external goal; an important component of this definition is intent. However, the problem with applying the term *malingering* to test takers is that although SVTs document behavior, they do not document intent. Some patients with marked somatoform disorders create symptoms that are not real, and in the process they fail measures used to document noncredible neurocognitive performances—but they do so nonconsciously, because they have come to believe that they are ill. Therefore, the term *malingering* should not be applied to them. *Malingering* should be reserved for those test takers who show evidence that they do not believe in their symptoms—that is, those who are engaging in *other*-deception rather than *self*-deception. Such evidence would include test scores/behaviors that are markedly at variance with evidence of normal function in daily life activities when the persons do not know that they are being observed.

In describing failed SVTs, it is generally preferable to use terms that do not make judgments about intent, such as *noncredible performance, nonphysiological patterns*, and *negative response bias*. The terms *poor effort* or *suboptimal effort* have also been employed, but the disadvantage of this terminology is that others can then claim that nonplausible performances on neurocognitive testing were due to lack of interest in the testing, leading to poor effort (such as the clinician may have observed in testing of some adolescents). But in the context of litigated cases, lack of interest or investment in the testing is not the operative issue; rather, the test taker is typically expending *considerable* effort to pretend to have symptoms that are not real.

Likewise, the objective, validated techniques for identifying noncredible neurocognitive performances are often referred to as *effort tests*, but preferable terms would be *SVTs* or *measures of response bias*.

PREVALENCE OF NEGATIVE RESPONSE BIAS IN COGNITIVE TESTING

Mittenberg, Patton, Canyock, and Condit (2002) surveyed members of the American Board of Clinical Neuropsychology (ABCN) regarding the number of probable cases of malingered cognitive symptoms they had encountered within the previous year. The reported rates of such cases were approximately 29% in personal injury litigation, 30% in disability or workers' compensation claims, 19% in criminal cases, and 8% in nonforensic cases. When data were analyzed by diagnosis within a compensation-seeking setting, estimates of rates of feigning were 39% for mild head injury, 35% in fibromyalgia or chronic fatigue syndrome, 31% in chronic pain or somatoform disorders, 26% in neurotoxic injury, 22% in electrical injury, 15% in depressive disorders, 14% in anxiety disorders, 11% in dissociative disorders, 11% in seizure disorder, 9% in moderate or severe head injury, and only 2% in vascular dementia.

Several studies have provided estimates of noncredible cognitive performance based on rates of positive findings on measures of response bias. Larrabee (2003c), in reviewing 11 published studies on rate of feigning of cognitive symptoms associated with mTBI in civil forensic cases ($n = 1,363$), concluded that the overall base rate was 40%. This percentage closely matches the rate of estimated excessive medical costs (35–42%) associated with auto accidents in a Rand Corporation study (Carroll, Abrahamse, & Vaiana, 1995). Similarly, rates of SVT failure in disability seekers have been reported as ranging from 42% to more than 50% (Chafetz, 2011a, 2011b; Chafetz, Pretkowski, & Rao, 2011).

Meyers and Diep (2000) reported that in individuals claiming cognitive deficits as results of chronic pain, 29% of the litigating group ($n = 55$) failed two or more cognitive SVTs; in contrast, none of the patients in the nonlitigating group ($n = 53$) failed more than one test. Gervais, Rohling, Green, and Ford (2004) provided data on a sample of 519 cases referred for assessment in connection with workers' compensation, long-term disability, or personal injury claims (66% orthopedic injuries, 9% fibromyalgia or chronic fatigue syndrome, 7% PTSD or other anxiety disorders, 5% repetitive strain injuries, and 3% depression). Ten percent ($n = 52$) of the sample failed two of three measures of cognitive response bias, and 7% ($n = 38$) failed all three. Richman et al. (2006) reported that 42% (45 of 106) of patients seeking compensation primarily for soft tissue injuries or fibromyalgia failed a cognitive SVT. Greve, Ord, Bianchini, and Curtis (2009) observed that in a sample of 508 compensation seekers with pain complaints (89% workers' compensation, 9% personal injury, 2% disability), 25.2% met criteria for probable or definite (8.9%) and malingered neurocognitive dysfunction, while upwards of 36% met criteria for malingered pain-related disability. Thus the rate of feigned cognitive symptoms in patients reporting pain and seeking compensation appears to range from 17% to 42%.

Van Hout, Schmand, Wekking, and Deelman (2006) documented that 27.4% (84 of 306) of solvent-exposed workers performed below expectations on at least two of three cognitive SVTs, while an additional 44.7% ($n = 137$) were judged to have provided "dubious effort" (failure on one SVT). Greve et al. (2006) reported that 40% of 128 persons seeking compensation for toxic exposure met criteria for definite or probable malingering of cognitive symptoms. Thus, in compensation-seeking claims of toxic injury, noncredible cognitive symptoms have been found in 27–40%.

Larrabee et al. (2009) have suggested that the available data argue for a new "magical number" for prevalence of feigned cognitive symptoms in compensation-seeking settings: 40% ± 10%.

Regarding the rate of feigned cognitive symptoms in criminal defendants, Ardolf, Denney, and Houston (2007) documented that 54% (57 of 105) of pretrial and presentence defendants undergoing neuropsychological evaluation for claimed cognitive deficits or neurological concerns met criteria for either definite or probable malingering of cognitive symptoms; >89% failed at least one SVT, while 70.5% failed two or more.

In conclusion, current research indicates that feigning of cognitive symptoms is highly prevalent in compensation-seeking and criminal evaluation contexts.

HOW IMPORTANT IS RESPONSE BIAS IN A NEUROPSYCHOLOGICAL EXAM?

As illustrated by Rohling, Larrabee, and Millis (2012) in their graphing of effect sizes for various conditions/diagnoses on cognitive test performance, malingering has a massive effect, essentially equal to that of a frank dementia (see Figure 2.1). In a study of head injury, negative correlations were observed between neuropsychological test scores and head injury severity in patients who passed cognitive SVTs, but not in patients who failed SVTs (Moss, Jones, Fokias, & Quinn, 2003). Similarly, Fox (2011) reported that documented evidence of brain damage was significantly correlated with neuropsychological test performance when SVTs were passed, but not when they were failed. He further observed much larger effect sizes for the impact of SVTs (d's = 1.01–1.22) than for brain damage (d = 0.64) on cognitive test performance, but the effect size for brain damage rose dramatically when only patients passing both SVTs were examined (d = 1.30). In contrast, presence of documented brain damage was not associated with SVT performance, indicating that it did not account for the failures.

Meyers, Volbrecht, Axelrod, and Reinsch-Boothby (2011) found that the number of failures on embedded SVTs was negatively associated with overall neuropsychological test battery mean scores (r = −.77)—a finding comparable to the relationship reported earlier by Green, Rohling, Lees-Haley, and Allen (2001) between a free-standing SVT and overall test battery mean scores. Both studies noted that 50% of variance in neuropsychological test scores was explained by SVT failures. In a study in Germany, Stevens, Friedel, Mehren, and Merten (2008) reported that effort accounted for 35% of score variance on measures of thinking speed, memory, and intelligence.

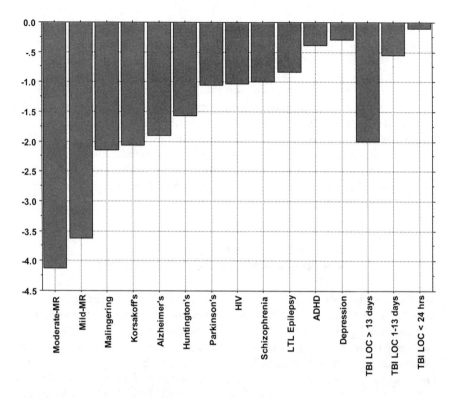

FIGURE 2.1. Effect sizes on cognitive test performance for various conditions/ diagnoses. MR, mental retardation; HIV, human immunodeficiency virus; LTL, left temporal lobe; ADHD, attention-deficit/hyperactivity disorder; LOC, loss of consciousness. From Rohling, Larrabee, and Mills (2012). Copyright by Taylor & Francis Ltd. *www.informaworld.com*. Reprinted by permission.

CAN NEGATIVE RESPONSE BIAS BE ADEQUATELY IDENTIFIED THROUGH INTERVIEW AND/OR STANDARD COGNITIVE TESTS?

Some neuropsychologists have opined that they do not need to use SVTs because they "know" when someone is feigning: "If Mr. X is faking, then he is the best actor since [fill in the blank]!" But what does the empirical literature indicate about the ability of psychologists to detect feigning without the use of validated techniques? In an early study by Heaton, Smith, Lehman, and Vogt (1978), the success of 10 neuropsychologists in identifying feigned neuropsychological data (16 out of 32 total protocols) when they knew that at least some of the records were feigned ranged from chance to slightly above chance. Similarly, Faust and colleagues documented poor ability to detect pediatric (Faust, Hart, & Guilmette, 1988) and adolescent malingering (Faust, Hart, Guilmette, & Arkes, 1988) in large samples of more than 125 clinicians. In fact, the literature has historically shown that mental health professionals have poor ability to detect pseudopatients (Rosenhan, 1973). Some testees engaging in malingering will show obvious "suspicious" behaviors (e.g., forgetting to maintain stuttering or tremors, failure to recall overlearned information such as birthdate), but these probably constitute a minority of the individuals engaging in symptom feigning. It is a frequent experience to evaluate an examinee who appears credible on interview, but, once testing begins, to see clear evidence of noncredible performance emerging.

But probably the most compelling evidence that psychologists are poor at detecting feigned performance solely on the basis of interview and standard psychological test performance is the fact that in the 1980s malingering was thought to be relatively rare in litigation (Binder, 1986), whereas now it is appreciated that 40% or more of litigants claiming mTBI are feigning cognitive symptoms (Mittenberg et al., 2002; Larrabee, 2003c). That is, before the advent of tests and techniques to identify response bias, psychologists were in fact not detecting the vast majority of noncredible individuals. Thus it is imperative that neuropsychologists use measures to document response bias, as various neuropsychological organizations have recommended (NAN—Bush et al., 2005; AACN—Heilbronner et al., 2009).

STRATEGIES FOR IDENTIFICATION OF NONCREDIBLE PERFORMANCE

Once in a deposition, opposing counsel asked, "You indicated that plaintiff was not credible on testing, but your determination of credibility—isn't that a subjective determination, a matter of 'art,' so to speak?" As listed in Table 2.1, a neuropsychologist has several methods for examining the credibility of neuropsychological test performance. Using some combination of these strategies provides converging evidence of noncredible test performance, and allows for objective determination and documentation of response bias. That is, it moves identification of noncredible performance from a subjective "hunch" to an objectively based decision. I devote most of the rest of this chapter to discussing use of measures of response bias (freestanding SVTs and embedded indicators, the first two categories in Table 2.1), but I briefly discuss the other types of strategies at the chapter's end.

TABLE 2.1. Strategies for Detection of Feigned Cognitive Symptoms

- Noncredible patterns on free-standing SVTs
- Noncredible patterns on embedded indicators derived from standard cognitive tests
- Inconsistency in scores within/across cognitive evaluation
- Inconsistency between test scores and ADLs
- Inconsistency between injury specifics and test scores (improbable outcomes)
- Elevated overreport scales on personality testing

MEASURES OF RESPONSE BIAS

The examiner can and should employ measures specifically designed to assess for response bias (*free-standing* or *dedicated* SVTs). However, emerging data show that SVTs derived from standard cognitive tests (*embedded indicators*) are of increasing importance in measuring the credibility of performance. These latter techniques have the advantage of measuring both response bias and specific cognitive skills, and thus do not add to test battery administration time. Furthermore, since the original and primary use of the tests is to measure cognitive skills, they are less likely to be identified as SVTs; thus it is less probable that test takers will be educated/coached about their use in measuring response bias.

How Do Neurocognitive SVTs Work?

The effectiveness of the majority of neuropsychological SVTs relies on the fact that the general public holds faulty beliefs about the effects of brain injury—specifically, that the following skills are impaired:

- Recognition memory
- Basic attention
- Overlearned information (alphabet, simple calculations, sight reading, and letter discrimination)
- Motor strength/dexterity

However, these domains are relatively spared in all but the most severe cases of brain injury (Baddeley & Warrington, 1970; Black, 1986; Heaton et al., 1978; Mittenberg, Rotholc, Russell, & Heilbronner, 1996; Rawling & Brooks, 1990; Rubinsky & Brandt, 1986; Wiggins & Brandt, 1988).

Several recognition memory tests employ a *forced-choice* paradigm, in which subjects have a 50% chance of selecting a correct answer on each trial (see Table 2.2). Overall scores significantly below chance have been used to document noncredible performance, in that even individuals who have not been exposed to the test stimuli would be expected to obtain approximately half of the items correct. However, < 15% of "real-world" noncredible patients score significantly below chance (Binder & Willis, 1991; M. S. Kim et al., 2010; Slick, Hopp, Strauss, Hunter, & Pinch, 1994; Wiggins & Brandt, 1988), indicating that this method of interpreting forced-choice test performance is rarely effective. A common mistake observed in neuropsychological reports is to refer to a score at or slightly below half correct (e.g., 25 out of 50) as "significantly below chance." However, "significantly below chance" actually refers to scores that are below chance at $p < .05$; this translates into scores of < 19 out of 50.

How Are SVTs Validated?

An effective SVT should have both high *sensitivity* and *specificity*. *Sensitivity* refers to the percentage of noncredible individuals identified as such by a measure, while *specificity* refers to the percentage of credible individuals identified as such by the test. A test might identify all malingerers (100% sensitivity), but this does not necessarily make it a good measure of response bias; if the test also misidentifies a high percentage of credible patients as noncredible (low specificity), it would be irresponsible to use this test given the likely possibility of harm to credible patients. Conversely, if a test does not misidentify any credible patients as noncredible, but detects few malingerers, it would be essentially worthless. As cutoffs are adjusted to increase sensitivity, specificity falls, and vice versa. Test cutoffs are traditionally set to maintain ≥ 90% specificity (Boone, Lu, & Wen, 2005; Boone et al., 2000; Greve, Ord, Curtin, Bianchini, & Brennan, 2008; M. S. Kim et al., 2010; N. Kim et al., 2010), reflecting the emphasis the field places on protecting credible patients even if this results in some sacrifice in detecting noncredible individuals. However, it is also helpful to have cutoffs available

---

TABLE 2.2. Available Forced-Choice Free-Standing SVTs

- Word Memory Test (WMT)
- Test of Memory Malingering (TOMM)
- Warrington Recognition Memory Test—Words
- Computerized Assessment of Response Bias (CARB)
- Victoria Symptom Validity Test (VSVT)
- Portland Digit Recognition Test
- Hiscock Memory Test
- Validity Indicator Profile (VIP)
- Medical Symptom Validity Test (MSVT)
- Nonverbal Medical Symptom Validity Test (NV-MSVT)

---

that correspond to 100% specificity (i.e., the score that no credible patient falls below). Although sensitivity may be low with this cutoff score, if a test taker in fact falls beyond the cutoff, it can be argued that there is virtually no likelihood of false positive identification.

The two major types of research designs employed in validation of measures of response bias are *simulation studies* and *known-groups* (or "criterion" groups) *designs*. In simulation studies, participants, typically normal volunteers (e.g., college undergraduates), are instructed to feign symptoms. The main concern about simulation studies is the questionable generalizability of results to real-world noncredible populations. Simulators typically do not match such populations in demographics (e.g., age, education); more important, incentives are markedly different for simulators versus compensation seekers, and this probably affects commitment to feigning. In fact, many simulation studies have shown that a subset of simulators in fact do not feign, despite instructions to do so (e.g., Lindstrom, Coleman, Thomassin, Southall, & Lindstrom, 2011). This has led Rogers (1997) to recommend that simulation studies require post-experiment questionnaires in which participants are queried on the extent of their compliance with simulation instructions. Simulation studies tend to show higher sensitivity rates than known-groups studies (e.g., the Rey Auditory Verbal Learning Test [RAVLT]: Boone et al., 2005; the California Verbal Learning Test–II [CVLT-II]—Donders & Strong, 2011; Wolfe et al., 2010). As a result, validation of SVTs on simulators will overestimate true effectiveness of the tests. Furthermore, some plaintiffs' attorneys will attack the use of SVTs by claiming they were not validated in real-world settings. In fact, SVTs developed on simulators should not be employed until the appropriateness of cutoff scores is verified in real-world populations.

In known-groups designs, patients are assigned to noncredible groups based on motive to feign, failure on independent SVTs, and evidence that low cognitive scores are at substantial variance with evidence of intact function in ADLs. Patients assigned to credible groups should have no motive to feign and should fail one or no SVTs (as discussed on p. 50, failure on a single SVT is not unusual in credible patient populations). They should also have no diagnoses of amnestic disorder/dementia or low IQ (< 70), given the high rates of SVT failures in these populations despite performance to true capability (Dean, Victor, Boone, & Arnold, 2008; Dean, Victor, Boone, Philpott, & Hess, 2009); if these participants are retained, cutoffs will have to be lowered to protect them, and will be so low as to have inadequate sensitivity. Some claim that a disadvantage of this approach is that accuracy of group assignment is not absolutely known, but in reality the likelihood of incorrect assignment to groups is low. As discussed on pages 50–51, failure on two or more SVTs is associated with at least 95% specificity—indicating that very few credible patients will be incorrectly assigned via this method, and virtually guaranteeing that all patients in noncredible groups are in fact feigning.

Some authors have argued that *positive predictive power* (PPP) and *negative predictive power* (NPP) of tests should be considered when examiners are interpreting findings from SVTs. PPP refers to the proportion of the sample predicted to have the condition who actually have it, while NPP describes the proportion predicted not to have the condition who in fact do not have it; both rely on the base rate of the condition in the testing context. For example, as Rosenfeld, Sands, and van Gorp (2000) illustrate, if a test cutoff achieves 77% sensitivity at 90% specificity for detection of noncredible performance, but the base rate of negative response bias is only 15%, almost half of subjects classified as noncredible would be in fact performing to true ability.

However, according to this line of reasoning, if the base rate of noncredible test performance is very low, it is questionable whether SVTs should be administered, because even if a test is failed the examiner is still more likely to be correct (from a probability standpoint) if he/she judges the patient to be credible. The problem with this argument is that in fact noncredible performance can be found in unusual and unexpected settings. For example, my colleagues and I once observed that a patient in a depression treatment study failed several SVTs but had no apparent motive for feigning. The treating therapist indicated that the patient's symptoms did not "add up," and that the patient was very vague and evasive when providing a history. The patient dropped out of the study, and it was eventually concluded that she probably had a factitious disorder. Similarly, a patient in an Alzheimer's disease treatment study was found to be noncredible on cognitive testing (she failed numerous SVTs and produced bizarre pencil-and-paper constructions, but when repeatedly pressed to redo the designs, she subsequently copied them flawlessly). Although she did not appear to have a motive to feign, her family eventually asked that disability paperwork be completed; whether the patient had a factitious disorder or was malingering was unclear. To have concluded that these individuals were credible simply because symptom feigning is rare is these settings would have been an error.

Furthermore, if as neuropsychologists we truly ascribed to the belief that base rates should inform diagnoses, why do we bother teaching our students about more unusual illnesses and their neuropsychological characteristics, if from a probability standpoint the students would be more accurate in never diagnosing such a condition than in concluding that it is indeed occasionally present? I recently evaluated a woman with parkinsonism related to anoxia; although I had not seen such a patient in over a decade, the constellation of shuffling gait, masked facies, micrographic handwriting, tremor, and extremely slowed response rate was unmistakable and irrefutable (although, granted, I was registering the combination of symptoms, not a test score in isolation). Frankly, if it looks like a duck, walks like a duck, and quacks like a duck, it most likely is a duck; it does not matter how many other ducks are around.

PPP and NPP refer to the predictive accuracy of a single test, but the field is in fact moving away from use of single tests to instead relying on data from multiple SVTs, rendering the predictive accuracy of individual tests in isolation less relevant. As discussed on pages 50–51, failures on two to three SVTs approach 100% specificity. Larrabee (2008) has shown that multiple positive SVT findings lead to high posterior probabilities of malingering, even in low base-rate settings.

How Should SVTs Be Selected, and How Many Should Be Administered?

Current recommended clinical practice is to "disperse SVTs or measures with symptom validity indicators throughout the evaluation, with administration of at least one SVT early in the evaluation process" (NAN—Bush et al., 2005, p. 424), including both free-standing and embedded indicators (AACN—Heilbronner et al., 2009).

Dozens of different neurocognitive SVTs (free-standing and embedded) have been described in the literature, many of which are reviewed in Boone (2007a) and Larrabee (2007). Administration of several neurocognitive SVTs, as discussed more fully on pages 50–51, provides increasing confidence in conclusions regarding presence of response bias.

In selecting measures of response bias for use, the *first consideration* would be test effectiveness as assessed by sensitivity while maintaining adequate specificity. Sensitivity values of < 40% are considered low; values of 40–69% are moderate; and values of ≥ 70% are high. Low- to moderate-sensitivity tests can be used to "rule in" but not "rule out" response bias. That is, cutoffs are set to protect credible patients at a sacrifice to sensitivity (i.e., ≥ 90% specificity). Thus a failing score is highly informative, while a passing score is less so. For low- to moderate-sensitivity SVTs, a passing score could still be present in a test taker who is faking deficits; he/she could simply be in the ±50% of noncredible patients who pass the measure.

When a neuropsychologist is providing testimony, it is not unheard of for him/her to be questioned about the sensitivity of SVTs employed. The following would not be effective testimony:

> DEFENSE COUNSEL: I started out asking questions about the two tests for effort and malingering that you gave: the Rey 15-Item

Memorization Test and the Validity Indicator Profile. Are there data or known success rates in picking up malingerers for those two?

PLAINTIFF NEUROPSYCHOLOGICAL EXPERT: I imagine there's some sort of published information in the manual.

The neuropsychologist should have a general idea of the sensitivity rates of SVTs used, or at least should have the information readily available to refer to. Table 2.3 shows real-world sensitivity levels of commonly used SVTs when cutoffs are set to > 88% specificity.

A *second consideration* in neurocognitive SVT selection is the need to sample response bias repeatedly during a neuropsychological exam. A recent survey of neuropsychological forensic assessment experts showed that approximately 79% of respondents reported giving at least one SVT in every litigant assessment, with the Rey 15-Item Memorization Test and TOMM cited as the most frequently administered tests (Slick, Tan, Strauss, & Hultsch, 2004). A survey of NAN members revealed that 56% reported often or always including a measure of response bias in neuropsychological evaluations: the TOMM, MMPI-2 (F-K and FBS), Rey 15-Item, and CVLT were endorsed as the most frequently administered SVTs (Sharland & Gfeller, 2007). However, reliance on a single SVT incorrectly assumes that response bias is constant across an exam. Instead, response bias typically fluctuates across an exam; therefore, *continuous sampling* of performance veracity is needed (Boone, 2009).

In a recent paper (Boone, 2009), I described two patients who feigned cognitive symptoms, but only during discrete parts of the neuropsychological exam. For example, a 51 year-old disability-seeking female claiming depression, anxiety, and fibromyalgia failed two SVTs—but only halfway through the exam, after she had spontaneously commented, "You do know that my brain is on overload!" Her response bias, occurring only during the second half of the exam, was serving to illustrate that she did not function when she was tired. Similarly, a 59-year-old disability-seeking male claiming panic attacks and depression failed four SVTs—but only while exhibiting "panic attacks," during which tears streamed down his face and his hands shook, causing the table to bang against the wall. Oddly, he made no comment regarding any distress or need to discontinue the testing temporarily. His response bias, confined to the attacks, was in the service of demonstrating severe dysfunction only during the attacks.

Other examples included a 31-year-old personal injury litigant claiming brain injury (with no loss of consciousness), who commented at the beginning of the exam, "I can tell you this is going to be affected by the

TABLE 2.3. Sensitivity Levels of Commonly Used SVTs

SVT	Cutoff	Sensitivity	Reference
	Free-standing SVTs		
Warrington Recognition Memory Test Words			M. S. Kim et al. (2010)
All-purpose cutoffs			
Accuracy	≤42	88.9%	
Time	≥207 sec.	65.5%	
b Test (E-score)			Boone, Lu, and Herzberg
All-purpose cutoff	≥150	64%	(2002a)
TBI-specific cutoff	≥90	77%	
Dot Counting Test (E-score)			Boone, Lu, and Herzberg
All-purpose cutoff	≥17	73–79%	(2002b); Boone and Lu
TBI-specific cutoff	≥19	72%	(2007)
Rey Word Recognition Test (combination score)			Nitch, Boone, Wen, Arnold, and Alfano (2006)
TBI-specific cutoff	≤9	82%	
Rey 15-Item Memorization Test			Boone, Salazar, Lu,
All-purpose cutoff			Warner-Chacon, and
Standard	<9	46%	Razani (2002); Boone and
With recognition trial	<20	56–71%	Lu (2007)
TOMM (Trial 2)	≤48	70%	Greve, Ord, Curtis,
TBI-specific cutoffs	≤45	48%	Bianchini, and Brennan (2008)
Pain-specific cutoffs	≤49	55%	
VIP			Ross and Adams (1999)
Verbal	Invalid	27%	
Nonverbal	Invalid	45%	
Portland Digit Recognition Test			Greve et al. (2008)
Easy			
TBI-specific cutoff	≤24	74%	
Pain-specific cutoff	≤26	47%	
Hard			
TBI-specific cutoff	≤19	56%	
Pain-specific cutoff	≤20	47%	
Total			
TBI-specific cutoff	≤44	70%	
Pain-specific cutoff	≤46	41%	
WMT			Greve et al. (2008)
Immediate recall			
TBI-specific cutoff	≤75	59%	
Pain-specific cutoff	≤87.5	60%	

TABLE 2.3. *(continued)*

SVT	Cutoff	Sensitivity	Reference
Delayed recall			
TBI-specific cutoff	≤77.5	63%	
Pain-specific cutoff	≤87.5	57%	
Inconsistency		63%	
TBI-specific cutoff	≤72.5		
Pain-specific cutoff	≤82.5	55%	
At published cutoffs		85% (but 30% false-positive rate)	

Embedded SVTs

SVT	Cutoff	Sensitivity	Reference
CVLT-II			Root, Robbins, Chang, and van Gorp (2006);
Forced-choice recognition			Wolfe et al. (2010);
All-purpose cutoff	≤14	44%	Donders and Strong (2011)
Logistic regression			
TBI-specific cutoff	.63	49.4%	
TBI-specific cutoff	.67	37.5%	
Wisconsin Card Sorting Test (WCST)			Greve, Heinly, Bianchini, and Love (2009)
Failure to Maintain Set			
TBI-specific cutoff	≥3	29%	
WAIS-III Digit Span			Babikian, Boone, Lu, and Arnold (2006); Babikian
Age-corrected scaled score (ACSS)			and Boone (2007); Greiffenstein, Baker, and
All-purpose cutoff	≤5	36–47%	Gola (1994)
Reliable digit span (RDS)			
All-purpose cutoff	≤6	38–57%	
TBI-specific cutoff	≤7	68–70%	
Three-digit time			
All-purpose cutoff	>3 sec.	38%	
Finger Tapping Test (dom.—three-trial mean)			Arnold et al. (2005)
Men			
All-purpose cutoff	≤35	50%	
TBI-specific cutoff	≤33	32%	
Women			
All-purpose cutoff	≤28	61%	
TBI-specific cutoff	≤32	67%	
WAIS-III Digit Symbol (recognition)			N. Kim et al. (2010)
All-purpose cutoff	≤57	79.9%	
WAIS-III Picture Completion (Most Discrepant Index)			Solomon et al. (2010)
All-purpose cutoff	≤2	65%	*(continued)*

TABLE 2.3. (continued)

SVT	Cutoff	Sensitivity	Reference
WMS-III Logical Memory (equation)			Bortnik et al. (2010)
All-purpose cutoff	≤39.5	55.6%	
Finger Agnosia Test (errors)			Trueblood and Schmidt
TBI-specific cutoff	>3	56%	(1993)
RO Figure (equation)			Lu, Boone, Cozolino, and
All-purpose cutoff	≤45	64–74%	Mitchell (2003); Boone and
Cross-validation sample	≤50	80%	Lu (2007); Reedy (2011)
RAVLT (equation)			Boone, Lu, and Wen (2005)
All-purpose cutoff	≤12	74%	
RAVLT/RO discriminant function			Sherman, Boone, Lu, and Razani (2002); Boone and
All-purpose cutoff	≤−.40	61–71%	Lu (2007)

Note. For information regarding additional symptom validity measures, including cutoffs and sensitivity–specificity rates validated in mTBI, the reader is referred to Victor, Kulick, and Boone (in press-a, in press-b).

time of day." She failed the first SVT administered (Rey Word Recognition Test = 6; combination score = 9; Nitch et al., 2006) and also obtained a borderline score on the next standard cognitive task administered (RO Figure, 3-minute delay = 3rd percentile for age). However, immediately afterward her cognitive performance "zoomed up." Specifically, on the next test, a visual-perceptual task, she scored in the superior range (WAIS-III Picture Completion = 95th percentile for age); all subsequent visual memory scores were above average, as were virtually all remaining neuropsychological scores (the patient ultimately achieved an overall IQ of 147), and all remaining SVTs (seven of eight) were passed. Her response bias only occurred when she was attempting to showcase that she was dysfunctional in the morning. Conversely, a 45-year-old male personal injury litigant claiming brain injury (but with no loss of consciousness) failed a single SVT during the morning portion of the exam, which would be equivocal evidence of negative response bias. However, after a lunch break with his attorney, he markedly failed subsequent measures of response bias. If measures of response bias had not been administered during all portions of the neuropsychological exams, the response bias in these cases would probably not have been documented.

In the Boone (2009) paper, archival data from 146 noncredible patients showed that when at least four SVTs were administered (with failure required on at least two), the average number of tests failed was 64%;

only 16% of the patients failed all SVTs; and approximately a third of the sample failed half or fewer of administered SVTs. These findings confirm that in fact negative response bias is not constant or static across a neuropsychological exam, at least for the vast majority of noncredible patients. Similarly, in a study of feigned amnesia for a crime involving 40 simulators who were administered seven measures of response validity (Giger, Merten, Merckelbach, & Oswald, 2010), 3 subjects failed none; 2 failed one; 7 failed three; 2 failed four; 10 failed five; 1 failed six; and 3 failed all seven. These results again show that noncredible participants do not display negative response bias on every SVT. In a second simulation study of individuals instructed to malinger, as compared to psychiatric patients who were instructed to respond honestly, "unanimous" findings on four SVTs occurred in only half of the cases, and 46% of the malingering sample were classified as honest by at least one test (Rosenfeld, Green, Pivovarova, Dole, & Zapf, 2010).

Some noncredible individuals will do well on some tests, but this does not negate the fact that they are not credible. Johnstone and Cooke (2003), in surveying strategies used by their simulators to feign mental retardation, noted that participants reported using strategic "honest" responses; this confirms that at least a subset of individuals intuit when feigning that it would not appear plausible to perform poorly on every test administered. During a neuropsychological exam, most individuals attempting to feign cognitive symptoms are deliberating and "picking and choosing" which tests to perform poorly. If only one or two SVTs are administered across a several-hour cognitive exam, it is very possible that an individual who is in fact feigning symptoms on at least some tasks will not be detected.

Ideally, every cognitive task should have attached validity indicators so that response bias can be measured in "real time," instead of extrapolated from tests administered adjacent to (or minutes or even hours separate from) the target test. Thus the relevant question is not "How many SVTs should be administered?" but rather "Has an attempt been made to select standard neuropsychological tests for administration that have SVTs embedded, so that response bias can be assessed continuously?"

A *third and related consideration* in determining which SVTs to administer is the need to employ SVTs that tap, or appear to tap, various neuropsychological domains. Use of just one or two SVTs assumes incorrectly that response bias presents in the same manner in all individuals (i.e., that all patients who are feigning use the same strategies). In fact, response bias may be confined to specific types of tasks. An individual intent on feigning cognitive symptoms during an exam has to decide what types of deficits he/she wishes to portray, and then select tests for underperformance that are perceived to measure the targeted skills. Fabricated cognitive symptoms can occur in the domains of memory, attention, processing speed, motor dexterity and strength, sensory function, language, visual-perceptual/visual–spatial skills, executive abilities, math, and overall intelligence. The decision as to what deficits to feign is probably based on the person's beliefs regarding what types of deficits accompany his/her claimed condition (e.g., head injury, fibromyalgia, ADHD, toxic exposure). In addition or alternatively, individuals may feign deficits observed in their environment; for example, they may have driven a bus for disabled children, lived with a grandmother who had a right-hemisphere stroke, or the like (which is why it is helpful to note during the interview whether the testee has been exposed to any such models).

In the Boone (2009) paper, I provided examples of two personal injury litigants claiming brain injury for head injuries (in which they did not lose consciousness), who failed different types of SVTs. For example, a 56-year-old female litigant failed SVTs associated with measures of finger dexterity (tapping), thinking speed, and visual-perceptual/memory skills; all other standard neuropsychological scores were within the normal range, with the exception of these three areas. Of note, she passed measures of response bias associated with other domains. Conversely, a 66-year-old male litigant failed three verbal memory SVTs, and his only lowered scores across the neuropsychological battery were in verbal memory; he passed all cognitive SVTs in other cognitive domains.

More recently, a colleague and I have described another personal injury litigant suing in the context of claimed TBI (with no loss of consciousness), who presented with noncredible symptoms only in language (acquired "foreign" accent, grammatical errors similar to those made by persons with English as a second language [ESL], articulation distortions, word retrieval problems) and sensory skills (noncredible hearing exam and excessive errors on finger localization; Cottingham & Boone, 2010). She failed three SVTs confined to letter discrimination, verbal repetition speed, and finger agnosia errors, but passed seven measures of response bias associated with the domains of verbal and visual memory, processing speed, attention, and motor dexterity. Low scores on standard neuropsychological tests were limited to tasks involving speech (rapid word reading and color naming, sentence repetition, and word generation) and auditory discrimination, with some impaired scores on some measures of processing speed and in finger tapping in her nondominant hand.

In these three case examples, the failed measures of response bias generally predicted which standard scores were differentially lowered. If SVTs had not been administered that covered these areas, negative response bias would not have been detected.

In fact, various studies have provided evidence for the use of different strategies when individuals feign cognitive symptoms. Simulators of mental retardation have reported using strategies of minimal responding (incorrect, absurd, or opposite responses), "near-misses" (e.g., off by one), noncompliance (refusal to complete tasks), and strategic "honest" responses (Johnstone & Cooke, 2003). Larrabee (2004), in a cluster analysis of scores on SVTs in noncredible litigants, found that the scores grouped into four clusters: impaired attention/memory, motor dysfunction, reduced problem solving, and poor perceptual problem solving. Osimani, Alon, Berger, and Abarbanel (1997) reported that their simulators attempted to make errors, increase reaction time, or both. Tan et al. (2002) canvassed their mild traumatic brain injury simulators about the strategies they used when feigning cognitive symptoms, and noted that 76% attempted to display memory loss; 33% adopted a reduced rate of responding; 12% showed poor concentration; 16% portrayed confusion; and 20% variously endorsed appearing nervous, dyslexic, or uncomprehending. Thus, while the majority of patients in fact targeted memory loss, approximately one-quarter did not; this suggests that if only memory SVTs are administered, some 25% of noncredible individuals will not be detected.

Further complicating the picture, symptom-feigning strategies may differ as a function of patient characteristics. Substantially higher detection rates were found for an SVT derived from WAIS-III Picture Completion in less educated as compared to more educated noncredible patients (Solomon et al., 2010), suggesting that the former thought poor performance on the task would best display their functional impairment. Similarly, particularly poor scores on grip strength were more prominent in noncredible patients of lower socioeconomic status (SES) than in those of higher SES, probably because the former may perceive that poor strength better illustrates disability in the types of unskilled and blue-collar occupations they have held (Arnold & Boone, 2007). Furthermore, in a recent investigation of the visual–spatial/visual processing speed component (employing WAIS-III Block Design, WAIS-III Digit Symbol, and RO Figure copy) of the Meyers and Volbrecht (2003) SVT equation for estimating finger tapping (Curiel, 2012), 77% of noncredible males were detected with the measure, as compared to 55% of noncredible females. This finding suggests that men may view poor performance on visual processing tasks as best displaying functional deficits. In other words, level of education, SES, and gender may dictate which deficits a noncredible patient perceives will best illustrate his/her disabilities.

The particular disorder the person is attempting to feign may also guide the types of cognitive symptoms that are fabricated, and this may mean that particular SVTs will be more effective in some contexts than in others. For example, the Rey Word Recognition Test, an SVT that involves verbal recognition, is more sensitive to symptom feigning in noncredible head-injury compensation-seekers as compared to a heterogeneous noncredible group alleging diverse conditions (Nitch et al., 2006). Similarly, Greve et al. (2008) observed that forced-choice memory SVTs were more effective in identifying noncredible TBI than noncredible chronic pain presentations. Conversely, WAIS-III Picture Completion (Most Discrepant Index), the Dot Counting Test, the b Test, and the Finger Tapping Test (Arnold et al., 2005; Solomon et al., 2010; Victor et al., in press-a, in press-b) appear to be more sensitive in groups of symptom feigners with heterogeneous alleged conditions than in subjects claiming cognitive dysfunction from mTBI. The WMT, though an effective measure of response bias in many contexts, performed worse in identifying simulated dyslexia than an SVT specifically designed to detect faked reading difficulties (Osmon, Plambeck, Klein, & Mano, 2006). Individuals feigning in a civil context (personal injury litigants and disability seekers) feigned less blatantly on the Dot Counting Test than did individuals feigning severe mental disturbance in a forensic hospital setting (Boone, Lu, Back, et al., 2002).

It may be possible to group neurocognitive SVTs by the type of faking strategy they detect. For example, in a study examining relationships among eight measures of response bias (Nelson et al., 2003), the Dot Counting Test was most closely related to WAIS-III Digit Span and the Rey 15-Item Memorization Test (26–37% shared variance); the three tests have numbers/counting in common, and as such are likely to identify individuals who are feigning dysfunction involving number manipulation. The Rey 15-Item Memorization Test was most strongly correlated with the RO Figure Equation (48% shared variance), no doubt due to the requirement in both tasks to remember visual information; these two tests are likely to capture individuals feigning visual memory deficits. WAIS-III Digit Span was also closely related to the RO Figure Equation (27% shared variance); both tasks require immediate free recall, and are likely to identify individuals attempting to feign deficits in this skill. The b Test was most closely correlated with the Dot Counting Test (24% shared variance); both are timed tests and are likely to detect individuals whose strategy for feigning is to appear "slow" in thinking. The RAVLT recognition trial was most closely correlated with the Rey Word Recognition Test (41% shared variance), but, interestingly, was not strongly correlated with the Warrington Recognition Memory Test ($r = .34$), probably due to the fact that information is presented orally in the first two tasks and visually in the third task. Individuals feigning deficits in the ability to recall auditorily presented verbal information are likely to underperform on the two former tests.

Table 2.4 lists neurocognitive SVTs by the domains they are likely to tap.

A *fourth consideration* in choosing SVTs is to attempt to select tests that are not strongly correlated with each other. If tests are highly related, the information they provide is likely to be redundant (Rosenfeld et al., 2000); thus even if several highly related tests are failed, it cannot be argued that they are providing converging evidence of noncredible performance (incremental validity). In a study of eight SVTs (Rey 15-Item Memorization Test, Dot Counting Test, Rey Word Recognition Test, RAVLT recognition, RO Figure equation, WAIS-III Digit Span, Warrington Recognition Memory Test–Words, and b Test), Nelson et al. (2003) found only modest to moderate relationships (<48% shared variance) in 105 noncredible patients, with the exception of the Dot Counting Test and WAIS-III Digit Span ($r = -.75$; 56% shared variance). Therefore, use of these tests in concert can be used as converging evidence of noncredible performance with the exception that failures on both the Dot Counting Test and WAIS-III Digit Span should be viewed as relatively redundant. Of concern, some research has shown substantial correlations across forced choice memory measures; for example, correlations between the TOMM, VSVT, and Letter Memory Test range from .66 to .78 (Nelson, Sweet, Berry, Bryant, & Granacher, 2007). Other research has shown high correlations between the WMT and Warrington–Words ($r = .731$), the WMT and TOMM ($r = .701$), and the TOMM and Amsterdam Short-Term Memory Test ($r = .982$) (P. Green, personal communication, 2008), which would argue that data from these tests are largely redundant.

A *fifth consideration* in selection of measures of response bias is the potential confound of patient characteristics/diagnoses. A priority in appropriate and ethical use of SVTs is to ensure that credible patients are not incorrectly identified as noncredible. Some populations are at risk for SVT failure despite performing to true ability; this is particularly true of patients with low intellectual level or dementia/amnestic disorder.

• *Low intelligence.* Recent data (Dean, Victor, et al., 2008) show that individuals with IQs of 60–69 and with no motive to feign failed on average 44% of SVTs, and persons with borderline IQs (70–79) failed approximately 17% of SVTs, within a neuropsychological exam (all patients with IQs < 70 failed at least one SVT). In contrast, those with IQs between low average and superior failed < 10% of SVTs. Finger tapping as a measure of response bias was the most robust to lowered IQ, while tests requiring attention/encoding showed the worst specificity rates (e.g., Rey 15-Item Memorization Test, Rey Word Recognition, WAIS-III Digit Span variables). Summaries of the available literature addressing performance of individuals with very low intellectual level are provided by Victor and Boone (2007), Dean, Victor, et al. (2008), and Salekin and Doane (2009). Table 2.5 shows specificity values for various SVTs in low IQ samples.

TABLE 2.4. Free-Standing and Embedded SVTs, Grouped by Domains They Are Likely to Tap

	Verbal Memory	Visual Memory	Attention/ vigilance	Processing speed	Language	Sensory–Motor	Executive	Visual perception/ construction	Numbers/ counting
Free-standing	MSVT Rey Word Recognition Test VIP (Verbal) Warrington Recognition Memory Test–Words WMT	CARB NV-MSVT PDRT Rey 15-Item plus Recognition TOMM VSVT	b Test Dot Counting Test	b Test Dot Counting Test Warrington Recognition Memory Test–Words (time score)	b Test VIP (Verbal)			VIP (Nonverbal)	Dot Counting Test CARB PDRT Rey 15-Item plus Recognition VSVT
Embedded	CVLT-II Rey Auditory Verbal Learning Test Equation WMS-III Logical Memory Equation	CVMT RO Effort Equation WAIS-III Digit Symbol Recognition WMS-III Faces	Conners CPT-II SRT TOVA WAIS-III Digit Span variables (ACSS, RDS, time to recite digits forward) WAIS-III WMI	Digit Span (time to recite digits forward) SDMT Trails A WAIS-III Digit Symbol Recognition WAIS-III PSI	Stroop Test SSPT Sentence Repetition Test Token Test WAIS-III VIQ/VCI	Finger Agnosia Errors Test Finger Tapping Test Grip Strength Test Grooved Pegboard Test	Category Test COWAT/ FAS WCST	Benton Facial Recognition Test JOLO RO Figure Equation; RO copy VFDT WAIS-III Picture Completion MDI WAIS-III PIQ/POI	WAIS-III Digit Span variables (ACSS, RDS, time to recite digits forward)

Note. b Test (Boone et al., 2002a); Benton Facial Recognition Test (Whiteside et al., 2011); Category Test (Greve et al., 2007); CARB (Computerized Assessment of Response Bias; Allen et al., 1997); Conners CPT-II (Continuous Performance Test-II: Ord, Boettcher, et al., 2010); COWAT/FAS (Controlled Oral Word Association Test/FAS; Curtis et al., 2008; Silverberg et al., 2008); CVLT—II (California Verbal Learning Test – II; Donders & Strong, 2011; Root et al., 2006; Wolfe et al., 2010); CVMT (Continuous Visual Memory Test; Henry & Enders, 2007; Larrabee, 2009); Dot Counting Test (Boone et al., 2002b); Finger Agnosia Errors Test (Binder et al., 2003; Trueblood & Schmidt, 1993); Finger Tapping Test (Arnold et al., 2005); Grip Strength Test (Arnold & Boone, 2007); Grooved Pegboard Test (Arnold & Boone, 2007); Hooper VOT (Hooper Visual Organization Test; Whiteside et al., 2011); JOLO (Judgment of Line Orientation; Iverson, 2001; Meyers & Volbrecht, 2003; Whiteside et al., 2011); MSVT (Medical Symptom Validity Test; Green, 2004); NV-MSVT (Non-Verbal Medical Symptom Validity Test; Green, 2008); PDRT (Portland Digit Recognition Test; Binder, 1993); Rey Auditory Verbal Learning Test Equation (RAVLT; Boone et al., 2005); Rey 15-Item plus Recognition (Boone, Salazar, et al., 2002); RO (Rey–Osterrieth) Effort Equation (Lu et al., 2003; Reedy, 2011) and RO Copy (Lu et al., 2003; Whiteside et al., 2011); Rey Word Recognition Test (Nitch et al., 2006; Bell-Sprinkel, 2012); SRT (Seashore Rhythm Test; Curtis et al., 2010; Ross et al., 2006); Sentence Repetition Test (Meyers, Morrison, & Miller, 2001; Meyers & Volbrecht, 2003; Schroeder & Marshall, 2010); SSPT (Speech Sounds Perception Test; Curtis et al., 2010; Ross et al., 2006); Stroop Test (Lu et al., 2004); SDMT (Symbol Digit Modalities Test; Backhaus, Fichentenberg & Hanks, 2004); Token Test (Meyers & Volbrecht, 2003); TOMM (Test of Memory Malingering; Tombaugh, 1996; Greve et al., 2008); TOVA (Test of Variables of Attention; Henry, 2005); Trails A (Iverson et al., 2002a); VIP (Validity Indicator Profile) NV (Nonverbal) and V (Verbal); Frederick, 1997); VFDT (Visual Form Discrimination Test; Larrabee, 2003c); VSVT (Victoria Symptom Validity Test; Slick et al., 1997); Warrington Recognition Memory Test–Words (M. Kim, 2010); WAIS-III Digit Span indicators (Babikian & Boone, 2007); WAIS-III Digit Symbol Recognition (Kim, N., et al., 2010); WAIS-III PIQ/POI (Performance IQ/Perceptual Organization Index; Curtis et al., 2009); WAIS-III Picture Completion MDI (Most Discrepant Index; Solomon et al., 2010); WAIS-III PSI (Processing Speed Index; Curtis et al., 2009); WAIS-III Verbal IQ/VCI (Verbal Comprehension Index (Curtis et al., 2009); WAIS-III WMI (Working Memory Index; Curtis et al., 2009); WMS-III Faces (Glassmire et al., 2003); WMS-III Logical Memory Equation (Bortnik et al., 2010); WCST (Wisconsin Card Sorting Test; Greve et al., 2009; Larrabee, 2003c; Ord, Greve, et al., 2010); WMT (Word Memory Test; Green, 2003)

43

TABLE 2.5. Specificity Values for SVTs in Low IQ Samples

SVT	Specificity	Reference
CVLT-II (recognition)		Marshall and Happe (2007)
Cutoff ≤ 14	89%	
Dot Counting Test (E-score)		Dean, Victor, et al. (2008); Marshall and
Cutoff ≥ 17	21–71%	Happe (2007)
Digit Memory Test		Graue et al. (2007); Shandera et al. (2010)
Cutoff < 90% correct	85–88%	
WAIS-III Digit Span		Graue et al. (2007); Dean, Victor, et al.
ACSS cutoff ≤ 5	19–33%	(2008)
ACSS cutoff ≤ 4	38%	Shandera et al. (2010)
RDS cutoff ≤ 7	78% (IQ < 80);	Mathias, Greve, Bianchi, Houston, and
RDS cutoff ≤ 6	31%	Crouch (2002); Marshall and Happe
	15–33%	(2007)
		Graue et al. (2007); Shandera et al. (2010)
		Dean, Victor, et al. (2008)
WAIS-III Vocabulary minus		Graue et al. (2007); Marshall and Happe
Digit Span		(2007)
Cutoff ≥ 4	98–100%	Shandera et al. (2010)
Cutoff ≥ 5	100%	
Digit Memory Test		Graue et al. (2007); Shandera et al. (2010)
Cutoff < 90% correct	85–88%	Graue et al. (2007); Shandera et al. (2010)
Cut-off < 80% correct	96%	
Finger Tapping Test	78–100%	Arnold et al. (2005); Dean, Victor, et al.
Cutoff for men ≤35		(2008)
Cutoff for women ≤28		
Letter Memory Test		Graue et al. (2007); Shandera et al. (2010)
Cutoff < 93% correct	58–61%	Graue et al. (2007); Shandera et al. (2010)
Cutoff < 70% correct	83–96%	
Rey 15-Item Memorization		Goldberg and Miller (1986); Hurley and
Test (IQ < 80)		Deal (2006); Marshall and Happe (2007)
Cutoff < 9	20–62%	Marshall and Happe (2007); Dean, Victor,
With recognition cutoff < 20	17–45%	et al. (2008)
Rey Word Recognition Test	57%	Dean, Victor, et al. (2008)
Cutoff for men ≤ 5		
Cutoff for women ≤ 7		
RO Figure Equation		Dean, Victor, et al. (2008)
Cutoff ≤ 47	64%	
RO/RAVLT discriminant	75%	Dean, Victor, et al. (2008)
function		
Cutoff ≤ −.40		

TABLE 2.5. (*continued*)

SVT	Specificity	Reference
TOMM		Graue et al. (2007); Hurley and Deal
Trial 2 cutoff < 45	55–95%	(2006); Simon (2007); Shandera et al.
Trial 2 cutoff < 30	96%	(2010)
Retention trial cutoff < 45	81–100%	Graue et al. (2007); Shandera et al. (2010)
Retention trial cutoff < 30	96–100%	Graue et al. (2007); Simon (2007);
		Shandera et al. (2010)
		Graue et al. (2007); Shandera et al. (2010)
VIP	5%	Frederick (1997)
VSVT		Loring, Lee, and Meador (2005)
Cutoff ≤ 20 for hard items	40%	
Warrington Recognition Memory Test–Words Cutoff ≤ 33	67%	Dean, Victor, et al. (2008)
WMT		Shandera et al. (2010)
Immediate recall		Shandera et al. (2010)
% correct < 82.5%	42%	Shandera et al. (2010)
Delayed recall		
% correct < 82.5%	42%	
Consistency		
% correct < 82.5%	25%	

- *Dementia.* Dean et al. (2009) examined SVT performance in patients diagnosed with dementia who had no motive to feign cognitive symptoms. Table 2.6 shows specificity rates for various free-standing and embedded SVTs as a function of Mini-Mental State Exam (MMSE) scores. Those with MMSE scores over 20 failed an average of 36% of SVTs administered, while those with MMSE scores of 15–20 failed an average of 47%, and patients with MMSE scores under 15 failed 83% of SVT cutoffs. As can be seen from Table 2.6, most indicators had specificities of only 30–70%, although cutoffs for some WAIS-III Digit Span indicators (Vocabulary minus Digit Span and four-digit time) maintained ≥ 90% specificity. In addition, specificity for Finger Tapping Test cutoffs was preserved in patients with Alzheimer's disease and frontal–temporal dementia, but not in those with vascular dementia. Other research (Merten, Bossink, & Schmand, 2007) has indicated that the WMT (5–10% specificity), Amsterdam Short-Term Memory Test (10% specificity), WAIS-III Digit Span RDS (30% specificity), and TOMM (Trial 2 and retention trials; 50–70% specificity) are problematic for use in individuals with Alzheimer's disease (see also Teichner & Wagner, 2004).

TABLE 2.6. Specificity Rates for SVTs as a Function of MMSE Scores

	MMSE scores in dementia patients		
	21–30	15–20	<15
WAIS-III Digit Span			
ACSS ≤ 5	84% (n = 44)	67% (n = 30)	33% (n = 9)
RDS ≤ 6	86% (n = 44)	60% (n = 30)	22% (n = 9)
Mean four-digit time >4 sec.	94% (n = 16)	83% (n = 12)	100% (n = 2)
Vocabulary minus Digit Span >5	94% (n = 35)	100% (n = 21)	100% (n = 7)
Dot Counting Test (E-score) ≥ 17	77% (n = 26)	44% (n = 18)	8% (n = 13)
TOMM (Trial) 2 <45	63% (n = 8)	33% (n = 9)	0% (n = 2)
Warrington Recognition Memory Test–Words (total) <33	73% (n = 15)	20% (n = 5)	0% (n = 3)
Rey 15-Item Memorization Test (plus recognition) <20	21% (n = 14)	0% (n = 8)	0% (n = 3)
Finger Tapping Test (men ≤ 35; women ≤ 28)	70% (n = 20)	83% (n = 12)	100% (n = 2)
b Test (E-score) ≥ 160	50% (n = 10)	38% (n = 8)	0% (n = 2)
Rey Word Recognition Test			
Total: men ≤ 5; women ≤ 7	64% (n = 11)	83% (n = 6)	50% (n = 2)
Equation ≤ 9	46% (n = 11)	50% (n = 6)	50% (n = 2)
RAVLT Equation ≤ 12	15% (n = 20)	0% (n = 9)	0% (n = 3)
RO Figure Equation ≤ 47	44% (n = 16)	15% (n = 13)	0% (n = 1)
RO/AVLT fx ≤ –.40	44% (n = 18)	29% (n = 7)	0% (n = 1)

Note. Data from Dean, Victor, Boone, Philipott, and Hess (2009).

Dean et al. (2009) provide SVT cutoffs that achieve ≥ 90% specificity in dementia, and the Dot Counting Test manual (Boone, Lu, & Herzberg, 2002b) reports cutoffs for mild (MMSE >20) and moderate (MMSE = 10 to 20) dementia that result in ≤ 10% false positive identifications (e.g., E-score ≥ 22 = 93.8% specificity in mild dementia; 62.4% sensitivity). However, adjusting cutoffs to adequately protect patients with dementia generally lowers sensitivity to unacceptable levels; thus new measures and/ or algorithms need to be developed for the differential diagnosis of actual and feigned dementia. In this vein, the Green Genuine Memory Impairment profile appears promising (Green, 2004; Howe & Loring, 2009), although the sensitivity rates of this technique may be problematic; Chafetz (2011b) documented that 42% of claimants who met criteria for malingering obtained the severe impairment profile, a rate also observed in simulators (n = 10; Singhal, Green, Ashave, Shankar, & Gill, 2009), and Axelrod and Schutte (2010) have also raised concerns regarding the effectiveness of this technique. Another viable approach might be to focus on symptom validity techniques incorporating skills that have been found to be intact in dementia (e.g., forward digit span). Yet another approach might be to rely on the total number of SVTs failed; for example, if a patient fails 85% of SVTs administered, this would be comparable to the performance of patients with advanced dementia (MMSE scores < 15), and such a test taker would not able to live independently, drive, handle finances, or manage other important ADLs. Thus, if a patient failing 85% of SVTs does not demonstrate markedly impaired function in ADLS, the SVT failure can be relied upon as evidence of noncredible neurocognitive performance.

• *Low math skills.* Preliminary data suggest that patients with poor math skills (i.e., WAIS-III Arithmetic subtest ACSS ≤ 5) are at increased risk for failing cutoffs on WAIS-III Digit Span SVTs and the Dot Counting Test (Ziegler et al., 2008a, 2008b). Therefore, math ability must be investigated before failures on these measures are interpreted as indicative of negative response bias. However, available evidence suggests that presence of learning disability, at least in college students, does not place patients at risk for failing SVTs (e.g., Rey Word Recognition Test, Rey 15-Item Memorization Test, b Test, and Dot Counting Test; Alfano & Boone, 2007).

• *Psychosis.* A subset of individuals with psychosis—namely, those with low educational level and low MMSE scores (≤ 24; likely meet criteria for dementia)—fail SVTs despite no external motive (Back et al., 1996). Psychotic individuals tend to perform poorly on continuous performance tasks (Cornblatt, Lenzenweger, & Erlenmeyer-Kimling, 1989; Nelson, Sax, & Strakowski, 1998) and for that reason are likely to be at increased risk for failure on SVTs employing this paradigm, such as the b Test; cutoffs can be adjusted for this population, but with a corresponding loss in test sensitivity (Boone, Lu, & Herzberg, 2002a). Psychotic patients (particularly those with poor concentration skills) also show increased false positive identification rates for WAIS-III Digit Span indicators, the Dot Counting Test, the Digit Memory test, and the Hiscock Memory Test, the Rey 15-Item Memorization Test, the Finger Tapping Test, and the WMT, although some research shows that performance is preserved on the Warrington Recognition Memory Test–Words, the TOMM (except in patients with concurrent concentration problems), and the VSVT (Goldberg, Back-Madruga, & Boone, 2007).

• *ESL/ethnicity*. Hispanic individuals and those with ESL status tend to perform more poorly than non-Hispanic individuals and native English speakers on WAIS-III Digit Span, placing them at risk for false positive identification as noncredible using recommended Digit Span cutoffs and necessitating that cutoffs be adjusted (Salazar, Lu, Wen, & Boone, 2007). Furthermore, as noted by Salazar et al. (2007), cutoffs for Hispanics also required adjustment for the RO equation and the Rey 15-Item Memoriza-tion Test with recognition trial, although the Dot Counting Test, RAVLT indicators, and the Warrington Recognition Memory Test–Words either required no adjustment or cutoffs could be made more stringent. For African Americans, while cutoffs for WAIS-III Digit Span indicators, the Dot Counting Test, the Rey 15-Item Memorization Test with recognition trial, and the Warrington Recognition Memory Test–Words required no or only minor adjustments, cutoffs for RO equation and RAVLT indica-tors required more dramatic modifications to maintain adequate specificity. These data should be viewed as preliminary, given differences in educa-tional level across groups.

The neuropsychological examiner has the obligation to be aware of published data on populations at risk for failure on particular SVTs and either to select SVTs on which these groups do not underperform or to adjust cutoffs to protect them. For example, on the Dot Counting Test, Table 2.7 shows cutoffs that maintain at least 88% specificity for various diagnostic groups, allowing the clinician to select the cutoff for the appro-priate differential diagnosis (e.g., actual vs. feigned psychosis).

A *sixth consideration* in SVT selection involves concern about educa-tion/coaching of patients in regard to passing SVTs. The traditional rule of thumb in neuropsychological examinations is to select tests that are the most commonly used and have the most research data. However, this may not be the most prudent approach to choosing SVTs. Unfortunately, some Internet sites potentially provide enough information regarding SVTs to allow motivated test takers to learn to pass the tests (Bauer & McCaffrey, 2006; Ruiz et al., 2002).

I conducted a record review in which an attorney, who was attempt-ing to secure disability benefits for amnestic disorder due to medication side effects, migraines, lupus, and colitis, failed an SVT (the WMT) on a first neuropsychological exam, scored at chance level on WMS-III Faces recognition, and inserted pauses in recitation of digits forward on WAIS-III Digit Span. She reported on a second exam 9 months later that she was "shocked" by the first neuropsychologist's assertion that she had not been performing to true capability. On the second exam, she passed commonly used free-standing SVTs (VIP, NV-MSVT), but performed at chance level on a visual forced-choice task embedded in a memory measure

TABLE 2.7. Dot Counting Test E-Score Cutoffs for Various Diagnostic Groups

Diagnostic group	*n*	Cutoff	Specificity (%)	Sensitivity (%)
Comparison groups combined	230	≥ 19	94.7	71.8
Advanced age	51	≥ 14	96.1	88.2
Major depression outpatient	64	≥ 14	95.3	88.2
Schizophrenia in day treatment	28	≥ 20	96.4	68.2
Moderate/severe TBI in rehab	20	≥ 20	95.0	68.2
Stroke in rehab	20	≥ 22	88.9	62.4
College learning disabilities	31	≥ 15	96.8	85.9
Mild dementia (MMSE > 20)	16	≥ 22	93.7	62.4

Note. Data from Boone, Lu, and Herzberg (2002b).

(Wide Range Assessment of Memory and Learning Design Memory forced choice; 47% correct)—a performance comparable to that of a blind person. She spontaneously reported that she recalled visual test stimuli from the first neuropsychological exam, which would not have been possible if her visual memory/learning skills were at chance levels. On two other forced-choice measures contained within standard memory tests administered on the second exam, she obtained 65–75% accuracy—also implausible performances. The claimant had been provided with the report from the first exam, which divulged the name of the SVT she failed, and also alerted her to the existence of cognitive SVTs. The most likely explanation for her performance on the second exam was that she had researched dedicated SVTs but was not aware of embedded measures.

In an initial validation study of the Rey 15-Item Memorization Test incorporating a recognition trial, data gathered from 1985 to 2000 showed test sensitivity rates above 70% (Boone, Salazar, et al., 2002). However, on cross-validation with data obtained from 2001 to 2005, sensitivities had dropped to 58% (Boone & Lu, 2007)—a decrease not observed in concurrent cross-validation of a less well-known test (the Dot Counting Test). We suspect that because the Rey 15-Item Test has been historically one of the most commonly used SVTs, it has become too accessible and its security has been breached. The publisher of the TOMM sent out a letter several years ago alerting users not to expose the acronym on the booklet covers during testing, because test takers were becoming aware of the test. I promptly pulled all the covers off the booklets, and more recently have typed up score sheets that do not contain the names or acronyms of SVTs.

Given the concern regarding coaching/education, as well as the extra time required to administer free-standing SVTs, the field is likely to focus more on embedded SVTs, as well as on discriminant functions and logistic regression analyses (e.g., see Schutte, Millis, Axelrod, & VanDyke, 2011;

Bernard, Houston, & Natoli, 1993; Bernard, McGrath, & Houston, 1996; Sherman et al., 2002; Mittenberg, Azrin, Millsaps, & Heilbronner, 1993; Mittenberg, Theroux-Fichera, Zielinski, & Heilbronner, 1995; Mittenberg et al., 2001) incorporating scores from many standard cognitive tests. The exposure/education concern requires that the examiner give many measures of response bias, not just the most popular.

A *final consideration* in SVT selection is brevity. Because of the need for multiple SVTs, it is preferable that the measures be relatively brief and/ or included in standard cognitive tests (embedded indicators), so as not to increase battery administration time substantially.

How Are Data from Multiple SVTs to Be Interpreted?

A common misapprehension is that use of multiple SVTs "complicates" test interpretation. Some neuropsychologists may say, "What do I do with all these data? Using fewer SVTs makes conclusions more straightforward and clear-cut. Adding SVTs just makes things murkier."

Another common misperception is that concurrent use of multiple SVTs dramatically raises the false positive rate for identifying a credible patient as noncredible. For example, one psychologist made the following statements:

> "Sometimes more than *half* the battery is just SVTs in forensic cases. I think that this constitutes a highly prejudicial exam and should be inadmissible. Odds alone suggest that the more of one kind of measure you give, the greater the probability that someone will do poorly on at least one or two of the measures. And with a cutting score approach, the odds of poorer performance seem to go up as well."

However, these views are not accurate. Various studies have shown that failure on two SVTs best discriminates credible and noncredible groups in terms of total classification correct, although some false positive identifications may occur at two failures. We (Victor, Boone, Serpa, Buehler, & Ziegler, 2009) reported that with cutoffs set to maintain specificity of at least 90%, failure on a single SVT (out of four) was not rare in credible patients at a neuropsychology clinic (41%), but only 5% failed two, 1.5% failed three, and none failed four. Meyers and Volbrecht (2003) examined performance on nine different SVTs, and while a single failure was not rare, failure on two or more SVTs in noninstitutionalized and nonlitigating groups was nonexistent (100% specificity). Similarly, Suhr, Tranel, Wefel, and Barrash (1997) reported that failure on two of four SVTs was associated with 100% specificity in non-compensation-seeking head injury patients; Larrabee (2003c) found that failure on two measures of response bias (out of five) was associated with 89% specificity in credible head injury patients, and failure on three SVTs was absent (100% specificity). Most recently, Chafetz (2011a) observed essentially 100% specificity with three failures out of four possible in a known groups study of Social Security applicants.

Comparable findings have been reported for simulation studies. In a study of simulated amnesia for a crime, 100% specificity was found for two failures out of seven SVTs (Giger et al., 2010); in a study of simulated ADHD, failure on three out of four indicators was associated with 100% specificity (Sollman, Ranseen, & Berry, 2010); and in a study of simulated TBI, 100% specificity was observed for failure on three of three indicators (Vickery et al., 2004).

As shown in Table 2.8, Dean et al. (2008) reported that in patients with IQ ≥ 80, failure on > 1 SVTs (out of ≤ 8) was unusual.

The best way to limit false positive identifications of patients as noncredible is in fact to administer *several* SVTs. Failure on an increasing number of indicators does not increase sensitivity, but it does increase specificity (i.e., when tests are very easy, failures are not likely to occur even when increasing numbers of tests are administered). Larrabee (2008a) illustrated that the likelihood of obtaining a false determination of malingering *decreases* with *each subsequently failed SVT*. Specifically, chaining of likelihood ratios showed an increase in probability of malingering with increasing numbers of SVTs:

- .713 to .837 for one failed SVT
- .936 to .973 for two failed SVTs
- .989 to .995 for three failed SVTs

TABLE 2.8. SVTs Failed by IQ Band in Heterogeneous Neuropsychological Clinic Patients with No Incentive to Feign

FSIQ band	n	Mean failed	Range	Mean %
50–59	3	4.0	1–6	60%
60–69	12	2.9	1–6	44%
70–79	48	1.1	0–4	17%
80–89	44	0.5	0–4	8%
90–99	39	0.3	0–2	7%
100–109	27	0.2	0–1	4%
110–119	11	0.4	0–2	6%
≥ 120	5	0.2	0–1	5%

Note. Data from Dean, Victor, Boone, and Arnold (2008).

Thus, rather than making test interpretation more problematic and error-ridden, administration of many SVTs has the potential to provide much greater confidence in conclusions about negative response bias than the use of one or two tests.

Note that this discussion relates to SVT cutoffs set to specificity rates of 90% to < 100%; to the extent that cut offs are used that are associated with 0% false positive rates, the probability of "chance" SVT failures will be even lower.

Another factor must also be considered in assessing the accuracy of SVT failures: In most SVT validation studies, some types of patients who are at increased risk for failure on SVTs are included (e.g., patients with psychosis, ESL, borderline IQ, or poor math skills). SVT cutoffs were selected to protect the credible patients, including these higher-risk patients. To the extent that a particular test taker does not fall within any of these higher-risk groups, the likelihood of false positive failures on SVTs will be even less likely.

From a Practical Standpoint, How Can the Suggestions about SVT Selection Be Implemented?

Testing can commence with the RO Figure copy, the Rey Word Recognition Test, and then RO Figure 3-minute delay. The result will be that in the first 5–10 minutes of testing, indicators of response bias from two different tests pulling for feigned deficits in verbal memory (the Rey Word Recognition Test) and visual-constructional skill/visual memory (the RO Figure Equation) will be available for review, and standard scores on a popular measure of visual–spatial ability/visual memory will also have been obtained. If the testee has failed one or two of the indicators, the question of performance veracity will need to be answered before testing proceeds to the standard battery. A good choice at this point may be a forced-choice SVT with excellent sensitivity and specificity, such as the Warrington Recognition Memory Test–Words (which again assesses for feigned verbal memory deficits). Subsequent administration of the WAIS-III Picture Completion, Digit Symbol, and Digit Span subtests will also do double duty: It will further clarify the issue of response bias (Picture Completion Most Discrepant Index, Digit Span indicators, Digit Symbol recognition) and will provide information regarding the cognitive domains of visual perception, information-processing speed, and attention. At this point, SVTs from six different tests will be available for review.

If only one or two SVTs have been failed, it will be prudent to continue with a standard battery, but performance veracity must continue to be examined at regular intervals through embedded indicators (RAVLT, CVLT-II, Finger Tapping Test, Finger Agnosia Test, WCST) as well as at least one more free-standing SVT. If additional failures are documented, it will be useful to increase the number of free-standing SVTs administered.

If, in contrast, the patient has failed three or four of the six initial SVTs, this will constitute compelling evidence that the patient is not credible. There is currently no consensus in the field as to whether a complete standard battery should be administered to individuals showing initial evidence of suboptimal performance, as opposed to either discontinuing testing or proceeding with only tests that provide data regarding presence of response bias. Arguments against proceeding with the battery include the following: (1) The patient will be exposed to tests, which could allow for some breach of test security, and the test results are neither accurate nor useful, so what is the value of exposing the tests to the test taker? (2) If tests are administered, the results will have to be reported, and the psychologist may very well lose control of how the reported scores are handled. Even though the psychologist may clearly state in his/her report that the results are not valid due to failed SVTs, subsequent experts (particularly ones in other professions) may "unyoke" the standard cognitive scores from the comments regarding presence of negative response bias, and refer to the test scores as valid. For example, extremely low IQ scores or very poor scores on attentional tasks may be referred to as valid and then used to explain the failed SVTs ("He had poor attention; that's why he failed the SVTs").

An argument in favor of administering a full battery despite evidence of response bias, is that standard scores can be compared against previous testing, with odd unexplainable fluctuations (i.e., declines) in scores taken as indicative of response bias; it can then be argued that the pattern of cognitive test scores does not match that expected for the condition in question. Also, if testing is abruptly discontinued after one or two tests, and the test taker subsequently discovers that he/she was determined to be noncredible, the patient will then know which are the "honesty" tests and may thus be enabled to navigate around them in subsequent exams. However, this latter problem can be circumvented by administering several free-standing and embedded SVTs.

The following three case examples show how test batteries can be adjusted for (1) initial evidence of response bias, (2) initial evidence of no response bias, and (3) initial equivocal evidence for response bias. All were young adults injured in the same motor vehicle accident, and all had sustained severe physical injuries but at most mTBI. They were tested 2½ years after the accident.

Case 1: Clearly Noncredible

This 22-year-old female may have been rendered unconscious, but she regained consciousness shortly after the collision, as evidenced by memories at the scene involving flashing lights and broken glass that "made it look like it was raining." Glasgow Coma Scale (GCS) score was gauged at 14 out of 15. Brain imaging was normal, and neurological exam was intact. She sustained substantial orthopedic and cosmetic injuries, for which future surgeries were planned.

At the time of the exam, she was reporting continuing orthopedic pain in multiple body areas (excluding the arms); she was prescribed no medications. In terms of cognitive symptoms, the patient reported that she "can't remember as good" and "can't focus as long," and that it "takes longer to learn things." She denied experiencing depression or suicidal ideation, but reported nightmares involving "a really loud crashing noise and then I wake up." She also described herself as "jumpy" and "easily scared," and she indicated that she could not tolerate loud noises, such as when a pan was dropped or a helicopter flew overhead. She denied significant stressors in the previous 5 years aside from the motor vehicle accident, but in other records, she had reported an assault 3 years previously. She had completed high school, and denied any history of learning disability or ADHD, but academic achievement scores showed that the patient scored "below basic" in English/language skills. Work history consisted of minimum-wage employment, and the patient had not worked since the accident.

The patient was very personable and charming, and did not appear to be in any physical or psychiatric discomfort during the exam. At the start of the neuropsychological exam, she was administered the RO Figure and was observed to copy it normally. After the stimulus was removed, the Rey Word Recognition Test was administered, which she failed (6 recognized; combination score = 9; Nitch et al., 2006). The 3-minute delayed recall of the RO Figure was then obtained, on which the patient obtained a low average performance (10th percentile), followed by the Meyers (1995) recognition trial. Calculation of the RO Figure Equation showed a passing score (51; Lu et al., 2003). Given that the patient had failed one out of two SVTs within the first 10 minutes of the exam, the question of whether she was performing to true ability needed to be addressed before administration of a standard cognitive battery could continue. Thus the planned goal of proceeding with cognitive testing to measure neuropsychological skills was put on hold, in order to ascertain whether the patient was in fact going to allow accurate measurement of neuropsychological skills.

The patient was then administered the b Test, which she failed (E-score = 342; Boone, Lu, & Herzberg, 2002a). Given converging evidence of inadequate negative response bias, the decision was made to administer only those standard cognitive tasks that have SVTs attached, as well as additional free-standing SVTs in various cognitive domains. If performance on these later measures of response bias had in fact normalized, administration of a complete battery could have been cautiously attempted under the assumption that any response bias attempted at the beginning of the exam had been discarded.

Administration of the WAIS-III was started. The patient obtained an average score on Picture Completion (25th percentile), and passed the SVT associated with this test, the Most Discrepant Index (5; Solomon et al., 2010). Test administration then continued with the Vocabulary subtest, and another average score was obtained (63rd percentile). However, on the Digit Symbol subtest, the patient scored at the 5th percentile, but she failed a recognition trial SVT associated with this task (4 correct; N. Kim et al., 2010). Furthermore, on the subsequent administration of Digit Span, the patient failed three SVTs (ACSS = 5; RDS = 6; mean four-digit time = 5 sec.; Babikian et al., 2006). At this point, the patient had failed indicators from four separate tests. The decision was made to administer three more dedicated SVTs, as well as three additional standard tests that contained SVTs. Although the exam could have been ended after failure on four measures of response bias—a performance essentially 100% predictive of noncredible performance (as discussed on pp. 50–51)—administration of additional measures would enable the examiner to screen most cognitive domains and perhaps to comment on the faking strategies employed by the test taker (i.e., to identify which skill deficits were being feigned). Furthermore, an increasing number of failed SVTs would provide irrefutable evidence of negative response bias and increase the examiner's confidence in conclusions, while not significantly raising the risk of false positive identifications (see discussion on pp. 50–51).

The patient ultimately failed a total of seven separate indicators of response bias. Although she obtained a passing E-score (12) on the Dot Counting Test, she committed 4 errors—a performance found in only 10% of credible patients with moderate to severe TBI (Boone, Lu, Back, et al., 2002). She passed the Rey 15-Item Memorization Test recognition trial (23; Boone et al., 2002); however, she then failed the Warrington Recognition Memory Test–Words on time (216 seconds) but not accuracy (44; M. S. Kim et al. 2010). She was then administered the RAVLT, scoring in the low average range by the 5th learning trial (12th percentile), but she performed in the borderline range after the interference trial (5th percentile). She then scored in the average range with both hands on the Finger Tapping Test, thus passing this test as a measure of response bias (dominant = 50.3; Arnold et al., 2005). However, she subsequently made an excessive number of errors on the Finger Agnosia Test (5), failing this test as an SVT (Trueblood & Schmidt, 1993). Neuropsychological testing was completed with delayed recall of the RAVLT list on which a low average score was documented (16th percentile). She performed normally on the recognition trial (14; 0 false positives). Although she passed SVTs associated with this task (RAVLT equation = 19, Boone et al., 2005; RAVLT/RO discriminant function = 1.343, Sherman et al., 2002), she failed two other verbal memory SVTs (Warrington–Words, Rey Word Recognition Test), which would argue that she was engaging in response bias when completing verbal memory tasks.

The failed SVTs clustered in verbal memory (Warrington–Words, Rey Word Recognition Test), visual memory (WAIS-III Digit Symbol recognition), attention (WAIS-III Digit Span, Dot Counting Test), processing speed (Warrington–Words time), and sensory function (Finger Agnosia Test errors). In contrast, normal performance was observed in language (WAIS-III Vocabulary range), finger speed (Finger Tapping Test), and visual-perceptual/constructional skill (WAIS-III Picture Completion, RO Figure copy). One could hypothesize that the strategy employed by the patient was to fake deficits only in the former skills. In fact, this strategy mirrored her reported cognitive deficits in the interview (i.e., "can't remember as good," "can't focus as long," and it "takes longer to learn things").

In the examiner's opinion, little would be gained by any further administration of neuropsychological tasks. The patient scored in the low average range on verbal and visual delayed recall, in the borderline range in processing speed and attention, and in the impaired range in sensory function, but she failed indicators of performance credibility associated with these skills; as a result, these scores could not be accepted as representative of true function. If the patient scored poorly on additional measures of memory, attention, processing speed (including timed executive tasks), and sensory skills, those scores would have been uninterpretable. In actuality, it is questionable whether any further poor scores in any cognitive domain could have been accepted as valid, given the 7 SVT failures. The patient had not undergone previous neuropsychological testing, and thus current scores could not be used to identify nonsensical fluctuations from earlier performances.

At the conclusion of the neuropsychological exam, the patient completed the MMPI-2–RF; scores on validity scales suggested noncredible overreport of physical/cognitive symptoms (FBS-r = 96T; RBS = 97T) as well as possible overreport of psychiatric symptoms (Fp-r = 77T) not explained by failure to comprehend test items or by random responding (VRIN-r = 63T, TRIN-r = 50T). She also scored at the cutoff on the Modified Somatic Perception Questionnaire (MSPQ), which has been recommended as indicating overreport of pain complaints (raw = 14; Larrabee, 2003d).

It was concluded that the patient had responded in a noncredible manner on cognitive testing and in her report of physical, cognitive, and psychiatric complaints, indicating that her claims of dysfunction in these areas could not be accepted as accurate.

Case 2: Clearly Credible

This 24-year-old male also may have been rendered unconscious in the accident, but his GCS score was 15 at the scene, and brain imaging was normal. He was subsequently placed in a drug-induced coma for management of his substantial internal and orthopedic injuries, and remained hospitalized for 2½ months. Brain imaging was normal. He reported problems in short-term memory and concentration. Psychiatrically, the patient described himself as angry, and indicated that he "did not know" whether he was depressed; he denied anxiety, but did report becoming "freaked out" by poor driving in other drivers and by nightmares whose content he could not recall. He continued to have symptoms related to damage to internal organs, as well as back pain and weakness/numbness in his right lower leg. His history was noteworthy for resource placement for English classes, but he had been able to complete an AA degree. At the time of testing, he was working fulltime in car repair. His only current prescribed medications related to ongoing gastrointestinal (GI) symptoms.

On exam the patient was initially sullen and wary of the examiner, but he gradually "warmed up" over the course of the interview, becoming friendly and animated.

He was administered the RO Figure and copied it normally. He was then administered the Rey Word Recognition Test, which he passed (8 recognized; combination score = 13; Nitch et al., 2006). The 3-minute delayed recall of the RO Figure was then obtained, which was average (59th percentile for age), followed by the Meyers (1995) recognition trial. Calculation of the RO Figure equation showed a passing score (61; Lu et al., 2003). Thus, within the first 10 minutes of testing, the patient had passed two of two SVTs. The decision was made to proceed with a full neuropsychological exam with performance credibility to be monitored through administration of one additional free-standing SVT and examination of several embedded measures of response bias.

Administration of the WAIS-III was then initiated. FSIQ was 98, Verbal IQ (VIQ) was 98, and Performance IQ (PIQ) was 97, and all individual subtest scores were average or higher with the exception of Similarities (16th percentile) and Digit Symbol (5th percentile). Indicators of response bias from Picture Completion (Most Discrepant Index = 5), Digit Symbol recognition (76; N. Kim et al., 2010), and Digit Span (ACSS = 13; RDS = 12; three-digit time = 1 second; Babikian et al., 2006) were all passed. The Warrington Recognition Memory Test–Words was administered after Block Design, and passing scores were obtained (total = 48; 138 seconds; M. S. Kim et al., 2010). After the WAIS-III, the WMS-R Logical Memory subtest was administered, and a low average score was obtained (LM I = 21; 24th percentile for age); on the WMS-R Visual Reproduction subtest, a nearly high average score was documented (VR I = 36; 70th percentile for age). Similarly, on the RAVLT, the patient learned an average number of words by the 5th learning trial (13; 52nd percentile for age); recall after interference was average/low average (10 words; 26th percentile for age).

On the Wide Range Achievement Test–4 (WRAT4) Math subtest, the patient scored within the average range for his age (45th percentile; 11.0 grade equivalent). The patient scored in the average range on Trails A (26 seconds; 40th percentile for age/education), but in the low average range on Trails B (69 seconds; 21st percentile for age/education), and in the average to low average range in rapid word reading (Stroop A = 28th percentile for age), rapid color naming (Stroop B = 20th percentile for age), and rapid response inhibition (Stroop C = 21st percentile). On WMS-R Logical Memory delayed recall, performance was again low average (LM II = 16; 22nd percentile for age); delayed recall on WMS-R Visual Reproduction was borderline (VR II = 8th percentile for age). RAVLT delayed recall was low average (8 words; 14th percentile for age). However, the patient only correctly recognized 7 words and committed 3 false positive errors. As a result, he failed both indicators of response bias from the RAVLT recognition trial (equation = 7, Boone et al., 2005; RAVLT/RO discriminant function = –1.6, Sherman et al., 2002).

The patient then obtained low average scores on the Word Reading (23rd percentile for age; 9.0 grade equivalent) and Spelling (18th percentile for age; 7.0 grade equivalent) subtests of the WRAT4. Phonemic fluency was in the impaired range (20; 2nd percentile for age/education), whereas performance on the WCST was normal (6 categories). Boston Naming Test performance was normal (54/60), as was Finger Tapping Test performance (right = 53.7, 44th percentile for age/gender; left = 52.7, 67th percentile for age/gender), and the patient passed a SVT cutoff applied to the latter task.

The patient then completed the MMPI-2–RF. Scores on validity scales were within normal limits (T = 50–63), although the patient showed a trend toward overreport of physical/cognitive symptoms (FBS-r = 77T). Across the 50 clinical scales, significant elevations were only found for RC1 (68T), Malaise (69T), GI Complaints (80T), Neurological Complaints (65T), and Anger Proneness (66T); with the exception of GI Complaints, the elevations were relatively mild. The patient obtained a score of 12 on the MSPQ, suggesting no significant overreport of pain complaints.

It was concluded that the patient had responded in a credible manner on cognitive testing. Failures on indicators of performance credibility from a single test (RAVLT) are not unusual in credible populations (Victor et al., 2009), and the fact that he underperformed on an SVT requiring reading words in a paragraph could reasonably be attributed to his history of reading difficulties (preliminary cross-validation data on the RAVLT as an SVT show that cutoffs must be lowered to protect credible patients with histories of learning disability).

The mildly lowered scores in processing speed (including timed executive tasks) and verbal skills (including verbal memory, rapid naming and word generation, spelling, and sight reading) were judged consistent with the patient's history of preexisting language-based learning disability (see pp. 180–181). Performance on visual memory tests was inconsistent (varying from borderline to average), and the significance of the isolated lowered score was unclear and judged as perhaps related to normal variability (see pp. 174–177). Lowered scores were not attributed to residual effects from a possible mTBI 2½ years earlier, given research showing no long-term cognitive abnormalities in this population (see pp. 227–228).

Personality testing results were summarized as showing mildly elevated physical symptom report consistent with continuing medical problems from the accident, and with no evidence of significant anxiety or depression.

Case 3: Inconsistently Noncredible

On arrival at the emergency department, the GCS score for this 22-year-old female was noted as 3, although this was related to respiratory distress and intubation. On exam she was found to have numerous orthopedic fractures and required removal of some internal organs. Brain imaging was normal, and she was not diagnosed with a TBI.

At the time of neuropsychological testing, the patient was reporting continuing orthopedic pain and some left-sided numbness. When queried as to cognitive symptoms, she reported decreased memory ("memory very bad"; "I used to have a very good memory, now it is not as good for anything"). She denied experiencing depression or suicidal ideation, but reported a "lot more anxiety" and panic attacks. She denied premorbid psychiatric symptoms, but records indicated that prior to the accident the patient tended to be an "anxious person"; that she was "extremely shy as a child, with separation anxiety and performance anxiety"; and that she had a "long-standing history of anxiety and phobia," including claustrophobia and fear of heights. Family psychiatric history was positive for depression and panic attacks in an aunt.

Complicating the picture, the patient had a preexisting seizure disorder (at least some tonic–clonic), possibly related to being born 2 months prematurely and/or to having had a high fever as an infant. She stated that her seizure frequency had markedly increased after the accident, although records indicated that she was not compliant in postaccident use of anticonvulsant medication and that seizures were related to her menstrual cycle and stress. It was also noted that she had observed memory problems before the accident, although she claimed they were worse afterward. Her only current medications were an anticonvulsant and an antidepressant.

The patient had finished high school and had almost completed an AA degree at the time of the accident; she stated that she had had to withdraw from school after the accident, but had recently completed a course in which she obtained an A. She denied any history of learning disability or ADHD, and claimed that she had been in some gifted classes. Job history consisted of work in public relations as an assistant; she had stopped working at 1 year postaccident, but was searching for a job at the time of the current evaluation.

The patient was pleasant and socially appropriate, and at no point appeared to be in any physical distress or discomfort. She claimed that she had experienced three panic attacks the morning before the exam, but at no time did she appear to be anxious during the evaluation. At the start of the neuropsychological exam, she was presented the RO Figure and was observed to copy it normally (34/36). After the stimulus was removed, the Rey Word Recognition Test was administered, which she failed (6 recognized; combination score = 10; Nitch et al., 2006). The 3-minute delayed recall of the RO Figure Equation was then obtained, on which the patient scored in the average range (51st percentile), followed by the Meyers (1995) recognition trial. Calculation of the RO Figure Equation showed a passing score (58; Lu et al., 2003). Given that the patient had failed one out of two SVTs within the first 10 minutes of the exam, the question of negative response bias needed to be addressed before administration of a standard cognitive battery could continue. As in Case 1, rather than proceeding with cognitive testing with the intent to measure neuropsychological skills, the examiner put the planned goal on hold in order to ascertain whether the patient was in fact going to allow accurate measurement of neuropsychological skills.

The patient was then administered the Warrington Recognition Memory Test–Words, and obtained a passing score (47; 184 seconds; M. S. Kim et al., 2010). She was then administered WAIS-III Picture Completion, scoring in the average range, and passing the symptom validity indicator associated with this task (Most Discrepant Index = 5; Solomon et al., 2010). Performance on the Vocabulary subtest was also average (63rd percentile for age), while Digit Symbol coding was superior (95th percentile for age), and the patient passed the recognition trial SVT for this task (76; N. Kim et al., 2010). At this point, the one failed indicator out of five was considered a possible anomaly, and the decision was made to proceed with the standard battery while still monitoring performance credibility. The patient scored in the average range on WAIS-III Similarities (25th percentile for age), in the superior range on Block Design (91st percentile for age), and in the average range on Matrix Reasoning (63rd percentile for age). However, the "boat was rocked" when the patient obtained a score nearly within the borderline range on Digit Span (9th percentile for age), and she failed RDS according to a cutoff appropriate for the differentiation of credible versus noncredible mTBI (RDS = 7; Greiffenstein et al., 1994). She also took longer than expected to recite digits forward (mean time per digit = 1.27 seconds; Babikian et al., 2006), and thus failed this additional Digit Span indicator. FSIQ IQ was 99, VIQ was 89, and PIQ was 113; all individual subtest scores were average or higher, with the exception of Digit Span and Information (9th percentiles).

By this juncture, the patient had failed SVTs from two separate tests and obtained passing scores on four. Testing proceeded with administration of the WRAT4, and the patient scored within the average to high average level (Word Reading = 53rd percentile for age, 12.5 grade equivalent; Spelling = 81st percentile for age, >12.9 grade equivalent; Math = 75th percentile, >12.9 grade equivalent). Administration of memory measures followed: The patient scored within the average range on WMS-R Logical Memory (LM I = 24; 39th percentile for age) and the average range on Visual Reproduction (VR I = 33; 42nd percentile for age), but in the low average range on the final learning trial of the RAVLT (10 words; 12th percentile for age) and in the impaired range after an interference trial (6 words; 2nd percentile for age).

Performance on Trails A (29 seconds) and Trails B (58 seconds) was average (32nd and 54th percentiles, respectively, for age/education). Insertion of the b Test at this point revealed a passing score (E-score = 27; Boone, Lu, & Herzberg, 2002a). Subsequent performance on Stroop was average to low average (Stroop A = 19th percentile; Stroop B = 47th percentile; Stroop C = 12th percentile), and a low average performance was obtained on phonemic fluency (FAS = 28; 10th percentile for age/education).

On delayed memory testing, WMS-R Logical Memory and Visual Reproduction were average (LM II = 18, 30th percentile for age; VR II = 33, 64th percentile for age), but RAVLT recall was impaired (4 words; 1st percentile for age). However, she only recognized 7 words (0 false positives), and thus failed two SVTs derived from this task (equation = 10, Boone et al., 2005; RAVLT/RO discriminant function = –1.55, Sherman et al., 2002); these results suggested that she was not performing to true capability on this test.

Boston Naming Test performance was normal (57), and Finger Tapping Test performance was average (right = 48.7, 50th percentile for age/gender; left = 47.3, 67th percentile for age/gender), with the patient passing an indicator of negative response bias cutoff applied to the latter task. She then made a single error on the Finger Agnosia Test, also passing this measure when used as an SVT. On the last test administered (the WCST), the patient scored normally, completing 5 categories within 1 deck of cards.

At this point the MMPI-2–RF was administered. It showed evidence of physical/cognitive symptom overreport (FBS-r = 99*T*, RBS = 84*T*, Fs = 74*T*, F-r = 83*T*) not attributable to random responding or failure to comprehend test items (VRIN-r = 63*T*, TRIN-r = 50*T*). Numerous elevations were found on the 50 clinical scales, with the highest observed for RC1 (86*T*), Malaise (81*T*), GI Complaints (88*T*), Neurological Complaints (80*T*), Cognitive Complaints (91*T*), and Anxiety (100*T*). A score substantially beyond cutoffs was obtained on the MSPQ (25), consistent with nonplausible overreport of pain complaints.

Of note, the patient had undergone cognitive screening within a month of her injury, and at that time had scored in the average range on WAIS-III Digit Span and delayed verbal recall. However, 9 months before current testing, scores on these measures had inexplicably plummeted to borderline to impaired (< 1st percentile to 7th percentile), comparable to the scores obtained on the current testing. The drop in test scores remote from the injury does not reflect expected outcome following TBI and provides additional evidence that current scores were not credible.

At the conclusion of cognitive testing, the patient had failed indicators from three separate tests involving verbal memory and attention, indicating that she was not performing to true capability in these areas and that scores from these tasks could not be accepted as valid. She passed seven SVTs related to processing speed, visual memory, visual perception and constructional skill, finger dexterity, letter identification, and sensory function, suggesting that her performance credibility in these areas was at least better than that for the attention and verbal memory tasks. In fact, scores in these latter domains were all average or higher, with the exception of low average to average scores in verbal processing speed and timed verbal executive tasks.

It was conceivable that some of the low average scores in rapid verbal processing could have been related to the patient's seizure disorder (post-accident electroencephalographic [EEG] telemetry had captured a single, poorly localized complex partial seizure). However, it was concluded that the patient did not have any cognitive residual effects from the injury 2½ years previously, given that research does not provide evidence of any such long-term sequelae (see pp. 227–228). Personality testing was summarized as showing noncredible reports of physical and cognitive symptoms; the marked endorsement of anxiety was also likely exaggerated, given no evidence of psychological distress during the exam, recent completion of a college course in which she obtained an A, and the fact that the patient was actively searching for employment at the time of testing.

These three examples are interesting companion cases, in that all of the patients had serious physical injuries but at most had mTBI, and they differed considerably on the dimension of cognitive response bias. The patient in Case 1 was blatantly noncredible on cognitive testing, failing 7 of 12 separate SVTs, which provided evidence that she was not performing to true capability on a wide range of skills (verbal memory, attention, sensory function, and processing speed). In contrast, the patient in Case 3 was highly selective in her response bias; she had been tested twice before and was probably more savvy and sophisticated in her feigning than the first patient, targeting only measures of attention and verbal memory, and failing only 3 of 10 separate measures of negative response bias. The patient in Case 2 was probably entirely credible, failing an index of response bias from a single test (out of eight); this case shows that negative response bias should not be inferred from failure on a single SVT, particularly when the test may require skills in which the patient is in fact weak (e.g., reading). The Case 2 patient also well illustrates that while credible patients with true medical disorders may show mild elevations on MMPI-2–RF scales associated with physical symptoms, they do not obtain markedly elevated scores on Fs, FBS-r, or remaining somatic scales. All three patients had sustained comparably serious physical injuries, yet only two (the two who also showed evidence of response bias on cognitive SVTs) exceeded T-scores of 80 on FBS-r ($96T$ and $99T$ vs. $77T$ for the credible patient).

In case 1, where cognitive symptom feigning was blatant, a full battery was not administered. Although the goal at the outset had been to objectively measure the patient's neuropsychological skills, she did not allow this. At times I have been criticized for not giving a full battery after ample evidence is obtained early in an evaluation that the patient is engaging in response bias. The neuropsychologist must carefully consider the utility of the data to be collected; if these data have no value, a compelling case can be made for stopping the exam once it is documented that response bias is pervasive. Neuropsychologists are contracted to conduct an exam, not to administer a set battery of tests. If patients do not allow accurate measurement of neurocognitive skills, then the goal of testing becomes instead to document the extent and nature of the response bias. Once that is done, the exam can be concluded.

A further argument against continuing with a full neuropsychological battery after response bias has been well documented is that the neuropsychologist may lose "control" over interpretation of the standard test scores, and other experts may attempt to argue that the low-standard cognitive test scores in fact "explain" the positive SVT findings (e.g., "the patient has compromised intelligence from this mild traumatic brain injury, and that's why several SVTs were failed"). That is, once standard cognitive test scores have been included in a report, they may become "unyoked" from the interpretation provided by the neuropsychologist who conducted the exam. Additionally, administration of psychological tests provides exposure of their content to nonpsychologists, and if the resulting data are not reliable and valid, test security has been risked to no useful end.

Conversely, an argument in favor of administering a full neuropsychological battery is that standard test scores can be compared against those obtained in a separate exam, and nonsensical fluctuations can then be used as evidence of failure to perform to true ability. Further, test takers may perform well on some difficult tasks, in contrast to highly abnormal performance on easy SVTs, thereby providing evidence of response bias superimposed on intact neurocognitive function.

Under What Circumstances Can Failed SVTs Be Discounted?

As discussed earlier in this chapter (pp. 41–48), some patient groups are at risk for false positive identification on SVTs, despite performing to true capability. In particular, patients with low intelligence or dementia typically fail a high percentage of administered measures of response bias. Some patients with severe TBI have a high rate of failure on SVTs, but these individuals are also likely to obtain low IQ scores and may carry diagnoses of dementia due to head trauma. Thus, as long as SVT cutoffs are considered in light of IQ and presence of dementia, patients with significant head injury are likely to be protected. As discussed on pages 47–48, some SVT cutoffs may require adjustment for ethnic minority groups and/or for those with ESL status or with poor math skills.

For every SVT failure, it is important that the neuropsychologist evaluate whether the patient's demographic or illness characteristics may have caused a false positive identification on the task. However, any decisions to dismiss failed SVT results should be based on empirical literature. For example, I have seen many neuropsychological reports in which the neuropsychologist claims that depression/distress, PTSD/or other anxiety disorders, poor attention/attentional lapses, fatigue, and/or pain/pain medications have caused false positive SVT failures. These are reasonable hypotheses, but it is not appropriate to assert them as definitive until the clinician examines the literature to verify that research has confirmed these assertions. And, in fact, the available literature does not show that these factors lead to SVT failure.

• *Depression.* In a review of the impact of psychiatric conditions on SVT performance (Goldberg et al., 2007), depression was consistently not associated with an increase in failure on SVTs.

• *Attentional lapses.* Research has shown that patients with actual ADHD exhibit a low rate of false positive identifications on neurocognitive SVTs (Sollman et al., 2010),

- *Pain*. Etherton and colleagues (Etherton, Bianchini, Ciota, & Greve, 2005; Etherton, Bianchini, Greve, & Ciota, 2005) reported that acute pain (administered through placing hands in ice water) during administration of SVTs did not result in lowered scores. Iverson, Lange, and Rose (2007) observed that patients with chronic pain did not showed increased rates of failure on SVTs.

- *Fatigue and/or PTSD/other anxiety*. There are no studies directly addressing the impact of fatigue or PTSD/other anxiety on SVT performance. However, it must be kept in mind that SVTs are "easy," which is why they are effective at detecting response bias (i.e., they appear hard but are in fact simple, allowing patients with true cognitive dysfunction to pass). Furthermore, cutoffs are set to err on the side of protecting credible patients (set to ≥ 90% specificity). If a patient fails 40% of SVTs administered, this is comparable to the performance of individuals with extremely low intelligence (IQ = 60–69; Dean, Victor, et al., 2008). If it is argued that fatigue or PTSD/other anxiety has caused this failure rate on SVTs, this would be analogous to claiming that fatigue or anxiety causes IQ to decline by 40+ points. If that were true, streets would be strewn with the wreckage from car accidents as individuals who began to feel fatigued and/or anxious suffered drastic declines in intellect and became unable to drive. Moreover, research has shown that anxiety does not affect performance on tests of attention, learning, memory, mental flexibility, and eye–hand coordination (Waldstein, Ryan, Jennings, Muldoon, & Manuck, 1997). If anxiety has no impact on standard neuropsychological tests, which are arguably much harder than SVTs, it does not make sense that it would cause failure on SVTs.

In some neuropsychological reports, it has been hypothesized that although depression, pain, poor attention, pain, PTSD/other anxiety, or fatigue may not cause SVT failures in isolation, *in combination* they probably do. But it is incumbent on the psychologist arguing this point to cite literature in support of this proposition—and there is none. However, there is a large literature on SVT performance in patients with moderate to severe TBI, who, given their injuries, are likely to be experiencing depression, pain, decreased attention, PTSD/other anxiety, and fatigue; yet many studies show that they outperform noncredible patients on SVTs (Binder, Kelly-Villaneuva, & Winslow, 2003; Fox, 2011; Heinly, Greve, Bianchini, Love, & Brennan, 2005; Greve, Bianchini, Mathias, Houston, & Crouch, 2003; Curtis et al., 2009; Iverson, 2001; Boone, Lu & Herzberg, 2002a, 2002b). It needs to be remembered that the only credible patients who fail SVTs at a high rate are those with very low intelligence or dementia, so the assertion that these conditions in combination cause SVT failure is equivalent to claiming that they lead to dementia-like cognition. If this were true, this would have been well documented in the literature.

Interestingly, although some neuropsychologists claim that the results of SVTs cannot be accepted as valid due to fatigue, stress, depression, and so forth, they still use the results of standard cognitive tests obtained during the same exam to verify the presence of brain damage. However, they cannot have it both ways: If the conditions discussed here were to affect performance on SVTs, they certainly would contaminate the results of neurocognitive tests.

Under What Circumstances Can Passed SVTs Be Discounted?

Many patients pass all of several SVTs, which is suggestive of performance credibility on the cognitive exam. But are there ever any exceptions? That is, are there instances in which SVTs are passed, but other evidence shows that obtained scores are underestimates of true ability? Again, neuropsychologists have several strategies for identifying noncredible performance (see Table 2.1), only one of which is performance on measures of response bias. I have on occasion tested litigants who passed all SVTs, yet showed a marked drop across postaccident test scores that could not be explained by any major neurological event in the interim.

For example, I tested a medical–legal defense attorney who sued in the context of a claimed mTBI after a motor vehicle accident, yet was not rendered unconscious in the accident and was noted at the scene to be "joking" with paramedics and making business calls while being transported in the ambulance. Her GCS score was 15, and there were no brain imaging abnormalities. On my exam of her, she passed SVTs from eight separate tests, including several with high sensitivity (b Test, Warrington Recognition Memory Test–Words, Rey Word Recognition Test, WAIS-III Digit Span variables, RAVLT variables, RO Figure Equation, WAIS-III Digit Symbol recognition, Finger Tapping Test). Yet she obtained average to low average IQ scores (VIQ = 104, PIQ = 85, FSIQ = 96), and variable scores were observed in processing speed (impaired to average), language skills (borderline to average), visual–spatial skills/visual memory (low average to average), and motor dexterity (low average to average). In contrast, verbal memory, basic attention, remote memory/fund of general information, math skills, and executive abilities were average. I concluded that "the patient's profile is puzzling in that overall intellectual scores are generally lower than would normally be expected for an attorney," and because she showed unexpected mild cognitive abnormalities remote from an equivocal brain injury (the rest of her medical and psychiatric history was noncontributory).

I was then provided with testing results from the plaintiff's neuropsychological expert from an exam 8 months previous to mine (but still almost 2 years after the accident), in which she had achieved a high average VIQ (118), an average PIQ (97), and a nearly high average FSIQ (109). The plaintiff had experienced no significant neurological event in the period between the evaluations that could have accounted for the marked drop in scores across exams. In this context, I judged that the most likely explanation was that she had been provided with feedback from the first exam, realized that those results would not be effective in securing monetary damages in the lawsuit, and decided to substantially lower her performance on my exam. (Although she passed five SVTs on her first exam, she still obtained an MMPI-2 FBS raw score of 29, suggesting that inflation of cognitive/physical symptomatology was also present on that exam.)

A defense attorney would be particularly well positioned to become sufficiently educated about SVTs to pass them while still feigning cognitive impairment. She would have been aware of the measures from reading neuropsychological reports as part of her job duties as a personal injury defense attorney. Research shows that when noncredible individuals are aware that SVTs will be included in a test battery, they still feign but attempt to do so more carefully, and are relatively accurate in identifying which tests are the "SVTs" (see discussion on pp. 8–9). Furthermore, some studies have shown that it is relatively easy to search for SVTs on the Internet, and unfortunately some tests have been described in sufficient detail to allow noncredible test takers to pass the tests (see discussion on p. 2).

In his deposition, the opposing neuropsychologist took issue with my suggestion that the plaintiff could have educated herself regarding measures of response bias, enabling her to pass them: "So how could someone memorize these, know all the questions, all the words? I mean, that's impossible for someone to memorize that." But what the psychologist seemed to be overlooking is that a test taker who has information about task formats, regardless of the actual stimuli, can pass SVTs. For example, if this plaintiff had learned that some SVTs are administered via computer, she could have decided to perform well on all computer-based tasks. Or if she had learned that some SVTs involve trials in which the test taker has to pick between two choices, she could have cautioned herself to perform well on those. Similarly, Internet research might have educated her to do well on tests involving number repetition, counting, and identification of letters. If she had learned some of the names of the tests of response bias, she could have looked for those test names and acronyms on the score sheets, and performed well when those tasks were administered. (To this end, I have started to type score sheets that show no test names/acronyms.) Several patients have let it "slip" during their exams with me that they searched my name on the Internet before the exams. For those of us who publish in the field of response bias testing, patients have the ability to access our publications prior to testing. Thus, ironically, measures of negative response bias may be less sensitive in identifying noncredible performance when they are used by the actual test developers.

When the opposing neuropsychologist was subsequently asked in the deposition what might have led to the plaintiff's 13-point drop in IQ if she was not in fact malingering, the psychologist responded: "I think it's mood disturbance, level of distress, the fact that it was a defense-related exam, which I think can be off-putting and foster quite a bit of anxiety, level of ambient pain; so it's a combination of factors." This statement contains a number of hypotheses that may appear possible, but statements attempting to account for atypical fluctuations in test scores must be based on published literature, not "hunches." Starting with the assertion that a mood disturbance might have led to a 13-point loss in FSIQ, the plaintiff in fact emphatically denied depression on the exam I conducted, although she did endorse "sadness" about losing her job. On the MMPI-2–RF, scores on scales measuring depression and anxiety were not significantly elevated (RCd = 64T, RC2 = 61T, RC7 = 48T). Thus no compelling evidence of significant depression was present. However, even if she were depressed, depression has been found to result only in mild lowering of PIQ, not VIQ (by an average of 8 points; Boone et al., 1995), and thus would not account for a 14-point loss in VIQ.

Regarding "level of distress," the plaintiff appeared relaxed and euthymic during my exam of her, and certainly the MMPI-2–RF did not show compelling evidence of significant "distress" (RCd = 64T). Regarding the claim that lower scores are obtained on defense exams than on exams conducted by plaintiff experts, there is no empirical support for this assertion. In fact, in a study of MMPI-2 protocols, no significant differences were documented in validity scale scores obtained by plaintiffs who underwent both defense and plaintiff exams (Greiffenstein, Baker, Tsushima, Boone, & Fox, 2010).

The final claim was that pain may have accounted for worse performance on the second exam; however, no pain behaviors (e.g., repositioning, massaging body areas, asking to stand, grimacing, etc.) were noted on the second exam. The plaintiff did not appear to be in any discomfort, did not spontaneously report any pain, and moved easily. Literature on IQ test performance in actual pain patients shows that scores on IQ indexes, such as the WAIS-III Processing Speed Index, are only mildly lowered by acute or chronic pain, and that "unexpectedly low scores in the absence of significant/documented brain dysfunction suggest poor effort or deliberate misrepresentation" (Etherton, Bianchini, Heinly, & Greve, 2006, p. 1218). Furthermore, Iezzi, Duckworth, Vuong, Archibald, and Klinck (2004) observed that pain severity does not predict lowered attention/

concentration (including the WAIS-III Digit Span and Arithmetic subtests) or reasoning skills (including WAIS-III Similarities and Picture Arrangement).

The astute defense counsel appropriately asked the opposing neuropsychologist what was different in terms of patient distress, mood, and pain across the two exams—a question that the neuropsychologist could not answer.

REMAINING STRATEGIES FOR IDENTIFYING NONCREDIBLE PERFORMANCE

As discussed above, failure on at least three SVTs is associated with nearly 100% specificity, which provides high confidence in the conclusion that a patient is not performing to true capability. Two SVT failures typically result in an approximately 5% false positive rate, which would suggest a strong although not definitive probability that a patient has not performed to true capability. However, additional strategies are available to provide the clinician with increasing certainty that the results of failed SVTs are accurate.

Inconsistency of Scores within/across Cognitive Evaluations

Of importance in evaluating the credibility of cognitive test scores is examining the consistency of scores within and across neuropsychological evaluations. At times nonsensical fluctuations (e.g., low–high–low) in individual test scores across sequential cognitive exams may be observed (e.g., first-year postinjury Picture Completion = 2nd percentile; second-year postinjury Picture Completion = 75th percentile; third-year postinjury Picture Completion = 2nd percentile). The reason why a patient would show this pattern may reflect the patient's misinformation about brain injury (e.g., that it causes "intermittent" brain dysfunction, similar to a plug incompletely inserted into a wall socket). Alternatively, the explanation may be as simple as the fact that if one feigns impairment on one several-hour exam, it may be difficult to recall the exact tests/items on which one underperformed, and to reproduce the same pattern accurately, on a subsequent exam 1 or more years later.

For example, we described a case of a litigant (Boone & Lu, 2003) with documented severe brain injury who demonstrated improved cognitive scores across two evaluations while in a rehab setting. Scores on the final exam reflected normal performance (low average or higher), with the exception of one impaired score (out of three) on testing of visual memory. However, 8 months later, when I evaluated the patient at the request of defense counsel, the patient displayed scores markedly lower than those shown on the second exam in rehab. After a brain injury, test scores remain the same or gradually improve, and there would be no brain mechanism to account for a sudden dropoff in cognitive scores remote from the injury in the absence of any intervening major neurological event.

Nonsensical fluctuations in performance on tasks measuring the same skill within an exam may also be observed and be informative regarding questions of negative response bias. I recall testing a litigant who could not repeat three words in sequence on the MMSE, but who, when asked to follow a three-step command, spontaneously repeated the lengthy instructions ("You mean you want me to take this in my right hand, fold it in half, and put it on the floor?"). If he could repeat that sentence, I am sure he could repeat "Ball, flag, tree." Some variability in scores from tests measuring similar skills is expected. But, for example, obtaining average scores in 30-minute delayed recall of WMS Visual Reproduction designs while claiming zero recall for any details in 3-minute delayed recall of the RO Figure would be implausible. Similarly, some patients can be observed struggling to recite digits forward, yet can subsequently rapidly and easily repeat number sequences in forward order in preparation for saying them backward. Likewise, other patients will be noted to struggle in reading words on the learning trial of the Warrington Recognition Memory Test–Words, yet show no trouble reading the same words when selecting responses on the recognition trial.

Inconsistency between Neurocognitive Test Scores and ADLs

An additional technique for identifying nonplausible test performance is comparing test scores with information about how the test taker actually functions in ADLs. Neuropsychological testing is of value precisely because test scores predict function; if they did not, there would be no point to the testing. A neuropsychologist has not only objective test data, but also observations of the patient's actual function *in vivo*, as well as information from patient self-report and medical/work/school records as to how the patient truly functions. Here are several examples.

• Boston Naming Test scores of 6 out of 60 would be consistent with a marked/profound word retrieval difficulty, which, if truly present, would be very apparent in the patient's spontaneous speech during interview and exam. In the absence of obvious word retrieval problems in conversation, a score of 6 on the Boston Naming Test would be noncredible.

• Claimed inability to repeat any numbers on WAIS-III Digit Span due to a postaccident "problem with numbers" would be inconsistent with surveillance tapes showing the patient engaging in banking transactions and counting out money for purchases in a pharmacy.

• Markedly poor attention and vigilance scores would be inconsistent with ability to complete the MMPI-2–RF in 1 hour with a normal-range VRIN-r score.

• Inability to accurately distinguish the letter *b* from similar-appearing letters on testing would be inconsistent with the presence of a handwritten memo by the patient (reproduced in medical records) that included multiple uses of the letter *b* on paperwork requesting that her physician complete forms for her disability application.

• Marked visual-perceptual/visual–spatial deficits would be inconsistent with ability to drive and navigate to new destinations, such as a neuropsychologist's office (assuming that a GPS device is not used). They would also be inconsistent with careful application of makeup and rather intricate grooming of facial hair.

• Chance-level memory scores, expected for patients with Alzheimer's disease, would be inconsistent with ability to live independently and handle one's own finances, to obtain average grades in school, to receive positive work evaluations and bonuses, and to provide detailed deposition testimony regarding the sequence of events prior to and following a motor vehicle accident.

• Finger Tapping Test scores of 15 would be indicative of marked/profound deficits in finger dexterity, and such dysfunction, if truly present, would impair the patient's ability to (1) shake hands on being greeted; (2) pick up and use a pen, and turn pages, on Coding, Symbol Search, copy and recognition trials of the RO Figure, and the b Test, (3) turn a knob and open a door when leaving the testing session; and (4) retrieve messages and text on a cell phone (nowadays most patients can be observed to use a cell phone at some time during the examination session). Such low scores would also be inconsistent with a surveillance recording that shows the patient, without looking, easily retrieving a cell phone from a pocket with one hand and flipping it open, or readily retrieving keys from a pocket with one hand, selecting a key, and easily inserting it into a car door. Similarly, such low finger dexterity performance would be inconsistent with neurological records documenting no motor deficits, as well as reported daily activities of playing drums, spending hours using a computer keyboard to play games, and drawing blood as a part of one's duties as a phlebotomist.

In other words, if evidence emerges that patients are in fact able to do things they claim/demonstrate they cannot do on testing, this provides further support for symptom invalidity.

Inconsistency between Injury Specifics and Test Scores (Improbable Outcomes)

A further method for identifying nonplausible cognitive performance is comparison of test scores to expected deficits for the claimed condition. As discussed later (pp. 227–228), research shows that there are no long-term cognitive abnormalities associated with mTBI. Yet some patients with claimed histories of concussion present with dementia-level performance on exam—an implausible pattern in the absence of other medical/neurological conditions that could account for the performance. Similarly, a mild circumscribed stroke in the left hemisphere might be expected to be associated with some lowering of Finger Tapping Test scores in the right hand, but not with impaired scores in both hands.

Elevated Overreport Scales on Personality Testing

Finally, results from personality testing can shed further light on the credibility of physical and cognitive symptom report. For example, as discussed on pages 112, 113–116, and 124–129, marked elevations in MMPI-2 FBS, and MMPI-2–RF FBS-r and RBS, indicate that a test taker has completed the inventory in the same way that individuals failing cognitive SVTs and/ or found to be malingering complete it. Similarly, as discussed on page 138, recent published data on the Personality Assessment Inventory (PAI) shows that a cutoff applied to the Somatic Complaints scale can be used to identify test takers failing cognitive SVTs.

In summary, neuropsychologists use all of the information discussed in this section together with the results of SVTs in deriving conclusions regarding veracity of symptoms on cognitive exam.

3

Assessment of Symptom Validity through Psychological Symptom Overreport Measures

Several tests have been developed to assess specifically for nonplausible psychological symptom report. Most commonly these tests look for feigned psychosis, but some also examine for noncredible report of depression, PTSD, low intellectual function, neurological impairment, and amnesia. The reseach underpinnings of these measures are summarized and analyzed in this chapter, and if information is available regarding the tests' ability to assess for noncredible cognitive symptom overreport, this is also included.

M TEST

The M Test (Beaber, Martson, Michelli, & Millis, 1985) is a 33-item true–false inventory designed to detect malingered schizophrenia through two types of detection strategies: improbable symptoms and rare symptoms. It originally contained three scales: Confusion (C; 8 items that reflect inaccurate beliefs about mental illness), Schizophrenia (S; 10 items that represent genuine symptoms of schizophrenia), and Malingering (M; 15 items that reflect bogus symptoms of schizophrenia). Beaber (personal communication in 1990 to Hankins, Barnard, & Robbins, 1993) apparently subsequently deleted the C scale from the measure, resulting in a 25-item instrument.

In the original validation (Beaber et al., 1985), the M Test was administered to 104 undergraduates first under honest and then simulating instructions (i.e., "Pretend you are in a situation where it would be to your advantage to look crazy"; participants then read a description of the *Diagnostic and Statistical Manual of Mental Disorders*, third edition [DSM-III] criteria for schizophrenia). Administration of the honest condition allowed pretesting of items to confirm that each item was not endorsed by ≥10% or more of normal individuals. In the simulation condition, participants were told to answer "true" to real symptoms of mental disturbance and "false" to items that were not actual symptoms of mental illness, and they were specifically instructed, "Remember, there will be some items which are not real symptoms." They had access to the DSM-III criteria for schizophrenia during completion of the test under the simulation condition. Under the feigning condition, significantly higher scores were obtained on all three scales. The undergraduates' scores were compared with scores of 65 male Veterans Administration (VA) inpatients in California with diagnoses of schizophrenia. The patients obtained significantly higher mean scores than controls in the honest condition on all three scales, but the magnitude of the differences was small (C scale, 1.19 vs. .69; M scale, 2.83 vs. 2.07; S scale, 4.37 vs. 2.46). Malingerers obtained significantly higher mean scores than patients on all three scales (C = 3.10, M = 8.07, S = 7.36) and the magnitude of the differences was large. With a C scale cutoff score of >2, sensitivity was 52.5% and specificity in patients was 93.7%. With an M scale cutoff of ≥4, sensitivity was 73.1% and specificity was 87.7%. However, while an S scale cutoff of ≥6 was associated with 77.9% sensitivity, specificity was only 64.6%.

The authors then reclassified subjects: S scale scores were deleted, and subjects with one or no failures on the remaining two scales were designated as credible, and those with two failed indicators were designated as malingering. This reclassification resulted in 78.2% sensitivity, with an overall classification accuracy of 72.6%. However, this was an ill-conceived modification of study methodology (turning a simulation study into a known-groups design and inappropriately using dependent variables to compose groups), which inaccurately enhanced test sensitivity; that is, known simulators with scores that failed to meet criteria for inclusion (i.e., less blatant malingerers) were excluded from the malingering group. True sensitivity values are those reported for the individual scales, although these are based on simulators and, as shown below, are not applicable to actual malingerers. Furthermore, given that the cutoff for the most effective scale, M, only achieved 88% specificity, the cutoff should actually be raised to ≥5. Finally, some item content is specific to British culture, and the authors do not indicate whether those items were modified for the VA patients in Los Angeles.

Gillis, Rogers, and Bagby (1991) subsequently studied the M Test in real-world malingerers (25 individuals determined to be malingering during a 1- to 2-month inpatient pretrial assessment), simulators (60 undergraduates [30 of whom were coached], 39 community, 25 forensic; total = 124), nonclinical honest responders (41 community, 26 correctional, 30 undergraduates; total = 97), and clinical honest responders (33 outpatient, 39 inpatient; mood, anxiety, psychotic, substance abuse, and Axis II diagnoses). Because two of the M test items are only applicable to male test takers, scores on these two items were prorated for female test takers by using the mean score on the remaining M scale items. The two honestly responding groups scored significantly lower than the feigning groups on the M and S scales, but the malingerers were not significantly different from the honest clinical group on the C scale; the honest clinical and nonclinical groups differed significantly on the S scale. When the criteria of surpassing the Beaber et al. (1985) cutoffs on M and/or C scales were used, 79.8% of simulators were identified, but only 40% of actual malingerers; specificity was 96.9% in nonclinical honest responders, but dropped to 86.1% of honest clinical patients. This study illustrates well the limitation of simulation studies (sensitivity rates are much higher in simulation studies than in studies of actual malingerers).

Smith and Borum (1992) obtained M Test data on 85 prisoners referred for pretrial evaluations; 23 were determined to be malingering, and 62 were judged to be credible. Application of M Test cutoffs captured 69.6% of the malingerers, but the false positive identification rate was 34%. No significant differences were found between groups on the M and C scales, but significant differences were present on the S scale. However, the methodology of this study was problematic: The method of determination of malingering was not specified, and therefore the error rate in group assignment is unknown (i.e., malingerers may have been retained in the credible group, and vice versa).

Hayes, Hale, and Gouvier (1997) obtained M Test data on pretrial defendants with mental retardation who were not malingering (n = 13); patients with mental retardation who were found not guilty by reason of insanity (n = 18); and individuals with mental retardation who met DSM-III-R or DSM-IV criteria for malingering (n = 6) as determined by treatment teams, and who all had shown behaviors that contradicted symptom report. Surprisingly, the malingerers were reported as endorsing fewer deviant items on the M Test than the other two groups, but no additional information was provided.

Schretlen, Neal, and Lesikar (2000) reported M Test (M and S scales) performance in 97 incarcerated defendants awaiting trial with an average of 11.4 years of education; based on interview data and available (nontesting) records, 86 defendants were judged to be credible, and 11 were deemed noncredible. Significant group differences were obtained for both scales;

the noncredible group obtained mean scores of 6.4 (*SD* = 4.1) and 7.0 (*SD* = 2.7) on the M and S scales, respectively, as compared to mean scores of 0.9 (*SD* = 1.4) and 3.2 (*SD* = 2.4) in the credible group. When a cutoff of > 3 for the M scale was used, specificity was 92% and sensitivity was 73%. Classification of groups was enhanced when M Test scores were combined with a forced-choice vocabulary definition task.

Rogers, Bagby, and Gillis (1992) identified a "Rule-In" scale for the M Test composed of 10 test items that had the highest positive predictive power, while a "Rule-Out" scale consisted of 10 items that had the highest negative predictive power. Interpretation Option A (incorporating a Rule-Out score of < 4 followed by a Rule-In score of < 2) was associated with 81% sensitivity and 83.8% specificity, while Option B (employing a Rule-Out score of < 4 followed by a Rule-In score of 0) achieved 95.2% sensitivity but only 70.6% specificity.

Smith, Borum, and Schinka (1993) subsequently attempted to replicate the Rogers, Bagby, and Gillis (1992) Option A and Option B algorithms in the same sample as the Smith and Borum (1992) publication. Of concern, the Rule-In scale was found to be significantly related to race. When Option A was used, specificity was only 65.6% and sensitivity was 68.2%; Option B resulted in 72.7% sensitivity but only 49.2% specificity. As described above, the methodology of this study was problematic vis-à-vis determination of malingering and group assignment.

Hankins et al. (1993) obtained M Test data (they omitted the first eight items, which constitute the C scale) on 79 "incompetent to proceed" inpatient defendants; a clinician read the M Test items if a defendant was unable to read. Determination of malingering was based on an independent interview by a forensic expert (*n* = 9; 11.4% of sample) and on a treating therapist's global rating of malingering (*n* = 13; 16.5% of sample) and psychotic symptoms (*n* = 7; 8.9% of sample); the diagnosis of malingering was not based on M Test results. The forensic expert and primary therapists agreed on 85% of cases. With the M scale cutoff, sensitivity was 11.1–30.8%, with specificity of 67.1–69.7%. For Option A, sensitivity ranged from 56% to 86%, but specificity was only 60–64%. Similarly, for Option B, sensitivity ranged from 67% to 86%, but specificity hovered between 50% and 53%. Because one item on the Rule-In scale was not administered, a constructed variable (not well explained) was employed. The obvious problem with this study is the very small size of the malingering groups, and the lack of complete agreement by raters on the presence of malingering also indicates that group assignment was not entirely accurate.

In a subsequent use of the Rule-In and Rule-Out scales, Heinze and Purisch (2001) reported M Test data on 57 male defendants who had been found incompetent to stand trial and hospitalized for the purpose of restoring them to competency. All had been determined to be malingering by both the multidisciplinary treatment team and the evaluating psychologist, based on behavioral observations and atypical self-reports—including "bizarre, unusual or overly intense symptoms such as, for example, visual hallucinations of mermaids swimming in toilet bowls, rainbow colored dinosaurs running down the corridors or auditory hallucinations that have transformed into black and white nightmare visual hallucinations" (p. 29). Judgments as to malingering status were not based on psychological testing. Mean Rule-In and Rule-Out scale scores were 2.73 ($SD = 0.29$) and 7.04 ($SD = 0.33$), respectively. With a Rule-In cutoff of >0, sensitivity was 88%, and with a Rule-Out cutoff of >3, sensitivity was 90%; a positive finding on either scale was associated with 93% sensitivity. A limitation of this study is the lack of a credible comparison group.

In conclusion, the available empirical data regarding the M Test suggest that specificity is unacceptably poor; however, if cutoffs were to be selected to maintain false positive identification rates $\leq 10\%$, sensitivity would be low (likely $<30\%$) and of very limited clinical use. Further, preliminary data suggest that individuals with extremely low intelligence may be particularly vulnerable to scoring beyond cutoffs. No data have been published regarding the ability of the M Test to identify feigned cognitive symptoms. Finally, no studies have appeared on the M Test in over 10 years; this fact suggests that while it may have been an impetus for subsequent test development, the time for its epitaph has arrived.

STRUCTURED INTERVIEW OF REPORTED SYMPTOMS

The Structured Interview of Reported Symptoms (SIRS; Rogers, 1992) is a 172-item structured interview that incorporates detailed inquiries (addressing specific symptoms and severity), repeated inquiries (testing for response consistency), and general inquiries (assessing specific symptoms, general psychological problems, and symptom patterns). Items are organized into eight primary scales:

- Rare Symptoms (RS; 8 items): infrequent among patients with actual illness
- Symptom Combinations (SD; 10 items): common symptoms that are rarely paired together
- Improbable and Absurd Symptoms (IA; 7 items): fantastic and/or preposterous quality and highly unlikely to be true
- Blatant Symptoms (BL; 15 items): "obvious" symptoms that the lay public would recognize as severe psychopathology
- Subtle Symptoms (SU; 17 items): characteristics common to mental

disorder; some are not immediately recognizable as evidence of major mental disorder
- Selectivity of Symptoms (SEL; 32 items): indiscriminant endorsement of symptoms
- Severity of Symptoms (SEV; 32 items): proportion of symptoms considered unbearable or potentially incapacitating
- Reported versus Observed Symptoms (RO; 12 items): easily observed behavioral characteristics to compare with the patient's reported characteristics

Supplementary scales are available, including Direct Appraisal of Honesty (DS; items asking about honesty and completeness of self-reports); Defensive Symptoms (DS; problems and worries that most people experience); Symptom Onset (SO; report of symptom onset as sudden or otherwise uncharacteristic); Overly Specified Symptoms (OS; symptoms described in an overly precise manner); and Inconsistency of Symptoms (INC; items allowing comparison of responses to similar items).

Identification of malingering is based on the following algorithm:

- Three or more primary scales in the "probable feigning" category
- One or more primary scales in the "definite feigning" category
- > 76 total SIRS score

Interrater reliability has been found to be high (.99), as has test–retest reliability (Rogers, Vitacco, & Kurus, 2010), and a Spanish version has been developed that shows comparable large effect sizes (Correa, Rogers, & Hoersting, 2010). In a survey of test usage in emotional injury evaluations, the SIRS was employed in 11% of assessments, and was utilized by 29% of those who classified themselves as "frequent assessors" (Boccaccini & Brodsky, 1999). In a survey of board-certified forensic psychologists (Lally, 2003), the SIRS was "recommended" for determinations of malingering by 58% of the respondents, and 89% judged it "acceptable" for this purpose.

Meta-Analytic Data

Green and Rosenfeld (2011) recently published a review and meta-analysis of the effectiveness of the SIRS based on 26 studies conducted between 1990 and 2009; 61.5% were published in peer-reviewed journals, and the remaining studies were unpublished doctoral dissertations. The composite effect size was large ($d = 2.02$), but individual effect sizes ranged from 0.11 to 6.93. Across individual scales, the BL scale was found to have the largest weighted mean effect size ($d = 1.79$), and the IA Symptoms scale was observed to have the lowest. Overall specificity was 89% and overall sensitivity was 73.9% for both simulators and suspected malingerers. Using cutoffs of one scale in the definite-malingering range, or at least three in the probable-malingering range, resulted in a mean specificity of 94.6% but sensitivity was only 48.6%. When a total score cutoff was used, mean sensitivity was 72.7%, but specificity was unacceptable (70.3%). With a cutoff of 2 or more scales in the probable malingering range, sensitivity was higher (87.3%) and specificity was nearly within acceptable limits (87.1%). The best overall classification rates were achieved with the use of discriminant-function analyses to discriminate groups (81.1% sensitivity, 93.8% specificity).

Comparison of initial validation studies with subsequent investigations showed a significant decline in weighted mean effect sizes for total score (d = 2.07 vs. 1.65), and in four out of the eight individual scales: SU, BL, RS, and SEV. Of particular concern, studies conducted after the initial validation obtained specificity rates that were on average >20 percentage points lower than in the original studies (78.1% vs. 99.5%). Moreover, some populations were at particular risk for false positive identification, such as patients with mental retardation and dissociative disorders (only two-thirds passed), although specificity rates varied widely even in conventional samples. In contrast, sensitivity rates were generally higher in later studies; in the initial validation studies, sensitivity was 48.5% but rose to 70.7% overall in postmanual studies (48.8% by probable- and definite-feigning algorithms, 72.7% for total score, 81.1% for discriminant-function analysis, and 87.3% for alternative techniques). In investigations published after the initial validation studies, identification of noncredible subgroups was superior in simulation as compared to known-groups designs (sensitivity = 74.4% vs. 62.3%). Not unexpectedly, effect sizes were larger in comparisons of noncredible groups and honestly responding nonclinical as compared to clinical samples (mean d = 2.19 vs. 1.65), leading the authors to caution that use of the former would result in artificially inflated classification rates.

Interestingly, abbreviated formats (self-report paper-and-pencil versions; versions only employing items for the eight primary scales; items for five primary and one supplementary scale; etc.) achieved specificity rates comparable to those for the full version (82.0% vs. 79.3%) and somewhat better sensitivity (74.7% vs. 63.1%).

Green and Rosenfeld (2011) conclude that the SIRS is effective, but probably less so than MMPI-2 validity indicators, and is questionably deserving of its "gold standard" designation. They argue that studies employing the SIRS for group classification should acknowledge the limitations of this standard. These authors also express concern that little information is available about the ability of the SIRS to discriminate test takers feigning differing types of Axis I disorders.

Use of the SIRS to Identify Noncredible Cognitive Symptoms

Hayes, Hale, and Gouvier (1998) obtained SIRS data in a forensic psychiatric setting on 21 individuals found incompetent to stand trial (an interdisciplinary staff determined 12 of these individuals to have mental retardation, while the other 9 were judged to be malingering; determinations were not based on psychological test results), and in 18 defendants with mental retardation found guilty by reason of insanity. Mean IQs across the three groups were 61.0 (*SD* = 5.6) for pretrial defendants with mental retardation, 66.0 (*SD* = 6.3) for malingerers, and 60.2 (*SD* = 4.9) for individuals with mental retardation judged not guilty by reason of insanity. All pretrial individuals with mental retardation were correctly classified, as well as 94% of those judged not guilty by reason of insanity; 89% of the malingerers were correctly identified.

However, these findings were not replicated in subsequent studies of the SIRS in samples with mental retardation. Hurley and Deal (2006) administered the SIRS to 39 individuals with IQs between 50 and 78 living in residential facilities. With a total cutoff of > 76, 53.8% of the sample were identified as malingering (mean of 93.8 ± 61.9, range of 2–238), while scores in the range of definite-malingering for one or more primary scales, or within the probable-malingering range on three or more scales, were associated with a 30.8% false positive rate.

Shandera et al. (2010) assessed the utility of the SIRS in the differential diagnosis of actual versus feigned mental retardation in a simulation study involving 24 individuals with actual mental retardation, who were compared to community volunteers with no more than 11 years of education and no history of psychotic or neurological illness or substance abuse. The volunteers completed the test honestly (*n* = 10) or under instructions to feign mental retardation (*n* = 25). Subjects with mental retardation were provided $20 for their participation, and the community volunteers were given $75. Simulators were asked to feign in a believable manner in the context of death penalty litigation; they were read a fact sheet on mental retardation and completed a quiz on the information, and at the conclusion of the testing they completed a questionnaire regarding instructions and their compliance. Mean WAIS-III FSIQs for the three groups were 63.21 (*SD* = 6.66), 84.80 (*SD* = 9.37), and 67.76 (*SD* = 8.78), respectively; group mean scores for the SIRS were 66.70 (*SD* = 39.77), 48.00 (*SD* = 16.89), and 82.20 (*SD* = 46.22), respectively. When a SIRS total cut-score of > 76 was used, sensitivity was 52% and specificity in the group with mental retardation was 65% (whereas in the community honest responders it was 58%!), leading Shandera et al. to report that the SIRS "fared poorly" (2010, p. 53).

Two studies have evaluated the SIRS with civil litigants and disability seekers, although it is unclear whether the data are independent since many of the authors in the two publications are the same. Rogers, Payne, Berry, and Granacher (2009) examined the ability of the SIRS, including the new Improbable Failure (IF) scale (requiring the test taker to provide antonyms or rhymes to simple words) to identify feigned symptoms in workers' compensation applicants (66%), civil litigants (18%), and disability applicants (16%). The presence of feigned cognitive disorder was based on the VSVT, TOMM, and Letter Memory Test. Subjects failing two or more of the measures were assigned to the cognitive-feigning group ($n = 79$); those passing all three measures were assigned to the genuine group ($n = 330$); and the remaining subjects were placed in an indeterminate category ($n = 89$). Effect sizes on SIRS scales between credible subjects and cognitive feigners averaged 1.33, while effect sizes between credible and indeterminate subjects ranged from 0.79 to 0.92. When SIRS standard decision rules were used, specificity was 97.5% (although this appeared to exclude the indeterminate cases); sensitivity rates were not provided.

In the sample of 276 subjects passing both cognitive SVTs and personality test validity scales, 29 credible individuals with cognitive disorders (dementia, amnestic disorder, or cognitive disorder not otherwise specified [NOS]) obtained higher SIRS scores than credible subjects without cognitive disorders ($n = 247$), although the effect size was modest (mean $d = -0.2$). Credible individuals (passing both cognitive SVTs and personality test validity scales) with IQ < 80 ($n = 18$) scored approximately 3 points higher on the total score than those with IQ ≥ 80 ($n = 258$); the mean effect size across primary scales was 0.15, and no comparisons were significant with the exception of those for the IF scale. Patients with low IQs failed approximately 3 of the 20 IF items as compared to less than 1 in the higher-IQ group, and scored comparably to the cognitive-feigning group. The IF scale was modified to include only those items that maintained specificity of $\geq 90\%$, and named the IF-Revised; however, while specificity was high for a cutoff of 0 (91%), sensitivity was low (31%). The authors conclude that "the present findings support use of the SIRS for persons with cognitive disorders but underscore its limited value for assessing FCI [feigned cognitive impairment]" (p. 223).

Vagnini et al. (2006) administered the SIRS to 122 compensation seekers (workers' compensation or civil litigation) undergoing evaluation to determine presence and extent of brain dysfunction, the majority in the context of a claimed head trauma ($n = 85$). Subjects were placed in honest, indeterminate, and probable-cognitive-feigning groups, based on their performance on three cognitive SVTs (TOMM, VSVT, and WAIS-III Digit Span). Those who passed all three measures were placed in the honest group ($n = 37$); those who failed a single indicator were assigned to the indeterminate group ($n = 32$) and removed from further analyses. Those subjects who failed two tests were placed in the noncredible group (n = 36) (testing had been terminated in the 17 subjects failing all three tests). Mean SIRS scores were 18.5 (SD = 15.1) in the honest responders and 37.2 (SD = 24.4) in the noncredible subjects. Although sensitivity and specificity data were not provided, it is apparent from mean scores that false positives would be low in credible patients (although indeterminate cases were excluded), but that sensitivity would also be low (although data were missing for more blatant feigners).

STRUCTURED INTERVIEW OF REPORTED SYMPTOMS–2

The Structured Interview of Reported Symptoms–2 (SIRS-2; Rogers, Sewell, & Gillard, 2010) is identical in content to the original SIRS, but provides new validation data from 206 protocols, and now incorporates a decision tree with two indeterminate classifications (evaluate: a > 50% likelihood of feigning, which requires further evaluation; general: distorted responding is likely, but not necessarily related to an attempt to feign symptoms). The SIRS-2 also includes the IF scale discussed above, as well as two index scores, the Modified Total (MT) index and the Supplementary Scale (SS) index; the SO scale and total score from the original SIRS have been dropped. The MT index, an adapted version of the SIRS total score, is employed to distinguish definite from indeterminate protocols, while the SS index measures disengagement (reduced investment in testing). Use of the measure with an interpreter is referred to as "unauthorized." The manual cites sensitivity rates of 80% at 97.5% specificity.

DeClue (2011) and Rubenzer (2010), in separate reviews of the SIRS-2, raise various concerns, including the fact that data directly comparing the accuracy of the SIRS-2 to the SIRS in terms of identifying feigning versus honest test takers have not been reported; and that information regarding the key validation study of the SIRS-2 is inaccurate (n's are not consistent), "seriously incomplete," or otherwise problematic, and has not been subjected to peer review. Specifically, such basic information regarding subjects such as age, gender, and ethnicity, or whether groups differed on these characteristics, is not provided; nor is it described how participants in the known-groups comparisons were identified as feigning or verified as credible. Also, protocols for the genuine subjects were obtained 20 years after protocols for feigning subjects, raising the possibility of cohort confounds. Of particular concern, apparently one-third of the protocols on presumed honest responders came from individuals diagnosed with dissociative identity disorder (some authors have commented that such symptoms are in fact fabricated and reflect a factitious disorder). In fact, data from the SIRS suggest that patients with dissociative identity disorder obtain mean scores above cutoffs indicative of feigning (Brand, McNary, Loewenstein, Kolos, & Barr, 2006). In addition, over 80% of the SIRS-2 test protocols for noncredible subjects came from simulators (only 36 of 207 presumed feigned presentations were real-world individuals feigning psychopathology). Also, more protocols were designated as indeterminate than feigned, and the indeterminate protocols were excluded in determining sensitivity and specificity; when indeterminates are included, sensitivity drops to 49%. Finally, in one of the case examples presented in the manual, compelling evidence of malingered cognitive dysfunction (performance significantly below chance on a forced-choice measure) was dismissed as due to "distractibility."

Use of the SIRS-2 to Identify Noncredible Cognitive Symptoms

Although the SIRS-2 manual (Rogers, Sewell, & Gillard, 2010) indicates that the instrument has been used successfully with examinees diagnosed with mild mental retardation (p. 14), no data are provided to support this assertion. Subsequently, Weiss, Rosenfeld, and Farkas (2011) obtained SIRS-2 data in 43 community-dwelling individuals with mild mental retardation (mean WASI FSIQ = 66.63 ± 6.17; range = 56–75). Mean SIRS-2 total score was 70.56 (SD = 29.14); when the cutoff of ≥76 was used 41.1% (n = 18) were misidentified as malingering. When the original scoring method for the SIRS was employed (one scale in the definite range or three in the probable range), 23.3% (n = 10) were classified as feigning, 53% (n = 23) were identified as credible, and 23.3% (n = 10) were indeterminate. Classification accuracy improved with use of the SIRS-2 interpretation algorithm: 7.0% (n = 3) were identified as feigning, 9.3% (n = 4) as indeterminate—general, 11.6% (n = 5) as indeterminate—evaluate (> 50% likelihood of feigning), and 72.1% (n = 31) as credible. Of the individual subscales, only two (SC and IA) identified all subjects as honest or indeterminate, while only two (SU and SEV) classified subjects as in the definite-feigning category (9.3% and 11.6%, respectively).

Examination of the supplementary scales showed that 5 subjects scored high on the INC scale; 3 were identified as feigning on the SIRS but not the SIRS-2. However, more problematic was the IF scale, which was specifically designed to detect feigned cognitive impairment (although the manual does warn that it is to be used to screen for feigned cognitive impairment in primary English speakers of low average intelligence or higher); mean score was 10.26 (SD = 5.41), with 33 subjects (76.7%) scoring above the cutoff. Total score, primary scales, and the INC scale were not significantly related to IQ, but the IF scale was negatively correlated with FSIQ and VIQ (r = −.53). Higher SIRS scores were associated with comorbid psychiatric conditions; mean scores rose exponentially from 56.70 (SD = 22.02) in subjects with no comorbid condition, to 77.14 (SD = 27.99) in those with one comorbid condition, to 108.33 (SD = 15.57) in those with two or more comorbid conditions.

Weiss et al. (2011) conclude that "the SIRS-2 clearly represents a dramatic improvement in the classification of feigned psychiatric symptoms, but the risk of misclassification, for individuals with ID (intellectual disabilities), as feigning symptoms remains elevated" (p. 288). They also note that the primary scales that identified their sample as definitely feigning are those measuring amplification of symptoms, and they suggest that this may be an artifact of "acquiescence and suggestibility" common in individuals with low intellectual function; however, the subscales that classified all subjects as honest or indeterminate are those that measure unlikely symptoms, "suggesting that evaluees with ID may not acquiesce to symptoms that are entirely unfamiliar" (p. 289).

In summary and conclusion, most research on the SIRS has been conducted in correctional settings and in the context of feigned psychosis, and it is not likely to generalize well to other settings/populations. Available data suggest that the SIRS instruments have adequate specificity in most settings, but sensitivity probably hovers at 50%. MMPI-2 instrument validity indicators appear to be more sensitive (see Chapter 4), and have the added advantage of requiring no examiner administration time. Validation data for the SIRS-2 appear to be problematic, and they raise questions regarding admissibility. Few studies have examined the ability of the SIRS instruments to identify feigned cognitive impairment, and most have involved the differentiation between actual and feigned mental retardation. SIRS measures have generally performed poorly in these investigations, although in fairness, cognitive SVTs also have low specificity in individuals of very low intelligence (Dean, Victor, et al., 2008; Victor & Boone, 2007). IF, a scale specifically designed to detect feigned cognitive impairment, may have adequate specificity in populations excluding mental retardation, but sensitivity is poor.

MILLER FORENSIC ASSESSMENT OF SYMPTOMS TEST

The Miller Forensic Assessment of Symptoms Test (M-FAST; Miller, 2001) is a 25-item structured interview designed to assess for malingered psychopathology in a forensic setting. It includes several subscales reflecting various detection strategies, including discrepancy between Reported versus Observed Symptoms (RO), Extreme Symptomatology (ES), Rare Combinations of symptoms (RC), Unusual Hallucinations (UH), Unusual Symptom Course (USC), Negative Image (NI; i.e., overly negative self-image) and

Suggestibility (S; i.e., symptoms provoked by examiner suggestion). A cut-off of ≥6 for total score is recommended.

Use of the M-FAST to Identify Noncredible Psychiatric Symptoms

Simulation Studies

The M-FAST test manual reports non-peer-reviewed data on 94 undergraduates, half of whom were instructed to feign mental illness without being "obvious," while the other half were instructed to provide honest responses. The simulators scored significantly higher (16.00 vs. 0.81).

Guriel et al. (2004) obtained M-FAST protocols for 68 college students assigned to either an honestly responding group (*n* = 10) or one of three groups instructed to simulate PTSD symptoms associated with a motor vehicle accident for a civil litigation lawsuit: uncoached feigning (*n* = 19), coached regarding symptoms (provided with a list of PTSD symptoms available from the Internet; *n* = 23), and coached regarding symptoms and strategies (provided with a list of PTSD symptoms available from the Internet, but also informed about strategies that would help them to evade detection; *n* = 16). Coached simulators had to pass a quiz on the information provided before they completed the measure. Honest responders obtained significantly lower mean M-FAST scores than the other three groups (1.40 vs. 9.74 in uncoached, 10.57 in PTSD information only, and 7.38 in PTSD information plus strategies to evade detection). With a cutoff of >5, sensitivity was 68% in uncoached simulators, 87% in simulators coached with information only, and 69% in simulators coached with avoidance of detection strategies; specificity was 90%.

Subsequently, Guriel-Tennant and Gremouw (2006; also described on pp. 154–155) recruited 113 undergraduates, 66 of whom had experienced a traumatic event. Participants were assigned to four simulation groups: positive for trauma and coached (*n* = 31), positive for trauma and not coached (*n* = 35), negative for trauma and coached (*n* = 25), and negative for trauma and not coached (*n* = 22). Mean M-FAST scores across the four groups were 13.4 ± 12.02 (trauma-positive/naïve), 6.4 ± 4.27 (trauma-positive/coached), 11.0 ± 5.66 (trauma-negative/naïve), and 6.9 ± 3.95 (trauma-negative/coached); coached participants obtained lower scores, but still scored on average above the cutoff of 5.

Jackson, Rogers, and Sewell (2005) collected M-FAST data on 147 jail inmates who took the M-FAST under standard conditions; 5–7 days later, 96 again completed the test under honesty conditions, and the other 51 were instructed to feign psychiatric symptoms "that would interfere with his or her competency to stand trial" (e.g., cause "major problems in working with your attorney" and "make you unable to think through what is going on in court"). Simulators were also warned that the interviewer would "try some trick questions to catch persons trying to fake." All subjects were paid $5, and simulators were offered an additional $5 if they were successful in feigning. Following their participation, the inmates were surveyed regarding their understanding of instructions, the amount of effort they put forth in the task, and how successful they were at feigning; 8 reported exerting little effort on the task, and their data were removed, resulting in a final simulator n of 43. M-FAST data were also available from 49 inmates undergoing a competency restoration program, 8 of whom were judged to be noncredible from their performance on the SIRS.

Group comparisons showed that noncredible groups differed from credible groups, that simulating and malingering groups did not differ (mean M-FAST scores of 8.58 and 10.25, respectively), and that control and credible patient groups did not differ (mean M-FAST scores of 1.60 and 2.15, respectively). When the cutoff of ≥ 6 was applied, sensitivity in combined noncredible groups was 76% and specificity in credible groups was 90%. Limitations of this study include the fact that, unfortunately, specificity rates were not provided for credible patients separately from controls, and thus data on true levels of specificity in real-world psychiatric populations cannot be gleaned from the study. In addition, data were available on only 8 real-world malingerers, precluding reliable sensitivity rates for this subgroup. Also of note, item 5 had been deleted from the M-FAST; although it was found to be uncorrelated with the total score, it is unclear whether omission of this item affected any of the classification statistics. Furthermore, participants had apparently taken the M-FAST in an "honest" condition prior to the simulation trial, and in a real-world setting malingerers have not typically had prior exposure to the instruments. Finally, the amount of incentive was low, and simulators were warned that "trick questions" would be used to identify the veracity of their presentations—conditions that do not correspond to actual incentives in the real world and standardized test administration procedures.

Guy, Kwartner, and Miller (2006) examined M-FAST scores in undergraduates instructed to simulate one of four diagnoses: schizophrenia (n = 48), major depressive disorder (n = 50), bipolar disorder (n = 51), and PTSD (n = 41). Simulators were instructed to imagine a scenario in which they were failing school, which placed their financial aid in jeopardy, and that this problem would be averted if a psychologist diagnosed them with a serious mental disorder that interfered with ability to complete schoolwork. They were also provided with specific characteristics of the disorder they were instructed to feign; were allowed 15 minutes to "mentally prepare" and write down strategies they might refer to; and were offered "double" extra credit if they were successful in feigning, while also being told that "only the smartest and most skilled students would be able to fake the test without getting caught." Fifteen percent of participants failed at least one of three questions from a postexperiment compliance-and-understanding check, and their data were excluded. Performances were compared against previously published samples of credible patients with the same diagnoses. Simulators obtained significantly higher scores than credible patient groups, with the largest differences observed for the schizophrenia and bipolar conditions. At a cutoff of 6, sensitivity was 88% (82% specificity) for feigned schizophrenia, 62% (79% specificity) for feigned depression, 84% (79% specificity) for feigned bipolar disorder, and 63% (85% specificity) for feigned PTSD. Guy et al. (2006) speculate that the M-FAST is better able to detect feigned psychosis because the majority of the items reflect psychotic content and/or highly unusual/improbable symptoms.

Messer and Fremouw (2007) obtained M-FAST data on four groups of undergraduates: those with high clinical PTSD ($n = 24$), those with moderate subclinical PTSD ($n = 41$), honest responders ($n = 39$), and coached simulators ($n = 41$). Presence of PTSD was determined by responses to the Detailed Assessment of Posttraumatic Symptoms (DAPS), and subjects with DAPS Negative Bias (NB) scores ≥ 12 were excluded. Those not showing clinical or subclinical PTSD were randomly assigned to the honest-responder and simulator groups. Simulators were instructed to feign PTSD symptoms associated with a motor vehicle accident for a civil suit; were provided with a description of PTSD symptoms and had to pass a quiz on the information before further participation; and were told that if they evaded detection, they would receive $25. The simulators scored significantly higher on the M-FAST than the other groups, averaging scores of nearly 10, whereas the remaining groups were indistinguishable (obtaining average scores of < 3). With a cutoff of > 5, sensitivity was 78%, but specificity was only 79.2% in the group with clinical PTSD (although specificity was 100% in the remaining two groups). A limitation of this study is that students attending college may not reflect the more disabling spectrum of PTSD symptoms, and thus specificity levels, already problematic, may have been overestimated.

Known-Groups Studies

In addition to various limitations listed for the studies above, a major disadvantage of simulation studies is that the results do not necessarily generalize to real-world noncredible subjects. Fortunately, five studies have examined validity of the M-FAST in real-world populations, although it is unclear to what extent the data from the first four studies overlap.

Miller (2004) reported M-FAST data from 50 male inpatients in a forensic psychiatric unit who had been deemed incompetent to stand trial.

Seventeen additional patients were not included because of either danger-ousness ($n = 5$), inability to comprehend the informed consent and assess-ment procedures ($n = 2$), or refusal to participate ($n = 10$). Subjects were assigned to credible and noncredible groups based on the SIRS (two pri-mary SIRS scales in the probable-feigning range and a total SIRS score greater than 76); 28% ($n = 14$) were identified as malingering. Noncred-ible patients scored significantly higher on the total M-FAST score (mean of 12.79 ± 4.94 vs. 2.44 ± 2.07) and the four individual scores on which there were enough items to run analyses: UH (2.36 ± 1.65 vs. 0.53 ± 0.88), RO (1.29 ± 1.14 vs. 0.25 ± 0.44), ES (3.50 ± 1.91 vs. 0.89 ± 1.21), and RC (4.00 ± 1.71 versus 0.47 ± 0.77). A cutoff of 6 applied to the total score was associated with 93% sensitivity and 83% specificity. Sensitivity rates for cutoff scores for the four individual scales (selected for ≥90% specific-ity) were as follows: UH (≥3) = 50%, RO (≥2) = 36%, ES (≥4) = 57%, and RC (≥3) = 86%.

Guy and Miller (2004) also administered the M-FAST to 50 incar-cerated males with an average of 11 years of education who were receiv-ing psychological treatment in a maximum-security prison. It was noted that not all had a motive to malinger, but no other information was pro-vided regarding incentive to feign. Of the 50 subjects, 21 were placed in the malingering group based on SIRS scores (total score of ≥76 and two primary scales within the probable range). They scored significantly higher on the M-FAST total score (mean = 11.38 ± 5.15) than did nonmalingerers (mean = 3.00 ± 2.55), and the groups also differed significantly on all indi-vidual scales. A total cutoff of ≥6 was associated with 86% sensitivity, but specificity was 83%; raising the cutoff to 8 maintained specificity of 93%, while dropping sensitivity to 71%. When the standard cutoff of ≥6 was used for total score, specificity was 90% in Caucasians, but 63% in African Americans and 83% in Hispanics. Across individual scales, RC actually exceeded the group classification accuracy of the total score (cutoff of ≥3 = 90% specificity and 76% sensitivity).

Miller (2005; also reported in the test manual) published M-FAST data (original 79-item pool) gathered on 280 incarcerated psychiatric inpa-tients who had been judged incompetent to stand trial; approximately 25% of the available hospital population did not participate because of either dangerousness, inability to comprehend the informed consent and assess-ment procedures, or refusal to participate. With the SIRS as the criterion for assignment to credible and noncredible groups, 26% of the sample was judged to be malingering. No significant differences were found in M-FAST scores between illiterate patients ($n = 58$) and literate patients ($n = 222$). In a second study involving 50 forensic inpatients administered the final 25-item M-FAST, 14 were judged to be malingering based on the SIRS, and 8 were illiterate. The noncredible patients obtained significantly higher M-FAST scores (12.79 vs. 2.44). Literacy was again unrelated to M-FAST scores: The mean total score for credible illiterate patients was 1.7 (SD = 3.2) as compared to 2.6 (SD = 3.1) in credible literate patients, while the mean score in noncredible illiterate patients was 10.5 (SD = 5.0) versus 13.2 (SD = 6.2) in noncredible literate patients. With a cutoff of 6, specificity was 83% in both literate and illiterate groups (with sensitivity of 92% to 100%). However, of concern, specificity at this cutoff was only 71% in African Americans (100% sensitivity); specificity was high in Caucasians (98%), but sensitivity was only 67%. Moreover, the data from this second study are of questionable reliability, due to small n's in the subgroups.

Veazey, Hays, Wagner, and Miller (2005) obtained M-FAST data for psychiatric inpatients (70 of 150 agreed to participate) with a mean of 2.1 psychiatric admissions; approximately 55% carried a mood disorder diagnosis. Mean IQ was 90.3. Mean M-FAST total score was 4.3 (SD = 4.0). Age, education, gender, ethnicity, and IQ were not related to M-FAST scores, nor were Global Assessment of Functioning scores, and M-FAST scores did not differ across diagnostic groups; however, number of psychiatric admissions was positively related to M-FAST scores. Forty-four inpatients subjects had completed the PAI; when a PAI Malingering Index (MAL) score of 3 was used for assignment to credible and noncredible groups, an M-FAST cutoff of 6 was associated with 80% sensitivity and 85% specificity. Raising the cut-score to ≥7 increased specificity to 90% while retaining sensitivity of 80%. However, these data are problematic, because it is not clear why some participants completed the PAI and others did not, and the number of patients assigned to credible and noncredible groups based on the PAI is not reported. Furthermore, it is not known how the greater than 50% refusal to participate affected the results of the study (i.e, the 70 patients who did not agree to participate may not have been representative of psychiatric inpatient samples).

Vitacco, Rogers, Gabel, and Munizza (2007) collected M-FAST data for 100 defendants undergoing competency-to-stand-trial evaluations. The defendants had a wide range of diagnoses, including psychosis (68%), mood disorder (17%), and cognitive disorder (1%); 21 were identified as malingering based on the SIRS. The mean M-FAST score for nonmalingerers was 2.38 (SD = 3.14) and for malingerers was 11.75 (SD = 4.60). With a cutoff of ≥6, sensitivity was 100% with specificity of 90%, and two individual scales had cutoffs also associated with good sensitivity at 90% specificity: RC ≥2 = 81% sensitivity, and UH ≥2 = 67% sensitivity.

Some additional known-groups studies that do not appear to have been published in peer-reviewed journals are reported in the test manual; all used the SIRS to assign subjects to the noncredible groups. Of 16 individuals seeking disability for psychiatric symptoms, 6 were found to be noncredible on the SIRS, and this subset obtained significantly higher M-FAST scores (9.69 vs. 2.60). In a sample of 20 forensic inpatients judged incompetent to stand trial, 9 who were deemed to be noncredible based on the SIRS obtained significantly higher M-FAST scores (11.50 vs. 1.33).

Use of the M-FAST to Identify Noncredible Cognitive Symptoms

Vagnini et al. (2006) administered the M-FAST to 122 compensation seekers (workers' compensation or civil litigation) undergoing evaluation to determine presence and extent of brain dysfunction (three-quarters in the context of a claimed head trauma; $n = 85$). Subjects were placed in honest, indeterminate, and probable-cognitive-feigning groups based on performance on three cognitive SVTs (TOMM, VSVT, and WAIS-III Digit Span); those who passed all three measures were placed in the honest group ($n = 37$), and those who failed a single indicator were assigned to the indeterminate group ($n = 32$) and removed from further analyses. Those who failed two tests were placed in the noncredible group ($n = 36$) (testing had been terminated in the 17 participants failing all three tests). Mean M-FAST scores were 1.8 ($SD = 1.4$) in the honest responders and 3.8 ($SD = 3.6$) in the noncredible subjects. Sensitivity and specificity data are not provided, but it is apparent from mean scores that false positives would have been low in credible patients (although indeterminate cases were excluded), but that sensitivity would also be low (although data were missing for more blatant feigners).

Graue et al. (2007) collected M-FAST data on a sample of participants with mild mental retardation ($n = 26$; mean WAIS-III FSIQ = 60.0) and on community volunteers with ≤11 years of education and with no histories of significant psychiatric/neurological disorder or substance abuse. The latter were assigned to either honest ($n = 10$; mean WAIS-III FSIQ = 80.7) or feigning ($n = 25$; mean WAIS-III FSIQ = 61.7) conditions. The patients with mental retardation were in day treatment settings but served as their own guardians; they were paid $20 for participation. Community volunteers were recruited via flyers at vocational assistance agencies and entertainment venues, and were paid $75. Feigners were presented with a scenario in which they would benefit if they successfully feigned mental retardation and were provided with symptoms of the condition; a bonus of $20 was offered for successful feigning. These participants completed a quiz regarding symptoms of mental retardation before completing the M-FAST, and they underwent debriefing after their participation in which they were asked to recount their instructions. M-FAST total scores averaged 8.9 ($SD = 6.5$) in malingerers, 6.7 ($SD = 5.5$) in subjects with mental retardation, and 3.3 ($SD = 3.4$) in honest responders. The total score cutoff of ≥6 is reported as resulting in 68% sensitivity, but specificity in the sample with mental retardation was 50%.

Alwes, Clark, Berry, and Granacher (2008) reported M-FAST data on 308 workers' compensation claimants or personal injury litigants; 23% claimed brain injury. Twenty-three were determined to be faking psychiatric symptoms based on the SIRS, and 75 were identified as feigning cognitive dysfunction, based on failing at least two cognitive SVTs (TOMM, VSVT, and Letter Memory Test) (55 subjects who failed one SVT were excluded from data analyses). The M-FAST mean scores for psychiatric feigners, psychiatric nonfeigners (n = 172), cognitive feigners, and cognitive nonfeigners (n = 178) were 9.0 (SD = 3.1), 2.4 (SD = 2.1), 5.5 (SD = 3.7), and 2.9 (SD = 2.3). At a cutoff score of ≥ 6, sensitivity in identification of feigned psychiatric symptoms was 83%, with specificity of 91%; however, sensitivity to cognitive feigning was 43% and specificity was 88%. The latter sensitivity and specificity rates are probably artificially elevated, owing to the exclusion of subjects failing a single cognitive SVT (i.e., less blatant malingerers who failed one SVT were excluded as well as more cognitively impaired credible subjects who failed one SVT).

Sollman et al. (2010) employed the M-FAST in an ADHD simulation study involving 73 undergraduates, including 29 with previously diagnosed and verifiable ADHD; subjects with histories of learning disabilities, diagnosed or self-perceived psychiatric conditions, and neurological disorders were excluded. The undergraduates without ADHD were assigned to either honest-responding (n = 14) or ADHD simulation (n = 30) groups; the latter were provided with a scenario in which they had used the ADHD medication of a roommate, found that it made studying easier, suspected that they might have ADHD, and subsequently feigned symptoms on exam in order to secure the medication. Simulators were provided with information from the internet regarding ADHD, were allowed to take notes regarding symptoms to fake, and were informed that they could receive $45 if they faked convincingly. Participants with ADHD were offered either $45 or course credit and $15. Postexperiment testing was used to document understanding of, and compliance with, task instructions. Mean M-FAST scores across the three groups were 0.21 (SD = 0.58; honest responders), 2.63 (SD = 3.03; simulators), and 1.07 (SD = 1.22; students with ADHD). Specificity was 100%, but sensitivity was only 10%.

In summary and conclusion, half of the studies providing validation data regarding the effectiveness of the M-FAST in detecting feigned psychiatric symptoms have relied on simulation designs, which have limited generalizability to real-world situations. Findings from real-world patient groups indicates that the recommended cutoff of ≥ 6 results in inadequate specificity (i.e., $\leq 90\%$), particularly for ethnic minorities, and that the cutoff for total score should probably be raised to at least 7. However, raising the cutoff from ≥6 will lower sensitivity rates from 70–80%+ to <70%. Furthermore, sensitivity rates may already be inflated by use of the SIRS for group assignment in the known-groups studies (i.e., as discussed on p. 84, the SIRS may only detect 50% of noncredible subjects, probably the more blatant feigners). The M-FAST appears to be robust to literacy—an advantage over self-administered personality inventories.

The few studies regarding use of the M-FAST in the context of feigned cognitive symptoms (ADHD and acquired brain injury) show that it is not effective (sensitivity rates are <50%); however, only two known-groups studies have been conducted, and they may have had overlapping data (Alwes et al., 2008; Vagnini et al., 2006). Specificity at a cutoff of ≥6 is problematic for patients with mental retardation, who show a 50% false positive rate.

STRUCTURED INVENTORY OF MALINGERED SYMPTOMATOLOGY

The Structured Inventory of Malingered Symptomatology (SIMS; Widows & Smith, 2005) is a 75-item true–false inventory that consists of five non-overlapping scales designed to detect feigned Low Intelligence, Affective Disorders, Neurological Impairment, Psychosis, and Amnestic Disorders. The SIMS incorporated items from the MMPI, SIRS, and WAIS-R that had demonstrated some effectiveness for detection of malingering, and qualitative items were added that had been shown in research to have similar utility. Detection strategies to identify feigned psychiatric and neurological disorders consist of rare and improbable symptoms, symptoms inconsistent with claimed conditions, and unlikely symptom combinations; additional detection strategies employed to capture feigned cognitive impairment include approximate answers and failure to answer simple questions correctly. Nine experienced psychologists rated an original pool of 200 items for how well they reflected malingering; those 75 items on which there was at least 67% agreement were retained (15 items per scale).

The original validation study (Smith & Burger, 1997) was based on 476 undergraduate simulators (90% Caucasian; 71% female) who received course credit for participation and who were randomly assigned to eight experimental groups: a control group and simulating conditions for each test scale, as well as groups of simulators of mania and depression for the Affective Disorders scale, and a "general" malingering group (the number of subjects in each group was not reported). Simulating groups were provided with symptom-specific vignettes in which they were to imagine simulating symptoms to reduce culpability for a serious assault charge. Participants were warned to endorse only symptoms of their particular condition so as to avoid detection. "Pilot testing" indicated that participants understood instructions and perceived that they were able to feign the conditions (however, of note, those instructed to feign psychosis did not differ from those in the honest condition on the MMPI F scale). All simulation groups scored significantly differently from the control group on SIMS scales and total score (it is unclear whether this means that participants feigning one type of disorder also scored significantly differently from controls on all remaining SIMS scales). All simulators were then combined to determine the sensitivity and specificity values for each SIMS scale and total score; Smith and Burger (1997) argued that this would "more closely mimic conditions found in the 'real' world (e.g., group membership is unknown) and would establish the heuristic value of each scale" (p. 187). The authors reported sensitivity values between 74.6% and 88.3% for individual scales, and 95.6% for total score, although the cutoffs associated with these values were not reported. The authors indicated that a total score of > 14 in conjunction with an MMPI F raw score of ≥ 26 is suggestive of malingering and that further evaluation is warranted.

Smith and Burger (1997) note that the problems with the validation study included the very high base rate of malingering (87.5%), lack of credible patient comparison groups, low incentive for faking in the simulation groups, failure to screen participants for actual psychopathology (although the fact that they were attending college suggests that they did not have disabling conditions or low intelligence), and unknown impact of gender and ethnicity on test scores. In addition, although the authors have argued that the SIMS is a screening test for malingering, specificity rates are unacceptable, particularly given that the comparison group consisted of honest responders and not actual patients. Of note, in college students taking the test under the honest condition, nearly half failed the cutoff on the Low Intelligence scale; arguably specificity would be even poorer in a credible noncollege sample (i.e., college students would be expected to be on the higher end of intelligence, relative to the non-college-student population). Furthermore, the high sensitivity values for the SIMS are an artifact of using cutoffs with poor specificity; if cutoffs were selected according to traditional guidelines requiring ≥ 90% specificity, sensitivity values would be poor. Finally, it is questionable whether the simulating subjects should have been combined when sensitivity values were calculated for each SIMS subscale; rather, sensitivity rates should have been provided for each scale for the simulating subgroup that was feigning those particular symptoms. In other words, the individual scales were not validated in terms of detecting the specific symptoms/conditions measured by the scale. However, no doubt clinicians using the test assume that if a patient falls beyond cutoffs for a particular scale, he/she was feigning symptoms specific to that scale.

Subsequent studies involving nonclinical control groups and simulators have shown high sensitivity and specificity rates, but cross-validation studies in real-world criminal and civil forensic populations have confirmed problematic specificity rates.

Simulation Studies

Rogers, Hinds, and Sewell (1996) obtained SIMS data on 53 primarily male, nonpsychotic juvenile offenders in a state hospital treatment unit; diagnoses included substance abuse, dysthymic disorders, PTSD, adjustment disorders, ADHD, and oppositional defiant and conduct disorders. All subjects completed the test under an honest condition and one of three feigning conditions (schizophrenia, major depression, and generalized anxiety disorder), and were provided with a description of the disorder and examples of symptoms; whether they completed the test first under honest or simulating instructions was randomized. Subjects were provided with financial compensation as well as a financial incentive for successful feigning. At a cutoff score of > 16, positive predictive power (PPP) was .87 while negative predictive power (NPP) was .62; at an optimized cutoff score (i.e., the best cut-score for the sample) of > 40, NPP was .94 while PPP was .49.

Edens, Otto, and Dwyer (1999) administered the SIMS twice to 196 undergraduates (once honestly and once simulating, in counterbalanced order). Simulators were assigned to one of three conditions: feigned psychosis ($n = 59$), feigned depression ($n = 65$), and feigned cognitive impairment ($n = 72$). Simulators were provided with descriptions of the conditions they were to feign and were instructed that they would receive additional financial incentive if they simulated successfully. Simulators obtained much higher SIMS scores than honest responders, with honest responders obtaining mean total scores of 7.78–8.09, and simulators obtaining means of 32.54 (feigned depression), 40.71 (feigned psychosis), and 38.60 (feigned cognitive impairment). Furthermore, among SIMS subscales, simulators scored the highest on subscales reflecting the specific symptoms they were to feign, although for psychosis all scores were uniformly high (means of 7.69–9.95). Also, the cognitive impairment simulators, while obtaining highest mean scores on the three scales most associated with cognitive impairment (Amnestic Disorders = 12.29, Neurologic Impairment = 8.16, Low Intelligence = 7.50), also scored high on Affective Disorders (mean = 7.28), while the depression feigners scored high on Amnestic Disorders (mean = 8.11) in addition to obtaining elevated mean scores on Affective Disorders (mean = 9.95). At an overall cutoff of > 14, specificity rates were adequate (89.2–93.2%; overall 91.3%) and sensitivity was high (92.3–98.6; overall 96.4%). Regarding cutoffs for individual scales, specificity was adequate for Psychosis (> 1; overall 89.3%; sensitivity = 91.5% for feigned psychosis), Neurologic Impairment (>2; overall 91.8%; sensitivity = 94.4% for feigned cognitive impairment), and Amnestic Disorders (>2; overall 90.3%; sensitivity = 95.8% for feigned cognitive impairment), but inadequate for Affective Disorders (>5; overall 82.1%; sensitivity = 100.0 for feigned depression) and Low Intelligence (>2; 71.3%; sensitivity = 91.7% for feigned cognitive impairment). Obviously, the concern is that specificity rates were poor for some scales in putatively normal individuals; specificity rates would be much lower in actual patients. In an attempt to obtain true specificity rates, Edens et al. (1999) identified 27 participants identified as experiencing current psychological distress as evidenced by the Symptom Checklist-90—Revised (Global Severity Index ≥45). Of concern, when the cutoffs above were used, specificity rates were 77.8% for total score, 51.9% for Affective Disorders, 58.2% for Psychosis, 73.1% for Neurologic Impairment, 74.1% for Low Intelligence, and 81.5 for Amnestic Disorders. Based on these results, the test authors conclude in the manual that "the SIMS may be less than optimal for differentiating malingering from emotional distress or psychopathology" (Widows & Smith, 2005, p. 29).

Rogers, Jackson, and Kaminski (2005) examined the ability of undergraduates to malinger disability (n = 17) or portray factitious presentations (dependent, n = 14, vs. demanding, n = 18). Subjects were told they would be provided $20 remuneration for successfully role-playing their instructions; no data regarding instruction compliance were obtained. Controls (n = 16) were instructed to assume the role of a patient in outpatient treatment with no acute mental health crisis. Simulators in the factitious/dependent group were provided with a descriptive paragraph and instructed to "role-play outpatients adulating their psychologists and wanting more services as needy patients, immersed in the sick role" (p. 28); participants in the factitious/demanding group were also provided with a descriptive paragraph and instructed to "role-play outpatients feeling hurt, frustrated, and neglected because their treatment needs were not being met" (p. 28). Participants instructed to malinger were given the scenario of being high-paid professionals in a company that was downsizing and deciding to feign unspecified symptoms to protect themselves from termination and to receive generous disability benefits in the interim. The controls (mean = 7.56, SD = 4.97) obtained significantly lower SIMS total scores than the malingerers (mean = 18.00, SD = 8.81) and factitious/demanding (mean = 16.76, SD = 8.13), but not factitious/dependent (mean = 15.07, SD = 10.03); the three simulation groups did not significantly differ from each other. On individual scales, controls obtained significantly lower scores than malingerers only on the Neurologic Disorders scale, and significantly lower scores than the factitious simulator groups only on the Affective Disorders scale; no other pairwise significant differences were detected. Computation of a new variable

(Affective Disorders minus Neurologic Disorders) resulted in a mean score of 1.5 in malingerers, versus 5.21 and 6.18 in the factitious groups; a cutoff score of ≥1 identified all factitious simulators and controls, but sensitivity was only 31% in malingerers. However, as the authors note, the difference in groups on this variable may have been due to more indiscriminate feigning of symptoms in the malingerers; specifically, they were not instructed about any particular symptoms to fake, whereas the factitious simulators were reporting symptoms in a manner intended to secure more psychological treatment (neurological symptoms would not be likely to further this goal).

Translated Versions

Merckelbach and Smith (2003) examined a Dutch translation of the SIMS (involving translation and back-translation and adaptation of content specific to the United States—e.g., U.S. dollar values) in 82 undergraduates (60 women), 25 of whom took the test under honest conditions, 28 of whom simulated amnesia, 14 of whom simulated schizophrenia, and 15 of whom simulated neurological problems. The simulation groups were provided with "a detailed vignette outlining a particular set of complaints" (p. 148). The authors also obtained SIMS data on 10 psychiatric inpatients who took the test honestly (diagnoses included substance abuse, borderline personality disorder, bipolar disorder, and schizophrenia). Across the three simulation conditions, those feigning schizophrenia scored the highest on the Psychosis and Affective Disorders scales; those feigning amnesia scored the highest on the Amnestic Disorders scale (but also relatively high on the Low Intelligence scale); and those simulating neurological problems scored the highest on the Neurologic Impairment scale (but also relatively high on the Amnestic Disorders scale). The simulators scored significantly higher than the patients, but the patients also scored significantly higher than the controls. The authors had access to additional college student samples of honest responders, for whom they examined test reliability and construct validity; these data were pooled with the above-described data to calculate sensitivity and specificity estimates. With a cutoff of >16, sensitivity was 93% and specificity was 98%—but the latter was based on 231 controls and only 10 actual patients, and it is of note that the patients scored significantly higher on SIMS total score than the controls. Also, though Merckelbach and Smith's (2003) data suggest that feigning particular types of complaints results in elevations on specific scales of the SIMS, if the simulators had been presented with a detailed report of symptoms for disorders just prior to completing the test, this would have artificially enhanced the correspondence between the disorder simulated and the specific SIMS scale (i.e., probably few real-world malingerers have access to a specific list of symptoms for the disorder they wish to feign just prior to evaluation).

Jelicic, Hessels, and Merckelbach (2006) assigned 60 undergraduates to either a control group (n = 15) or one of three simulation groups instructed to feign psychosis in the context of evading criminal prosecution for manslaughter: naïve (n = 15), informed (provided with some information regarding symptoms; n = 15), and coached (provided with information regarding psychosis and warning not to exaggerate symptoms; n = 15). All participants were given a small remuneration ($6). The three simulator groups obtained significantly higher scores on the Dutch version of the SIMS scores than controls, but did not differ from each other; mean SIMS total scores were approximately 5 in controls, 40 in naïve simulators, 35 in informed simulators, and 32 in coached malingerers. Specificity was 100%, and sensitivity rates (at a cutoff of > 16) in the three simulator groups were 93%, 100%, and 80%, respectively.

Jelicic, Merckelbach, Candel, and Geraerts (2007) then conducted a simulation study using the Dutch version of the SIMS with 90 college undergraduates (control, n = 30; naïve simulators, n = 30; and coached simulators, n = 30), who were again provided a small remuneration for their participation ($6). Naïve simulators were given a brain injury scenario and asked to feign believable symptoms associated with that injury, but were given no additional information; coached simulators were provided with the same scenario, but were also given information regarding cognitive dysfunction after brain injury and warned not to exaggerate symptoms unduly. The mean SIMS scores for honest responders, naïve malingerers, and coached malingerers were 5.0 (SD = 3.3), 30.3 (SD = 11.2), and 25.5 (SD = 10.4), respectively. At a cutoff of 14, specificity was 100% and sensitivity was 90% for both simulator groups.

That same year, Jelicic and colleagues reported on a separate study (Jelicic, Peters, Leckie, & Merckelbach, 2007) in which they assessed whether knowledge of psychiatric conditions enhanced ability to feign psychosis. Sixty-one undergraduates (30 who had never taken a course in psychopathology and 31 who had taken at least one course) were instructed to complete the Dutch version of the SIMS honestly and also to complete it while feigning psychosis in an attempt to avoid criminal responsibility for manslaughter (test order was counterbalanced); all students received a small remuneration for their participation (5 euros). Participants without knowledge of psychopathology scored higher in both honest and feigning conditions than their counterparts who had taken a course in psychopathology, but more so in the feigning condition (means in honest condition: 5.3 ± 3.5 vs. 3.3 ± 2.7; means in feigning condition: 45.9 ± 14.2 vs. 37.0 ± 12.8). However, at a cutoff of 16, specificity was 100%, and sensitivity was

100% in the group without knowledge of psychopathology and 97% in the group with knowledge; these results led the authors to conclude that this information does not help simulators to feign successfully.

Giger et al. (2010) obtained data for the German version of the SIMS in Swiss German-speaking volunteers (community members [n = 24] and Swiss Army soldiers [n = 39]) who did not receive compensation for their cooperation. Three SIMS items (14, 63, and 67) were adapted for Swiss German culture, and a cutoff specific to the German version was employed. In a novel experiment, participants acted out a crime that involved intent to steal secret information but that subsequently involved murder of a witness (the participants were instructed to hit a dummy with great force). They were asked to imagine that a judge had ordered a forensic examination as a part of the legal process. One-third of the participants were instructed to respond honestly to psychological testing; another third were instructed to feign amnesia for the crime; the last third were also instructed to feign amnesia but not to be detected, and were told that special tests might be administered to check the veracity of their presentation. Simulators had to pass a test of their understanding of the task, and were told that a $100 award would be given for a convincing demonstration of amnesia. After the experiment, two simulators indicated that they had not complied with the task, and their data were excluded. Mean SIMS scores were 5.8 (SD = 3.7) for honest responders, 37.9 (SD = 13.8) for naïve simulators, and 22.3 (SD = 12.6) for warned simulators. For a total score cutoff specific to the German version, specificity was 95%, while sensitivity was 95% in naïve simulators and 65% in warned simulators. Across individual scales, specificity was consistently ≥95% with the exception of the Psychosis scale (75%). In naive simulators, sensitivity ranged from 60% (Low Intelligence) to 100% (Amnestic Disorders), and in warned simulators, sensitivity ranged from 40% (Low Intelligence and Affective Disorders) to 90% (Amnestic Disorders).

Merten, Lorenz, and Schlatow (2010) examined SIMS data for the German version in four groups of simulators (n for each = 20), nearly three-quarters of whom were college undergraduates. The participants were asked to feign in the context of an armed robbery experienced on the way home from work, which would qualify them for workers' compensation benefits. Group 1 was provided with no additional information; Group 2 was given information regarding symptoms of PTSD; Group 3 was informed about the presence of validity scales on the various instruments administered and warned not to overly exaggerate symptom report; and Group 4 was given information on PTSD and warned about validity indicators. A preexperimental check on task instructions (cutoff of > 1 error) necessitated reinstruction in 26 cases. An award of 50 euros was offered to subjects who most successfully feigned (one award was provided in each group). A postexperimental check was also implemented to check for role compliance. Across the four groups, mean total scores were 29.60 (SD = 9.48), 30.55 (SD = 10.56), 26.55 (SD = 10.34), and 22.95 (SD = 7.40), respectively; groups did not significantly differ on total score or any individual score, although a trend was present ($p < .10$) for group differences on the total score and the Psychosis scale (means of 3.35, 3.60, 2.40, and 1.75, respectively). Sensitivity rates for the total score cutoff specific to the German version were 90%, 90%, 85%, and 70%, respectively, for an overall rate of 84%. Sixteen percent of the sample identified the SIMS as a likely measure of symptom exaggeration or fabrication.

Jelicic, Ceumen, Peters, and Merckelbach (2011) conducted a brain injury simulation study using the Dutch versions of the SIMS and the TOMM with 86 undergraduates or otherwise university-affiliated participants, who were paid $8 for their participation. Of the 86, 29 completed the SIMS honestly. The other 57 completed the SIMS under instructions to feign believable symptoms of brain injury from an accident and were provided with information about cognitive deficits following brain injury, but were also told that at least one of the tests was designed to detect feigning. Twenty-eight of the simulators were also warned that patients with actual brain injury would score like nondisabled individuals on the tests to detect faking and were specifically instructed to perform normally on those tests. Mean SIMS scores in the three groups were 4.6 (SD = 2.7), 25.8 (SD = 6.8), and 27.2 (SD = 9.8), respectively. With a cutoff of 16, specificity was 100%; sensitivity was 93% in the first simulation group, and 86% in the more test-coached simulation group. These findings led the authors to conclude that the SIMS is relatively resistant to coaching.

Known-Groups Studies

Some real-world studies of individuals with incentive to feign have shown high hit rates, but, these studies have not examined corresponding specificity rates. For example, Heinze and Purisch (2001; study described on pp. 76–77) documented 87% sensitivity in 57 inmate malingerers (using a total SIMS score cutoff of > 13), as well as sensitivities for individual scales of 89% (Psychosis cutoff of > 0; Affective Disorders cutoff of > 4) to 100% (Neurologic Impairment cutoff of > 1, Amnestic Disorders cutoff of > 1, Low Intelligence cutoff of > 1); however, no data were reported for credible subjects. Furthermore, Merten, Thies, Schneider, and Stevens (2009) reported 51% failure rate on the SIMS on the German version, using a cutoff score of 16 for 61 claimants alleging PTSD. However, sensitivity rates cannot be obtained from this study, given that not all compensation seekers feigned symptoms.

When real-world studies of credible populations have been conducted, disappointingly poor specificity rates have been documented.

Correctional Settings

Poythress, Edens, and Watkins (2001) obtained SIMS data for 116 males from a general prison population assigned to either honest responding (*n* = 30) or simulation of serious mental illness (*n* = 30) conditions, and inpatients on a forensic inpatient psychiatric unit, determined by staff psychiatrists to be either credible (*n* = 30) or malingering (*n* = 26). The SIMS was read to all participants because of concerns about reading level. The SIMS total cutoff score of > 14 identified 90% of simulators and 85% of real-world malingerers; specificity, while 97% in controls, was only 40% in credible clinical patients.

Subsequently, Lewis, Simcox, and Berry (2002) administered the SIMS to a sample being evaluated for competency to stand trial or mental state at time of offense (24 malingerers, 7 indeterminate, and 33 credible, based on the SIRS); the indeterminates were excluded, leaving a final sample of 57. The noncredible group scored higher on total SIMS score and all subscales; mean scores in this group were 42.8 (*SD* = 10.6) for total score, 9.5 (*SD* = 3.6) for Neurologic Impairment, 9.0 (*SD* = 1.6) for Affective Disorders, 9.0 (*SD* = 3.4) for Psychosis, 5.8 (*SD* = 2.8) for Low Intelligence, and 9.5 (*SD* = 3.6) for Amnestic Disorders. In comparison, mean scores for the credible group were 14.5 (*SD* = 8.8) for total score, 2.4 (*SD* = 2.1) for Neurologic Impairment, 5.2 (*SD* = 2.6) for Affective Disorders, 1.2 (*SD* = 2.1) for Psychosis, 3.2 (*SD* = 2.1) for Low Intelligence, and 2.5 (*SD* = 3.5) for Amnestic Disorders. Using a total score cutoff of > 16, the authors obtained 100% sensitivity, but specificity was only 61%.

Edens, Poythress, and Watkins-Clay (2007) studied 56 incarcerated men who had been admitted to a mental health unit: 30 were determined to be credible and 26 were judged to be malingering symptoms by the admitting psychiatrist. Sixty additional incarcerated men were drawn from the general prison population and were judged to be free of mental disorder; half were instructed to feign psychiatric symptoms (one was excluded because he did not obtain *T* scores ≥ 70 on the PAI Schizophrenia, Paranoia, Depression, or Mania scales). At a cutoff of > 14, sensitivity was excellent (85% in suspected malingerers and 90% in simulators), but specificity was poor in patients (40%) as compared to 97% in controls. The authors note that it is possible that the psychiatrists who identified patients as credible and noncredible were in error at least part of the time; SIRS results showed only approximately 50% correspondence with the clinician-based group assignments. When the SIRS was instead used as the "gold standard" for group assignment, 25 of the original 56 patients were identified as malingering.

When the SIMS cutoff of > 14 was applied to the reconstructed groups, sensitivity was 100%, but specificity was still low (52%).

Vitacco et al. (2007) reported SIMS data as well as M-FAST data for 100 defendants undergoing competency-to-stand-trial evaluations (see p. 89 for details). The mean total SIMS score and mean scores for the Neurologic Impairment, Affective Disorders, Psychosis, Low Intelligence, and Amnestic Disorders scales in the feigning group were 45.33 (SD = 11.77), 9.43 (SD = 3.59), 8.52 (SD = 2.32), 9.57 (SD = 2.96), 7.52 (SD = 3.19), and 10.29 (SD = 4.01), respectively. In the nonmalingering group, mean scores were 14.94 (SD = 9.35), 2.51 (SD = 2.61), 4.94 (SD = 2.38), 2.46 (SD = 2.58), 2.57 (SD = 1.79), and 2.46 (SD = 3.16), respectively. As can be intuited from these data, the authors' use of a total score cutoff of > 14 was problematic (i.e., the mean score for nonmalingerers exceeded the cutoff). Whereas sensitivity was 100%, specificity was only 65%, and the cutoffs for remaining scales, while achieving sensitivity rates of 90% or higher, were associated with specificity rates of 51–71%.

Concerns regarding most of the studies discussed here include the use of the SIRS for group assignment. As discussed earlier (see p. 84), sensitivity of the SIRS approximates 50%. Thus when the SIRS is used to identify credible subjects, the resulting group includes noncredible subjects who were not detected by the SIRS, which lowers specificity rates.

Workers' Compensation/Civil Litigation Settings

Alwes et al. (2008) also reported SIMS data as well as M-FAST data on 308 workers' compensation claimants or personal injury litigants; 23% claimed brain injury (see p. 91). The SIMS total mean scores for psychiatric feigners, psychiatric nonfeigners, cognitive feigners, and cognitive nonfeigners were 31.6 (SD = 8.9), 14.4 (SD = 6.5), 24.8 (SD = 10.8), and 15.6 (SD = 7.1), respectively; mean scores for the nonfeigners exceeded test cutoffs. Sensitivity in identification of feigned psychiatric symptoms at a cutoff score of > 16 was 96%, but specificity was only 67%; sensitivity to cognitive feigning was 75%, but specificity was only 60%. The latter sensitivity and specificity rates were probably artificially elevated by the exclusion of subjects failing a single cognitive SVT; that is, less blatant malingerers were excluded (those failing one SVT), as well as more cognitively impaired credible patients who failed one SVT.

Wisdom, Callahan, and Shaw (2010) obtained SIMS scores for 33 individuals who were primarily personal injury litigants (60% with cognitive, physical, and emotional symptoms; 10% with cognitive and physical and/or emotional symptoms; 30% with physical and/or emotional but no cognitive symptoms). Two-thirds of them were identified as showing response bias (5 definite malingered neurocognitive dysfunction [MND],

17 probable MND; Slick, Sherman, & Iverson, 1999) across several measures of symptom validity. Sensitivity of the SIMS at a cutoff score of 14
was 96%, but specificity was only 64%; the mean score of the honest-
responding group was 15.3 (SD = 4.7), with a range of 10–23. Raising the
cutoff score to ≥23 resulted in 91% specificity, but sensitivity dropped to
only 55%. A problem with this study, aside from the small group n's, is that
subjects were warned that SVTs would be administered during the exam;
evidence suggests that this procedure results in individuals still attempting
to fake although more carefully and therefore more successfully (for discussion, see Boone, 2007b). The use of this instructional set raises the possibility that at least some of the "honest responders" were in fact faking but
not detected, as further indicated by the fact that in the honest-responding
group the range of FBS scores on the MMPI-2 included a raw score of 37,
and the range of MSPQ scores included a raw score of 25! The impact
of including feigners in the honest-responding group would have been to
lower test specificity rates.

Community Samples

Graue et al. (2007; study described on pp. 90–91) reported SIMS data for a
sample of individuals with mild mental retardation (n = 26) and community
volunteers with lowered levels of education assigned to either honest (n =
10) or feigning (n = 25) conditions. SIMS total scores averaged 36.0 (SD=
16.3) in malingerers, 28.7 (SD = 12.5) in subjects with mental retardation, and 18.3 (SD = 11.0) in honest responders; for the Low Intelligence
scale, mean scores were 6.7 (SD = 2.5), 5.6 (SD = 1.6), and 4.2 (SD = 1.9),
respectively. The total score cutoff of > 16 is reported as resulting in 100%
sensitivity, but specificity in the sample was mental retardation was zero.
In contrast, the Low Intelligence cutoff of >2 was described as capturing
no malingerers and as having 100% specificity in individuals with mental retardation, although these findings appear to have been inadvertently
reversed.

Van Beilen, Griffioen, Gross, and Leenders (2009) reported data on
the Dutch version of the SIMS data in 26 patients diagnosed with psychogenic movement disorders (paralysis = 12, walking disorder = 5, dystonia
= 5, muscle contractions = 3, tremor = 1) and with no apparent motive to
feign; 26 patients with docoumented neurological disorders (tremor = 3,
multiple sclerosis = 5, epilepsy = 5, migraine = 3, radicular syndrome = 3,
back pain = 2, poly- or mononeuropathy = 2, systemic lupus erythemato-
sus = 1, Parkinson disease = 1, and borrelia = 1); and 18 controls. Mean
SIMS scores in the three groups were 11.48 (SD = 7.44), 7.8 (SD = 3.9), and
4.58 (SD = 2.27), respectively. Twenty-three percent of the psychogenic

patients (*n* = 6), 3.8% of the neurological patients (*n* = 1), and no controls fell beyond a cutoff of 16.

Dandachi-FitzGerald, Ponds, Peters, and Merckelbach (2011) provided data on the Dutch version of the SIMS for a mixed psychiatric sample (*n* = 183) who did not have obvious external incentives to feign; 28% were referred for general cognitive assessments, 43% were evaluated for ADHD, 28% were tested in the context of possible autism spectrum disorder, and 1% were seen for possible mixed ADHD and autism spectrum disorder. Ten subjects with clinically obvious cognitive impairment were excluded, and data from outliers were replaced by using the mean from the sample plus 2 *SD*s. At a cutoff of 16, 21% (*n* = 38) failed the SIMS. Higher scores were correlated with lower educational levels (r = −.25), and failure on the SIMS was associated with lower IQ (mean of low average to borderline) and greater psychiatric symptom report.

In summary and conclusion, available data from real-world samples indicate that the recommended SIMS cutoff of >14 results in unacceptable specificity. The test authors (Widows & Smith, 2005) argue that they intended the measure as a "screen," and thus they wanted to err on the side of capturing the majority of potential malingerers, with more comprehensive testing in positive cases to rule out false positives. However, it can be argued that use of a cutoff that that has a false positive rate approaching 40% is irresponsible and harmful to credible patients, who will have an indication of possible malingering memorialized in their records.

Studies examining use of the SIMS in detection of feigned cognitive symptoms have focused primarily on use of the total score. Specificity rates in real-world credible samples are generally ≤65% with use of the recommended total score cutoff of >14; raising the cutoff to ensure adequate specificity (≥23; 91% specificity) drops sensitivity in real-world test takers feigning cognitive impairment to <60%. Cutoffs for the total score and the Low Intelligence scale appear to have zero specificity in samples with true mental retardation. Also of note, elevated SIMS scores have been reported in patients with psychogenic neurological conditions but with no apparent motive to feign, suggesting that high scores on the SIMS are not necessarily reflective of frank malingering.

MOREL EMOTIONAL NUMBING TEST

The Morel Emotional Numbing Test (MENT; Morel, 1998b, 2010) is a forced-choice facial expression discrimination test designed to assess for feigned PTSD. It consists of a booklet containing black and white photographs of an African-American male and a European-American male depicting various facial expressions. The initial clinical comparison groups included 17 veteran inpatients who were receiving treatment for substance abuse and had no history or evidence of PTSD, and 17 veterans with diagnoses of schizophrenia who were receiving services in an inpatient unit for chronic patients. An additional sample of veterans undergoing psychological evaluation for documentation of PTSD as a part of their claim for disability compensation were assigned to four groups: disability claimants diagnosed with PTSD (n = 17); disability claimants not diagnosed with PTSD (n = 17); older disability claimants (age 63 or older, half with PTSD; n = 17); and disability claimants with no history of psychosis or neurological/neurocognitive dysfunction and with suspect PTSD (n = 17), based on an MMPI-2 F minus K score of ≥ 15, mismatch between reported and actual military occupation/status (e.g., claiming to be a Navy SEAL but actually a cook, claimed combat exposure in Vietnam or conferring of medal but no military documentation of such), and highly improbable symptoms on the Quick Test for PTSD (Q-PTSD; Morel, 2008b). The latter group committed significantly more errors than all other groups, and the older claimant group made significantly more errors than the younger claimants diagnosed with PTSD. Selection of a cutoff to maintain < 5% false positive identifications in credible claimants (and 1 SD above the mean of patients with schizophrenia) resulted in 82% sensitivity. A slightly higher cutoff is recommended for older test takers (≥ 9 vs. ≥ 8).

Of concern, different instructions were apparently given in the different validation groups (Guriel & Fremouw, 2003). Specifically, the groups undergoing disability evaluation for PTSD were told that individuals with the condition at times have difficulty with recognition of facial expressions and were instructed to guess if they were not sure of the correct answer, but were not specifically told to perform with their best effort. In contrast, the inpatients with substance abuse or schizophrenia were instructed that the test was "designed to measure how well you are able to identify facial expression" (Guriel & Fremouw, 2003, p. 894) and were told to perform with their best effort. In defense of the test developer, it would have seemed irrelevant to patients not claiming PTSD symptoms to be administered a test in which they were instructed that individuals with PTSD have difficulty identifying facial expressions. Nonetheless, it is problematic when test development groups are given differing test instructions.

Morel (2008a) subsequently reported data on 37 veterans undergoing neuropsychological evaluations who were administered both the MENT and the WMT; 31 of these patients had service-connected disabilities, and 14 patients were attempting to obtain or increase disability compensation. The chief complaint involved memory loss, although 8 patients were reporting symptoms of PTSD. Subjects were divided into credible (*n* = 15) and noncredible (*n* = 22) groups based on WMT scores. At published MENT cutoffs, sensitivity was 64% and specificity was 100%, and decreasing scores on the WMT were associated with increasing errors on the MENT. However, the obvious concern for this investigation as a validation study for the MENT is that only a minority of patients (<20%) were actually claiming PTSD, and it is not reported how many of these were in the noncredible group. Furthermore, the subjects included in the study were those who had been administered the WMT, whereas the majority of patients in the archival database had not, raising questions as to whether patients in this subset were suspected of malingering by the examiner. If so, they may have been more "blatant" malingerers, resulting in the artificial enhancement of sensitivity rates.

The MENT has been modified for use in Europe, but of concern, substantial changes were made, including presenting color photographs of a Caucasian male and female presented on a computer screen (Geraerts et al., 2009). The instructions also apparently contain the statement that patients with PTSD "suffer from emotional numbness" (Geraerts et al., p. 281)—information not provided in the original instructions (Morel, 1998)—yet the original cutoffs are applied to the adapted measure. Geraerts et al. studied compensation-seeking (*n* = 49; 49% diagnosed with PTSD) and non-compensation-seeking (*n* = 70; 85% diagnosed with PTSD) Croatian veterans, finding that the former committed significantly more errors than the latter group (9.76 vs. 6.48). A cutoff of 9 correctly identified 91.8% of the compensation seekers, with only 4.2% false positive identifications in the non-compensation-seeking group. Although sensitivity and specificity values were excellent, it is of concern that the sensitivity rate was so high in a compensation-seeking group that apparently contained both credible and noncredible subjects (i.e., nearly half of compensation seekers were in fact diagnosed with PTSD). The authors cite research indicating that 37% of Croatian veterans undergoing psychological evaluation actually have PTSD; thus, to achieve ≤100% sensitivity, the European MENT should identify at most 63% of compensation-seeking veterans as faking (otherwise, it would be identifying veterans with actual PTSD as noncredible). Yet, as noted above, over 90% of the compensation-seeking sample in this study fell beyond the cutoff. Furthermore, the reported data are odd: The mean number of errors in the compensation-seeking group was only 9.76, yet 91.8% of this group was cited as exceeding the cutoff of 9.

In a second study of the Croatian version of the MENT applied to detection of simulated amnesia for a crime (Giger et al., 2010; see further description of study on p. 98), mean number of errors in honest responders was 2.6 (SD = 1.6), but 29.6 (SD = 18.6) in naïve simulators and 20.3 (SD = 14.3) in warned simulators. Specificity was 100% in honest responders, while sensitivity was 80% in naïve simulators and 65% in warned simulators.

Merten et al. (2009) utilized a German version of the MENT along with other symptom validity measures in 61 claimants alleging PTSD; 40% fell beyond cutoffs on the German MENT, 70% scored positive on at least one out of three free-standing SVTs, and 25% failed all three SVTs. In a subsequent study of the German version of the MENT (Merten et al., 2010; see pp. 98–99), four groups of simulators (n for each = 20) were asked to feign PTSD. Mean numbers of errors were 13.60 (SD = 10.24) for uncoached simulators, 22.15 (SD = 7.86) for simulators provided with information regarding PTSD only, 14.35 (SD = 9.26) for simulators warned regarding presence of validity indicators and told not to overexaggerate, and 11.80 (SD = 8.20) for simulators both provided with information regarding PTSD and warned; sensitivity rates were 70%, 95%, 75%, and 65%, respectively, for an overall rate of 76%. Merten et al. (2009) conclude that "informed and warned participants committed only half as many errors as informed participants. For this instrument, information without warning resulted in a deterioration of test performance" (p. 145) but this conclusion does not appear to match the actual results (i.e., Group 2 [informed participants] made more errors than Group 1 [uninformed participants]). Thirty-three percent of the sample identified the MENT as a likely measure of symptom exaggeration or fabrication.

Messer and Fremouw (2007) describe validation data on the "MENT-R," their adaptation of the MENT in which a selection of the Ekman and Friesen (1976) Pictures of Facial Affect (of 4 males and 4 females) replaced the original pictures of facial expressions in the test (the number of pictured emotions was reduced from 10 to 6). The total number of trials was increased from 60 to 72 (24 items per set), and test instructions were also slightly altered from Morel's (1998b) original validation study. Four groups of undergraduates were studied: students with high clinical PTSD (n = 24), students with moderate subclinical PTSD (n = 41), honest responders (n = 39), and coached simulators (n = 41). Presence of PTSD was determined by responses to the DAPS, and subjects with NB scores of ≥ 12 were excluded. Those not showing clinical or subclinical PTSD were randomly assigned to the honest-responder and simulator groups. Simulators were instructed to feign PTSD symptoms associated with a motor vehicle accident for a civil suit; were provided with a description of PTSD symptoms and had to pass a quiz on the information before further participation; and were told that if they evaded detection, they would receive $25. The simulators scored significantly higher on the MENT-R than the other groups did, averaging 30 errors, whereas the remaining groups were indistinguishable (averaging < 5 errors). At a cutoff of ≥ 9, sensitivity was 56% at 95.9% specificity; lowering the cutoff to ≥ 7 resulted in 91.7% specificity and raised sensitivity to 63%. Subjects judged that test instructions indicating that patients with PTSD have difficulty recognizing facial expressions were "somewhat believable" (i.e., ratings of 2.5–2.9 on a Likert scale of 0–4). A limitation of this study is that students attending college may not reflect the more disabling spectrum of PTSD symptoms; thus specificity may have been overestimated.

Singh, Avasthi, and Grover (2007) concluded that data in support of various measures of malingered PTSD, including the MENT, "have not been encouraging" (p. 129). This prompted Morel and Shepherd (2008) to claim that "evidence in the scientific literature on the efficacy of the MENT as a symptom validity test (SVT) for PTSD is unequivocal in the positive" (p. 128), based on data averaged across five studies. However, two of the studies cited were for different versions of the test, and it is not clear whether the three remaining studies relied on some of the same data (all were published by Morel). Furthermore, in the 2008 study, which was a validation study of the Q-PTSD, Morel used the MENT as the standard by which effectiveness of the Q-PTSD was measured (i.e., sensitivity of the Q-PTSD was reported as the percentage of subjects detected by the test who had already been determined to be noncredible by the MENT); however, when summarizing the data from this study in his response to Singh et al. (2007), he appears to have done the reverse (i.e., reporting sensitivity of the MENT as the percentage of subjects falling beyond cutoffs who had been determined by be noncredible by the Q-PTSD). If MENT data are used to validate the Q-PTSD, those same Q-PTSD data cannot then be used to argue for the validity of the MENT.

In summary and conclusion, at least three different versions of the MENT are in existence. None of these have been adequately validated in known-groups comparisons, and the data for different versions on the MENT cannot be used interchangeably. Furthermore, the sensitivity rates reported for simulators do not necessarily generalize to real-world noncredible subjects, and sensitivity rates cannot be obtained from the studies involving generic compensation seekers because not all compensation seekers in fact feign symptoms (see Mittenberg et al., 2002). By my estimate, the original version of the MENT (the one sold in the United States) has only been validated with 39 real-world noncredible subjects, all of whom may have been feigning in a highly blatant manner, thus skewing sensitivity rates upward. Moreover, a sizable subset of these subjects were not claiming PTSD symptoms; it can be argued that, since the majority of the 39 subjects were apparently claiming memory impairment rather than PTSD, the MENT has more validation data as a general neuropsychological SVT than as a PTSD SVT. Also of concern, test instructions for the original version of the MENT were not standardized across validation and comparison groups. Finally, the specificity rates obtained for normal individuals cannot be relied upon because they substantially underestimate false positive rates in clinical settings. That said, specificity is likely to be excellent at recommended cutoffs; true sensitivity rates are unknown, but probably well below 65%.

4

Assessment of Symptom Validity through Psychodiagnostic and PTSD Symptom Measures

Personality testing often imparts critical information in medical–legal neuropsychological exams. The MMPI-2–Restructured Form (MMPI-2–RF) in particular includes a variety of validity scales that provide data on the veracity of physical, cognitive, and psychiatric symptom reports, and that furnish useful adjunctive information to cognitive SVTs. Clinical scales on psychological inventories generate objective data on the levels of depression, anxiety, somatization, and so forth. Without this information, the extent of depression/anxiety and other Axis I symptoms cannot be objectively and reliably determined. In particular, it is problematic to identify the presence of somatization without use of psychological inventories, because only a minority of patients with somatoform conditions display obvious histrionic behaviors; rather, many present as conscientious and "earnest/sincere."

In a forensic context, it is imperative to know whether a person has been responding truthfully when completing psychological tests; thus some tests that might be useful in some clinical settings are not appropriate in forensic contexts, because the instruments are not very effective in identifying noncredible reports/responses. The reviews and critiques in this chapter focus on the ability of personality and PTSD symptom measures to detect noncredible report of psychological symptoms. When available, literature on the use of these instruments to identify noncredible cognitive and somatic symptom report is also summarized.

PERSONALITY INVENTORIES

Minnesota Multiphasic Personality Inventory–2

The Minnesota Multiphasic Personality Inventory–2 (MMPI-2; Butcher, Dahlstrom, Graham, Tellegen, & Kaemmer, 1989; Butcher et al., 2001) includes 567 true-false items and is designed to be used in adults ages 18 and older with fourth- or fifth-grade reading skills. It contains 9 validity scales (including Variable Response Inconsistency [VRIN], True Response Inconsistencies [TRIN], Infrequency [F], F=Ppsychopathology [Fp], F back [Fb], Symptom Validity [FBS], Correcion [K], Lie [L], and Superlative Self-Presentation [S]), and 10 clinical scales (Hypochondriasis, Depression, Hysteria, Psychopathic Deviate, Masculine–Feminine, Paranoia, Psychasthenia, Schizophrenia, Hypomania, and Social Introversion), as well as numerous supplementary scales. It also includes the 9 restructured clinical scales (RCd, Demoralization; RC1, Somatic Complaints; RC2, Low Positive Emotions; RC3, Cynicism; RC4, Antisocial Behavior; RC6, Ideas of Persecution; RC7, Dyfunctional Negative Emotions; RC8, Aberrant Experiences; and RC9, Hypomanic Activation).

Normative data for the MMPI-2 consisted of 2,600 individuals. It is the most researched psychological test, with more than 800 peer-reviewed publications identified in PubMed as of November 2011. About a decade ago, it was ranked first in frequency of usage in internship programs (Piotrowski & Belter, 1999), was the most frequently administered test in forensic evaluations (Pope, Butcher, & Seelen, 2000), was used in 89% of emotional injury personal injury cases (Boccaccini & Brodsky, 1999), and was employed by 100% of those who classified themselves as "frequent assessors" (Boccaccini & Brodsky, 1999). The Lally (2003) survey of board-certified forensic psychologists showed that they rated the MMPI-2 in the "recommended" category in terms of detecting malingering. In a survey of NAN and International Neuropsychological Society members, more than 80% used the MMPI-2 in their neuropsychological evaluations (Smith, Gorske, Wiggins, & Little, 2010).

Detection of Fake Bad Responding on the MMPI-2

In light of the recent publication and increasing use of the MMPI-2–RF; (Ben-Porath & Tellegen, 2008), discussion of the MMPI-2's effectiveness in detection of "fake bad" responding will be limited to a meta-analysis of this literature published in 2003 (Rogers, Sewell, Martin, & Vitacco, 2003). This investigation incorporated 62 studies of dissimulation, as well as 11 MMPI-2 diagnostic studies to increase credible patient samples, and examined F, Fb, Fp, F minus K, the Gough Dissimulation Index (Ds), and Obvious–Subtle (O-S) scales. Effect sizes were larger for comparisons of simulators versus healthy controls (mean d = 2.48) than for comparisons of simulators versus actual patients. In the latter analyses, the largest effect sizes were observed for F (mean d = 2.21) and Fp (mean d = 1.90). Rogers et al. (2003) concluded that a raw score cutoff of 24 for the F scale resulted in few false positives, although for patients with PTSD and psychotic disorders, a cutoff of > 30 is recommended. The authors argue that Fp is the best score to employ, because cutoff scores are more consistent across studies (e.g., > 4 to > 9) and they appear appropriate across a wide range of psychiatric disorders. However, the authors refer to Ds as the "premier specialized validity scale with its sophisticated strategy and minimal risk of false-positives" (p. 173) and indicate that it is superior to the revised Ds (Ds-r). In contrast, the authors warn that Fb is confounded by genuine psychopathology, with extreme elevations occurring in a minority of presumed credible patients. They also caution that use of F minus K is problematic due to huge variability in cutoff scores (–8 to 32), and they similarly conclude that O-S is "unlikely to be clinical useful except in rare cases of extreme endorsement levels" (p. 173).

A major problem with most of the known-groups studies on the effectiveness of MMPI-2 validity scales in detecting overreport employed in the Rogers et al. (2003) meta-analysis is the fact that investigators have not been attentive to excluding subjects with motive to feign from the clinical comparison samples. Furthermore, a large patient comparison sample used by Rogers et al. (2003) to augment cutoff scores was in part derived from Caldwell's (1997) large archival data set, but an unknown percentage of these patients were in fact engaged in litigation, raising questions as to whether this is an appropriate comparison sample. Rogers, Gillard, Berry, & Granacher (2011) have since acknowledged that "genuineness of these patient samples was assumed rather than systematically tested" (p. 357) and that a "presumably small percentage of clinical samples may be undetected cases of malingering," but argue that "their inclusion in these normative estimates likely will decrease the number of false-positives found with these cut scores" (Rogers, Sewell, Martin, & Vitacco, 2003, p. 173). However, inclusion of noncredible subjects in the credible sample results in greater overlap in scores between groups and requires higher cutoffs to maintain adequate specificity, thereby reducing cutoff sensitivity.

Scales Specific to Physical and Cognitive Symptom Overreport

Research has shown the MMPI-2 F family of validity scales to be minimally related to feigning of cognitive and somatic symptoms (Greiffenstein, Gola, & Baker, 1995; Greiffenstein, Fox, & Lees-Haley, 2007; Larrabee, 1998, 2003a; McCaffrey, O'Bryant, Ashendorf, & Fisher, 2003). These findings have necessitated the development of other scales from MMPI-2 items to identify noncredible symptoms in these areas.

SYMPTOM VALIDITY SCALE

The Symptom Validity Scale (FBS; Lees-Haley, English, & Glenn, 1991) was specifically designed for a litigation setting. It is constructed to tap a compensation-seeking response "constellation" of overreport of physical/cognitive symptoms, exaggerated postinjury emotional distress, and underreport or minimizing of preincident personality problems (Greiffenstein et al., 2007). The strategy is to appear honest and psychologically normal "but for" the effects of the incident.

The large literature on FBS is well summarized in Greiffenstein et al. (2007) and in a monograph published by the University of Minnesota Press (Ben-Porath, Graham, & Tellegen, 2009); therefore, only results of a recent meta-analysis by Nelson et al. (2010) are summarized here. The Nelson et al. (2010) investigation included 32 studies reflecting 2,218 overreporting and 3,123 comparison subjects. Large effect sizes emerged for FBS (d = .95), O-S (d = 1.00) and Ds (d = 1.03), with moderate effect sizes for Fb (d = 0.68), F minus K (d = 0.69), F (d = 0.71), Fp (d = 0.51), and Ds-r (d = 0.62). The authors note that "FBS exhibited larger effect sizes when (1) effort is known to be insufficient and (2) evaluation is conducted in the context of traumatic brain injury" (p. 701) as compared to the F-family scores. They thus conclude that "FBS shows relatively greater utility than the F-family as a response validity measure within the context of common forensic neuropsychology applications" (p. 715), and that "current results summarize an extensive literature that continues to support use of FBS in forensic neuropsychology practice" (p. 701). In fact, survey data from neuropsychologists have shown that it is the third most frequently used measure of response bias during neuropsychological examinations (see Sharland & Gfeller, 2007), and the legal literature shows growing acceptance of FBS in this area (Chuk, 2009; Hoyt, 2009).

A revision of the FBS (including 30 of the original 43 FBS items) appears in the MMPI-2–RF; studies reporting FBS-r data are summarized on pages 122–129.

MEYERS INDEX

Meyers, Millis, and Volkert (2002) developed a weighted algorithm involving seven MMPI-2 scales (F, FBS, Fp, F minus K, Ds-r, Ego Strength, O-S) in compensation-seeking (litigants, workers' compensation claimants, or disability seekers; n = 100) and non-compensation-seeking (n = 100) individuals referred for neuropsychological testing secondary to complaints of cognitive dysfunction; all were also receiving treatment for chronic pain. Thirty simulators who were knowledgable about chronic pain (e.g., physicians, nurses, case managers, etc.) were asked to perform on the MMPI-2 and on a neuropsychological test battery in a manner that would demonstrate chronic pain and pain-associated cognitive/emotional difficulties stemming from a work-related injury for the purposes of securing workers' compensation total disability benefits. At a cutoff of ≥ 5, specificity was 100%; 86% of the simulators and 36% of the compensation seekers were detected.

Aguerrevere, Greve, Bianchini, and Meyers (2008) subsequently examined an abbreviated Meyers Index (they deleted the O-S and Ds-r scores, which are not routinely provided by the Pearson computerized scoring system) in a large sample, some of whom were included in the original validation study. These authors found classification accuracy comparable to the original formula in 270 non-compensation-seeking individuals referred for neuropsychological or pain/psychological evaluations; in patients with incentive only and no SVT failure (TBI = 73, chronic pain = 34); in patients with probable (n = 80) and definite (n = 14) malingered neurocognitive dysfunction in the context of TBI or malingered pain-related disability (n = 32); and in two groups of chronic pain simulators (medically sophisticated = 30, undergraduates = 26). The original Meyers formula cutoff could be lowered to ≥ 3 while still maintaining specificity of $\geq 90\%$ in subjects with no incentive, resulting in sensitivity of 65% in those with TBI-related noncredible cognitive symptoms and 77–81% in those with noncredible cognitive symptoms in the context of claimed chronic pain. A cutoff of ≥ 2 on the abbreviated formula was associated with specificity of $\geq 89\%$ and resulted in 68% sensitivity in the noncredible TBI claimants and 82–88% in the noncredible chronic pain patients. (The incentive-only group showed false positive rates above 10%, but it can be argued that this group included malingerers who were not detected by the SVTs administered, given that SVT sensitivity is < 100%.)

In summary, while the Meyers Index was initially validated primarily in simulators, subsequent research in a large sample of real-world noncredible and credible subjects has suggested high sensitivity rates that may exceed those of other somatic/cognitive overreport scales.

RESPONSE BIAS SCALE

Gervais, Ben-Porath, Wygant, and Green (2007) identified 28 MMPI-2 items that predicted failure on cognitive SVTs in 1,152 non-head-injured individuals seeking compensation (e.g., workers' compensation, litigation). They primarily claimed chronic pain, anxiety, and depression, and they had passed or failed at least one neurocognitive SVT (89% were administered the WMT, 98% completed the CARB, 59% were administered the TOMM, and a smaller percentage completed the MSVT; 39% failed one or more SVT). Validation of the resulting Response Bias Scale (RBS) was conducted in two additional samples: (1) 209 individuals referred for psychological assessment, 87% of whom were seeking disability or in litigation, and who presented with claimed symptoms similar to those of the original sample; and (2) 108 persons referred for neuropsychological assessment, the majority of whom were compensation-seeking, and with a third claiming head injury but with another subset claiming depression or miscellaneous conditions. At a cutoff of 16, specificity was 89% and sensitivity was 34% in those passing versus failing the WMT or MSVT, but specificity was only 82% in the subgroup claiming anxiety. Raising the cutoff to 17 ensured adequate specificity (≥90%) in all subgroups, but sensitivity was lowered to 25–29%.

Whitney, Davis, Shepard, and Herman (2008) examined the ability of RBS to predict TOMM performance in 46 patients referred for neuropsychological evaluation and who had completed both the MMPI-2 and TOMM (24 passed and 22 failed). Comparison of groups showed the largest effect size for RBS ($d = 0.98$), followed by the Henry–Heilbronner Index (HHI) ($d = 0.90$); among the remaining MMPI-2 F-family validity scales, effect sizes ranged from 0.51 to 0.65, with the exception that the effect size associated with FBS was only 0.23. At an RBS cutoff of 17, specificity was adequate (92%) and sensitivity was 50%. The study methodology was problematic in that selection bias was probably present (i.e., participants had only completed the TOMM if their presentation was suspicious for malingering of cognitive symptoms). Thus it is likely that only more blatant malingerers were included in the sample, which would account for the relatively high sensitivity rate.

Smart et al. (2008) applied a hierarchically optimal classification tree analysis to MMPI-2 clinical and validity scale data (including FBS, the Malingered Depression [Md] scale, and RBS), as well as cognitive SVT data (VSVT, TOMM, WMT, Multi-Digit Memory Test, Letter Memory Test), in 198 compensation seekers versus 109 individuals with no secondary gain (a total of 125 subjects failed ≥1 SVT). RBS was most effective in identifying cognitive response bias (cutoff of > 16.5), followed by the Hysteria scale (cutoff of 79.5T), with scores above cutoffs for the two scales identifying nearly 60% of the noncredible sample (at 75.8% specificity). Hysteria was found to moderate interpretation of RBS; if Hysteria was less than 79.5T, even if RBS was > 16.5, sufficient effort on cognitive tasks was likely to be present.

Giger et al. (2010) obtained RBS data for Swiss German-speaking volunteers (community members [$n = 24$] and Swiss Army soldiers [$n = 39$]) who did not receive compensation for their cooperation. In a novel experiment, subjects acted out a crime (see p. 98) and were then asked to imagine that a judge had ordered a forensic examination as a part of the legal process. One-third of the subjects were instructed to respond honestly to psychological testing; another third were instructed to feign amnesia for the crime; and the last third were also instructed to feign amnesia but not to be detected, and were told that special tests might be used to check the veracity of their presentation. Simulators had to pass a test of their understanding of the task, and were told that a $100 award would be given for a convincing demonstration of amnesia. The mean RBS score for the honest responders was 6.4 (SD = 3.2), as compared to 16.2 (SD = 4.0) and 12.5 (SD = 5.4) in the two simulation groups. Specificity was 100% at recommended cutoffs, with sensitivity of 40% and 25%, respectively, in the two simulation groups.

Wygant et al. (2010) examined the effectiveness of RBS in 127 criminal defendants who had been diagnosed with substance abuse or psychiatric disorders (with the exception of 14% who were determined to be malingering), and in 141 litigants or disability seekers (described on p. 126). Among the compensation seekers, comparison of those failing versus passing the SVTs showed the largest effect size for RBS (d = 1.24), although this was not meaningfully higher than the effect sizes for FBS (d = 1.18), Fs (d = 1.14), and FBS-r (d = 1.13). In contrast, in the criminal defendant sample, largest effect sizes were found for Fp (d = 1.65) and F (d = 1.61), although these were not meaningfully different from RBS (d = 1.48), F-r (d = 1.48), or Fp-r (d = 1.46). In the compensation seekers, an RBS T-score of 90 was associated with 91% specificity and 38% sensitivity; a cutoff of 120T resulted in no false positive identifications, but sensitivity was only 2%. In the criminal forensic sample, a cutoff of 100T resulted in 89% specificity and 59% sensitivity; a cutoff of 120T was associated with 99% specificity and 24% sensitivity.

Most recently, Jones and Ingram (2011), as described on page 126, provided RBS data for 288 military personnel evaluated in the context of head, blast, or heat injuries, or brain disease; 70% were subject to medical discharge with possibility of disability compensation. Significant differences in RBS were documented (mean of 13.21 [approximately 84T] in noncredible subjects and 8.98 [67T] in credible subjects). Schroeder et al. (2012), as also described on page 126, reported that a cutoff for RBS of >92T was associated with ≥90% specificity in credible neurological groups (43% sensitivity), although the specificity rate was unacceptably low in the psychiatric group (71%).

Tsushima, Geling, and Fabrigas (2011) reported RBS data in 118 litigants (71.2% TBI-related) and 163 clinical patients undergoing psychological evaluation for health-related issues (e.g., obesity, sleep disorders) or emotional and behavioral problems (e.g., depression, anxiety, somatization). An RBS raw score cutoff of ≥13 was associated with 90.8%

specificity and resulted in 39.0% sensitivity; at a cutoff of ≥17, specificity was 98.2%. These findings are very interesting because they show that when the credible comparison group is noncompensation-seeking, the RBS cutoff can be lowered substantially and still maintain at least 90% specificity. The Schroeder et al. (2012) study above reported low specificity of RBS in a noncompensation-seeking mixed psychiatric group, but sample size was small (n = 21), rendering findings unreliable. The other studies that recommended the higher RBS cutoffs had used "credible" comparison groups that were compensation-seeking but passed SVTs, and it is likely that undetected noncredible subjects who were in fact engaging in response bias were inadvertently retained in the credible group. This would serve to lower specificity, and require higher cut scores to maintain few false positive identifications.

Additional research has shown that RBS is a better predictor of memory complaints than FBS or F-family MMPI-2 validity scales (Gervais, Ben-Porath, Wygant, & Green, 2008) and other MMPI-2–RF validity scales (Gervais, Ben-Porath, Wygant, & Sellbom, 2010); when subjects who failed an SVT were excluded from analyses, RBS scores did not significantly correlate with actual memory performance (CVLT scores; Gervais et al., 2008). In individuals undergoing neuropsychological evaluation (Nelson et al., 2007), comparison of those with secondary gain (n = 157) versus those without (n = 54) on MMPI-2 scales showed highest effect sizes for Hypochondriasis (d = 0.91) and Hysteria (d = 0.70), followed by RBS (d = 0.65), FBS (d = 0.60), and the L scale (d = 0.51). In the Tsushima et al. (2011) study above, RBS had a higher sensitivity rate (39.0%) than HHI (27.1%), FBS (29.7%), and F (21.2%).

The MMPI-2–RF manual (2008/2011) indicates that RBS T-scores of 80–99 are suggestive of possible noncredible memory complaints, while scores above 100 reflect an unusual pattern of responses strongly indicative of overreported memory deficits. The studies described above show that cutoffs of 90–96T achieve adequate specificity (≥90%) in compensation-seeking groups, with associated sensitivity of 34–43%. However, cutoffs at this level may have inadequate specificity in psychiatric groups, necessitating cutoffs of approximately 101T to maintain false positive identifications below 10%. RBS scores are higher in noncredible individuals in a criminal forensic setting (with resulting sensitivity rates approaching 60%) than in a compensation-seeking setting, which may reflect the higher likelihood of feigned frank dementia in the former.

HENRY–HEILBRONNER INDEX

Henry, Heilbronner, Mittenberg, and Enders (2006) developed the 15-item Henry–Heilbronner Index (HHI) to identify a "pseudosomatic" presentation from items from the FBS and the Shaw and Matthews (1965) Pseudoneurologic Scale. The authors report that the HHI was superior to the original scales in classifying 45 compensation seekers who failed at least one neurocognitive SVT versus 74 noncompensation-seeking patients with TBI; a cutoff of ≥ 8 was associated with good specificity (89%) and sensitivity (80%). In a subsequent study by the same lab (Henry, Heilbronner, Mittenberg, Enders, & Stanczak, 2008), HHI and FBS were found to be better predictors of group membership (63 compensation seekers who failed at least one SVT vs. 77 noncompensation-seeking head-injured patients) than RC1. The authors suggest that HHI and FBS measure the construct of "exaggerated disability," while RC1 is a purer measure of "physical–somatic complaints."

However, Dionysus, Denney, and Halfaker (2011) reported that in a sample of 37 litigants who met the Slick et al. (1999) criteria for probable malingered neurocognitive dysfunction (including failure on ≥ 1 neurocognitive SVTs) and 42 litigants who did not fail SVTs, the groups differed on FBS, RBS, and HHI, but the effect sizes were larger for the two former scales ($d = 1.31\text{-}1.34$ vs. 1.11). At cutoffs associated with 90% specificity, sensitivity rates were 60% for FBS (cutoff of ≥ 25), 58% for RBS (cutoff of ≥ 14), and 45% for HHI (cutoff of ≥ 12). Logistic regression analyses showed that the predictive accuracy of FBS was increased with the inclusion of RBS, whereas HHI did not significantly contribute to group prediction and actually lowered the effectiveness of FBS. This study design is less desirable that that employed by Henry et al. (2006; Henry, Heilbronner, Mittenberg, Enders, & Stanczak, 2008), in that Henry and colleagues' comparison group was non-compensation-seeking, whereas the credible group employed by Dionysus et al. (2011) was litigating but did not fail any SVT. Because SVTs do not have perfect sensitivity, inadvertent inclusion of noncredible subjects in the credible group is likely in the latter study design.

As discussed above, Whitney et al. (2008) examined the effectiveness of MMPI-2 validity scales in 46 patients referred for neuropsychological evaluation and who had completed both the MMPI-2 and TOMM (24 passed and 22 failed). Comparison of groups showed the largest effect size for RBS ($d = 0.98$), following by the HHI ($d = 0.90$); among the remaining MMPI-2 F-family validity scales, effect sizes ranged from 0.51 to 0.65, with the exception that the effect size associated with FBS was only 0.23. Again, however, this study methodology was also problematic in that selection bias was likely to have been present (i.e., subjects were only administered the TOMM if their presentation was suspicious for malingering).

In the Tsushima et al. (2011) study described previously, an HHI cutoff of ≥ 11 was associated with 90.2% specificity in 163 clinical patients undergoing psychological evaluation for health-related and behavioral conditions; sensitivity was 27.1%, but this was an unselected sample of 118 litigants, not all of whom were likely malingering. The sensitivity rate for HHI was lower than that documented for RBS (39.0%).

Thus, although initial validation of the HHI by the scale developers was promising, subsequent (albeit methodologically problematic) research has raised questions as to whether HHI contributes unique information not already provided by FBS and RBS.

Scales Specific to Feigned Depression and Psychosocial Distress

Steffan, Clopton, and Morgan (2003) obtained MMPI-2 protocols from 68 college students instructed to feign depression; all were provided with information about symptoms of depression, and 45 were also told about MMPI-2 validity scales. To ensure that data were only retained for "successful" simulators, only those protocols that showed evidence of depression but no "excessive" elevations on validity scales were used, and the five most successful simulators were awarded prizes of $10 to $75. MMPI-2 protocols were also obtained on 33 students with minimal to mild depression ratings on the Zung Self-Rating Depression Scale. The 32 items that were the most divergent between groups were termed the Malingered Depression (Md) scale; simulators who were provided information about MMPI-2 validity scales did not differ on the scale from simulators not provided this information. Mean Md scores were 24.84 for simulators and 10.06 for depressed participants; a cutoff of > 16 was associated with 90.9% specificity and 88.2% sensitivity.

In a second study reported in Steffan et al. (2003; additional information in Walters & Clopton, 2000), MMPI-2 protocols were obtained from 172 college simulators (83 "warned" about MMPI-2 validity scales, and 89 "naïve") who were instructed to feign depression (i.e., they were told to imagine feeling slightly depressed because of poor grades and fear of losing scholarships/other financial problems, and were also told that if they were found to be significantly depressed on the MMPI-2 they might be eligible for monthly payments, deadline extensions, and rescheduling of exams). The warned simulators were provided with six malingering strategies they could use to avoid detection on MMPI-2 validity scales, and they were quizzed on the information. All simulators were cautioned to complete the test in a believable manner, and were reminded to feign both at the beginning of the MMPI-2 and again at 20 minutes and 40 minutes into test completion. MMPI-2 protocols were also obtained on 46 depressed students tested at a counseling center; profiles with elevated VRIN scores and with no evidence of depression were excluded. Simulators and depressed patients differed on all validity scales and the Md scale. F and Fb showed the largest effect sizes between naïve simulators and patients, while the

Md scale achieved the highest effect size between sophisticated malingerers and patients; the scores of naïve simulators averaged 2 points higher on this scale than those of sophisticated malingerers (24.80 vs. 22.87; 12.26 in depressed students). In the second study, the Md cutoff had to be raised to >21 to maintain at least 90% specificity, with sensitivity at 69.2%.

Bagby, Marshall, and Bacchiochi (2005) examined the effectiveness of the Md scale in identifying feigned depression in 23 mental health professionals instructed to simulate depression. The comparison group consisted of archival MMPI-2 data on 39 patients diagnosed with mild to moderate major depression and 42 patients diagnosed with severe major depression without psychotic features; patients had no other Axis I or Axis II disorder, and none were seeking disability compensation. Across clinical scales, simulators showed the highest elevations on the Depression scale ($105T$; as compared to $88T$ in patients with severe depression and $79T$ in those with mild to moderate depression). Simulators scored significantly higher than the two depression groups on all four validity scales studied (Md, F, Fb, and Fp); specifically, the simulators obtained mean scores on these scales of 26.26, 105.61, 115.22, and 79.70, respectively, as compared with means of 19.07, 77.26, 86.64, and 65.45 in patients with severe depression and 16.13, 72.23, 76.31, and 61.69 in those with mild to moderate depression. The largest effect size was found for Fb ($d = 2.09$), and the next largest for Md ($d = 1.83$) which was essentially comparable to F ($d = 1.78$); Fp showed the smallest effect size ($d = 0.87$). The authors conclude that although Md was able to discriminate feigners from nonfeigners, its clinical utility is "likely minimal as it did not 'pick up' many additional cases compared to Fb and the F and Fp combination" (p. 309).

Subsequently, Lange, Sullivan, and Scott (2010) investigated the Md scale in small groups of undergraduate simulators asked to feign depression ($n = 14$) or PTSD ($n = 15$), or to complete the MMPI-2 honestly ($n = 20$). Simulators were provided information about depression or PTSD, and then had to pass a quiz; on completion of the experiment, questionnaire data were obtained regarding understanding of instructions, and perceived ability in, and strategies for, feigning. All subjects were given course credit and informed that they would be eligible for a cash award of $400, depending on the quality of their responses. Groups did not differ on the Md scale (means of 18.6 in controls, 20.3 in depression simulators, and 19.5 in PTSD simulators), and every other MMPI-2 validity scale was more effective than Md in separating groups. However, the high Md scores in control participants are a nonsensical finding, perhaps related to small N.

Sweet, Malina, and Ecklund-Johnson (2006) also found no significant difference in Md scores in a large sample of neuropsychological referrals with actual or potential secondary gain (disability-seeking, in litigation, or contemplating litigation; $n = 89$) versus clinical referrals ($n = 71$). The two groups obtained highly similar scores on Md (11.76 in subjects with sec-ondary gain versus 11.61 for those without). However, this was a problem-atic design, in that not all subjects with actual or potential secondary gain feign symptoms, but even in those subjects with actual/potential secondary gain who failed at least one cognitive SVT ($n = 23$), only 35% exceeded an Md cutoff of 15, and only 4% exceeded a cutoff of 22. These findings led the authors to conclude that "the utility of the scale to clinical neuropsy-chologists appears low" (p. 541).

Henry, Heilbronner, Mittenberg, Enders, and Roberts (2008) derived a 15-item MMPI-2 subscale called the Malingered Mood Disorder Scale (MMDS) from the Md scale in a study of 62 compensation seekers (liti-gants or disability claimants) presenting for neuropsychological evaluation who met the Slick et al. (1999) criteria for probable malingered neurocogni-tive dysfunction (PM) versus 76 nonlitigants undergoing neuropsychologi-cal evaluation for TBI (NM; 85% mTBI). Groups differed on Md (means of 14.87 in PM vs. 8.59 in NM); at a cutoff of 14, specificity was 92.10% with associated sensitivity of 45.20%, and a cutoff of ≥17 produced no false positive identifications. The 15 of the original 32 Md items most closely associated with group membership were used to create the MMDS; a cutoff of ≥7 maintained 93.40% specificity, with a modest increase in sensitivity over Md (54.80%), and a cutoff of ≥8 achieved 100% specificity (46.80% sensitivity).

Subsequently, this group (Henry, Heilbronner, Mittenberg, Enders, & Domboski, 2009) compared effectiveness of the MMDS to the MMPI-2 RCd and Depression scales, in mostly the same sample as utilized in the 2008 publication (84 PM vs. 77 NM participants; 85% of the NM sample were evaluated for mTBI). The Depression scale was more effective than the MMDS, which was in turn more accurate than RCd. A cutoff score of ≥26 on Depression was associated with a 8% false positive rate while detecting 86% of noncredible subjects, and an RCd cutoff of ≥16 resulted in 87% specificity and 50% sensitivity (cutoffs associated with ≥90% specificity were not reported).

Crawford, Greene, Dupart, Bongar, and Childs (2006) investigated the ability of MMPI-2 validity indicators (F, Fb, Fp, FBS, F minus K, Ds-r) to detect simulated depression associated with a physical workplace injury in the context of litigation. College simulators ($n = 27$) were asked to feign major depression associated with facial disfigurement in a workplace acci-dent, but not to feign psychosis or to answer deviantly on all the items, because MMPI-2 validity scales would detect this; subjects were entered into a $50 lottery if they followed instructions to feign depression and did not engage in random responding. The simulation data were compared against archival records of inpatients with major depression ($n = 33$). FBS achieved the largest effect size ($d = 1.17$ vs. 0.50 for F, which registered the next highest effect size). The authors assert that FBS is "superior in detecting malingered psychological distress generated by a supposed physical injury" (p. 219). An FBS cutoff of >24 was associated with 63–67% sensitivity at 76–80% specificity; unfortunately, cutoffs limiting false positive identifications to ≤10% were not provided.

Henry et al. (2011) developed and cross-validated a 20-item scale (the Psychosocial Distress Scale, or PDS) from MMPI-2 items to identify over-reported psychosocial complaints in 90 noncredible patients (litigants or disability seekers who failed at least two cognitive SVTs) and 77 postacute non-compensation-seeking patients with TBI (85% with mTBI) tested within 1 month of injury. The noncredible group obtained significantly higher scores; at a cutoff of ≥10, specificity was adequate (≥90%), with sensitivity of 82–83%.

In summary, although scales have been developed to identify feigned depression (Md, MMDS), the original MMPI-2 validity and/or Depression scales may outperform these newer scales. Unfortunately, the only studies to examine feigning of depression per se employed simulators, and these simulators obtained markedly higher Md scores than "real-world" noncredible individuals feigning cognitive dysfunction in the Sweet et al. (2006) and Henry, Heilbronner, Mittenberg, Enders, and Roberts (2008) studies. A possible reason for the substantially higher simulator Md scores obtained by Steffan et al. (2003) was that the researchers reminded simulators to feign on the MMPI-2 at three separate points during test completion—a highly unusual procedure, which could serve to artificially enhance differences between simulators and depressed participants. However, it should be noted that Bagby et al. (2005) obtained comparable Md scores for mental health professional simulators who were not reported to have been given these nonstandardized test instructions. Of concern, some of the Md simulator scores were comparable to Md scores obtained in bona fide patients with severe depression, and mean Md scores in the latter exceeded scores of real-world feigners in the Henry et al. (2008) and Sweet et al. (2006) studies. However, research indicates that there are limited relationships between feigning of psychiatric symptoms and feigning of cognitive symptoms (Boone, Savodnik et al., 1995; Nelson et al., 2007; Sumanti, Boone, Savodnik, & Gorsuch, 2006), and thus data from the Sweet et al. (2006), Henry, Heilbronner, Mittenberg, Enders, and Roberts (2008), and Henry et al. (2009) studies may underestimate the true effectiveness of the Md and other scales in identifying feigned depression in isolation. Real-world studies of feigned depression without feigned cognitive dysfunction are problematic to implement, because there are no methods to assign subjects to noncredible groups (i.e., there are no "depression" analogues to neurocognitive SVTs).

A recently developed scale to identify feigned psychosocial distress, validated in a relatively large sample of real-world credible and noncredible patients, appears to have promise in detecting distress overreport.

Minnesota Multiphasic Personality Inventory–2–Restructured Form

The Minnesota Multiphasic Personality Inventory–2–Restructured Form (MMPI-2–RF; Ben-Porath & Tellegen, 2008) is a 338-item version of the MMPI-2 that includes 9 validity scales (VRIN-r, TRIN-r, F-r, Fp-r, Infrequent Somatic Responses [Fs], FBS-r, RBS, K-r, and L-r), 3 higher-order scales, the 9 restructured clinical scales described earlier for the MMPI-2, and 30 additional substantive scales. The restructured clinical scales remove the item overlap and the saturation with demoralization present in the original MMPI-2 clinical scales, and therefore are purer measures of the underlying constructs. The remaining MMPI-2–RF scales are theoretically grounded and hierarchically structured, and have benefited from test construction methods not available when the MMPI was originally developed. At this writing (May 2012), there have been > 140 peer-reviewed publications on the MMPI-2–RF, and its clinical use is escalating.

Detection of Fake Bad Responding on the MMPI-2–RF

Sellbom, Toomey, Wygant, Kucharski, and Duncan (2010) examined the effectivess of MMPI-2–RF validity scales in discriminating credible (*n* = 98) from noncredible (*n* = 27) criminal defendants (as determined by SIRS scores). The noncredible group obtained significantly higher scores on overreporting validity scales (F-r, Fp-r, Fs, and FBS-r), with the largest effect sizes found for F-r and Fp-r. Groups also significantly differed on all restructured clinical scales with the exception of RC3 and RC9; the highest elevations in the noncredible group appeared on RC6 and RC8. Mean validity scale scores in the noncredible group were F-r = 141.92, Fp-r = 122.38, Fs = 98.94, and FBS-r = 86.47, while all credible patient scores were < 70 with the exception of F-r (79.10–82.00). An F-r cutoff of 120 was associated with 88–91% specificity and 89% sensitivity, while an Fp-r score of > 100 resulted in 90–92% specificity and 74% sensitivity.

Sellbom and Bagby (2010) accessed archival data from an MMPI-2 simulation study involving 177 college students who completed the MMPI-2 honestly and then were instructed to feign psychiatric illness as a part of a disability claim; 70 of these students were provided information about the presence of validity scales and the best ways to avoid detection. The simulators were paid for their participation, and the most successful simulators were awarded a cash prize. For the present study, the MMPI-2 data were converted to MMPI-2–RF data, and the simulator profiles were compared with those from 127 psychiatric inpatients (47% with depression, 35% with schizophrenia, and 18% with bipolar illness). Uncoached simulators scored higher than patients on all four validity scales (F-r, Fp-r, FBS-r, and Fs), whereas coached simulators scored higher than patients on all scales except FBS-r; the largest effect size was observed for Fp-r ($d = 1.36$). Mean scores for the patients were 82.43 for F-r, 63.02 for Fp-r, 69.76 for Fs, and 70.93 for FBS-r, while uncoached simulators obtained mean scores of 109.89, 106.50, 99.36, and 81.44, respectively, and coached simulators obtained mean scores of 92.43, 90.16, 79.00, and 72.54, respectively. With cutoffs set to maintain at least 90% specificity, sensitivity for F-r in uncoached simulators was 64%, but only 27% in coached simulators (cutoff of $120T$); sensitivity for Fp-r was 79% in uncoached simulators and 49% in coached simulators (cutoff of $> 90T$).

Marion, Sellbom, and Bagby (2011) also accessed archival MMPI-2 data (converted to MMPI-2–RF data) collected as a part of a simulation study involving feigned major depression, schizophrenia, and PTSD. The simulators were either naïve (college students) or sophisticated (mental health experts), and they were asked to complete the MMPI-2 as if they had one of the three disorders. The students were provided with DSM-IV information on the disorder they were to feign (depression $n = 67$; schizophrenia $n = 30$, PTSD $n = 60$), and after completion of the MMPI-2 they were administered a post-test questionnaire to assess for compliance with study instructions. They were given $10 for participation, with an additional $100 awarded to the most successful simulator. Mental health experts simulated depression ($n = 30$) and schizophrenia ($n = 52$). Data for sophisticated PTSD simulators were obtained by recruiting individuals who had previously been diagnosed with PTSD, who were then instructed to feign PTSD when completing the MMPI-2–RF ($n = 77$). Simulator data were compared to MMPI-2–RF data for 237 patients who had been diagnosed with either major depression ($n = 75$), schizophrenia ($n = 56$), or PTSD ($n = 106$). Across the four validity scales, simulators scored higher than patients; naïve simulators also scored higher than sophisticated simulators, with the exception of the PTSD condition and FBS-r in the depression condition. The Fp-r cutoff score associated with at least 90% specificity in the depression condition was $\geq 85T$ (50–78% sensitivity); for the schizophrenia condition, it was $\geq 100T$ (67–80% sensitivity); and for the PTSD condition, it was $\geq 100T$ (37–47% sensitivity).

In a simulation study of feigned ADHD (Harp, Jasinski, Shandera-Ochsner, Mason, & Berry, 2011), college student simulators (students without ADHD who were asked to simulate ADHD, $n = 22$; students with ADHD who were asked to exaggerate ADHD symptoms, $n = 18$) received course credit or $20 for participation, with the possibility of an additional $50 if they feigned successfully. They were provided with information from the Internet about symptoms of ADHD, and were asked to complete the MMPI-2–RF in a manner than would indicate that they had ADHD without being detected as faking. Following the administration of the MMPI-2–RF, they completed a posttest questionnaire assessing their understanding of, and compliance with, task instructions. Feigners without ADHD scored higher than students with ADHD in the honest condition (n = 20) on F-r, Fp-r, Fs, RC1, RC4, RC8, RC9, Neurological Complaints, Cognitive Complaints, Behavior-Restricting Fears, Anger Proneness, Juvenile Conduct Problems and Activation, whereas the feigners with ADHD scored higher than honest students with ADHD on F-r, Fs, RC8, Behavior-Restricting Fears, and Activation. When cutoffs were employed that achieved at least 90% specificity, sensitivity rates were higher in the feigners without ADHD than the feigners with ADHD: Fp-r (cutoff of ≥77T), 63.6% versus 27.8%; F-r (cutoff of ≥70T), 40.9% versus 16.7%; Fs (cutoff ≥91T), 36.4% versus 33.3%.

In a specificity-only study, Purdon, Purser, and Goddard (2011) described MMPI-2–RF validity scale performance in 103 patients referred in the context of first-episode psychosis. Mean scores across overreporting validity scales were F-r = 75.12, Fp-r = 70.61, Fs = 67.21, FBS-r = 58.88, and RBS = 66.44; cutoffs of 120, 110, 100, 80, and 90, respectively, approximated 90% specificity.

In summary, available data suggest that in the differential diagnosis of feigned versus actual psychosis, an F-r cutoff of 120 should be employed. This may detect more than 90% of noncredible psychotic individuals, although these may be more blatant feigners (they are among the 50% captured by the SIRS; this issue is discussed on p. 84). For Fp-r, cutoffs can be lowered to ≥85T in the differential of actual and feigned depression and still maintain specificity of at least 90% (50–78% sensitivity), and in feigned ADHD they can be lowered to ≥77T (28–64% sensitivity). However, in PTSD and schizophrenia, cutoffs of at least ≥100T must be employed (67–80% sensitivity for feigned schizophrenia; 37–47% sensitivity for feigned PTSD). Unfortunately, the data available to date regarding feigned depression, PTSD, and ADHD have involved simulators and must therefore be viewed as preliminary.

Relationship between MMPI-2–RF Scales and Neurocognitive SVTs

Gervais et al. (2010) reported that MMPI-2–RF validity scales were more strongly related to memory complaints than were MMPI-2 overreporting scales, leading the authors to conclude that the MMPI-2–RF overreporting scales are "more efficient and sensitive measures of symptom overreporting" (p. 274).

Thomas and Youngjohn (2009) provided MMPI-2–RF restructured clinical scale data for litigants claiming TBI (primarily mTBI) who either passed all (n = 49) or failed at least one (n = 34) of three cognitive SVTs (Portland Digit Recognition Test, WMT, and Dot Counting Test). The largest group difference was detected for RC1, with the noncredible group averaging an RC1 T score of 82, and with those litigants passing SVTs averaging a T-score of 62. In a subsequent study employing essentially the same archival data (Youngjohn, Wershba, Stevenson, Sturgeon, & Thomas, 2011), groups were compared on MMPI-2–RF somatic/cognitive scales (Malaise, GI Complaints, Head Pain Complaints, Neurological Complaints, and Cognitive Complaints) and validity scales (F-r, Fp-r, Fs, FBS-r, L-r, and K-r). Mean overreport validity scale scores in the noncredible group were F-r = 84.09T, Fp-r= 60.59T, Fs = 78.71T, and FBS-r = 77.88T, and in the credible group the means were all ≤69T. Among the somatic/cognitive scales, mean scores in the credible group ranged from 53.42 (GI Complaints) to 69.48 (Neurological Complaints), and in the noncredible group they ranged from 66.41 (GI Complaints) to 79.97 (Neurological Complaints). The Head Pain Complaints scale alone showed a paradoxical inverse relationship with TBI severity. The largest amount of SVT variance was accounted for by the Malaise scale (the authors note that all eight Malaise scale items were contained in the original MMPI-2 Hysteria scale), and all somatic/cognitive scales accounted for significant amounts of symptom validity test variance except the Cognitive Complaints scale; the somatic/cognitive scales as a group were more effective predictors of SVT failure than were the validity scales. Among validity scales, only FBS-r accounted for a significant amount of symptom validity test variance—leading the authors to conclude that "the MMPI-2–RF's Somatic/Cognitive scales, rather than an exclusive focus on the Validity scales, may be useful in determining the likelihood of symptom overreporting in litigating patients" (p. 473), and that "the MMPI-2–RF scales FBS-r, RC1, and the newly created Somatic/Cognitive scales retain much of the sensitivity to somatization and overreporting that might have been lost when the MMPI-2 was restructured" (p. 474).

Wygant et al. (2009) examined MMPI-2–RF data for 151 compensation seekers (42% claiming work-related stress, 33% mTBI, 16% orthopedic injury, and 7% other neurological injury); 93 passed all SVTs (TOMM, WMT, CARB, VSVT), and 47 failed at least one SVT (21 failed one SVT and 26 failed two to three SVTs). When cutoffs were selected to maintain at least 90% specificity (F-r ≥90T, Fp-r ≥60T, Fs ≥80T, and FBS-r, ≥90T), sensitivity in the group failing at least two SVTs ranged from 38.5% (F-r, Fp-r, and FBS-r) to 61.5% (Fs). (Findings for simulation groups were also described in this study, although given questions about the generalizabilty of simulation data and the relatively large number of known-groups studies now available on the MMPI-2–RF, the simulation data are not included here.)

Wygant et al. (2010) published a subsequent study apparently involving essentially the same population of compensation seekers (42% claiming work-related stress and 56% neurological or somatic injury), who were assigned to credible (n = 96) and noncredible (n = 42) groups based on failure on the TOMM and/or the WMT (78 were administered the TOMM, 65 were given the WMT, and 16 received both; those failing one or both SVTs were assigned to the "fail SVT" group). Groups differed on all MMPI-2–RF validity scales, with the largest effect sizes found for FBS/FBS-r and Fs (d's = 1.05–1.18). In the credible group, means on overreport validity scales ranged from 52.1 (Fp-r) to 69.2 (FBS-r). In the noncredible group, mean Fp-r was 60.5, but means for the remaining scales were above 80 (F-r = 85.7, Fs = 80.0, FBS-r = 85.9).

Schroeder et al. (2012) examined MMPI-2–RF validity scale performance in litigants claiming TBI who met Slick et al. (1999) criteria for probable malingering (n = 21) and four credible comparison groups (litigants with TBI who passed SVTs, n = 27; nonlitigants with primary neurologic conditions who passed SVTs, n = 28; nonlitigants with primary psychiatric conditions who passed SVTs, n = 21; and inpatients with video-EEG-confirmed epilepsy, n = 50). The noncredible group scored significantly higher than the three neurological comparison groups on F-r and RBS, and a nearly significant difference was observed in comparison with the psychiatric group on RBS. In the noncredible group, mean T-scores were 87.5 for F-r, 61.0 for Fp-r, 81.1 for Fs, 89.0 for FBS-r, and 93.3 for RBS. In contrast, no mean score exceeded $69T$ in the three neurological groups, although in the psychiatric group means above 70 were observed for F-r ($83.5T$) and RBS ($79.4T$). Cutoffs associated with at least 90% specificity in the three neurological groups were $>88T$ for F-r (38% sensitivity), $>89T$ for FBS-r (48% sensitivity), and $>92T$ for RBS (43% sensitivity), although specificity rates for F-r and RBS were unacceptably low at these cutoffs in the psychiatric group (64% and 71%, respectively).

FBS-r and Fs data were provided by Jones and Ingram (2011) on 288 military personnel evaluated in the context of head, blast, or heat injuries, or brain disease; 70% were subject to medical discharge with the possibility of disability compensation. The sample was divided in credible (n = 171) and noncredible (n = 117) groups based on failure on one or both cognitive SVTs (TOMM, VSVT). Significant differences in raw FBS-r (mean of 15.41 in the noncredible group and 10.88 in the credible group) and Fs (mean of 4.15 in the noncredible group and 2.22 in the credible group) were documented.

Gervais, Wygant, Sellbom, and Ben-Porath (2011) observed that increasing numbers of neurocognitive SVT failures (WMT, CARB, MSVT,

TOMM) were associated with higher elevations on MMPI-2–RF overreporting scales in 1,003 compensation-seeking individuals (264 passed all
SVTs, 86 failed one, 36 failed two, and 29 failed three). Comparison of participants passing all SVTs to those failing three on validity scales showed
the largest effect size for FBS-r in both men and women ($d = 1.11/1.04$), but
with a nearly equally large effect size observed for the Emotional/Internal-
izing Dysfunction higher-order scale ($d = 1.01/0.82$) and three restructured
clinical scales (RC2, $d = 1.11/0.88$; RC1, $d = 0.98/1.04$; RCd, $d = 0.95/0.80$).
However, among clinical scales the largest effect size was documented for
the Cognitive Complaints scale ($d = 1.31/1.01$), which had a larger effect
size than the remaining somatic/cognitive scales (d's = ≤0.96). Among the
other substantive scales, large effect sizes in comparison of subjects failing
no versus three SVTs were documented for Behavior-Restricting Fears ($d =$
$0.93/1.11$), Social Avoidance ($d = 0.81/1.06$), Suicidal Ideation in women (d
$= 0.93$), Introversion/Low Positive Emotionality—Revised ($d = 0.92/1.03$),
and Negative Emotionality/Neuroticism—Revised in men ($d = 0.93$).
Gervais et al. (2009) had previously shown that in samples screened for
adequacy of cognitive effort, elevations on the Cognitive Complaints scale
were associated with cognitive and emotional complaints, but not objectively measured cognitive deficits.

Rogers et al. (2011) examined effectiveness of MMPI-2–RF validity
scales in 645 seekers of compensation (workers' compensation, litigation,
disability). Of these, 32 were assigned to a noncredible mental disorders
group based on the SIRS-2, and 42 were assigned to a noncredible cognitive
dysfunction group based on performance significantly below chance on the
VSVT, TOMM, or both (4 participants also identified as feigning psychiatric symptoms were excluded). Participants ($n = 345$) who scored in the valid
range on the VSVT and TOMM, and whose SIRS-2 scores indicated a high
likelihood of genuine responding (indeterminate cases were removed), were
retained in the credible cognitive symptom group.

In the group with noncredible mental disorders, means for validity
scales were as follows: F-r = $129.3T$, Fp-r = $74.4T$, Fs = $102.9T$, FBS-r =
$95.3T$, and RBS = $111.9T$. In the group with noncredible cognitive disorders, means were F-r = $103.8T$, Fp-r = $62.3T$, Fs = $86.6T$, FBS-r = $91.6T$, and
RBS = $103.4T$. In the genuine-responders group, means were F-r = $78.8T$,
Fp-r = $53.5T$, Fs = $66.2T$, FBS-r = $74.5T$, and RBS = $75.8T$. The subgroup
with major depression within the genuine-responders groups averaged substantial elevations (i.e., ≥$80T$) on F-r, FBS-r, and RBS, whereas moderate
elevations (i.e., ≥$70T$) were generally observed for the subgroup with PTSD
($n = 18$). Application of cutoffs showed problematic false positive rates; for
example, adequate specificity could not be achieved with an RBS cutoff
of 100T (88% specificity); a cutoff of $100T$ for FBS-r was associated with
95% specificity, but was only 62% at a cutoff of 80T. Rogers and colleagues

concluded that MMPI-2–RF and RBS are problematic in determination of noncredible cognitive presentations.

However, the methodology of the study was problematic. The base rate of noncredible presentation was only 17.2%, which is approximately half that estimated for compensation-seeking settings (Mittenberg et al., 2002). This would suggest that as many noncredible participants were missed as were detected, and that at least some of the undetected non-credible participants were assigned to the genuine group. As discussed on page 84, the SIRS instruments only detect approximately half of individuals feigning psychological symptoms, and they primarily have efficacy in identifying feigned psychosis but not the psychiatric symptoms claimed in most compensation-seeking settings (e.g., depression and anxiety). Thus it is likely that well under half of the subjects who were actually feigning psychological symptoms were detected. Similarly, traditional TOMM cut-offs detect only approximately half of noncredible cognitive performances (Greve et al., 2008), indicating that a not insubstantial subset of patients was probably feigning cognitive symptoms but was not detected. Regarding the VSVT, while simulation studies have reported high sensitivity rates (81–82%; see Sollman & Berry, 2011), no known-groups studies of actual noncredible subjects have been conducted; therefore, the true sensitivity rates of the VSVT are unknown, but are likely to be substantially lower than the simulation studies would suggest. When noncredible subjects are inadvertently retained in a credible sample, means will be elevated on over-reporting scales and cutoff specificities will be underestimated. In this vein, it is relevant to note that the mean FBS-r scores in the credible responders were essentially comparable to the mean FBS-r scores in the Youngjohn et al. (2011) noncredible group described above.

Furthermore, subjects were only included in the noncredible cognitive group if they scored significantly below chance on one or more of the two SVTs. Using this criterion results in an atypical noncredible sample, in that < 10% of noncredible cognitive patients actually perform at levels significantly below chance (e.g., M. S. Kim et al., 2010); thus these participants would reflect only the extreme of the cognitive negative response bias continuum, rendering generalization of results to the larger noncredible population problematic. In fact, the Rogers et al. (2011) MMPI-2–RF means for noncredible participants are much higher than those reported in the other studies described above.

In conclusion, most of the known-groups studies summarized above (Gervais et al., 2011; Schroeder et al., 2012; Wygant et al., 2009; Youngjohn et al., 2011) have reported remarkably consistent overreport validity scale data in noncredible participants (i.e., F-r = 82–90T; Fpr = 60–63T, Fs = 77–81T; FBS-r = 78–89T), despite relatively small n's (21–42). The much higher scores in the Rogers et al. (2011) study are probably related to the methodological issues raised above. Across studies, scores of credible subjects have also been consistent (all mean overreport T-scores generally < 70), with the exception of some elevations on F-r and FBS-r scores in psychiatric patients (Rogers et al., 2011; Schroeder et al., 2011). Sensitivity rates associated with cutoff scores set to ≥ 90% specificity have been modest (38–48%), indicating that data from self-report validity scales are not interchangeable with performance-based symptom validity information. Effect sizes for some of the substantive scales (Cognitive Complaints, Neurological Complaints, RCd, RC1, RC2, Emotional/Internalizing Dysfunction, Behavior-Restricting Fears, Social Avoidance, Suicidal/Death Ideation, Introversion/Low Positive Emotionality—Revised, Negative Emotionality/ Neuroticism—Revised) have been equal to or even higher than those for the overreport validity scales, suggesting that additional investigation of these scales as indicators of symptom overendorsement in a neuropsychological population is warranted.

Personality Assessment Inventory

The Personality Assessment Inventory (PAI; Morey, 1991) has 344 items rated on a 4-point Likert scale (totally false, slightly true, mainly true, very true) and is intended for use with individuals 18 years or older who have a least a fourth-grade reading level. It contains a total of 22 nonoverlapping scales: 4 validity (Inconsistency, Infrequency, Negative Impression, Positive Impression); 11 clinical (Somatic Complaints, Depression, Anxiety, Anxiety-Related Disorders, Paranoia, Schizophrenia, Mania, Borderline Features, Antisocial Features, Alcohol Problems, Drug Problems); 5 treatment consideration (Aggression, Suicidal Ideation, Stress, Nonsupport, Treatment Rejection); and 2 interpersonal (Dominance, Warmth). Normative data were obtained on 1,000 community-dwelling adults matched to 1995 U.S. Census demographic data; there are no separate gender norms. Clinical comparison data were collected on 1,246 patients from a wide variety of settings.

Approximately a decade ago, the PAI was ranked fourth in frequency of usage in internship programs (Piotrowski & Belter, 1999), was employed in 11% of emotional injury personal injury cases (Boccaccini & Brodsky, 1999), and was utilized by 17% of those who classified themselves as "frequent assessors" (Boccaccini & Brodsky, 1999). In a recent review of case law involving the PAI (Mullen & Edens, 2008), 125 cases published between 1991 and 2006 were identified. Of these, two-thirds involved civil cases (primarily child custody, personal injury, and workers' compensation); the criminal cases involved a wide range of preadjudication and postadjudication issues. The Lally (2003) survey of board-certified forensic psychologists showed that they rated the PAI in the "acceptable" category in terms of detecting malingering. In the survey of NAN and International Neuropsychological Society members, 50% of respondents reported some use of the PAI in their neuropsychological evaluations (Smith et al., 2010).

The reader interested in a review of research investigating the effectiveness of the PAI in identifying psychiatric diagnosis and suicidal ideation, assessing risk, predicting treatment amenability and response, and measuring defensiveness/positive impression management is referred to Edens, Cruise, and Buffington-Vollum (2001). In the following discussion, I focus on the PAI's ability to detect symptom overreport. I examine the four original validity scales and three subsequent overreport scales:

ORIGINAL VALIDITY SCALES

- Inconsistency: Inconsistent responses to pairs of highly correlated items
- Infrequency: Careless, random, and/or idiosyncratic endorsement of items
- Negative Impression (NIM): Items rarely endorsed in normal and clinical samples
- Positive Impression (PIM): Presentation of very favorable impression or reluctance to admit minor faults

LATER OVERREPORT SCALES

- Malingering Index (MAL; Morey, 1996): Measure of eight profile characteristics associated with attempts to feign mental illness
- Rogers Discriminant Function (RDF; Rogers et al., 1996): Weighted combination of 20 PAI scale scores designed to detect malingering
- Negative Distortion Scale (NDS; Mogge, Lepage, Bell, & Ragatz, 2010): Set of 15 items from eight clinical scales rarely endorsed by psychiatric inpatients

Of these seven scales, the NIM, MAL, and RDF have received the most research attention.

Detection of Fake Bad Responding on the PAI

As shown in the second list above, in addition to the four validity scales originally published with the PAI, three overreport scales have since been developed. Further, Hopwood, Morey, Rogers, and Sewell (2007) have suggested that analysis of the difference between actual and NIM-predicted clinical scales can provide information about the specific nature of the symptoms being feigned (e.g., depression, anxiety, or schizophrenia).

In 2008, Sellbom and Bagby provided a comprehensive review of the literature on the ability of the PAI validity and newer scales to detect symptom overreport. They conclude that for three of these scales (NIM, MAL, RDF), "high false-positive rates (except for extreme cut scores) negate accurate classification of malingering" (p. 198), and they recommend use of the following algorithm (*nonforensic* refers to clinical/civil settings, and *forensic* refers to criminal/corrections settings):

- Low likelihood of malingering:
  - Nonforensic: NIM < 73T, MAL < 3, and low RDF
  - Forensic: NIM < 77T
- Malingering should be further evaluated:
  - Nonforensic: NIM ≥ 73T, MAL ≥ 3, or high RDF
  - Forensic: NIM ≥ 77T
- High likelihood of malingering:
  - Nonforensic: NIM ≥ 110T or very high RDF (≥ 1.80 raw)
  - Forensic = NIM ≥ 110T or MAL ≥ 5

Subsequently, Hawes and Boccaccini (2009) published a meta-analytic review of 26 studies examining the PAI's effectiveness in detecting overreport of psychopathology. NIM showed the largest effect size (d = 1.48), followed by MAL (d = 1.15) and RDF (d = 1.13). Effect sizes (especially for RDF and NIM) and greater variability were more pronounced for simulation studies than for known-groups investigations, and for comparisons involving normal control participants than for those involving genuine patient groups. In addition, validity measures were more effective in detecting severe mental disorders than mood or anxiety disorders, but more variability was also noted for the former group. In terms of cutoff scores, the recommended NIM score of ≥ 77 detected 75% of noncredible individuals, but was only associated with a mean specificity value of 77%; the score had to be raised to between 95T and 100T to achieve specificity of at least 90%, but sensitivity was reduced to less than 50%. At a cutoff of ≥ 3, MAL nearly reached a mean 90% specificity rate (86%), but with an associated sensitivity of only 58%; raising the cutoff to ≥ 4 achieved 100% specificity, but mean sensitivity declined to 35%.

RDF scores were not examined because few investigations employed the same RDF cutoffs, but Hawes and Boccacchini (2009) noted that RDF was "no better than chance" (p. 113) in identifying overreport in known-groups studies (perhaps because it is less closely related to SIRS and M-FAST scores, the typical measures used to assign subjects to credible and noncredible groups). Also of note, Kucharski, Toomey, Fila, and Duncan

(2007) cautioned that "research to date on the PAI has underscored the external validity problems of simulator designs in that the findings in simulation studies of the RDF . . . have not been found to generalize in studies of actual forensic participants" (p. 31).

Given the comprehensiveness of these reviews and the concerns regarding simulation studies, I focus in the following discussion of PAI overreport studies on those employing known groups and on simulation studies published subsequent to the reviews cited above.

Wang et al. (1997) identified 40 PAI protocols out of 334 obtained at a corrections inpatient psychiatric hospital for which PAI indicators (NIM, MAL, and mean clinical elevation [MCE]) or behavioral indicators (discrepancies between inmate report and behavior) of malingering were present. Fifteen of the 40 patients were detected as malingering on the SIRS, and the remaining 25 patients were designated as nonfeigning (honest or indeterminate ratings). The feigning group obtained significantly higher elevations on NIM (mean = 100.53 vs. 81.08) and MAL (mean = 2.93 vs. 1.84), as well as a higher MCE (mean = 86.07 vs. 76.64), but not a higher RDF. Similarly, significant correlations were obtained between SIRS primary scales and NIM, MAL, and MCE (r's = .32 to .54), but not RDF (r's = −.25 to .11). The study design was problematic in that only individuals obtaining elevations on PAI malingering indicators were administered the SIRS, and this accounts for the elevated NIM scores in the credible group.

Subsequently, Rogers, Ustad, and Salekin (1998) examined the relationship between SIRS and PAI data in 80 individuals who had undergone mental health evaluations in an urban jail setting; 16 showed evidence of feigning on the SIRS. NIM and SIRS scales were significantly correlated (r's = .4 to .7, median of .61), and highly significant differences were found on NIM between feigners (mean = 91.19) and credible patients (mean = 58.32). At a cutoff score of > 10 (> 80T), NIM identified 62.5% of feigners while correctly classifying 95% of credible patients.

Rogers, Sewell, Cruise, Wang, and Ustad (1998), in a study of 115 male forensic patients, used performance beyond cutoffs on the SIRS as the criterion for malingering (57 malingerers, 58 credible patients). They found that the NIM cutoff of ≥77T achieved 84% sensitivity but had inadequate specificity (74%). MAL cutoff of ≥3 and RDF cutoff of 0.12368 performed even worse, reaching only 47% and 51% sensitivity, respectively, and with specificities of only 86% and 72%. Raising NIM and MAL cutoffs to ≥110T and ≥5, respectively, increased specificity to 98% and 100%, respectively, but at sacrifice to sensitivity (23% and 16%, respectively).

Bagby, Nicholson, Bacchiochi, Ryder, and Bury (2002) compared PAI protocols of 45 undergraduates to those of 75 inpatients and outpatients with various psychiatric diagnoses (nearly 75% with a mood or anxiety disorder). The students were instructed to complete the PAI honestly and then in either a coached (n = 23) or uncoached (n = 22) simulation condition in which they were instructed to feign psychological symptoms in the service of obtaining disability compensation. In the coached condition, they were informed of the presence of validity scales and strategies to avoid detection. The students received $40 compensation and were told that the participant who feigned most successfully would received an additional $100. Patients and simulators did not differ on NIM and MAL, but simulators scored significant higher on RDF (which outperformed MMPI-2 validity scales); coached and uncoached simulators did not differ on any validity/overre-port scales. Across clinical scales, the highest scores in the simulators were obtained on Depression and Paranoia, suggesting that they were primarily feigning in these areas. In contrast, the only scale on which simulators and honest responders did not differ was Mania, indicating that they were not feigning this type of symptoms.

Boccaccini, Murrie, and Duncan (2006) evaluated cutoffs for NIM and MAL in 166 defendants undergoing pretrial court-ordered evaluations, with the SIRS again used as the criterion for assignment to the malinger-ing group (n = 45; 29%). "Indeterminate" cases (n = 44; 29%) and honest responders (n = 65; 42%) were combined. At a cutoff of $\geq 81T$ for NIM, sensitivity was 91%, but specificity was unacceptable (72%); raising the cutoff to $\geq 92T$ still did not achieve adequate specificity (84%; sensitivity = 78%). A cutoff of ≥ 5 for MAL resulted in excellent specificity (97%), but sensitivity was poor (13%); a cutoff of ≥ 3 showed virtually identical specificity and sensitivity values to those in the Rogers, Sewell, et al. (1998) study (53% sensitivity at 84% specificity).

Kucharski et al. (2007) examined the ability of the PAI to detect feign-ing in 116 criminal defendants with an average of 10.5 years of education; 73.3% were classified as not malingering, and 26.7% were classified as malingering based on the SIRS (subjects who had refused to participate in the SIRS had been excluded). SIRS scores were significantly related to NIM and MAL but not RDF. When logistic regression analysis was used, only the NIM differentiated groups, and MAL and RDF did not add incremen-tal prediction. At a NIM cutoff of $92T$ (raw score = 13), specificity was 89% and sensitivity was 71%. The authors note that the strategy of the malingerers appeared to have been to "portray oneself as ill across a wide array of symptoms," including "psychotic, somatic, anxiety, and affective symptoms as well as symptoms of personality disorder" (p. 29), but group differences were not found on the Antisocial Features and Mania scales (both groups scored low) or on Suicidal Ideation (both groups scored high). The authors conjecture that the low Mania scores in the malingerers were due to their perception that they could not have maintained feigned manic symptoms consistently for any length of time.

Edens et al. (2007) studied the PAI in a postadjudication population, including 56 incarcerated men who had been admitted to a mental health unit; 30 of these were determined to be credible and 26 were judged to be malingering symptoms by the admitting psychiatrists, based on self-report symptoms inconsistent with the psychiatrists' or staff's observations of patient behavior, and/or endorsement of blatant symptoms, overly severe symptoms, unusual symptom combinations, or other unusual symptom reports. Sixty additional incarcerated men were drawn from the general prison population and were judged to be free of mental disorder. Half of these 60 were instructed to feign serious mental illness while avoiding detection; they were offered $50 as an incentive for successful feigning (1 was excluded because he did not obtain T scores ≥ 70 on the PAI Schizophrenia, Paranoia, Depression, or Mania scales). The PAI was read to all subjects. Total score on the SIRS was significantly correlated with NIM ($r =.75$), but less closely related to MAL ($r = .57$) and RDF ($r = .40$). Of concern, all PAI cutoff scores appeared to be unacceptable; for example, a NIM cutoff of $\geq 77T$ identified 76% of simulators but only detected 58% of malingerers, while misclassifying 50% of credible patients. A MAL cutoff of ≥ 5 captured between 46% (malingerers) and 52% (simulators) of noncredible participants, but had a 27% false positive rate for credible patients. An RDF cutoff of $\geq 70T$ behaved very differently across noncredible groups, identifying 90% of simulators but only 39% of malingerers, and specificity in credible patients was only 73%. The authors note the possibility that the psychiatrists who identified patients as credible and noncredible were in error at least part of the time; examination of SIRS results showed only 50% sensitivity and 60% specificity for the clinician-based group assignments. When the SIRS was instead used as the "gold standard" for group assignment, 25 of the original 56 patients were identified as malingering. With this group assignment, the NIM cutoff showed 80% sensitivity, MAL was associated with 52% sensitivity, and RDF identified 36% of SIRS-determined malingerers, but all three scales still had inacceptable specificity (68%, 77%, and 71%, respectively).

Three simulation studies have been published since the Sellbom and Bagby (2008) and Hawes and Boccaccini (2009) reviews.

King and Sullivan (2009) studied the effect of "warning" (i.e., being told that the tests could detect malingering) in warned ($n = 24$) and unwarned ($n = 20$) college student simulators and controls ($n = 22$). Simulators were instructed to "believably fake psychological impairment" (p. 39) and were provided with a list of "characteristic disorder symptoms" (p. 39), but were not instructed to fake any particular disorder. Unwarned simulators obtained significantly higher scores on NIM, MAL, RDF, and 11 clinical scales relative to controls, with the exception of the Antisocial Features and Mania scales. Warned simulators obtained

NIM, MAL, RDF, and clinical scale scores that were significantly lower than those of unwarned simulators, and were only significantly different from controls on the Depression scale; warned simulators and controls did not differ on the three overreport indicators. At cutoffs of $\geq 92T$ for NIM (100% specificity), ≥ 5 for MAL (100% specificity), and > 0.12368 for RDF (82% specificity), sensitivity in warned simulators was only 8%, 4%, and 29%, respectively, and for unwarned simulators was 48%, 26%, and 89%, respectively. When queried about the specific faking strategies they employed, most simulators (70%) indicated that they used knowledge gained from the provided list of symptoms, and a minority of both warned and unwarned simulators reported that they were careful not to report extreme or bizarre symptoms.

Lange, Sullivan, and Scott (2010) compared the effectiveness of the PAI and MMPI-2 in identifying protocols of college undergraduates instructed to feign depression ($n = 14$) or PTSD ($n = 15$), or to take the tests honestly ($n = 20$). Simulators scored significantly higher than controls on the NIM and MAL scales, and for RDF, depression simulators scored higher than both PTSD simulators and controls, who did not differ from each other. At a cutoff of $\geq 70T$ for NIM, specificity was adequate (95%), but sensitivity was 53% for feigned PTSD and 71% for feigned depression; at a cutoff of $\geq 80T$, specificity was 100%, but sensitivity was 33% for feigned PTSD and 64% for feigned depression. MAL performed the best of the overreport indicators: A cutoff of ≥ 2 achieved 90% specificity with sensitivity of 73% in the feigned-PTSD group and 79% in the feigned-depression group. A MAL cutoff of ≥ 3 was associated with 100% specificity, but 50–53% sensitivity; when the cutoff was raised to ≥ 5, sensitivity was only 7–14%. For RDF, a cutoff of ≥ 1.80 was associated with 100% specificity, but 7% sensitivity for feigned PTSD and 29% for feigned depression.

Sullivan and King (2010) reported PAI scores in college undergraduates, 22 of whom completed the test under honest conditions, and 19 of whom were instructed to feign psychopathology. Simulators were offered a chance of winning a $100 prize for successful feigning, and were provided with a list of wide-ranging symptoms (the first five of which were somatic symptoms). Postexperimental questionnaires were administered to assess compliance with task instructions. The group feigning psychopathology scored significantly higher on NIM, MAL, and RDF, and on all clinical scales with the exception of Mania and Antisocial Features; overreport of somatic complaints, depression, psychoticism, and phobic anxiety was most flagrant (but was probably a function of the specific list of symptoms provided). When cutoffs of ≥ 73 for NIM, ≥ 3 for MAL, and 0.69 for RDF were applied, specificities were 91–95%, and sensitivities were 74%, 42%, and 84%, respectively. The authors concluded that RDF was most sensitive to feigning.

The problems with applying the findings of the studies cited above to actual clinical practice include likely unreliability of findings due to small n's and/or questionable generalizability of results due to use of simulators. Furthermore, in the studies by King, Sullivan, and colleagues, specificity rates were based on normal individuals, which are not comparable to specificity rates in patients. What is needed is information about how the PAI validity/overreport scale cutoffs behave in actual "real-world" credible and noncredible patient samples.

Mogge et al. (2010) reported on the development of a new PAI validity scale, the Negative Distortion Scale (NDS), intended to discriminate psychiatric inpatients with higher levels of psychopathology from malingerers. The authors note that of the three most commonly used PAI validity/overreport scales (NIM, MAL, and RDF), only NIM relies on rarely endorsed symptoms, but it consists of only eight items, none of which are drawn from the clinical scales. This led the authors to conclude that this limits use of an infrequency strategy, because it "cannot fully measure over-endorsement of rare symptoms across diverse areas of psychopathology" (p. 79). PAI records were accessed from archival data on 475 involuntarily committed inpatients at a state psychiatric hospital who had an average educational level of 11.6 years. The sample was divided in half for purposes of scale development and cross-validation. Data on 82 participants were excluded based on inconsistent responses (Inconsistency scale $> 72T$) or infrequent responses (Infrequency scale $> 74T$), as well as 33 protocols containing missing data. The final sample included of 360 protocols (194 in one group and 166 in the other). The NDS consisted of 15 items from eight clinical scales (Somatic Complaints, Anxiety, Anxiety-Related Disorders, Depression, Mania, Paranoia, Schizophrenia, and Borderline Features) that were rarely endorsed (i.e., were 1.28 SDs below the average item score of the scale from which they were drawn in both samples). NDS was most highly correlated with NIM ($r = .753$), followed by MAL ($r = .638$) and RDF ($r = .389$). In the second study, PAI and SIRS data were accessed from inpatients in a forensic program who had been suspected of noncredible symptom report based on either staff observations or PAI validity scales. Using the SIRS, 56 of 91 were determined to be malingering; mean NDS score in this group was 18.77 ($SD = 7.03$), as compared to 9.89 ($SD = 5.40$) in patients passing the SIRS. At a cutoff score of ≥ 17, NDS specificity was 91%, with sensitivity of 61%. When NIM, MAL, and RDF were entered into a logistic regression along with the NDS, NDS was the only variable retained in the equation. Thus, these preliminary data suggest that NDS has promise in the differential diagnosis between actual and feigned severe psychopathology.

Relationship between PAI Scales and Neurocognitive SVTs

Sumanti et al. (2006) examined the PAI protocols of 233 workers' compensation "stress" claimants who were also administered two cognitive SVTs (Dot Counting Test, Rey 15-Item Memorization Test). Nine percent exceeded the NIM cutoff ($\geq 84T$), and 16% fell beyond the MAL cutoff (≥ 3), but 29% failed RDF ($\geq 60T$).

NIM and MAL were moderately correlated with each other (35% shared variance), but neither was related to RDF (< 1% shared variance). Participants higher on NIM and MAL had elevations on the majority of PAI clinical scales, suggesting indiscriminate endorsement of psychiatric symptoms. Those scoring high on RDF did not report global psychopathology, but only scored higher on Depression and Paranoia. Therefore, RDF appears to be assessing unique parameters of response distortion, distinct from those tapped by NIM and MAL. RDF appears to be more appropriate for use in a workers' compensation "stress" claim population, in that it detects two to three times as many noncredible claimants and captures feigned depressive and paranoid symptoms (which are more plausible in a work stress situation than indiscriminate endorsement of psychiatric symptoms).

Fifteen percent failed the Dot Counting Test (E score ≥ 15), while 8% obtained < 9 items on the Rey 15-Item Memorization Test; 5% failed both. A weak relationship between psychiatric malingering indicators and cognitive SVTs was found; only 2–4% failed both a PAI validity indicator and a cognitive SVT, and correlations between the two sets of tests were modest (< 10% shared variance). Thus, consistent with other literature (see Haggerty, Frazier, Busch, & Naugle, 2007; Nelson et al., 2007; Whiteside, Dunbar-Mayer, & Waters, 2009), the two categories of credibility indicators seem to be measuring different aspects of noncredible symptom production.

It was hypothesized that the PAI profiles of participants failing cognitive SVTs would be higher on the Somatic Complaints, Antisocial Features, and/or Borderline Features scales. However, these subjects scored higher on Somatic Complaints, Depression, Anxiety, and Anxiety-Related Disorders, but not on Borderline or Antisocial Features. These findings suggest that antisocial and/or borderline characteristics do not predispose individuals to symptom feigning, or that when feigning, individuals try to minimize "personal flaws" (such as not being truthful) and will not endorse these characteristics, even if present.

Haggerty et al. (2007) studied the relationship between the PAI NIM scale and the VSVT (Slick, Hopp, Strauss, & Thompson, 1997) in a neuropsychology clinic population. Based on VSVT results, 276 patients were judged to be credible, and 24 were assigned to the noncredible group. Significant although modest correlations were observed between NIM and

VSVT variables (number correct on easy items, $r = -.116$; number correct on difficult items, $r = .125$; easy response latencies, $r = .170$; hard response latencies, $r = .140$).

Subsequently, Whiteside et al. (2009, 2010) evaluated the relationship between the TOMM and PAI validity/overreport and clinical scales in 222 outpatients referred for neuropsychological evaluation, approximately 9% of whom had a motive to feign (they were referred for forensic or disability-related evaluation); 10.5% ($n = 21$) of the sample fell below cutoffs on the TOMM. TOMM Trial 2 was significantly correlated with NIM ($r = -.32$; MAL and RDF were not investigated) and with the Somatic Complaints scale ($r = -.25$), and more minor relationships were found for the Schizophrenia ($r = -.17$), Anxiety ($r = -.16$), and Depression ($r = -.15$) scales. Of note, these four clinical scales are mostly the same ones that Sumanti et al. (2006) found were elevated in subjects failing different SVTs. A cutoff of $>87T$ for the Somatic Complaints scale achieved 76% sensitivity and 93% specificity in identifying those patients who failed the TOMM, leading the authors to conclude that "the evidence suggests that extreme scores on SOM should prompt careful evaluation for suboptimal cognitive effort" (p. 315). However, concerns about this study would include the small percentage of noncredible subjects in the sample (approximate $n = 23$), which renders sensitivity values unreliable. Also, nonsensically, specificity *and sensitivity* levels dropped when the somatic complaints cutoff was lowered to $>70T$ (72% and 67%, respectively). Finally, the percentage of subjects failing the TOMM exceeded the percentage with motive to feign, a finding which is difficult to explain.

In summary and conclusion, PAI overreport studies involving simulators and normal controls show more marked effect sizes than studies employing known groups and actual patient comparison samples, and also at times result in findings opposite to those observed in known-groups studies. For instance, Lange, Sullivan, and Scott (2010), found RDF to be the least effective PAI overreport indicator in identifying simulated depression and PTSD, whereas Sumanti et al. (2006) found that it detected more noncredible workers' compensation "stress" claim applicants than did NIM or MAL. As such, simulation studies of the PAI appear to have limited application in clinical practice.

Seven known-groups studies addressing psychiatric symptom overreport on the PAI in correctional settings have been published; however, in at least six of the seven studies, the credible-patient group appears to have had motives to feign symptoms, and all studies used the SIRS to assign patients to credible and noncredible groups. Regarding the latter issue, some studies (discussed in Chapter 3) show that the SIRS may identify only approximately 50% of noncredible subjects. As a result, when the SIRS is used to assign individuals to research groups, perhaps up to 50% of actual malingerers will be placed in the nonmalingering group (particularly when indeterminate cases are included with honest responders). The result of this error will be to lower the specificity values of test cutoffs; for example, in the Wang et al. (1997) study, the mean NIM score in credible subjects was 81.08, which is above the NIM cutoff score employed in most studies. Thus, while some of the specificity rates reported above are unacceptable, they may be underestimated, and true specificity values may actually be substantially higher. To obtain accurate measures of specificity, studies are needed in which credible comparison groups do not have a motive to feign; this will lessen the need for reliance on overreport measures in assigning subjects to groups.

Available data suggest that to restrict false positive identifications to 10% or less, cutoffs of approximately $\geq 95T$ should be used for NIM and ≥ 5 should be used for MAL in a correctional population; however, associated sensitivity rates are likely to fall between 50% and 65% for NIM and $< 20\%$ for MAL. Whether these cutoffs are useful in a civil population is unknown, but they are probably not, given that individuals in a civil setting do not generally feign severe psychopathology. The most appropriate cutoffs in a civil setting will likely be lower, because the credible comparison group would be individuals with less severe psychiatric disorders (depression, PTSD); these individuals will obtain lower scores on validity scales than do patients with severe psychopathology, allowing cutoffs to be lowered. However, this conclusion requires empirical verification.

The various investigations found that NIM is more effective than MAL and RDF in identifying malingerers in a correctional setting, but this may be at least partially due to the fact that the SIRS was used for group assignment. The SIRS is most highly correlated with NIM, has a more modest relationship with MAL, and has virtually no association with RDF, indicating that RDF is measuring a different aspect of symptom malingering than that tapped by the SIRS. RDF does not appear useful in a correctional population, although some evidence suggests that it has the potential to be the most effective PAI overreport indicator in such civil settings as workers' compensation evaluations and disability seeking. NIM and MAL are likely to be more appropriate for the detection of feigned severe psychopathology, while RDF may be more effective in identifying feigned psychiatric presentations involving more subtle and circumscribed disorders (e.g., depression, paranoia)—symptoms that would be more plausible in a work stress setting or disability seeking than the feigning of severe mental disorders found in a incarcerated population. However, no known-groups studies to date have identified RDF cutoffs in civil settings that limit false positive rates to $\leq 10\%$. Preliminary data on a very new overreport scale (NDS) suggest that it may be more effective than NIM in identifying feigned psychopathology in a correctional setting.

Three known-groups studies have been conducted regarding the relationship between measures of cognitive symptom validity and PAI validity/overreport and clinical scales. The Somatic Complaints scale appears to have more utility in identifying feigned cognitive presentations (at a cutoff of $>87T$; 73% sensitivity at 93% specificity) than any of the PAI overreport/validity scales.

Some studies have suggested that malingerers/simulators do not exhibit elevations on the PAI Mania and Antisocial Features scales. Failure to exaggerate the former symptoms may be due to relative lack of familiarity with characteristics of mania, as well as the fact that fatigue is commonly reported in neuropsychiatric disorders. Furthermore, endorsement of narcissism and/or exploitation of others (the former for mania and the latter for antisocial disorders) may be perceived as counterproductive when a person is attempting to convince others of, and elicit sympathy for, fabricated symptoms.

Millon Clinical Multiaxial Inventory–III

The Millon Clinical Multiaxial Inventory–III (MCMI-III; Millon, 1994), designed for individuals ages 18 and older, is a 175-item true–false inventory that includes 11 Clinical Personality Patterns, 3 Severe Personality Pathology Scales, 7 Clinical Syndrome Scales, and 3 Severe Syndrome Scales. It also incorporates 4 Modifying Indices: V (a "validity" scale consisting of three improbable, low-endorsement items used to detect random responding or content-nonresponsive dissimulation), X (Disclosure Index—self-revealing inclinations toward symptoms), Y (a Desirability Index reflecting fake good responding), and Z (a Debasement Index to measure fake bad responding). In 2009 an inconsistency scale (W) was added.

The original normative data were derived on 998 clinical patients in 26 U.S. states and Canada (600 for scale development and 398 for cross-validation), and in 2009 gender norms derived on 752 males and females were incorporated.

In a survey of test usage in emotional injury evaluations, the MCMI-II or -III was employed in 39% of assessments, and was utilized by 46% of those who classified themselves as "frequent assessors" (Boccaccini & Brodsky, 1999). The survey of NAN and International Neuropsychological Society members cited in earlier sections showed that slightly more than 40% reported some use of the MCMI-III in their neuropsychological evaluations (Smith et al., 2010).

In a meta-analysis of 33 studies examining the convergent and discriminant validity of MCMI instruments in identifying Axis II pathology (Rogers, Salekin, & Sewell, 1999), the authors concluded that the MCMI-III does not meet *Daubert v. Merrell Dow Pharmaceuticals, Inc.* (1993)

criteria for admissibility, because positive findings of personality disorder appear to be incorrect in four out of five instances (although negative findings are acceptably accurate), and minimum requirements for construct validity have not been demonstrated. Error rates have not be reported for the MCMI-II, although research suggests that the Avoidant, Schizotypal, and Borderline scales have good construct validity, in contrast to the moderate construct validity reported for the Schizoid, Dependent, Histrionic, Narcissistic, Antisocial, Aggressive, Negativistic, Self-Defeating, and Paranoid scales, and no demonstrable convergent discriminant validity for the Compulsive scale. Craig (1999) provides further discussion of forensic-related use of MCMI instruments, including recommendations regarding testimony.

Detection of Fake Bad Responding on the MCMI Scales

Daubert and Metzler (2000) note that the MCMI-III was kept brief to protect against fatigue and to be more efficient than longer inventories, but that as a result, less attention was given to incorporating items to assess test-taking validity. Furthermore, the items are mostly "face-valid"; 84% of statements of relevant diagnostic criteria in DSM-IV (105 of 125) have a directly corresponding item on the MCMI-III, and the inventory was intentionally developed to include "obvious" items and to exclude "subtle" criteria. Daubert and Metzler further noted that as of 2000 there had been surprisingly little research on the Modifying Indices.

Bagby, Gillis, Toner, and Goldberg (1991) obtained MCMI-II data for 75 psychiatric inpatients and for 150 college undergraduates who were allowed to chose assignment to one of three conditions: standard ($n = 50$), fake bad ($n = 50$), and fake good ($n = 50$). In the fake bad condition, paticipants were given various scenarios in which feigning of psychiatric symptoms might occur, such as attempting to be acquitted of a criminal charge by reason of insanity, applying for rehabilitation services, and obtaining disability benefits. The fake good scenarios included attempting to obtain custody of children in a divorce, trying to be released from a psychiatric hospital, and applying for a job. Participants were paid $5 and told that if they feigned successfully, they would be entered into a lottery for $100; controls were also entered into the lottery. A discriminant function involving the X, Y, and Z Indices correctly classified between 78% and 87% of inpatients, and between 64% and 68% of fake bad simulators. In the fake good condition, the discriminant function only correctly classified between 64% and 68% of controls, as compared to between 76% and 80% of simulators.

Lees-Haley (1992) examined the MCMI-II Modifying Indices in personal injury litigants who claimed psychological disability from a trauma that did not meet DSM-III-R criteria as an index trauma (e.g., supervisor interrupted claimant's completion of paperwork two to three times per day; supervisor expected claimant to work when not on breaks; claimant received contradictory instructions from two different supervisors; supervisor told claimant to work faster, etc.). The participants were divided into a group with spurious PTSD ($n = 55$) and a control sample ($n = 64$), based on MMPI-2 Keane PTSD scale and Schlenger and Kulka PTSD scale scores of $\geq 65T$ and $\leq 60T$, respectively (and only 1 control obtained a T-score > 65 on the F scale); claimants with actual PTSD were excluded from the control sample. MCMI-II X and Z Index cutoffs of base rate (BR) ≥ 60 identified 73% and 87%, respectively, of the group with noncredible PTSD while correctly classifying 97% of controls. However, the control sample is odd in that those participants were apparently not reporting nonplausble disabling psychological symptoms when completing the personality inventories, but did so on interview.

Wierzbicki (1997) used MCMI-II items rated for subtle versus obvious in a simulation study of 304 college undergraduates who received course credit for participation and who were assigned to six groups: honest responding, fake bad ("appear as pathological or psychologically disturbed as possible"), fake good ("appear as healthy or free of psychological disturbances as possible"), fake antisocial (appear as though "you have a history of severe antisocial aggressive behavior"), fake depression (appear as though "you were suffering from depression or extreme sadness"), and fake alcohol/drug abuse (appear as though "you have a history of severe alcohol and/or drug abuse"). Students in the three latter groups were provided with three common symptoms associated with the disorders. As students endorsed more obvious than subtle items, Z scores rose ($r = .92$) and Y scores declined ($r = -.71$). In discriminant-function analyses, subtle–obvious items correctly classified a similar percentage of group members as the V, Y, and Z Indices (between 69% and 98%).

Daubert and Metzler (2000) administered the MCMI-III to 160 psychiatric outpatients attending day treatment programs who were given the test under standard instructions and fake bad ($n = 80$) or fake good ($n = 80$) instructions; a free meal at a local restaurant was awarded to patients completing the tests accurately. For the fake bad condition, specificity and sensitivity of the X, Y, and Z Indices were relatively poor (X BR ≥ 85 = 81% specificity, 61% sensitivity; Y BR ≤ 35 = 76% specificity, 58% sensitivity; Z BR ≥ 85 = 79% specificity, 55% sensitivity). For the fake good condition, specificity values were better (75–98%), but sensitivity was poor to moderate (10–64%).

Morgan, Schoenberg, Dorr, and Burke (2002) compared MCMI-III and MMPI-2 overreport indicators in 191 psychiatric inpatients, two-thirds of whom were diagnosed with a mood disorder (62%) and 15.5% of whom were diagnosed with an anxiety disorder. The authors noted that the MCMI-III X Index remained valid until the MMPI-2 F scale score approached 120T and Fp exceeded 105T, and they observed that the "MMPI-2 was found to be invalid due to overreport at a rate 29 times greater (29 vs. 1) than the MCMI-III" (pp. 295–296). The authors concluded that the MCMI-III has a "very high tolerance for overreport" (p. 288).

Subsequently, the same authors (Schoenberg, Dorr, & Morgan, 2003) examined the MCMI-III performance of 217 undergraduate students (111 were given standard instructions and 106 were instructed to feign) and of what appeared to be essentially the same clinical sample described above (n = 181). Simulators were asked to complete the MCMI-III as if they were personal injury litigants with severe psychological problems; were provided with symptom information; were told to feign so that they would meet hospital admission criteria; and were also told that if they were success-ful in feigning, they would be entered into a lottery for $200. Simulators were specifically informed that the MCMI-III had four validity scales that checked for symptom exaggeration and random responding. After comple-tion of the MCMI-III, the student subjects were asked to rate the extent to which they exaggerated symptoms, what strategies they used, and how convincingly they feigned. At the published cutoff for the X Index of > 178 (raw score), specificity was 100%, but sensitivity was zero. Using an X Index BR cutoff of > 89, specificity was 88% and achieved 35% sensitivity. Sensitivity of remaining Indexes ranged from 33% to 59%, but specificity was only 66% to 85%.

Relationship between MCMI-III Scales and Neurocognitive SVTs

Ruocco et al. (2008) examined the MCMI-III protocols of 105 compensation-seeking patients primarily claiming TBI (94%; unreported severity), who were also administered two cognitive SVTs (TOMM and the Reliable Digit Span [RDS] from the WAIS-III) as a part of a neuropsychological evalua-tion. Thirty percent of the sample fell below cutoffs for the TOMM, while 34% scored below cutoff scores for the RDS. Among the MCMI-III Modi-fying Indices, however, only 2.9% exceeded cutoffs for X (≥ 85), 1.9% fell below cutoffs for Y (< 24), and 9.5% exceeded cutoffs for Z (≥ 85). TOMM Trials 1 and 2 were significantly related to RDS (r = .31-.32), but no signifi-cant relationships were observed between the MCMI-III Modifying Indices and the two cognitive SVTs (r's ranged from –.22 to .10); only 3.5% of the sample failed both cognitive and psychiatric validity indicators. Also, no significant relationships were observed between the cognitive SVTs and the MCMI-III Clinical Syndrome Scales, including the Somatoform scale (r's of −.01 to −.19), and no differences in MCMI-III profiles were found when the groups passing and failing the TOMM were compared. Factor analysis showed that the MCMI-III Modifying Indices and cognitive SVTs loaded on two different factors representing malingering of psychiatric versus cognitive symptoms.

In contrast, Aguerrevere, Greve, Bianchini, and Ord (2010) found a stronger relationship between malingering of cognitive symptoms and MCMI-III Modifying Indices (X, Y, and Z) in 107 patients with TBI who were referred for neuropsychological evaluation; no significant differences in the Modifying Indices were documented between patients with mTBI (n = 76) and those with moderate/severe TBI (n = 31), and so the groups were collapsed. All but 6 participants had financial motives to feign symptoms, and the sample averaged nearly 2 years postinjury. None had a significant preaccident psychiatric history, and none had been psychiatrically hospitalized postinjury. Of the total sample, 55 met criteria for malingered neurocognitive dysfunction (Slick et al., 1999), 26 were "indeterminate," and 26 were judged to be credible. The group with malingered neurocognitive dysfunction had significantly less education than the credible group (11.5 years vs. 13.8 years), but education was not significantly correlated with MCMI-III Modifying Indices. The malingering group scored significantly differently on all Modifying indices as compared to indeterminate and credible groups, and the indeterminate group's scores were intermediate between those of the two other groups. At cutoffs associated with ≥90% specificity in the credible group, sensitivity was 51% for X (cutoff of ≥65 BR) and Y (cutoff of ≤54 BR), and 55% for Z (cutoff of ≥71 BR). When cutoffs were set to allow no false positive errors (X ≥80, Y ≤50, and Z ≥75), presence of at least one score falling beyond cutoffs resulted in 56% sensitivity. Aguerrevere et al. (2010) suggest that scores falling outside the cutoffs can be indicative of symptom overreport in patients with TBI, including psychological symptom overreport. However, they caution that because their sample excluded patients with significant psychopathology, the cutoffs should not be used as evidence of feigning in psychiatric populations, or in patients with TBI who have a documented history of severe psychiatric illness.

The difference in findings between the Ruocco et al. (2008) and Aguerrevere et al. (2010) studies is likely related to the less stringent MCMI-III cutoffs employed in the latter study, and also perhaps the fact that those with a psychiatric history were excluded from the latter study (as discussed above, the MCMI-III Modifying Indices tend to misidentify psychiatric patients as feigning). In addition, the latter study required that the malingering group meet strict standards (i.e., not just failure on a single SVT), and it was in this group that the relationship between MCMI-III Modifying Indices and feigning of cognitive symptoms emerged.

In summary and conclusion, minimal data are available regarding the ability of the MCMI-II or -III scales X, Y, and Z Indices to identify feigned psychiatric symptoms, and most studies suggest that they perform poorly, even for simulators. Sellbom and Bagby (2008) concluded that due to the paucity of research on the effectiveness of the MCMI-III Modifying Indices, "this shortage precludes the use of these scales for the classification of defensiveness and malingering . . . we do not recommend routine use of these scales in ruling in or ruling out malingering" (p. 188), and they ultimately caution, "Under no circumstances should practitioners use this measure in forensic evaluations to determine response styles" (p. 205). In the Lally (2003) survey of board-certified forensic psychologists, the MCMI-II and -III were rated as "equivocal–unacceptable" in detection of malingering.

Only two studies have investigated use of the MCMI-III in neuropsychological evaluations, and the results appeared contradictory. However, the Aguerrevere et al. (2010) data show that the MCMI-III Modifying Indices have promise if cutoffs are adjusted and if patient samples match the characteristics of those in this study.

PROJECTIVE TECHNIQUES

Rorschach Inkblot Test

The Rorschach Inkblot Test (Rorschach, 1921) consists of 10 ambiguous inkblots shown individually to the test taker with instructions to report what they look like. The rationale behind the test is that individuals "project" aspects of their personalities when trying to decipher unstructured test stimuli, and that their responses will reflect how the persons experience their world, as well as their internal needs, thought processes, interpersonal relationships, and emotions.

In a survey of test usage in emotional injury evaluations in the 1990s, the Rorschach was employed in 28% of assessments, and was utilized by 63% of those who classified themselves as "frequent assessors" (Boccaccini & Brodsky, 1999).

Detection of Fake Bad Responding on the Rorschach

Few studies have examined feigning of psychiatric symptoms on the Rorschach, and all were published prior to 1997; the present discussion includes studies published since 1980. The reader interested in studies published prior to 1980 is referred to the review by Perry and Kinder (1990). Because of the paucity of studies conducted in real-world settings (only one known-groups design), studies employing simulation designs are also included.

Albert, Fox, and Kahn (1980) provided Rorschach protocols to 46 fellows of the Society for Personality Assessment who were asked to provide a diagnosis and informed that the protocols might have "questions of possible malingering." The protocols were obtained on 6 inpatients diagnosed with paranoid schizophrenia, 6 controls, and 18 male undergraduates; 12 of the undergraduates were asked to fake paranoid schizophrenia on the Rorschach (half of these were given a 25-minute tape describing paranoid schizophrenia), and the other 6 took the test under honest conditions. All protocols were scored by the second author (Fox); the scoring system employed was not identified. Each of the 24 protocols was examined by 6–9 fellows. Uninformed malingerers were given diagnoses of psychosis as often as the real patients (46% vs. 48%); informed malingerers were given psychotic diagnoses more often than the real patients (72%); and 24% of normal protocols were diagnosed as psychotic.

Kahn, Fox, and Rhode (1988) obtained 50% of the protocols from the Albert et al. (1980 study) and had them rescored by a professional experienced in the Exner Comprehensive System (Exner, 1974); half of these protocols were rescored by yet another psychologist experienced in the Exner system. Interrater reliability ranged from 64% to 88% depending on the type of response scored, which was deemed adequate. The scoring for each protocol was then analyzed via the "Systematic Interpretation of the Rorschach Protocol Utilizing the Comprehensive System" (Exner, 1985). The computer-generated interpretations did not designate any of the controls as psychotic, whereas virtually all truly psychotic patients were unidentified as psychotic as compared to 50% of uninformed simulators and 80% of informed simulators. These findings led the authors to conclude, "Clearly, the computer-scoring method was taken in to an extreme degree by the fakers" (p. 522). The coauthor of the computer interpretation system subsequently argued (Cohen, 1990) that the Kahn et al. (1988) study suffered from methodological problems, including using the computer-generated statements to make diagnoses; overlooking the fact that the program was not designed to detect malingering, and only identifies invalidity in terms of inadequate number of responses; probable nonstandard administration of the original protocols; too much variation in procedures across studies to allow direct comparison; and unacceptably small n.

Seamons, Howell, Carlisle, and Roe (1981) administered the Rorschach twice to four groups of inpatients hospitalized at a state prison: patients without schizophrenia ($n = 12$), patients with "latent schizophrenia" (past psychotic behavior and current disordered thought processes; $n = 12$), patients with "residual schizophrenia" (past but not current psychotic behavior; $n = 12$), and patients deemed "schizophrenic–psychotic" (past and current psychotic behavior; $n = 12$). Patients were told to provide responses "as if you are a normal well-adjusted individual" and "as if you are mentally ill, as if you are psychotic" (p. 132) in a counterbalanced design; the average time between administrations was 25 days. One examiner administered and scored all protocols according to the Exner Comprehensive System, and a random 20% were rescored by a second person, with at least 90% interrater reliability achieved. Group comparisons showed that under instructions to appear psychiatrically normal, subjects provided more popular responses; under feigning conditions, they produced more dramatic responses (defined as depression themes, sex, blood, gore, mutilation, confusion, hatred, fighting, decapitation). No other significant differences across Exner variables were found, including number of responses. However, a "clinical psychologist with many years of experience with the Rorschach" (p. 132) was reported as achieving 80% accuracy in assigning protocols to feign mental illness and portray mental health conditions. Diagnostic groups differed on several Exner variables, but there were virtually no interactions between extent of psychiatric pathology and instructional set.

Brems and Johnson (1991) examined MMPI and Rorschach data in 292 psychiatric inpatients who were divided into "overreporter" (top quartile; $n = 73$), "standard reporter" (second and third quartiles; $n = 146$), and "underreporter" (bottom quartile; $n = 73$) groups based on MMPI O-S items. Reporting style was unrelated to diagnosis. Overreporters were elevated on MMPI F and clinical scales compared to the other groups, while underreporters were elevated on K and scored the lowest across clinical scales. However, when the Rorschach indices of schizophrenia, suicidal potential, affective ratio, and depression were examined (scoring system not specified), no group differences were found.

Netter and Viglione (1994) assigned 40 normal individuals to either faking or honest conditions; the simulators were given a description of symptoms of schizophrenia and were instructed to convince the examiner that they had schizophrenia. Protocols from 20 patients diagnosed with schizophrenia were also obtained. Rorschach protocols were scored according to the Exner Comprehensive System, and interrater reliability was at least 90% across three raters (one experienced and two graduate students); scores were averaged across raters. The simulators had longer reaction times than the other groups, and half of the malingerers obtained scores of 4 or higher on the Schizophrenia Index (SCZI), which would suggest a moderate likelihood of the condition. The simulators tended to give modified responses, including "mod-spoiled" (initially reporting a normal percept and then making it atypical), "mod-alive" (pretending percept is alive), "mod-circumstantial" (creating a dramatic story about the image), and "mod-distress" (referring to personal distress). In addition, simulators tended to "spoil" popular responses on Card V, and only the malingerers criticized the cards or offered aggressive or provocative comments such as

"How ugly!" or "The color is awful!" One-third of simulators successfully feigned psychosis; the strategies employed included trying to appear aloof/withdrawn; avoiding eye contact; appearing confused, nervous, or uncomfortable; and pretending to hear voices (but atypically, like talking to an imaginary friend).

Ganellen, Wasyliw, Haywood, and Grossman (1996) evaluated Rorschach and MMPI data in 48 defendants who were undergoing evaluation for fitness to stand trial and/or sanity at the time of the offense; the majority were accused of crimes that carried long prison sentences or the death penalty. Thirteen of the subjects were determined to have malingered psychiatric symptoms when an MMPI F T-score cutoff of 90 was used. Rorschach protocols were scored according to the Exner Comprehensive System, and interrater reliability was 95% across at least two of three experienced psychologists. It was hypothesized that credible and noncredible groups would differ on measures of perceptual accuracy (X+%, X–%, Xu%) and thought disorder (Sum 6 Special Scores, Level 2 Special Scores, Deviant Responses); percent positive on the SCZI; and number of populars, a summary measure of Dramatic Content, and number of responses. Significant group differences were only found for Dramatic Content.

In the only study to investigate faked depression on the Rorschach (Meisner, 1988), 58 undergraduates screened for absence of depression took the Rorschach under standard administration, with half again taking the test under instructions to fake depression. They were provided with descriptions of the disorder, and were offered a cash incentive for faking depression in a convincing manner. The Rorschach protocols were scored according to the Exner Comprehensive System; all five raters had scored more than 50 protocols prior to their scorings of the study protocols. Protocols obtained under the faking condition contained more morbid responses but fewer overall responses; no other changes were noted. However, this study does not provide information about how individuals feigning depression score relative to individuals with actual depression.

In the single investigation of feigned PTSD on the Rorschach (Frueh & Kinder, 1994), protocols of 20 male undergraduates asked to fake PTSD were compared to those of 20 veterans with PTSD. Protocols were scored according to the Exner Comprehensive System by a graduate student, with 33% of protocols scored by a second graduate student; interrater agreement was at least 82%. The simulators achieved scores similar to those of patients with PTSD on some Rorschach variables (e.g., number of responses, indicators of disturbed/psychotic thinking, depression, social withdrawal, low stress tolerance). However, the simulators provided more dramatic responses, pure form responses, and color responses, and showed more social ineptness and poor reality testing. Methodological problems with the study include the fact that at least some of the veterans themselves may have been malingering (patients whom the clinical treatment team suspected of malingering were excluded, but some remaining patients were described as "suspicious" toward the testing; presence of secondary gain was not reported).

Of concern, included in the case examples provided in the original publication on the Exner Comprehensive System (Exner, 1974) is a defendant who was probably faking symptoms (Case 3; pp. 374-385), although he is presented as a credible example of an "impulsive" individual. This test taker was under indictment for aggravated assault and attempted homicide, and was referred by the court to determine whether he was "insane" or had neurological or psychological impairments that would constitute mitigating factors (i.e., factors that would advocate for hospitalization rather than trial). The patient claimed to have "no memory for the event," and was also noted to have "marked memory lapses for his various jobs"— assertions that would not be consistent with known patterns of organically based memory impairment. On exam, this defendant was described as "picks his words carefully" and having a "ready smile that seems to have 'cooperativeness' written all over it." Rorschach responses included exaggerated reactions to stimulus cards (e.g., "Holy Christ!," "Oh, you're kidding me aren't you? Am I supposed to tell you what this really looks like to me?", and "Well, I said I'd be honest, you'll probably lock me up and throw away the key . . . "), and upon providing a response with sexual content, he asked, "How's that?" The patient's pattern of responses was interpreted as indicative of "very limited emotional controls," but the possibility of a feigned presentation was not entertained, despite the presence of substantial motive.

Draw-A-Person Test

The Draw-A-Person Test (Goodenough, 1926) requires test takers to complete separate drawings of a man, a woman, and themselves, and was originally developed to measure intelligence, although it is more commonly used as a "projective" measure to assess for personality characteristics. Lilienfeld, Wood, and Garb (2000) have concluded that there are no reliable scoring systems for this test, with the possible exception of Naglieri's (1988) system.

Detection of Fake Bad Responding on the Draw-A-Person Test

Carmody and Crossman (2011) report the only study that could be identified as providing data about feigning on the Draw-A-Person Test. The first experiment involved 61 undergraduates who received course credit for participation; the study was replicated on 65 undergraduates who also received course credit, and 40 high school students who volunteered their time. Undergraduates in the second study completed a debriefing form documenting their knowledge of experiment instructions. All participants were instructed to draw pictures of a man, a woman, and themselves; they were told to draw complete figures and their best possible figures. Participants in the replication study were also encouraged to use the entire time limit of 5 minutes per picture. Undergraduates were tested in small groups (2–5 participants), while the high school students were tested in groups of 12–15. They were then instructed to imagine that they had been in a car accident and stood to gain a large amount of money if they claimed psychological distress. They were told that they would be undergoing a psychological evaluation, during which they would be asked to draw figures, and that they were to "draw the figures as if you are claiming distress as a result of the motor vehicle accident" (p. 3). Drawings were scored according to Naglieri's Quantitative Scoring System, which involves 64 points per figure. The simulation condition was associated with higher scores for emotional disturbance (Experiment 1: 10.46 ± 0.54 vs. 8.00 ± 0.48; Experiment 2: 17.85 ± 0.69 vs. 14.50 ± 0.57), as well as with lower scores for cognitive function; that is, in the simulation condition, figures were more "primitive" (Experiment 1: 93.43 ± 2.86 vs. 120.02 ± 2.48; Experiment 2: 125.43 ± 2.04 vs. 142.45 ± 2.34). The authors conclude that the Draw-A-Person Test is susceptible to malingering, but they suggest the possibility that malingering could be detected if "estimates of cognitive ability based on the drawing scores are much lower than those on an independent cognitive assessment" (p. 7). However, the obvious problem with this study is that no data are reported regarding how actual patients perform.

In summary and conclusion, available data regarding the detection of feigned psychiatric symptoms on the Rorschach and Draw-A-Person Test are problematic, given the small number of studies, reliance on simulation designs, and failure of some investigations to compare feigned protocols with those of actual patients. The studies generally show that simulated symptoms are not detected as such on Rorschach protocols, with the exception that more dramatic responses, criticism of the cards, and longer reaction times may signal the presence of feigning. Furthermore, Rorschach findings do not correspond to MMPI evidence of overreport. No data are available regarding the Rorschach's ability to identified feigned cognitive symptoms, and no published research regarding feigning on the Rorschach has appeared in over 15 years, suggesting that this line of empirical inquiry has dead-ended. The single simulation study of the Draw-A-Person Test revealed that simulators were able to alter their responses to show more signs of emotional distress and cognitive dysfunction, but it is unknown whether simulated responses would differ from those of patients. When board-certified forensic psychologists were surveyed regarding tests they judged to be appropriate for determination of malingering, the Rorschach and other projective drawing techniques were assigned to the "unacceptable" category (Lally, 2003).

PTSD SYMPTOM MEASURES

Trauma Symptom Inventory

The Trauma Symptom Inventory (TSI; Briere, 1995) is a 100-item inventory designed to assess for posttraumatic stress and other psychological symptoms of exposure to traumatic events, such as rape, spouse abuse, physical assault, combat, major accidents, natural disasters, and child abuse/other early trauma. The 10 clinical scales assess for Anxious Arousal, Depression, Anger/Irritability, Intrusive Experiences, Defensive Avoidance, Dissociation Behavior, Sexual Concerns, Dysfunctional Sexual Behavior, Impaired Self-Reference, and Tension Reduction Behavior. Three validity scales are scored: Response Level (RL; measuring underreport), Atypical Response (ATR; assessing for overreport or psychosis/extreme distress), and Inconsistent Response (INC).

Normative data were obtained from a stratified, random sample based on geographic locations of registered owners of automobiles and/or individuals with listed telephones; 1,442 participants had deliverable addresses, and 836 completed the survey including the TSI. Gender distribution was approximately equal (50.5% male), and the majority of the sample was Caucasian (77.5%; 10.3% African American, 6.1% Hispanic, 2.9% Asian, and 2.3% Native American). Ethnic differences were only found on validity scales, and the manual includes the following caution to the clinician: "Because African Americans and Hispanic respondents in the standardization sample scored an average of 3 to 5 points above the expected T score on the three validity scales, those interpreting TSI scores of African American or Hispanic respondents may wish to adjust the cutoff score for a valid profile accordingly for these two groups" (p. 31).

In a survey of psychological test usage in emotional injury evaluations, the TSI was employed in 15% of assessments, and was utilized by 29% of those who classified themselves as "frequent assessors" (Boccaccini & Brodsky, 1999).

Detection of Fake Bad Responding on the TSI

The test manual indicates that protocols with an ATR scale T-score of ≥ 90 should be considered invalid. This cutoff was derived by identifying the

T-score associated with the top 1.5% of item endorsers. Thus this cutoff would be associated with 98.5% specificity in normal individuals, but since no noncredible subjects were studied, no information is available regarding cutoff sensitivity.

A few subsequent studies have investigated the effectiveness of the ATR scale in simulators. Edens, Otto, and Dwyer (1998) examined this scale in 155 college student simulators (77% female), who were instructed to complete the TSI in an honest condition and in a simulation condition in which they were told to respond to the inventory as if they were plaintiffs in a personal injury lawsuit and were claiming emotional trauma. All male participants and half of the female participants were instructed to assume that their psychological claims were related to an automobile accident, while the remaining female participants were told to complete the inventory as if they had been sexually assaulted and were seeking damages. All participants were given a one-page description of PTSD symptoms that they were able to refer to while completing the TSI under simulation conditions. Half the students completed the TSI under honest conditions first, while the other half completed the TSI under feigning conditions first. Participants were informed that 1 out of 30 who feigned most effectively would be provided with a $30 reward. After completion of the TSI, participants were surveyed regarding their understanding of task instructions; after completion of the simulation trial, they were queried about the level of their motivation to follow test instructions, and they also completed a checklist asking for strategies they used when feigning. Evidence of inconsistency associated with random responding (>65T on the INC scale) or incorrect responding when asked about understanding of task instructions resulted in deletion of data from 35 subjects (final n of 155).

The two simulation groups did not differ on ATR scores (sexual assault = 73.29T, automobile accident = 76.16T), and no test order effects were found; as a result, simulation groups were collapsed. Participants obtained significantly higher scores on ATR and INC and significantly lower scores on RL in the simulation condition as compared to the honest condition. Students with histories of moderate trauma (n = 63) did not perform significantly differently from those without trauma histories when completing the TSI in simulation conditions. When an ATR cutoff of >61T was applied to the first half of the sample, sensitivity was 82% and specificity was 92%; comparable results were obtained when this cutoff was applied to the second half of the sample (73% sensitivity, 92% specificity). With application of the recommended ATR cutoff of 90T, specificity was >99%, but sensitivity was only 27%.

Lowering the ATR cutoff to 61T resulted in 81% sensitivity while specificity was 95.2% in the 63 participants with trauma histories; 83% in 18 participants with histories of attempted or actual sexual abuse; 90% in

10 participants with at least a moderately traumatic auto accident within 6 months; and 85% in 20 participants with histories of at least moderate trauma within 6 months and with at least one elevated clinical score. This cutoff was also applied to available archival datasets and revealed specificity rates of 85% in 73 participants in the TSI normative sample in therapy; 81% in an unpublished data set of 243 female college students with reported history of physical or sexual abuse in childhood; 84% in 97 psychiatric outpatients; 45% in 114 patients in partial hospitalization; 86% in 21 patients with PTSD resulting from physical abuse; 96% in 27 patients with traumatic sexual abuse; 94% in 32 patients with major depression; 94% in 32 patients with personality disorder; and 75% in 20 patients with PTSD associated with a recent life-threatening event. Raising the cutoff to $\geq 65T$ increased specificity to generally acceptable limits ($\geq 87.7\%$), with the exception of psychiatric outpatients (85.6%), patients in partial hospitalization (52.8%), and patients with PTSD associated with a recent life-threatening event (75%); sensitivity rates at this cutoff were not reported.

Guriel et al. (2004) obtained TSI protocols from 68 college students assigned to either an honest-responding group ($n = 10$) or one of three groups instructed to simulate PTSD symptoms associated with a motor vehicle accident for a civil litigation lawsuit: uncoached feigning ($n = 19$), coached regarding symptoms (provided with a list of PTSD symptoms available from the Internet; $n = 23$), and coached regarding symptoms and strategies (provided with a list of PTSD symptoms available from the Internet, but also informed about strategies that would help them to evade detection; $n = 16$). Coached simulators were required to pass a quiz regarding the information provided before they completed the TSI. Honest responders obtained significantly lower ATR scores than the other three groups (mean of 49.80 vs. 83.53 in uncoached, 79.35 in PTSD information only, and 75.56 in PTSD information plus strategies to evade detection). When cutoffs for ATR of $> 61T$, INC of $> 65T$, and RL of $> 65T$ were used, sensitivity was 73.7% in uncoached simulators, 73.9% in those coached with information only, and 81.3% in those coached in avoidance of detection strategies. However, specificity was only 80% (and these were normal subjects!)

Elhai et al. (2005) reported that the ATR scale discriminated poorly between a sample of 47 victims of violent crime who were diagnosed with PTSD and had received treatment, and 63 college student simulators who were allowed 25 minutes to study information on PTSD, on which they were later quizzed (those scoring $< 70\%$ correct were excluded). Simulators selected among scenarios involving feigning of PTSD in the contexts of motor vehicle accidents, gang physical attack, or sexual assault, and prizes were awarded to simulators whose protocols most resembled those of patients. Following completion of the TSI, simulators were surveyed regarding confidence in portrayal of PTSD, motivation to feign, clarity of the training material, understanding of PTSD, and previous familiarity with PTSD. Protocols with high INC scale scores were excluded, as were protocols of simulators who had endorsed histories of possible PTSD. At the recommended ATR cutoff of $\geq 90T$, specificity was high (95.7%) but sensitivity was just 22.2%. Lowering the cutoff to $61T$ increased sensitivity to 65.1%, but specificity was only 55.3%. Fewer than 5% of patients scored higher than $87T$, but, unfortunately, a cutoff associated with 90% specificity was not reported.

Carmody and Crossman (2005) conducted a simulation study with 100 undergraduates who received course credit for participation (in lieu of completing a paper, deemed "motivated by avoidance") and with a second sample of 50 undergraduates who received $8 for participation (with the incentive of an additional $50 for successful feigning; deemed "motivated by money"). Participants first completed the TSI under standard conditions; they then received a 10-minute training session on the symptoms of PTSD accessed from information on the Internet, as well as a three-page handout on the material. They were then instructed to complete the TSI as if they had been in a motor vehicle accident and were attempting to feign trauma associated with that accident but not to fabricate psychosis, including hallucinations, or respond inconsistently. Participants completed a posttest questionnaire to ensure that they had understood instructions. The two groups did not differ in test scores, and scores in the simulation condition were significantly higher than scores in the honest condition. In the honest condition, 9 protocols exceeded validity scale cutoffs (ATR = $90T$, INC $75T$, RL $73T$) and 35 protocols surpassed the trauma summary scale cutoff ($65T$); all data from these subjects were excluded from further analyses. Successful feigning in the simulation condition was defined as an ATR score of $< 90T$ and scores of $> 65T$ on the trauma scales; 86 of the 106 participants had elevated scores on trauma scales and 47 passed the validity scales, indicating that 44% successfully feigned (41% in the course credit group and 51% in the compensation group).

Guriel-Tennant and Fremouw (2006) recruited 113 undergraduates, 66 of whom had experienced a traumatic event. The students were assigned to four simulation groups: positive for trauma, coached ($n = 31$); positive for trauma, naïve ($n = 35$); negative for trauma, coached ($n = 25$); and negative for trauma, naïve ($n = 22$). Coaching was provided through a 15-minute video and accompanying handout of information on PTSD accessed from attorney internet sites, DSM-IV criteria for PTSD, and strategies for avoiding detection. All participants then were administered a quiz on the material; coached simulators were required to obtain 90% accuracy, and none of the naïve simulators achieved 90% accuracy. Simulators were instructed to feign symptoms of PTSD secondary to a motor vehicle accident in order to obtain a lawsuit award of $1,000,000. They were provided with extra course credit and were told about the potential of receiving a $50 award via lottery for successful feigning. Mean ATR *T*-scores across the four groups were 80.9 ± 18.97 (trauma-positive/naïve), 60.8 ± 19.06 (trauma-positive/coached), 80.2 ± 21.85 (trauma-negative/naïve), and 61.1 ± 18.66 (trauma-negative/coached), and showed that coached participants obtained lower scores. No credible groups were studied.

Rosen et al. (2006) instructed 161 college students to complete the TSI under honest (*n* = 60) or simulation conditions in which they were to portray litigants either feigning symptoms of trauma from a motor vehicle accident (*n* = 52) or workplace sexual harassment (*n* = 49). Instructions described the traumatic events and symptoms of PTSD. Simulators obtained significantly higher scores on the ATR scale and 9 of 10 clinical scales. The two simulation groups only differed on 2 clinical scales, so scores from the two groups were collapsed. At a cutoff of >60*T* on the ATR, sensitivity was 68.3% but specificity was 80% (cutoffs that corresponded to at least 90% specificity were not provided). When the ATR cutoff of >61*T* was applied to the subset of the sample under honest conditions who obtained 2 or more elevated scores on clinical scales, specificity was only 57.9%.

Porter, Peace, and Emmett (2007) collected TSI data on 126 undergraduates who had reported experiencing at least one lifetime significant trauma event since age 16. Subjects were asked to write about their actual traumatic event or a fabricated trauma event (counterbalanced order), and to complete the TSI. For fictionalized events, the subjects were instructed to pretend as if the fake trauma had occurred and to complete the TSI "as convincingly as possible. " Those fabricating an event obtained a mean ATR scale *T*-score of only 59.06 (*SD* = 15.32) versus 51.32 (*SD* = 8.1) in those reporting an actual event. Peace, Porter, and Cook (2010) subsequently obtained data for both actual and fabricated trauma events (counterbalanced order) for three TSI administrations (Time 2 was an average of 91 days after Time 1, and Time 3 was an average of 72 days after Time 2) in 291 college undergraduates, all of whom reported a highly traumatic event after the age of 16 that could be externally verified. Course credit or monetary compensation was provided, and bonus extra credit was offered to those subjects who faked successfully. The majority of TSI protocols were valid in both groups at all three points in time (truthful, 88.5–94.4%; deceptive, 84.4–87.3%); the mean ATR *T*-score on all three administrations was 57.3 in fabricators versus 52.6 in truthful reporters. The ATR scale (cutoff not reported, but assumed to be ≥91*T*) was not effective in identifying feigned protocols (<16% sensitivity); it also had a not insignificant false positive rate (5.6–11.5%).

Efendov, Sellbom, and Bagby (2008) administered the TSI to 60 patients with "remitted" trauma who first took the TSI honestly, and then were instructed to fake workplace PTSD for disability compensation in a "convincing and believable manner" and were presented with a context and scenario for feigning (half received information about the ATR scale); all received $75 for participation and were told that the participant who feigned most effectively would receive an additional $200. TSI protocols were also obtained on 84 patients with workplace trauma who were applying for disability (individuals in whom malingering was diagnosed were excluded, although the number excluded was not specified; unspecified psychological test data were used to identify malingering). The mean ATR T-score was 78.31 in uncoached simulators and only 67.39 in coached simulators, but was 64.85 in patients with PTSD. At an ATR cutoff of $\geq 90T$, specificity was 87% and sensitivity was 34% in uncoached simulators and 16% in coached simulators. When the cutoff was dropped to $\geq 61T$, sensitivity was 72% in uncoached simulators and 55% in coached simulators, but specificity was only 51%. These results led the authors to conclude: "The results of the current investigation suggest the ATR is largely ineffective in detecting feigned PTSD. The ATR showed nonsignificant group effects between the validity scale coached participants and PTSD claimants, demonstrated poor classification accuracy, and conferred no significant increase in incremental validity over the original family of F scales" (pp. 323–324). However, the rather elevated ATR T-score in the supposedly true PTSD group raises questions as to whether malingerers were retained in this group, which then would have artificially lowered cutoff specificity.

In a study examining specificity only, Nye, Qualls, and Katzman (2006) obtained TSI data on 47 male veterans who had been diagnosed with PTSD by trained clinicians and whose combat zone experience had been verified; all were currently receiving treatment. Veterans with psychotic disorder or organic brain dysfunction were excluded. Nine TSI protocols were invalid (eight with ATR scores exceeding the "recommended" cutoff = 83% specificity, and one with an INC score exceeding the cutoff). No differences in demographic or historical variables were found between those obtaining valid and invalid profiles. Furthermore, those with invalid profiles were already service-connected for PTSD (i.e., condition was judged to be related to military service and, therefore eligible for compensation) at ratings between 70% and 100%, and none had claims to increase ratings; however, these veterans may have been concerned that their ratings might be lowered, and thus secondary gain may have been a possibility.

In the service of learning more about this test, I myself completed the TSI as if I were faking PTSD symptoms secondary to a motor vehicle accident. I was not tentative about reporting PTSD symptoms, as evidenced by the nearly ceiling scores on the Anxious Arousal (raw = 23 out of 24, 79T), Anger/Irritability (raw = 25 out of 27, 77T), Intrusive Experiences (raw = 20 out of 24, 75T), and Defensive Avoidance (raw = 23 out of 24, 76T) scales. Yet my ATR T-score was only 61—well below the test manual cutoff, but interestingly, the cutoff employed in several of the studies cited above. However, use of this latter cutoff cannot be recommended because of the poor specificity rates noted above.

To summarize the problems with the TSI, ethnic minority representation in the normative sample was problematic, with ethnic minorities scoring higher on validity scales. Furthermore, no study could be identified that provided TSI overreport data (ATR scores) for real-world noncredible individuals; all investigations have involved use of simulators, and thus applicability of findings to actual clinical practice is problematic. In addition, available data indicate that the ATR cutoff of $\geq 90T$ recommended in the manual is ineffective (< 30% sensitivity), but that this cutoff cannot be substantially lowered without decreasing specificity to unacceptable levels. Of note, none of the examples in the manual indicated whether the cases had motive to feign (e.g., were seeking compensation), suggesting that the test was not developed with concerns about malingering in mind, despite the fact that DSM-IV-TR specifically advises ruling out malingering in the diagnosis of PTSD (American Psychiatric Association, 2000, p. 467). Resnick, West, and Payne (2008), in a review of techniques to assess for feigned PTSD, asserted: "Currently, research has demonstrated significant limitations of the ATR scale when utilized within genuine trauma populations" (p. 121). Gray, Elhai, and Briere (2010) acknowledged that the original ATR was not effective in identifying malingering, attributing this finding to the fact that "the ATR was not designed to detect PTSD malingering specifically" (p. 448). Finally, Briere (2001) noted that "because the TSI measures traumatic responses that may have occurred in the prior 6 months and does not address all of the DSM-IV-TR symptoms of post-traumatic stress, it cannot be used to generate a PTSD or an ASD (Acute Stress Disorder) diagnosis" (p. 6).

Trauma Symptom Inventory–2

The Trauma Symptom Inventory–2 (TSI-2; Briere, 2011) was standardized with 678 U.S. residents recruited through an independent survey company who were between the ages of 18 and 90. Exclusion criteria included incarceration; inpatient medical or psychiatric hospitalization; current treatment for psychotic disorder; uncorrected vision or hearing loss; inability to understand English or read at the third-grade level; and inability to provide informed consent. Three-quarters were Caucasian, gender distribution was relatively equal, and the mean age was 53; no differences in scores across ethnic groups were found. Thirty-two percent of the sample reported experiencing a traumatic event, and 8% had sought psychological counseling within the previous 6 months.

Detection of Fake Bad Responding on the TSI-2

According to the TSI-2 manual, the TSI-2 includes an eight-item revised ATR scale containing items that appear to be plausible symptoms of PTSD but in fact are less likely to be endorsed by actual sufferers from PTSD, in contrast to the bizarre and extreme symptom items contained in the original ATR. An elevation on the TSI-2 ATR scale is judged to reflect generalized overendorsement of psychiatric symptoms, overendorsement of PTSD symptoms, random responding, or "very high levels of distress"("cry for help"; Briere, 2011, p. 14). A raw score cutoff of 15 (which corresponds to a T-score of 110) is recommended for clinical and forensic contexts, while a cutoff of 8 is suggested for screening contexts and testing of normal individuals. It is noted that although the items on the revised ATR are unlikely to be true of the majority of actual patients with PTSD, on occasion isolated items will accurately reflect a particular patient's functioning, in which case the item is to be deleted and the average of the remaining ATR items substituted for the discarded item.

The TSI-2 manual reproduces data obtained from 32 combat veterans, 30 individuals with diagnoses of borderline personality disorder, 32 victims of sexual abuse, and 31 victims of domestic violence; 84% were Caucasian and 68% were female. All of these groups scored significantly higher on the revised ATR scale than did matched controls from the larger standardization sample; whereas control groups averaged a revised ATR T-score between 47 and 52, combat veterans obtained a mean of 64.1 (SD = 16.6), the group with borderline personality averaged 67.9 (SD = 22.5), victims of sexual abuse averaged 70.3 (SD = 21.2), and victims of domestic violence averaged 69.7 (SD = 21.7). In a sample of 124 university students divided into PTSD simulators and those who met criteria for PTSD on the PTSD Checklist and were instructed to take the test honestly, a raw score cutoff of 8 was associated with 83% specificity and 65% sensitivity. The raw score cutoff of 15 was associated with at least 95% specificity in incarcerated women and patients with borderline personality disorder, and resulted in a 10.9% false positive rate in patients with PTSD; sensitivity rates associated with the cutoff of 15 could not be located in the manual.

Gray et al. (2010) reported TSI-2 data for 49 college students with genuine PTSD symptoms (i.e., they reported experiencing an index event and endorsed symptoms of PTSD on the PTSD Checklist) and 75 college student simulators reporting no PTSD index events. Over 87% of the sample was Caucasian. Simulators were allowed to study informational materials on PTSD, and were quizzed regarding their knowledge (none scored below 70% on a 10-point quiz); they were also provided with monetary incentives. The authors indicated that the revised ATR scale (at a raw score cutoff of 7) performed better than the original ATR, in that it correctly classified approximately 75% of students with genuine PTSD and 74% of simulators. However, even when the cutoff was raised to 8, specificity still did not reach acceptable levels (83%) and sensitivity dropped to 65%. Concerns about the methodology of this study include the fact that individuals with PTSD currently attending college are likely to represent the more functional end of the PTSD population, and thus the specificity values derived in this sample probably represent overestimates.

In summary, although it has been argued that that the revised ATR scale on the TSI-2 is an improvement on the original ATR, no sensitivity data are available for the recommended raw score cutoff of 15. A "screening" cutoff of 8 is associated with unacceptably low specificity in persons with arguably only mild PTSD, and sensitivity is only moderate in simulators.

Detailed Assessment of Posttraumatic Stress

The Detailed Assessment of Posttraumatic Stress (DAPS; Briere, 2001) is a 104-item inventory designed to assess for trauma exposure and posttraumatic response through four Trauma Specification scales (Relative Trauma Exposure, Onset of Exposure, Peritraumatic Distress, and Peritraumatic Dissociation), five Posttraumatic Stress scales (Reexperiencing, Avoidance, Hyperarousal, Posttraumatic Stress—Total, and Posttraumatic Impairment), and three Associated Features scales (Trauma-Specific Dissociation, Substance Abuse, and Suicidality). Two validity scales are also included: Positive Bias (PB; underreport) and Negative Bias (NB; overreport). Normative data were obtained from a stratified, random sample based on geographic locations of registered owners of automobiles and/or individuals with listed telephones. Of the 620 with completed surveys (including the DAPS), 71% reported at least one DSM-IV-TR-level traumatic event in the past; the DAPS was developed and normed on the latter group. Gender distribution was fairly equal (52.7% male), and a significant gender effect was found, necessitating separate gender norms. The majority of the sample was Caucasian (83.4%; 6.5% African American, 4.0% Hispanic, 2.8% Asian, and 1.9% Native American). No differences among ethnic groups were found, but analyses probably lacked sufficient power to detect any actual differences.

Detection of Fake Bad Responding on the DAPS

Like the overreport scale for the TSI, the NB scale on the DAPS was derived by identifying a *T*-score cutoff representing endorsement of statistically unusual phenomena in the validation group. Thus, although this provides specificity data, no information is available regarding cutoff sensitivity, since no noncredible participants were studied.

The manual recommends that an NB *T*-score of 75 or higher be considered invalid. A search of research databases shows *no* studies investigating the effectiveness of the NB scale, however. Furthermore, as for the TSI, case examples contained in the DAPS manual do not indicate whether the cases had a motive to feign PTSD. In the interest of test security, the NB items are not reproduced here, but they can be found in the manual. Perusal of them reveals that they would not appropriately detect faked PTSD symptoms in a litigation setting. That is, the items are preposterous and would only be endorsed by individuals who might be trying to feign severe psychosis.

I also completed the DAPS as if I were faking PTSD symptoms secondary to a motor vehicle accident. Again, I was not tentative about reporting PTSD symptoms, as evidenced by the nearly ceiling scores on the Reexperiencing (raw = 36; 95*T*), Avoidance (raw = 40; 99*T*), Hyperarousal (raw = 50; ≥100*T*), Posttraumatic Stress—Total (raw = 126; ≥100*T*), Posttraumatic Impairment (raw = 24; ≥100*T*), and Trauma-Specific Dissociation (raw = 11; 99*T*) scales. Yet my NB score was 72*T* (raw score of 11), below the test manual cutoff.

To summarize the problems with the DAPS, the overreport scale (NB) has not been empirically validated, and whether there are ethnicity-related differences in test scores has not been adequately tested.

5

Test Scoring/Interpretation
and the Neuropsychological Report

TEST SCORING

The Need to Recheck Scoring

Before memorializing any conclusions in a report, a neuropsychologist should recheck test scoring, particularly in areas where errors will have a major impact on the conclusions. On two occasions, I have testified oppo- site neuropsychologists who made gross errors in calculating IQ scores. One administered four of five WAIS-III Performance subtests, but failed to use the table in the test manual for prorating the sum of Performance subtest scaled scores; the reported PIQ was incorrect by a magnitude of 10 points. In the second case, a plaintiff was tested on four separate occa- sions in the clinic of the plaintiff-retained neuropsychologist; on the first exam, VIQ was 10 points lower than PIQ, while on the subsequent three exams, the two IQ scores were essentially comparable. The plaintiff neuro- psychologist attempted to make the case that the plaintiff's claimed expo- sure to carbon monoxide had caused a transitory lowering of VIQ, which had subsequently normalized. However, on rescoring of the WAIS-III, it was found that the initial examiner had misadded the Verbal subtest scores in computing the sum used to obtain the VIQ. In fact, the true VIQ was 10 points higher and comparable to the PIQ. Scoring of IQ tests is a skill taught in the first year of clinical psychology graduate training, and it is doubtful whether psychologists can rehabilitate their testimony if the IQ scores they report are substantially in error.

161

The Need for Careful Selection of Normative Data

For those tests that do not have up-to-date normative data in the test manuals, care should be taken in selecting norms for use in interpreting a patient's scores. Preferably, normative data should be selected that match the patient in demographic characteristics—particularly age and educational level, and in the case of motor and verbal memory tests, gender. However, this is a bit more complicated than it appears.

First is the problem of correcting for educational level. Correcting for age and gender is straightforward; age and gender have a *unidirectional* relationship with cognitive scores. For example, advancing age leads to lower performance in cognition, but lower cognitive ability does not influence age. Similarly, gender influences specific neurocognitive skills, but neuropsychological functioning does not have any impact on gender. However, education has a *bidirectional* relationship with cognitive scores: Lower education leads to lowered cognitive scores, but lower cognitive ability also limits educational level. Specifically, individuals of very low intellectual levels do not get very far in school. Thus it is appropriate to control for/adjust for the impact of age and gender on cognitive scores, but it is not *necessarily* appropriate to control for the impact of educational level on cognitive scores. That is, it is only appropriate to adjust for educational level if the person did not have an opportunity to obtain education; it is not appropriate if the person has low cognitive ability and would not have benefited from further education. A neuropsychologist who adjusts for low educational level in a patient of low cognitive ability is likely to "correct" the patient out of his/her low cognitive scores. This may inappropriately cause the patient not to qualify for services or disability compensation, make him/her eligible for the death penalty, or have other very negative results. On the other hand, if the neuropsychologist does not correct for educational level in a patient who has adequate intellectual capability but who discontinued education because of environmental factors (e.g., having to go to work to support the family, pregnancy, etc.), the person will be judged to be of lower cognitive ability than is actually the case, and may be deprived of scholarships, or work opportunities.

But how are neuropsychologists to determine when to make education corrections? At this point, the decision is based on qualitative analysis of school records and psychosocial data. If the patient was performing adequately in school but left because of pregnancy, decision to join the workforce, or the like, then education adjustments should be applied to test scores. However, if a patient struggled in school, was placed in special education, had very low scores on academic testing, and discontinued school in the ninth grade because he/she was not "getting it," it is highly questionable whether corrections for truncated education should be applied to neuropsychological test scores. In other words, in the former case, the patient would likely have benefited from additional education in terms of increase in cognitive skills; in the latter case, no amount of education would have altered the patient's cognitive functionality.

A second problem regarding the use of demographically corrected norms is the propensity to "forget" that the norms were demographically corrected when one is drawing conclusions about cognitive function. I have seen many reports in which the neuropsychologist opined that average scores were below expectation for a patient with above-average intelligence, but upon closer examination of the patient's neuropsychological test scores, they had been corrected for educational level. Thus the scores were "average," but only as compared to individuals of above-average educational level (and thus not likely to be truly "average").

This raises the obvious issue that if neuropsychologists are primarily interested in determining how a patient is performing relative to the "average" individual, then normative data from individuals of average levels of education (e.g., high school) should be employed. Alternatively, a neuropsychologist could report scores both ways—that is, against absolute "average" individuals and against individuals of the patient's age and educational level. This would enable the neuropsychologist to give an opinion about how the patient compares to "average" individuals (allowing for documentation of "absolute" levels of cognitive dysfunction), but also to draw conclusions about how the patient performs versus individuals of the same educational level (allowing for judgments about cognitive deficits relative to the patient's peer group). Such data would allow for nuanced conclusions. For example, a surgeon undergoing evaluation for disability compensation might have average scores as compared to those of similar-age peers. However, when compared to peers of similar age *and* education, he might be performing poorly, indicating that he should probably not return to the field of surgery. If only the first norms were used, he might be deemed cognitively intact and adequately equipped to function as a surgeon, but I myself would not want someone of only average cognitive abilities conducting surgery on me. If only the latter norms were used, showing the patient as "below average," not only would he be judged to be unable to return to work as a surgeon; his lowered scores might lead the psychologist to conclude (inaccurately) that there are concerns regarding his ability to drive, handle his own finances, or perform other tasks that an individual of average skills can certainly engage in.

It is critical that neuropsychological reports indicate not only raw scores, but also which normative data were used. In this era of "evidence-based" practice and transparency (i.e., showing exactly how one's conclusions were derived), the normative data employed should be referenced so that subsequent psychologists can follow the report writer's "road map" as to how the conclusions were generated. I cannot begin to count the number of neuropsychological reports I have read that contain mysterious "percentiles," the origins of which cannot be deciphered. For those of us who attended graduate school a generation ago, it was common practice not to report test scores, let alone the normative data employed. The rationale at that time was that the reader was not adequately sophisticated to understand the scores and would misinterpret them. In retrospect, probably the major reason for omission of test scores from reports was that psychologists did not want to have anyone to "check" their work or to be held accountable for the bases for their conclusions.

Referencing the normative samples used can open a neuropsychologist to criticism over why particular norms were chosen, and thus it is incumbent upon the clinician to have a reasonable rationale for why particular norms were selected (e.g, that these norms best matched patient demographic data, corresponded to the specific test administration format followed, etc.).

IMPORTANT ASPECTS OF INTERPRETATION AND REPORTING

Maintaining Test Security

Although test raw scores and referenced percentiles should be contained in neuropsychological reports, neuropsychologists should be vigilant about maintaining test security. Therefore, actual test paradigms should not be described. Unfortunately, I have seen many reports that described test stimuli and administration formats in intricate detail. The descriptions appeared to be "boilerplate"—inserted into all reports, and were apparently intended to lengthen the product and thereby to provide justification for the amount of the billed fee. However, if test formats are summarized in neuropsychological reports, then that information can be used to prepare future test takers to evade detection on SVTs and to alter their performance on standard neuropsychological measures. Neuropsychological tests are only effective in measuring cognitive ability and response bias when test takers are naïve to the test content and format.

Labeling of Percentiles

After scores are converted to percentiles or standard scores, the neuropsychologist must then label the performance. Guilmette, Hagan, and Giuliano (2008) note that "the descriptive label for a range of scores may significantly impact the trier of fact who must apply the law to the evidence.

It can have an impact of a lifetime for the injured person and the defendant" (p. 124). They further warn that "the interests of the court and the image of the field are likely not advanced when opposing experts in the field of neuropsychology examine the same test data produced by the same individual at the same time and then assign divergent qualitative labels to that test performance data" (p. 123). Their survey of 110 board-certified neuropsychologists showed variability in labels, although on average 71% of the sample endorsed the two most common descriptors for the 12 standard scores presented.

Lezak, Howieson, and Loring (2004) recommend that neuropsychologists, in describing ability levels, employ the labels provided in the Wechsler test manuals. The advantages of these labels are that they (1) are yoked to the Wechsler intelligence tests, the most commonly administered psychological measures (Lees-Haley, Smith, Williams, & Dunn, 1995; Rabin, Barr, & Burton, 2005; Watkins, Campbell, Nieberding, & Hallmark, 1995), thereby providing consistency between IQ test result descriptors and those of remaining neuropsychological tests; and (2) incorporate acknowledgment of the bell-shaped distribution of scores in the normal population into interpretation. For example, WAIS-III IQ scores of 80–89 are found in 16% of the normal population; the WAIS-III manual labels these as "low average," in recognition that such scores, though below average, are not unusual in the standardization sample. Although some neuropsychologists refer to scores from the 9th to the to 25th percentile as "mildly impaired," "moderately impaired," "borderline impaired," or just "impaired" (Guilmette et al., 2008), such scores are not rare and therefore should not be designated as "impaired." The term *impairment* refers to an anomalous condition, and by definition, 16% of persons in the normal population are not anomalous. The forensic neuropsychologist should be able to articulate why he/she has employed particular labels in describing scores in a report, as well as to provide references concerning the origin of the labels.

A related issue is what constitutes functional "impairment." Some clinicians assume that an "impaired" score constitutes "impairment" in ADLs. Although this may be the case, it is not always. An impaired score refers to distance from the normative mean, but may not translate into true substantial dysfunction in a skill. For example, given the small standard deviations on the Comalli version of the Stroop Test, a rapid word-reading score may fall more than 2 SDs from the mean (mean = 45 seconds, patient's score = 70 seconds; SD = 6.7). Nevertheless, taking 70 seconds to complete a task that others of the same age can complete in 45 seconds is not likely to indicate a true functional impairment in rapid word reading (i.e., individuals with the former score would probably be able to read words at a speed required for most work settings).

Estimating Premorbid Cognitive Function

Estimating Premorbid IQ

Many neuropsychologists employ various equations and tests in an attempt to estimate premorbid IQ. Two primary approaches to premorbid IQ estimation have been adopted: demographic equations, and performance on so-called "hold" tests (i.e., tests of skills thought to be preserved in brain injury; Green, Rosenfeld, Dole, Pivovarova, & Zapt, 2008). The interested reader is referred to an excellent review on this topic summarizing conceptual issues and research through 1997 (Franzen, Burgess, & Smith-Seemiller, 1997).

DEMOGRAPHIC EQUATIONS

Barona, Reynolds, and Chastain (1984) used the WAIS-R standardization sample to develop an equation utilizing demographic variables to predict WAIS-R VIQ, PIQ, and FSIQ. Of the eight demographic variables examined (sex, education, race, occupation, age, urban–rural residence, handedness, and geographic region of residence), education, occupation, and race were the most powerful predictors, although the squared zero-order correlations between race and IQ scores were .08–09. Despite the fact that gender did not contribute to explained variance in estimating IQs, it was incorporated in the final formula for FSIQ: 54.96 + 0.47 (age) + 1.76 (sex) + 4.71 (race) + 5.02 (education) + 1.89 (occupation) + .59 (region). It is inflammatory, if not outright discriminatory, to assign higher points for male gender, geographic location (residence in the northeast section of the United States was awarded more points), and ethnicity. Furthermore, the 95% confidence interval for predicted IQ was ±23.8 points, indicating very problematic estimation in the individual case.

Paolo, Ryan, Troster, and Hilmer (1996) documented that the Barona prediction equation underestimated IQ in individuals with IQ scores >119 and overestimated IQ in subjects with scores IQ <80. Barona and Chastain (1986) provided a revised equation described as providing greater accuracy in predicting IQs in Caucasians and African Americans, but Wrobel and Wrobel (1996) found both equations to overestimate IQ, while Basso, Bornstein, Roper, and McCoy (2000) observed both to be inaccurate predictors of IQ at the outer ranges. Some authors have argued that demographic equations perform at no better than chance levels in IQ range classifications in psychiatric patients and persons with brain injury (Sweet, Moberg, & Tovian, 1990).

"HOLD" TESTS

National Adult Reading Test (and variations). British reading tests, including the National Adult Reading Test (NART; Nelson, 1982) and the NART–Revised (NART-R; Nelson & Willison, 1991), and their North American counterparts, the North American Adult Reading Test (NAART) and the American National Adult Reading Test (AMNART; Blair & Spreen, 1989; Grober & Sliwinski, 1991), have been used to estimate premorbid cognitive function. The NART and the other tests utilize word-reading ability, which has been found to be highly correlated with overall intellectual function (Nelson & McKenna, 1975) and resistant to intellectual decline (Crawford, Parker, & Besson, 1988), as a method of estimating premorbid IQ. However, research on the tests' effectiveness (especially that of the NART) has raised concerns.

Crawford, Deary, Starr, and Whalley (2001) reported that NART scores at age 77 were highly correlated with IQ scores obtained at age 11 (r = .73), and earlier data from Crawford, Parker, Stewart, Besson, and De Lacey (1989) indicated that NART scores accounted for 66%, 75%, and 33% of the variance in WAIS FSIQ, VIQ, and PIQ scores, respectively, in normal individuals. However, less robust findings have been documented in other studies. While Berry and colleagues (1994) found that the NART-R scores underpredicted WAIS-R FSIQ scores obtained 3½ years earlier in normal individuals by only 3.8 points on average, correlations between the two instruments were rather modest (for FSIQ, r = .70; for VIQ, r = .68; for PIQ, r = .61). Moreover, Wiens, Bryan, and Crossen (1993) observed that in normal individuals, the NART overestimated IQ scores when actual IQs were below 100, and underestimated IQ when IQ scores were above 100. In another examination of normal individuals, Willshire, Kinsella, and Prior (1991) noted that NART scores accounted for 26% of WAIS-R FSIQ variance, but education accounted for 31% of variance; the two variables together accounted for 46% of IQ score variance, but the association was most pronounced for older persons (67% of score variance). The authors recommend using the NART in combination with demographic information. Gladsjo, Heaton, Palmer, Taylor, and Jeste (1999) reported that AMNART scores "added modestly" to prediction of WAIS-R FSIQ and VIQ over that obtained by demographic information in isolation, particularly in outliers with poor reading skills and higher education.

Initial studies found no differences in NART scores between patients with TBI and healthy and orthopedic controls (Crawford et al., 1988; Watt & O'Carroll, 1999), and this finding was used to argue that NART scores were accurately measuring premorbid function; however, these studies either did not specify the severity of the brain injuries or reported data on mixed severity samples. Subsequently, Bate, Mathias, and Crawford (2001) and Mathias et al. (2004) observed that NART scores were significantly lower in patients with moderate to severe TBI than in controls, and Morris, Wilson, Dunn, and Teasdale (2005) reported that NART scores were significantly correlated (r = –.31) with GCS scores in a mixed-severity brain injury sample. Riley and Simmonds (2003) showed that in a group with severe brain injury, test scores obtained at least 12 months after initial administration were more than 5 points higher in nearly half of the sample, and over 10% showed an improvement of 20 points. The authors further note that in a subsample on whom VIQ scores had been obtained on first assessment, the initial NART scores would have missed intellectual impairment in at least 25%, and they caution clinicians regarding use of the NART in the context of acute injury. Furthermore, Freeman, Godfrey, Harris, and Partridge (2001) found that NART scores indicated impairment in 30% of their sample with moderate to severe TBI.

Boekamp, Strauss, and Adams (1995) observed similar differences between AMNART and WAIS-R scores between African American and white patients with and without dementia, but reported that the AMNART overestimated IQ in nondemented individuals of lower intelligence, while underestimating IQ in more demented patients. McGurn and colleagues (2004) did not find significant NART differences between nondemented individuals and patients with mild to moderate dementia, and Bright, Jaldow, and Kopelman (2002) found no significant differences between NART/NART-R scores and demographic-based IQ estimates in controls, patients with Korsakoff's dementia, and patients with frontal and temporal lobe lesions. However, Storandt, Stone, and LaBarge (1995) documented significant deficits on the AMNART in patients with very mild and mild Alzheimer's disease as compared to healthy controls, while Stebbins and colleagues (1990) observed significantly lower NART scores in patients with mild and moderate/severe dementia as compared to controls and patients with very mild dementia. These findings led Storandt et al. (1995) to conclude that "use of this test as an indicator of premorbid intelligence in people with dementia of the Alzheimer type does not appear wise" (p. 174). Likewise, Taylor and colleagues (1996) found that AMNART estimates of VIQ were lower in patients with Alzheimer's disease than in controls, and that scores decreased with increasing severity of dementia. Taylor (1999) thus argues that NART scores are "clearly influenced by severity of dementia," and warns that "use of the NART as a comparator in estimating the severity of established dementia will lead to systematic underestimation of severity" (p. 291).

Supporting the use of the NART as a measure of premorbid IQ in schizophrenia, O'Carroll et al. (1992) found that NART scores did not differ among medicated acutely ill patients, unmedicated acutely ill patients, and controls, and NART estimates did not differ from IQ estimates based on demographic information, but NART scores were significantly higher than measured IQ in the patients. However, Russell et al. (2000) observed that in their sample of patients with schizophrenia, IQ scores recorded in childhood did not differ from those obtained upon presentation for psychiatric treatment in adulthood, which would argue for no loss in IQ as a function of illness. Furthermore, NART IQ estimates did not match actual IQ scores, particularly in those patients whose IQ scores differed from average.

Binder, Iverson, and Brooks (2009) argue that tests of word reading will frequently overestimate premorbid cognitive function, and they point out that the NART-R prediction of IQ was associated with a 95% confidence interval of ±15 points. Schretlen, Buffington, Meyer, and Pearlson (2005) found a 95% confidence interval of ±19.8 points for NART-R estimates of abbreviated WAIS-R/WAIS-III IQ; 5% of their healthy sample obtained FSIQs > 15 points deviant from predicted NART-R scores.

Wide Range Achievement Test–Revised and Wide Range Achievement Test–3. The Reading subtests of the Wide Range Achievement Test–Revised (WRAT-R; Jastak & Jastak, 1978) and WRAT3 (Wilkinson, 1993) have also often been used to estimate premorbid cognitive function. Weins et al. (1993) reported that in normal individuals, WRAT-R Reading subtest scores correlated .45 with WAIS-R FSIQ (a rather modest association), and that these scores underestimated IQ in higher IQ groups (the highest standard score possible is 118; Ball, Hart, Stutts, Turf, & Booth 2007). Johnstone and Wilhelm (1996) found no decline in WRAT-R Reading scores in patients tested longitudinally who either showed intellectual decline or remained stable, but, interestingly, reading scores increased in patients who demonstrated improvement in IQ scores. The authors warn that "significant variability in reading score decline/improvement suggests that caution must be used when estimating premorbid intelligence based on WRAT-R/WRAT3 Reading scores" (p. 282). Furthermore, Orme, Johnstone, Hanks, and Novack (2004) documented that in patients with TBI, WRAT-3 Reading scores improved upon retest 1 year after injury, particularly in patients with more severe injuries.

Oklahoma Premorbid Intelligence Estimate. The Oklahoma Premorbid Intelligence Estimate (Krull, Scott, & Sherer, 1995), developed on the WAIS-R standardization sample (half for validation and half for cross-validation), includes demographic variables (age, education, race, and occupation) in combination with current scores on two WAIS-R subtests (Vocabulary and Picture Completion). Vocabulary is utilized in the equation for VIQ, Picture Completion is included in the equation for PIQ, and both are used in predicting FSIQ. Krull et al. (1995) reported that the correlations between actual and predicted IQs were .87 for VIQ, .78 for PIQ, and .87 for FSIQ. This formula did not result in the restriction of range and overestimation of IQ found with other methods; however, of concern, only two-thirds of the cross-validation sample obtained actual and predicted

IQs within the same IQ band, and the authors note that "thirty-five percent of the cases were misclassified by only one category" (p. 85). Although the authors seem to view this as positive, to have a third of predicted IQs fall outside the actual IQ range is problematic for actual clinical use.

Schoenberg, Scott, Duff, and Adams (2002) adapted the OPIE to incorporate four WAIS-III subtest raw scores (Vocabulary, Information, Matrix Reasoning, and Picture Completion), and examined its accuracy in the WAIS-III standardization sample (half for validation and half for cross-validation). Correlations between actual and predicted IQ scores were .92 for FSIQ, .88 for VIQ, .84 for PIQ, .89 for the Verbal Comprehension Index (VCI), .83 for the Perceptual Organization Index (POI), .66 for the Working Memory Index (WMI), and .59 for the Processing Speed Index (PSI). However, only two-thirds of the sample obtained predicted FSIQ within the same category and within 5 points of actual FSIQ, although 93% obtained predicted FSIQ within 10 points and within one category of actual FSIQ. The authors do acknowledge that estimates for individuals with FSIQ > 129 were "poor," with only 50% of the sample obtaining IQ scores within 10 points of actual IQ. They note that the four-subtest OPIE outperformed the original OPIE, the BEST-3 approach, and the WTAR (see below for discussions of the latter two). Specifically, the proportion of OPIE four-subtest IQ estimates within 10 points of actual IQ scores was 75–93%, in comparison to 70% for the WTAR, 73% for WTAR plus demographic information, and 63–73% for the BEST-3 approach. The authors note that the algorithm may not behave as well in patient populations, particularly in those populations in which performance on "hold" subtests in fact declines (e.g., patients with dementia).

BEST-3 Approach. Like the original OPIE, the BEST-3 approach (Vanderploeg & Schinka, 1995; Vanderploeg, Schinka, & Axelrod, 1996) utilizes demographic information and WAIS-R subtests, and includes the Information subtest in addition to Vocabulary and Picture Completion. Vanderploeg, Schinka, and Axelrod (1996) reported that the BEST-3 approach generated IQ estimates were more highly correlated with WAIS-R IQ in the standardization sample than were Barona estimates, although the BEST-3 overestimated IQ by 5 points on average. However, Axelrod, Vanderploeg, and Rawlings (1999) found that BEST-3 scores were related to brain injury severity.

Wechsler Test of Adult Reading. More recently, the Wechsler Test of Adult Reading (WTAR; Wechsler, 2001), co-normed with the WAIS-III, has been used to estimate premorbid IQ; correlations between the WTAR and WAIS-III are .75 for VIQ and .73 for FSIQ (Wechsler, 2001). However, research on the accuracy of the measure has again been contradictory. Green and colleagues (2008) reported on a relatively small sample of patients with severe TBI, showing that WTAR scores did not appreciably change from administration at 2 and 5 months postinjury, and they concluded that the high stability of scores provides evidence for the test's utility as a measure of premorbid IQ. However, their patients were carefully screened and may not be representative of the larger population with TBI (i.e., exclusion criteria included dysarthria, semifluent English usage due to ESL or aphasia, acquired reading disorder, and history of learning disability). In fact, Mathias, Bowden, Bigler, and Rosenfeld (2007), while documenting only small improvement in WTAR scores longitudinally (similar to Green et al., 2008), found that groups with severe TBI scored significantly lower than samples with mTBI and moderate TBI, despite matching on demographic data. They concluded that WTAR performance is affected by severe TBI and thus is likely to underestimate premorbid IQ in this population.

COMPARISON OF APPROACHES TO ESTIMATING PREMORBID IQ

Kareken, Gur, and Saykin (1995) observed that WRAT-R Reading scores in combination with race and parental education provided estimates that approximated those obtained by the Barona equation. Johnstone, Callahan, Kapila, and Bouman (1996) reported that in a large sample (n = 232) of patients with TBI, dementia, and other neurological impairments, the WRAT-R and NAART IQ estimates were equivalent and accurate in patients with average VIQ, but at higher IQ levels these estimates (although equivalent across instruments) both underestimated VIQ. The WRAT-R was more accurate in predictions for individuals with low VIQ, but both instruments overestimated VIQ in these individuals; the authors conclude that the WRAT-R is the preferred estimator of verbal intelligence. Bright, Jaldow, and Kopelman (2002) found no difference in predictive accuracy between NART/NART-R data and demographic variables in patients with Alzheimer's disease, patients with Korsakoff's syndrome, patients with frontal or temporal lobe lesions, and healthy controls; they report that combining data from the NART/NART-R with demographic variables did not increase the amount of variance in IQ scores accounted for by the instrument. Powell, Brossart, and Reynolds (2003) compared the Barona equation with the OPIE, and concluded that the purely demographic equation provided better clinical utility in patients with cognitive impairment.

However, Griffin and colleagues (2002), in their comparison of the OPIE, Barona equation, NAART, and WRAT3 in a pain sample, found that the three former methods overestimated IQ, while the WRAT3 Reading subtest underestimated IQ. When the sample was stratified into IQ subgroups, the OPIE was found to be more accurate in subjects with above-average intelligence, while the WRAT3 Reading subtest was more effective in individuals with below-average intelligence; the NAART, OPIE, and WRAT3 Reading were equivalent for subjects with average IQ. The Barona equation was reported to "systematically under- and overestimate FSIQ across the intelligence continuum" (p. 497).

Axelrod, Vanderploeg, and Schinka (1999) compared the BEST-3, OPIE, and Barona equations in neurological patients and controls and found no difference in accuracy across methods. Basso et al. (2000), in examining the Barona equations, OPIE, and BEST-3 approaches, reported that while the OPIE and BEST-3 performed better, "their accuracy remained relatively weak," leading the authors to conclude that "regression-based estimates of premorbid IQ are very susceptible to error, particularly in outer ranges of intellectual function" (p. 325).

Veiel and Koopman (2001) have challenged the use of regression-based equations in general, because of regression to the mean; they argue that such an approach "grossly overestimates the probability of an IQ decline in the below-average range and grossly underestimates it in the above-average range" (p. 356). They provide a formula for computing "unbiased estimates of IQ decline," but a subsequent commenter has argued that this method "quadruples error" (Grove, 2001).

In conclusion, although the results of empirical studies are often contradictory, the preponderance of the research suggests that prediction methods (particularly those approaches involving demographic information) overestimate premorbid IQ in individuals with low IQ and underestimate premorbid IQ in more intelligent persons. Furthermore, evidence suggests that even with use of the most effective equations, only two-thirds of individuals obtain predicted IQ scores within 5 points and in the same IQ range as actual IQ. Binder et al. (2009) note that word-reading prediction of IQ (with the NART-R) is associated with a 95% confidence interval of ±15 points, confirming imprecise estimation of IQ in the individual case. They likewise question the "best performance method" of estimating premorbid abilities (e.g., assuming that the highest obtained scores represent premorbid ability, and using those as the standard by which other scores are compared and interpreted); they argue that this method is likely to overestimate premorbid abilities. In support of this conclusion, Binder and Binder (2011) cite the large amount of subtest scatter in the WAIS-IV standardization sample, particularly in subjects with high maximum test scores, to illustrate that "a few scores much higher than other scores do not mean that premorbid mental abilities were at the same level as the highest scores" (Binder et al., 2009, p. 43). Finally, performance-based methods, even those involving sight reading, appear to be affected by significant brain dysfunction (e.g., dementia, moderate/severe TBI) as well as by language-based learning disability, and will underestimate premorbid IQ in these conditions.

In my clinical work, I base my estimates of overall premorbid intellectual ability (i.e., average, below average, above average) on preinjury educational attainment (i.e., years completed in school and grade point average, results of formal academic achievement testing, and history of learning problems) and occupational background (e.g., professional, managerial, clerical, blue-collar, unskilled, etc.). No study has investigated whether statistical methods outperform such clinical judgments; the "veneer" of accuracy and sophistication ascribed to formally published statistical approaches may in fact be illusory.

Estimating Premorbid Neuropsychological Function

Diaz-Asper, Schretlen, and Pearlson (2004) found that normal individuals grouped by NART-R scores (below average, average, and above average) differed on neuropsychological tasks. Duff (2010) observed that a combination of demographic variables and WRAT3 Reading scores accurately predicted visual and verbal memory performance in normal older individuals and patients with mild cognitive impairment; specifically, current memory scores were 16–25 points lower than premorbid estimates in patients, but were comparable in the normal individuals. Duff, Chelune, and Dennett (2011) subsequently extended their findings to a larger sample with dementia, and employed either the WTAR or its new incarnation, Test of Premorbid Functioning. They again found that premorbid estimates of memory scores were 25–31 points higher than actual scores, consistent with a decline of 2 SDs. Similar findings have been reported for the Test of Premorbid Functioning and the WMS-IV in a sample with Alzheimer's disease (Psychological Corporation, 2009).

However, Williams (1997) concluded that demographic variables predicted memory scores at a much lower level of accuracy than they do intellectual scores, and Gladsjo et al. (1999) reported that while AMNART scores "added modestly" to prediction of WAIS-R FSIQ and VIQ in normal individuals over that obtained by demographic information in isolation, particularly in outliers with poor reading skills and higher education, AMNART information did not improve prediction of PIQ, Halstead–Reitan Average Impairment Rating, or verbal and visual memory scores.

Subsequently, Schretlen, Munro, Anthony, and Pearlson (2003) observed that in a healthy sample, the average lowest cognitive score was 1.9 SDs below NART-R IQ estimates, while 18% of the sample obtained a cognitive score 3 SDs below the NART-R IQ prediction. Schretlen et al. (2005) reported that although correlations between WAIS-R and WAIS-III abbreviated formats correlated at a high level with NART-R scores (r's $\geq .72$), correlations between NART-R and neuropsychological scores were much lower (mean r of .31). The relationship was nonsignificant for

Conners CPT data; $r = -.276$ for processing speed (Trails A); r's = .384 to .481 for language tasks (Boston Naming Test and verbal fluency tasks); r's = .284 to .328 for visual-perceptual/constructional tasks (RO Figure copy, Benton Facial Recognition Test); r's ≤.422 for verbal memory (WMS-R Logical Memory, Hopkins Verbal Learning Test—Revised), r's = .119 to .318 for visual memory (WMS-R Visual Reproduction, Brief Visual Memory Test—Revised), r's = $-.276$ to $-.286$ for grip strength; and r's = $-.528$ to .403 for executive tasks (WCST, Design Fluency, Trails B). NART-R prediction of neuropsychological performance was associated with a 95% confidence interval of ±25–29 points, and the authors note that "at least 5% of healthy adults produced standard scores that fell more than 24 points below their own NART-R estimated IQ scores" (p. 787).

Furthermore, the WTAR manual (Wechsler, 2001) shows that only 22% of WAIS-III Immediate and General Memory Index score variance was accounted for by WTAR scores, and Hawkins and Tulsky (2001) were able to demonstrate in the WAIS-III/WMS-III standardization sample that "a superiority of memory score over FSIQ is typical at lower IQ levels, whereas the converse is true at higher IQ levels. These data indicate that the use of IQ–memory score unstratified 'simple difference' tables could lead to erroneous conclusions for clients with low or high IQ" (p. 875).

Thus the available data suggest that although premorbid estimates of memory function do accurately capture the loss in memory ability observed in patients with confirmed dementia and those in the transitional stage, the problem is that large discrepancies between premorbid estimates and actual memory test data are also found in at least some normal individuals, particularly those with higher IQ. In other words, whereas sensitivity is likely to be high, specificity of the techniques appears to be problematic. Furthermore, the validation of these techniques has been limited to patients with dementia and predementia, and Duff et al. (2011) note that "the accuracy of these premorbid formulae in other clinical samples (e.g., traumatic brain injury) is unknown and needs to be examined and validated before they can be used clinically" (p. 704). Finally, although demographic and reading scores may be significantly *related* to current neuropsychological scores, the associations are probably not large enough in nondemented samples to accurately *predict* neurocognitive scores, particularly in the individual case.

Interpreting Lowered Scores

Normal Variability

One of the most valuable experiences I have had as a neuropsychologist was to test "normal controls" as a part of research projects. Prior to this experience, I assumed that "normal" individuals would obtain "normal" scores on all tests—but in personally testing well over 100 healthy control subjects carefully screened for neurological disorder, head injury, psychiatric conditions, substance abuse, and grossly abnormal laboratory findings, and in subsequently supervising the testing on well over 100 more, I realized that this is not the case. For the first 132 subjects (Palmer, Boone, Lesser, & Wohl, 1998), we demonstrated that three-fourths of these predominantly Caucasian, middle-aged or older controls with a mean of 14 years of education and mean IQ within the high average range obtained one borderline score (≤ 1.3 SD below mean of age-matched peers) across a flexible neuropsychological battery, and 48% obtained at least two borderline scores. When we lowered the cutoffs to ≤ 2 SDs below the mean of age-matched peers, 37% of the sample obtained at least one impaired score, while 24% obtained at least two. Furthermore, 44% of the sample obtained at least two scores in the borderline or lower range on two distinct tests, while 20% showed at least two scores in the impaired range on at least two different tests. We concluded that "any strong assertions regarding the occurrence of neurocognitive injury appear difficult to justify solely on the basis of a few unrelated and isolated 'abnormal' test scores" (Palmer et al., 1998, p. 510).

In a different approach, Schretlen and colleagues (2003), in studying neuropsychological performance in 197 older individuals screened for significant health problems, computed the difference between each individual's highest and lowest z-transformed scores (out of 32 from 15 tests), and found that the smallest difference was 1.6 SDs and the largest difference was 6.0 SDs; 66% of subjects had discrepancy values that exceeded 3 SDs. They note that "if one defines 'consistent' neuropsychological test performance by scores that all fall within ± 1 SD of each other, no participant demonstrated 'consistent' performance" (p. 868). The authors conclude that the findings indicate that "marked intraindividual variability is very common in normal adults, and underscore the need to base diagnostic inferences on clinically recognizable patterns rather than psychometric variability alone" (p. 864).

Ivnik, Smith, Malec, Petersen, and Tangalos (1995), in examining relationships between various cognitive domains (verbal and nonverbal intellect, attention/concentration, learning, and retention) in 397 normal older individuals, showed that even the mostly closely related dyad (verbal comprehension and perceptual organization) only shared 31% score variance, and the least related pair (attention/concentration and retention) shared only 5% score variance. These findings led the authors to conclude that the findings "challenge the assumption that performance in one cognitive ability domain can be used to predict performance in another" (p. 160).

A few studies have examined score variability of the standardization samples of some neuropsychological batteries and Wechsler instruments. Heaton et al. (2004) noted that 72% of controls scored < 40 on ≥ 2 out of 25 demographically adjusted T-scores on the expanded Halstead–Reitan battery, while Schretlen, Testa, Winicki, Pearlson, and Gordon (2008) found nearly the same percentage (75%) on a different set of 25 neurocognitive measures. In the normative sample for the Neuropsychology Assessment Battery, 30.8% of healthy adults obtained one or more memory scores 1.5 SDs below the mean (56.5% of subjects with low average IQ, and 21.1% of those with high average IQ; Brooks, Iverson, & White, 2007). More recently (Brooks, Holdnack, & Iverson, 2010), 47% of normal individuals were found to obtain at least one WAIS-IV/WMS-IV Index ≤ 16th percentile; 20% had one or more Indexes ≤ 5th percentile; and 82% of those with 9–11 years of education obtained at least one WAIS-IV/WMS-IV Index ≤ 16th percentile as compared to 20% of those with 16 or more years of education. Similarly, Gregoire, Coalson, and Zhu (2011) reported that > 70% in the WAIS-IV normative sample obtained one or more Index scores significantly different from the mean Index scores, while nearly 50% showed two or more Index scores significantly different from the mean; only a quarter did not obtain an Index score significantly different from the mean. Furthermore, the rate of deviation from mean Index scores increased with IQ level: 24% of those with FSIQ < 70 obtained two Index scores significantly different from the mean, in comparison to 56% of those with FSIQ ≥ 130. Binder and Binder (2011) examined variability in scores across subtests in the WAIS-IV standardization sample (n = 2,200), and found a mean variability of 6.6 (highest subtest score minus lower subtest score), leading them to conclude that "a high frequency of large subtest variability [is] to be expected" (p. 68).

Binder et al. (2009), in an excellent review article on the variability among normal individuals on cognitive test performance, conclude that "abnormal performance on some proportion of neuropsychological tests is psychometrically normal" (p. 15) and provide several "key psychometric principles" (p. 6):

> (a) obtaining some low scores from a battery of tests is the rule, not the exception, (b) the more tests that are given, the more likely the person is to have a large spread between high and low scores, (c) people with fewer years of education and/or lower levels of intellectual abilities are expected to have more low scores compared to those with more years of education and/or high intellectual abilities, and (d) people with more years of education and/or higher intelligence obtain some low scores.

The authors specifically caution that "people with less than high school education, those with below average intelligence, and individuals from diverse ethnic or cultural background are more likely to get more low scores, and are thus at greater risk for being misdiagnosed with cognitive impairment" (p. 42). Schretlen et al. (2008) caution that adjustment of scores for demographic factors does not eliminate the abnormal scores documented in normal populations.

High IQ Scores Do Not Translate to Uniformly High Scores on Neuropsychological Measures

The "best-performance" method of interpreting neuropsychological scores assumes that the highest scores obtained by patients represent their true premorbid capability and that in assessment for acquired cognitive dysfunction, neuropsychological scores are to be compared against this "highest-score" standard. However, as discussed below, investigations of cognitive performances of normal samples show that variability in test scores is the rule rather than the exception in individuals with high IQ.

In the Schretlen et al. (2003) study described above, each subject's lowest z-score fell on average 1.9 SDs below premorbid IQ estimates (based on NART-R FSIQ), leading the authors to conclude that "these findings clearly refute the notion that most individuals are endowed with equal ability across the spectrum of cognitive functions" (p. 868).

In the Palmer et al. (1998) study noted earlier, the normal volunteers had a mean IQ in the high average range, yet three-fourths of them obtained one borderline score across the test battery, and 20% obtained at least two impaired scores.

Examination of the WAIS-III technical manual shows that a VIQ–PIQ split of ≥ 15 occurs in 13% of individuals with low average IQ and in 7% with borderline IQ, but in 25% of individuals with superior or very superior IQ. Similarly, a 20-point difference between VCI and PSI is present in only 8% of individuals with IQ < 80, but is found in 29% of individuals with IQ ≥ 120.

More recently, Binder and Binder (2011), in their analysis of WAIS-IV standardization sample data, documented that individuals with higher IQs had more variability across subtests. Although it is a common clinical practice to denote as abnormal those subtest scores falling > 1 SD below the subtest score overall mean, nearly 20% of individuals with a maximum subtest score of 16 obtained an "abnormal" subtest score when this method was used. The authors further note that a difference score of 9 points from highest to lowest subtest scores (equivalent to 3 SDs) was present in 35.1% of subjects with a highest subtest score of 16, in 45.6% of those with a highest subtest score of 17, and in 68.6% of those with a highest score of 18.

In a fascinating study, Zakzanis and Jeffay (2011) administered a brief neuropsychological battery (RO Figure, WAIS-III Digit Span, Judgment of

Line Orientation, Finger Tapping Test, CVLT-II, and WASI Vocabulary and Block Design) to 20 university faculty members (mean age = 40.9), all of whom had obtained PhD degrees (average WASI IQ was 124 [SD = 5]), and none of whom had remarkable medical or psychiatric histories. However, marked intraindividual variability in test scores was observed, with all but 3 subjects obtaining some scores > 1.5 SDs below IQ level, and in 20% (n = 4), more than half of the neurocognitive scores were > 1.5 SDs below IQ level. Sixty-five percent of the sample (n = 13) obtained at least one average score; 30% were found to have at least one low average score (n = 6); 10% achieved at least one borderline score (n = 2); and an impaired score was documented in 15% (n = 3). The authors comment that "the results of the study are not surprising from biological and environmental perspectives. Consistent endowment of all types of cognitive abilities in any individual is highly unlikely, as is consistency of the distribution of neuro-cognitive abilities across individuals" (p. 297).

A reasonable conclusion that can be drawn from the data cited above, as well as other studies showing that individuals with high intelligence do not obtain uniformly elevated scores on cognitive exam (Diaz-Asper et al., 2004; Hawkins & Tulsky, 2001; Russell, 2001), is that the typical pattern for high-IQ individuals is to have particular strengths in circumscribed areas, with remaining skills average or perhaps even lower. The more unusual pattern would be to have high scores across all domains. This evidence led Greiffenstein (2009) to posit that the belief that above-average scores should be consistently found across cognitive tasks in individuals with above average-IQ is a neuropsychological "myth."

Determining Etiology of Lowered Scores

Below are summaries of the effects of various conditions/exposures and patient characteristics on cognitive function, to help the clinician determine whether these factors are contributing to low cognitive scores in tested patients.

Psychiatric Disorders

DEPRESSION

In a sample of middle-aged and older unmedicated adults diagnosed with major depression, mild declines were noted in only four cognitive domains: information-processing speed, executive skills, PIQ/visual–spatial skills, and visual memory (Boone, Lesser, et al., 1995). No declines relative to controls were documented in language, verbal memory, attention, and VIQ. Low scores in PIQ and visual memory were unrelated to severity of depression, suggesting that these might be trait findings in depressed individuals. In contrast, the losses in processing speed and executive skills were only found in subjects with at least moderate depression, indicating that these are likely to be state findings that occur once a threshold of depression severity is reached. Although no effect of depression was noted on the verbal memory tasks employed in this investigation (story recall and forced-choice recognition), other studies have observed that depressed patients exhibit difficulties in learning and recall of rote verbal information (e.g., CVLT; Basso & Bornstein, 1999; Otto et al., 1994).

Thus it can be concluded that depression is associated with mild declines in PIQ, visual-constructional skills, and visual memory, and that with increasing severity of depression, mild losses are found in processing speed, executive skills, and rote verbal learning/recall.

In a study examining the impact of depression specifically within a head-injured population, depression was found to be associated with reduced word list recall (but not recall of word pairs and stories) in patients, even after the researchers controlled for cognitive status and symptom validity/response bias (Keiski, Shore, & Hamilton, 2007). Treatment of depression in patients with mTBI results in improvement in psychomotor speed, verbal and visual memory, and general cognitive efficiency (Fann, Uomoto, & Katon, 2001). These findings indicate that depression should be considered when attempting to determine etiology of low cognitive scores in this population.

Some may then argue that perhaps depression is causing the cognitive problems, but that the accident caused the depression. However, a recent meta-analysis of the relationship between mTBI and psychiatric symptoms (depression, anxiety, psychosocial disability, reduced coping) sheds light on this issue Panayiotou, Jackson, & Crowe, 2010). Effect sizes ranged from −.28 to 0.26, did not significantly differ from zero ($p = .76$), and were considered "meaningless." Effect sizes were smaller when studies were weighted, indicating that unweighted effect sizes were unduly influenced by studies with small n's and highly variable findings. The authors concluded that "mTBI may have a very small to no measurable effect on psychological and psychosocial symptom reporting" (p. 468).

BIPOLAR ILLNESS

In a review of the neuropsychological characteristics of bipolar disorder, Bearden, Hoffman, and Cannon (2001) noted that cognitive impairment may be confined to a subset of chronic patients (older, psychotic, or with multiple episodes); primarily involves executive, attentional, and memory skills; and overall is less pronounced than that observed in patients with schizophrenia. In a subsequent review of studies on cognitive findings in bipolar disorder published between 1980 and 2000, Quraishi and Frangou

(2002) noted that in acutely symptomatic patients, abnormalities were detected in perceptual reasoning aspects of intellectual scores, attention, memory and executive functions, with abnormalities in the latter three domains remaining in remitted patients. No significant differences were found between patients with bipolar illness and unipolar depression, and bipolar patients outperformed patients with schizophrenia when remitted but not when acutely symptomatic.

A recent meta-analysis (Yucel, Pantelis, & Berk, 2011) of cognitive abnormalities in patients with bipolar I versus bipolar II disorder (the latter have hypomanic rather than manic episodes) showed that patients with bipolar II disorder achieved better scores in verbal memory ($d = 0.52$), visual memory ($d = 0.38$), global cognition ($d = 0.27$), and semantic fluency ($d = 0.31$), but showed no differences in sustained attention, working memory, planning/reasoning (WCST), Trails A or B, Stroop C, or phonemic fluency. Comparison of patients with bipolar II and controls showed better performance (d's = 0.29–0.55) in the latter in six of six domains (global cognition, processing speed, working memory, planning/reasoning, verbal memory, and visual memory). Other research has found that patients in the euthymic stage of bipolar illness exhibit significantly lowered scores in attention/processing speed (d's = 0.62–0.79), episodic memory (d's = 0.43 for recognition to 0.81 for learning trials), and executive functioning (d's = 0.47–0.71), suggestive of a "trait" neuropsychological deficit in bipolar illness (Torres, Boudreau, & Yatham, 2007; similar findings in Arts, Jabben, Krabbendam, & van Os, 2007, and Robinson et al., 2006). Moreover, first-degree relatives obtain lower scores than controls in executive function (Stroop; $d = 0.49$) and verbal memory ($d = 0.42$–0.56; Arts et al., 2007). Meta-analysis has shown that treatment with lithium is associated with significantly lowered scores in immediate verbal learning/memory ($d = 0.24$) and associational fluency/verbal association ($d = 0.33$), but not in delayed verbal memory, visual memory, attention, executive skills, processing speed, or finger dexterity skills (Wingo, Wingo, Harvey, & Baldessarini, 2009). However, long-term lithium treatment is associated with moderate losses in processing speed ($d = 0.62$).

Developmental Disorders

ADHD AND LEARNING DISABILITIES IN ADULTS

The reader is referred to an excellent review by Mapou (2008) regarding ADHD and learning disabilities in adults, which I have utilized in the following summary.

The cognitive symptoms of ADHD include primary problems in self-regulation and self-motivation, predominantly due to distractibility, procrastination, and problems with organization/prioritization. ADHD is now viewed as a chronic condition that typically persists throughout a person's lifetime; 70% of children with ADHD will continue to have ADHD symptoms in adulthood, and 50% of these will have occupational challenges. Some 3–5% of adults are reported to have ADHD, but only 10% of these have been diagnosed. Meta-analyses have shown medium effect sizes for verbal memory ($d = -0.56$), focused attention ($d = -0.55$), visual/verbal fluency ($d = -0.52$), sustained attention ($d = -0.52$), and abstract problem solving/working memory ($d = -0.51$), but small effect sizes for simple attention ($d = -0.38$), verbal intelligence ($d = -0.27$), executive functions ($d = -0.21$), visual problem solving ($d = -0.26$), and figural memory ($d = -0.18$; Schoechlin & Engel, 2005).

Some 80% of learning disabilities involve problems in reading; it is estimated that disability in written language occurs in 10% of school children, math disability is present in 1–6%, and nonverbal learning disabilities constitute 1–10% of the learning-disabled population. Learning difficulties do not resolve in adulthood, and it has been estimated that 3–20% of adults have learning disabilities. In adults with reading disability, neuropsychological testing reveals lower mean scores in naming speed, verbal learning and recall, word generation, rapid word reading, and vocabulary, as well as lower VIQ than PIQ (Felton, Naylor, & Wood, 1990; Kinsbourne, Rufo, Gamzu, Palmer, & Berliner, 1991; Ransby & Swanson, 2003). In contrast, mathematics disability is associated with abnormalities in executive skills and/or constructional skill (Osmon, Smerz, Braun, & Plambeck, 2006).

SEX CHROMOSOME ABNORMALITIES

In a study of men with Klinefelter syndrome (Boone et al., 2001), three cognitive subgroups were identified on the basis of VIQ–PIQ discrepancies. In men with VIQ ≤7 points below PIQ, associated deficits were identified in reading, spelling, verbal processing speed (Stroop A and B), and verbal executive skills (Stroop C, Auditory Consonant Trigrams [ACT], word list false positives, word-sequencing errors); in the men with PIQ ≤7 points below VIQ, losses in motor speed (Grooved Pegboard Test) and nonverbal executive skills (including tasks such as tracing of tangled lines and WCST perseverative errors) were found.

Substance Abuse

ALCOHOL

The following summary of the literature on alcohol overuse and its effect on the brain and cognitive functions is based on Oscar-Berman and Marinkovic

(2007) and Rourke and Grant (2009). Risky drinking patterns in men are characterized as more than 14 drinks per week, or more than 4 drinks per day at least 1 time per month; they are described in women as more than 7 drinks per week, or more than 3 drinks per day. The brain areas most affected by alcohol include the neocortex (especially frontal lobes), the limbic system (hippocampus, amygdala, hypothalamus), and the cerebellum, with some evidence suggesting that the right hemisphere is more affected than the left. There may be a genetic predisposition to frontal lobe dysfunction in families with histories of alcoholism, suggesting that in some individuals frontal lobe disturbance may predate actual use of alcohol. Of the estimated 18 million people with problem drinking in the United States, half do not appear to have cognitive, sensory, or motor impairments; however, slightly more than 10% become incapacitated and require residential placement. The remaining individuals have mild neuropsychological deficits that improve within 12 months of abstinence, although 10–30% of these will show continuing mild cognitive abnormalities. In alcoholics who recently detoxified, IQ scores are generally within the normal range (but with PIQ < VIQ), although impairments are reported in executive skills, learning/memory, visual–spatial skills, processing speed, and simple motor skills. Some literature suggests that the impact of alcohol on the brain is mediated by age: Older individuals with alcoholism exhibit cognitive impairments relative to age-matched controls, but no significant differences are found in cognitive function between younger individuals and their age peers.

METHAMPHETAMINE

According to a review by Scott et al. (2007), the acute effects of methamphetamine may include increased attention and processing/psychomotor speed, but methamphetamine use may also lead to deficits in inhibition and in filtering out irrelevant information. The results of a meta-analysis conducted by Scott and colleagues on the cognitive effects of chronic methamphetamine use show medium effect sizes in learning/memory ($d = -0.59$ to -0.66), executive skills ($d = -0.63$), information-processing speed ($d = -0.52$), motor skills ($d = -0.48$), attention/working memory ($d = -0.39$), and visual-constructional skills ($d = -0.37$), but some of the deficits may reflect premorbid neurocognitive abnormalities that predispose these persons to substance abuse. Forty percent of individuals with methamphetamine dependence may exhibit global neuropsychological impairment. Men show more pronounced deficits than women—perhaps due either to the protective effects of estrogen, or to more extensive use by men and a higher prevalence of comorbid substance abuse and closed head injuries in males. Older age is associated with more cognitive abnormalities in those who use methamphetamine, but it may also be a function of longer use. In early abstinence, deficits are equivalent to those observed in currently using individuals; with longer abstinence there may be recovery of cognition, although some deficits still remain, especially in episodic memory and cognitive inhibition.

Chronic methamphetamine use is also associated with psychiatric complications, including increased risk for positive and negative symptoms of psychosis (most often in those who inject the drug, but also in individuals with a predisposition to psychotic symptoms, including those with schizotypal or schizoid traits and family histories of psychotic disorders). Methamphetamine-related psychosis is usually transient (occurring during acute effects and withdrawal). Persons who use methamphetamine have high rates of comorbid ADHD; it is unclear whether methamphetamine use results in a similar symptom profile to ADHD, or whether individuals with ADHD symptoms have a predilection to methamphetamine use because of its initial positive effects on attention.

OPIATES

For reviews, see Gruber, Silveri, and Yurgelun-Todd (2007) and Ersche and Sahakian (2007). Acute effects of opioid use on cognitive function include losses in verbal memory. Contradictory findings have been reported regarding the effects of chronic opioid use: Several studies report no difference in cognitive function in chronic users relative to controls, but other investigations cite losses in visual–spatial skills, visual–motor function, spatial working memory, visual memory, and executive skills (although some authors argue that the abnormalities normalize with continuing abstinence). Similarly, acute methadone use appears to interfere with verbal memory, whereas long-term methadone treatment may lower psychomotor speed, working and long-term memory, visual–spatial attention, and executive skills. Again, there may be some recovery with abstinence, although some literature suggests that methadone treatment itself may improve memory in those who abuse opiates. Oxycodone (Oxycontin) has been reported to cause losses in psychomotor speed, executive skills, reaction time, eye–hand coordination, and memory. Acute use of hydrocodone with homatropine (Hycodan) was found to be associated only with losses in psychomotor speed; hydrocodone with acetaminophen (Vicodin) was also documented to reduce verbal recall and eye–hand coordination, but only at dosages two to four times recommended levels. Data on morphine use have shown acute declines in psychomotor speed, verbal memory, and auditory reaction time, but there are no detectable cognitive losses with long term treatment in patients with chronic pain as compared to patients who discontinued such treatment.

CANNABIS

A meta-analysis by Grant and colleagues (2003) provided evidence for a statistically significant "residual cannabis effect" that was of small magnitude ($d = -0.15$), indicating that the performance of persons using cannabis was one-fifth of a standard deviation below that of controls. In specific cognitive domains, the only significant findings were for memory (learning, $d = -0.21$; forgetting, $d = -0.27$), suggesting detectable but small effects.

Gonzalez (2007), in his review of the literature on effects of cannabis on cognitive function, notes consistent evidence for acute effects of marijuana in lowering short-term recall of verbal (word lists, story details) and visual information learned during intoxication, and in contributing to intrusions and false positive errors. In contrast, recognition is relatively intact, and no impairment is found in long-term or semantic memory or information learned prior to the cannabis ingestion. Some data suggest that memory deficits improve with continuing abstinence. Various investigations have found that neuropsychological abnormalities are confined to groups with current heavy cannabis use (4-point loss in IQ, memory problems, slower processing speed), but effect sizes were small; no differences in performance were observed among those with light use, those with former heavy use, and controls. In a study of identical twins discordant for cannabis use who were administered a comprehensive neuropsychological battery, a single small difference was detected on constructional skill (WAIS-R Block Design). There is equivocal evidence for losses in attention and executive abilities.

Gonzalez (2007) concludes:

> When taken together, investigations on non-acute effects of cannabis use indicate that abstinent cannabis users experience poorer neuropsychological performance than noncannabis-using controls. These deficits appear to be of small magnitude, generally circumscirbed to memory, and appear to resolve within weeks. Furthermore, the totality of the evidence suggests that any deficits observed are most likely to be seen only among heavy, frequent users of cannabis, notwithstanding acute cannabis intoxication. Some evidence suggests that heavy cannabis use may produce deficits on measures of decision-making and inhibitory control that persist for longer. At this time, however, it has not been determined if such deficits are a result of cannabis use of if they represent premorbid problems that may have contributed to the development of a cannabis use disorder. (p. 355)

ECSTASY

A recent meta-analysis showed that Ecstasy use was associated with small to medium effect sizes in verbal learning/memory (d's = 0.73–0.85), nonverbal learning/memory (d's = 0.58–0.57), motor/psychomotor speed (d's = 0.53–0.55), executive functions (d's = 0.49–0.52), and attention/concentration (d's = 0.38–0.40; Kalechstein, De La Garza, Mahoney, Fantegrossi, & Newton, 2007). Smaller although still significant effect sizes were reported in a second meta-analytic study (learning/memory, $d = -0.55$; verbal comprehension, $d = -0.36$; processing speed, $d = -0.33$; attention/concentration, $d = -0.27$; executive function, $d = 0.26$; perceptual organization, $d = -0.11$; motor skill, $d = -0.17$; Zakzanis, Campbell, & Jovanovski, 2007). A third meta-analysis of the impact of Ecstasy use on memory function confirmed a large effect size for verbal memory ($d = -1.00$) versus a small effect size for visual memory ($d = -0.27$); long-term memory was as impacted as short-term memory (Laws & Kokkalis, 2007).

COCAINE

Gonzalez, Vassileva, and Scott (2009), in reviewing the effects of cocaine on cognitive function, note that acute administration may enhance attention, information-processing speed, and inhibition. However, they indicate that some studies report that long-term use of cocaine, even after months of abstinence, can be associated with subtle declines in cognition—primarily in executive skills, but including attention, processing speed, and verbal and visual memory. Jovanovski, Erb, and Zakzanis (2005) examined effect sizes in the literature and reported that the median effect size was 0.35. The largest effect size was reported for attention, followed by visual memory, and then executive functions; minimal effect sizes were present for language and sensory-perceptual data. However, a limitation of this study was inclusion of studies where participants were concurrently abusing other substances (typically alcohol). Concurrent abuse of cocaine and alcohol is typical (up to 84%), and the effect of abusing both substances on cognitive function is unclear. Another limitation was a large range of abstinence periods (0–1,075 days); some studies were thus likely to have been gathering data during intoxication.

Chronic Medical Illnesses

HYPERTENSION

Arterial hypertension is associated with declines in executive skills and attention (Verdelho et al., 2007). Smith, Blumenthal, Babyak, Hinderliter, and Sherwood (2011) observed that higher levels of flow-mediated dilation of the brachial artery were associated with better scores on measures of executive function, while greater carotid artery intima–media thickness was correlated with reduced processing speed in overweight individuals with hypertension. A meta-analysis involving 19,501 subjects showed that improvement in blood pressure was associated with increased scores on the MMSE and on Logical Memory tasks (Birns, Morris, Donaldson, & Kalra, 2006).

CORONARY ARTERY BYPASS SURGERY/CARDIAC DISEASE

In a recent review and commentary, Selnes and Gottesman (2010) concluded from more recent, methodologically sound studies that postoperative cognitive decline in coronary artery bypass graft may occur in some individuals, but that it is mild and normalizes by 3 months postsurgery. The late cognitive changes attributed to the surgery have not been found to be specific to cardiopulmonary bypass. Lipid-lowering drugs have been reported to reduce the probability of developing cognitive impairment (Etminian, Gill, & Samii, 2003).

WHITE MATTER DISEASE

In a review of the impact of white matter abnormalities on cognition (Gunning-Dixon & Raz, 2000), losses in processing speed, executive skills, immediate and delayed memory, and indicators of global cognitive function were found, while fine motor performance and overall intelligence were spared. Some evidence suggests that cognitive declines occur once a threshold of white matter lesions is exceeded (Boone et al., 1992).

CHRONIC OBSTRUCTIVE PULMONARY DISEASE

In a review of the relationship between chronic obstructive pulmonary disease and cognitive dysfunction (Dodd, Getov, & Jones, 2010), it was noted that more than 90% of samples in all studies demonstrated cognitive dysfunction, and that nearly all studies reported abnormalities in attention, motor function, and memory, with the majority also citing losses in executive skills, visual–constructive skills, and language.

SLEEP APNEA

A meta-analysis of the effect of sleep apnea on neurocognitive function revealed a substantial effect for motor speed ($d = 1.21$) and vigilance ($d = 1.40$); medium effects for executive skills ($d = 0.73$), nonverbal intelligence ($d = 0.68$), and visual memory (d's $= 0.55$–0.56); and smaller effects for verbal memory (d's $= 0.16$–0.27) and verbal intelligence ($d = 0.08$) (Beebe, Groesz, Wells, Nichols, & McGee, 2003)

CANCER TREATMENT

A meta-analysis of the effects of various systematic therapies on cognition in patients with non-brain cancers (Anderson-Hanley, Sherman, Riggs, Agochant, & Compas, 2003) showed large effect sizes in two domains (executive, $d = -0.93$; verbal memory, $d = -0.91$), and a moderate effect size for motor function ($d = -0.55$); mean performance of patients was 0.33 to 1 SD below those of normative samples or control groups. In a second meta-analysis of the specific effects of chemotherapy of non-brain cancers on cognitive function (Jansen, Miaskowski, Dodd, Dowling, & Kramer, 2005), low to medium effect sizes were documented in visual memory ($d = -0.51$), information processing speed ($d = -0.44$), verbal memory ($d = -0.37$), motor function ($d = -0.36$), language ($d = -0.33$), executive function ($d = -0.26$), attention ($d = -0.17$), and visual–spatial skills ($d = -0.11$).

DIABETES

Type 2 diabetes is associated with losses in executive function, attention, speed and motor control, memory, and naming (Verdelho et al., 2007). A meta-analysis of studies on the impact of Type 1 diabetes on cognitive function showed that this condition was associated with declines in overall intelligence ($d = 0.7$), psychomotor speed ($d = 0.6$), cognitive flexibility ($d = 0.5$), visual attention ($d = 0.4$), visual perception ($d = 0.4$), speed of information processing ($d = 0.3$), and sustained attention ($d = 0.3$), but not in language, selective and divided attention, motor speed, verbal and visual memory, or working memory. Lower cognitive function was related to evidence of microvascular disease, but was not associated with severe hypoglycemic episodes or poor illness control (Brands, Biessels, de Haan, Kappelle, & Kessels, 2005).

SURGERY

Cognitive declines were reported for up to 3 months after orthopedic surgery in 56% of patients over age 64 (Ancelin et al., 2001); at 9 days, nearly three-quarters of the sample showed an abnormality in at least one test score. Risk factors included age over 75 years, low educational level, and preoperative cognitive dysfunction and depression.

As summarized by Gasquoine (2011), the empirical literature shows that acute respiratory stress, cancer, chronic kidney disease, chronic obstructive pulmonary disease, coronary heart disease, hypertension, obesity (as found in bariatric surgery candidates), obstructive sleep apnea, and Type 2 diabetes have all been found to be associated with cognitive decline, although the literature has been compromised by failure to control for comorbid conditions (including psychiatric disorders), effects of treatment (adjuvant therapy for cancer and bypass surgery for coronary artery disease), demographic variables, and limited premorbid cognitive function. The proposed mechanisms of impact of these medical illnesses on brain function are hypoxic–ischemic encephalopathy and/or cytokine-mediated immune dysregulation resulting in ischemic injury. Gasquoine (2011) concludes that because many participants in various studies probably had several concurrent conditions, the impact of any single condition was likely to have been overestimated. He further notes that no disease-specific profiles emerged; rather, all conditions were associated with mild decrements in attention, processing speed, memory, and executive skills, suggestive of bilateral frontal–subcortical ischemic injury. He also observes that this profile was only present in subgroups of patients, was related to disease severity and high levels of emotional distress, and might be reversible in some cases.

Other Neurological Conditions

On occasion I have observed symptoms of a primary neurological illness to be misattributed to the effects of claimed injury. For example, I once evaluated a middle-aged woman whose family was suing her treating physician for overprescribing large amounts of pain medication, claiming that it had caused her substantial cognitive dysfunction. However, on exam, the plaintiff's behavior and test performances were clearly indicative of a frontal variant of frontal–temporal dementia—a condition that would be unrelated to her opioid use. In another case, a plaintiff and his family were suing for malpractice because he had experienced a right-hemisphere stroke following an endarterectomy. On first neuropsychological evaluation 1 year after the stroke, his scores were average or higher, with the exception of isolated borderline to low average scores in visual memory, processing speed, motor strength, and executive skills. However, on my retesting of him 4 years after the stroke, his neurocognitive scores had markedly dropped (impairments present in visual memory and right-hand motor dexterity; borderline performance in processing speed and left-hand dexterity; and a 16-point decline in overall IQ). Thus, despite the stroke, his cognitive scores had been almost normal on first testing 1 year after the event; however, the second test results clearly revealed that he had subsequently developed a vascular dementia (the plaintiff's attorney declined to have the plaintiff undergo repeat brain imaging at the time of my exam, or at least he did not disclose the results). A third plaintiff claimed symptoms from mTBI, but had a history of operated brain tumor with subsequent radiation treatment prior to the accident. Although she claimed that her headaches were due to the accident, medical records revealed that in the months prior to the accident she had reported headaches, and on imaging a recurrence of her tumor was found.

Culture/Language

Research shows that individuals with ESL status obtain lowered scores on WAIS-III Digit Span, the Boston Naming Test, and Verbal Fluency (FAS) relative to native English speakers (Boone, Wen, Razani, & Ponton, 2007). In the WAIS-III/WMS-III standardization sample, language preference was found to account for significant portions of variance on the VCI, the PSI, and the Auditory Memory Composite score (Harris, Tulsky, & Schultheis, 2003). Studies also indicate that the percentage of English spoken while growing up is positively related in adults to performance on language tasks and tasks involving the English alphabet and numeric system (WAIS-III/WASI Vocabulary, Boston Naming Test, Digit Span, Stroop B [rapid color naming], Trails A and B), but not on visual–spatial/visual-constructional tests (WAIS-III Block Design, Matrix Reasoning; Boone et al., 2007; Razani, Murcia, Tabares, & Wong, 2006; Razani, Burciaga, Madore, & Wong, 2007). In an Australian sample with brain injury, ethnically and linguistically diverse patients who were educated in English scored lower than monolingual English speakers on WAIS-III VIQ and Vocabulary and Similarities subtests (Walker, Batchelor, Shores, & Jones, 2010); ethnically and linguistically diverse patients not educated in English scored lower than the monolingual English speakers on WAIS-III PIQ, Picture Completion, Block Design, and Similarities, as well as WMS-III Logical Memory I.

However, ESL status does not entirely account for lower performances on language/verbal tasks in ethnic minorities. Razani et al. (2006, 2007) observed that a fluent-English-speaking ethnically diverse (Middle Eastern, Asian, Hispanic) sample scored significantly below monolingual Anglo English speakers on language, verbal processing speed, and attention tasks (WASI Vocabulary and Similarities, Stroop B and C, Trails B, WAIS-III Digit Span, ACT 18-second delay), but not on visual–spatial/visual-constructional tests or tests of nonverbal processing speed (WASI Block Design and Matrix Reasoning, Trails A, WAIS-III Digit Symbol). However, the ESL and non-ESL subjects within the diverse group did not significantly differ on the language tests. Similarly, we found that in Hispanic patients, no significant differences were found on language tasks between those who were native English speakers (or who learned English concurrently with Spanish) and those with ESL status (Boone et al., 2007); native-English-speaking Hispanics, as compared to non-Hispanic white patients, averaged 10 points lower on the Boston Naming Test, > 6 points less on Verbal Fluency (FAS), and > 2 points lower on WAIS-III Digit Span. White foreign-born subjects, even if they have lived in the United States for decades, score lower than American-born subjects on some verbal tasks (Similarities, Boston Naming Test, and category and phonemic fluency)—a finding not mediated by language preference (i.e., there were no differences in performance between foreign-born subjects who spoke English at home and those who spoke another language; Touradji, Manly, Jacobs, & Stern, 2001).

The relevant factor for lowered scores in non-ESL ethnic minority groups appears to be level of acculturation to mainstream culture. Razani et al. (2006, 2007) found that ratings on an acculturation measure were positively related to several WAIS-III scores (Digit Symbol, Digit Span, Trails A, and Stroop B (rapid color naming), as well as WASI scores (Similarities, Vocabulary, and VIQ), while percentage of time English was currently spoken significantly predicted performance on language tasks (WASI Vocabulary and VIQ), but not other tasks. Although reduced scores for African Americans relative to white participants have been reported in several studies (see Walker, Batchelor, & Shores, 2009), Manly et al. (1998) observed that most of these differences disappeared (with significant differences remaining only in story learning) after adjustment for level of acculturation to the dominant culture. In immigrants, level of acculturation is more predictive of test scores than is number of years' residence in the United States (Razani et al., 2006, 2007), although number of years in the United States is related to scores on language tasks and tasks involving the English alphabet (Boston Naming Test, WAIS-III Digit Span, letter and category fluency, WAIS-III/WASI Similarities, Stroop B, Trails B; Boone et al., 2007; Razani et al., 2007; Touradji et al., 2001).

These data suggest that use of normative data developed on native English speakers and European Americans will "overpathologize" cognitive functioning in ethnic minorities and speakers of ESL. However, "race-based" norms do not appear to be the solution. Criticisms of such norms include (1) the impossibly large number of potential race/ethnic groups for which to generate norms; (2) nonscientific definitions of race/ethnic groupings; (3) overlooking of factors likely to be responsible for group racial differences (acculturation, socioeconomic status, quality of education, etc.); (4) the harm associated with false negative errors (i.e., cognitive deficits misdiagnosed as "normal"); and (5) potential use in justifying inferior or superior treatment of different racial groupings (Gasquoine, 2009). Ultimately, norms based on race should be discarded in favor of normative data that permit adjustment for level of acculturation, socioeconomic status, and the quality of education and where it was obtained (see below).

Educational Level/Illiteracy

Educational level has a significant impact on most neurocognitive scores (Mitrushina, Boone, Razani, & D'Elia, 2005; Walker et al., 2009), even nonverbal tasks that do not have obvious correlates with academic skills (e.g., Raven's Colored Progressive Matrices, WAIS-R Block Design, WMS-R Visual Reproduction; Marcopulos, McLain, & Guiliano, 1997). Furthermore, research shows that in general the greater the percentage of education completed outside the United States, the poorer the performance on neurocognitive measures obtained in the United States (Boone et al., 2007; Razani et al., 2006, 2007; Walker et al., 2010).

In addition, the quality of education, although difficult to assess, appears to have a significant impact on cognitive scores. Manly, Jacobs, Touradji, Small, and Stern (2002) observed that African Americans scored significantly worse than white Americans in word list learning/memory, figure memory, abstract reasoning, verbal fluency, and visual–spatial tasks, but after covarying for quality of education (with WRAT3 Reading serving as proxy), nearly all differences disappeared; reading level was most closely associated with verbal fluency, abstract reasoning, and naming (Manly, Byrd, Touradji, & Stern, 2004). The problem with this research is that determination of quality of education is based on a performance measure (WRAT3 Reading); individuals of low ability will perform worse on performance measures, regardless of education quality. Thus these findings, though clearly important, need to be supplemented by research employing indicators of education quality that are independent of test performance (e.g., published school ratings).

Illiterate individuals (defined as persons with no formal schooling and an inability to read) score more poorly than literate individuals on word list recall, but not on recall of pictured objects (Nitrini et al., 2004). They may also underperform on tasks involving digit span, verbal abstraction, long-term semantic memory (Information subtest), calculations, visual–spatial/visual-constructional skills, complex language comprehension, verbal repetition and fluency, and naming (Ardila & Rosselli, 1989; Castro-Caldas, Reis, & Guerreiro, 1997; Manly et al., 1999; Nitrini et al., 2004; Ostrosky-Solis, Ardila, Rosselli, Lopez-Arango, & Uriel-Mendoza, 1998; Reis, Guerreiro, & Petersson, 2003; Rosselli, Ardila, & Rosas, 1990).

Controlling for the Effects of Practice on Repeat Neuropsychological Testing

Many plaintiff attorneys send their clients for neuropsychological testing just prior to the defense neuropsychological exam; they appear to be under the belief that doing so will "ruin" the defense exam through practice effects (i.e., the increase in test scores will not be due to improvement in cognition, but rather to prior exposure to the tests). Vague (and unreferenced) statements such as "Neuropsychological testing cannot be completed within

6 months of the first exam" are proffered, although no such admonitions have actually been published, as others have pointed out (Greiffenstein, 2009; Heilbronner et al., 2010). Plaintiff counsel may also argue that it is an undue hardship on the client to undergo a second neuropsychological exam, particularly if one has just been completed, and that the defense neuropsychologist should forgo testing and simply accept the raw data generated from the plaintiff neuropsychological exam.

However, the defense neuropsychologist should typically attempt to complete his/her own exam, for several reasons. First of all, practice effects can be adjusted for if data are available from the first exam; a discussion of this issue is contained in the guidelines provided by the AACN regarding repeat assessments (Heilbronner et al., 2010). The presence of practice effects themselves may provide useful information regarding brain function and integrity, because the more severely impaired the patient, the fewer practice effects are observed (see Heilbronner et al., 2010); conversely, it can be argued that the more robust the practice effects, the more cognitively intact the patient is likely to be. Second, data from two separate exams can provide crucial comparison data, as in the case of scores *declining* precipitously on subsequent exams following a TBI. After a brain injury, test scores remain the same or gradually improve, and there is no brain/behavioral mechanism to account for a drop in scores. In addition, noncredible individuals often show odd changes in scores across various exams (probably because it is difficult to completely recall the exact tests on which one has deliberately underperformed in order to produce comparable results on an exam months or years later). Third, at times initial testing has been conducted during the acute recovery period (i.e., the first 12–18 postinjury months), and only testing completed outside that window will provide information about the permanence of any cognitive deficits. Fourth, the defense examiner may want to have data on particular tests that were not administered by the first psychologist; unless the defense neuropsychologist is allowed to conduct his or her own exam, including test selection, the ability to provide complete conclusions will be limited. Fifth, unless the testing is completed by the the defense neuropsychologist (or someone under this clinician's supervision whose skills he or she can vouch for), it will not be known whether the tests were in fact administered correctly. Finally, the fact that both sides can conduct their own exams keeps the exams "honest;" if only one side was allowed to do testing, unscrupulous practitioners might be disposed to "concoct" data helpful to the side that retained them. Knowing that other neuropsychologists will also be conducting exams helps safeguard against the fabrication of test scores, in that scores across exams should be grossly replicable (unless the patient is in an acute recovery period and is quickly improving, or has a rapidly deteriorating condition).

Stability of Test Findings

In cases of TBI, spontaneous recovery generally occurs within the first 12–18 postinjury months; as a result, test data obtained during this window may not be reflective of permanent cognitive residual effects. When testing is conducted during an acute recovery period, statements clarifying whether the findings can be expected to represent permanent function should be contained in the report.

Obtaining and Incorporating Medical and School Records

Medical, school, and work records are usually very helpful in corroborating the patient's report of injury and premorbid as well as postinjury function. Some neuropsychologists elect to provide a brief summary of each record, but I prefer to incorporate relevant data directly into my reports (not all records will be directly relevant). Some agencies will provide a review of records at a fee, but I prefer to read the records myself; other readers do not necessarily know what will be critical and relevant from a neuropsychological perspective. For example, in a case of claimed exposure to workplace toxins and in which the plaintiff denied any substance use/abuse to me, nursing notes buried in hospital admission records quoted the patient as admitting that "cocaine is ruining my life."

Medical and school records can be used to confirm (or disconfirm) the patient's report of pre-accident symptoms and academic function. Lees-Haley et al. (1997) documented that litigants underreported premorbid emotional and cognitive symptoms as compared to nonlitigants, and Greiffenstein, Baker, Gola, Donders, and Miller (2002) observed that head injury litigants inflated premorbid academic histories in comparison to nonlitigant controls.

Description of Performance on SVTs

Most neuropsychological reports contain a section on behavioral observations, and many still contain the previously ubiquitous statement that the "patient appeared to be exerting adequate effort on the various tests, and thus test results are judged to be an accurate reflection of actual cognitive function." It is now time to discard this statement. With the widespread use of SVTs, judgments about the quality of test responses must not be based solely on "behavioral observations." Such observations have no empirical validation (i.e., many individuals may appear credible on interview and during test administration, but are found to be engaging in response bias upon scoring of SVTs), and the error rate is unknown but is likely to be very high. Such "observations" were no doubt responsible for early reports that malingering was rare.

It is important to use well-validated SVTs and to employ the most up-to-date cutoffs. Doing so requires keeping abreast of the current literature. In the interest of transparency, current guidelines recommend providing the names of the measures of response bias employed and the scores in reports (Heilbronner et al., 2009), but in a way that protects test security. On occasion I have seen reports in which the entire SVT stimuli and administration procedures are detailed—a practice that clearly compromises test security and also violates the APA ethics code (see p. 164, and APA, 2010, Standard 9.11). On the other hand, other reports err in the opposite direction, providing no information about which measures were employed other than to indicate that unnamed "SVTs" were administered. Determining the balance between protecting tests and allowing one's work product and conclusions to be available for independent analysis is problematic, and there is no perfect solution.

As neuropsychologists, we are justifiably enamored of our tests, but professionals in medical and other related fields do not have the same understanding and appreciation of these measures' effectiveness that we do. In this regard, it is useful to attempt to make report data "alive" and comprehensible to the reader. For example, when a report concludes that a patient is not credible on cognitive testing, a neurologist or psychiatrist may ask, "Well, the neuropsychologist says the patient is faking, and she seems to be presenting objective test data that support her view, but I don't know the tests and I don't know if she is right. So maybe I should err on the side of giving the patient the benefit of the doubt?" Figure 5.1 below presents a sample report of a patient who was found to be noncredible on cognitive testing. As shown there, not only should scores on SVTs be reported, but it can also be useful to graph the patient's performances on SVTs in comparison to means for credible and noncredible patients. The question that can then be posed and answered for the reader is this: "Which group does the patient resemble? Credible patients or malingerers?" These visual aids are likely to be more convincing for juries and other medical professionals than written regurgitations of test scores.

However, some verbal descriptions can still render a patient's feigned performance particularly salient for nonpsychologists. For example, if a patient scores significantly below chance on the TOMM (a test that involves presentation of sequential pictures), the psychologist can indicate in the report that the patient scored worse than a blind person (who would be expected to perform at chance levels by guessing alone).

Personality Test Interpretation

The MMPI-2–RF publishers are moving toward "transparency," in which interpretive statements are referenced to specific research citations, so that the clinician will know the exact sources for particular interpretive statements. When preparing a report, it is recommended that interpretive statements for personality test data be referenced, and/or that interpretive material be directly quoted from narrative information provided by the test publishers (with quotation marks included). The latter approach is effective because it shows that it is the interpretation acknowledged by the test developers, who constitute a "disinterested" third party (i.e., they have no vested interest in the outcome of the case).

SAMPLE REPORT OF A NONCREDIBLE PATIENT

The sample report in Figure 5.1 illustrates how evidence of negative response bias can be documented.

REASON FOR REFERRAL

Ms. RG, a 57-year-old medical technician, was referred for neuropsychological testing by attorney KK for evaluation of cognitive and psychological functioning after an accident that resulted in a head injury. (Testing was completed 17 months after Ms. RG's accident.)

RECORDS REVIEWED

_____
_____
_____
_____

PRESENTING SITUATION AND BACKGROUND INFORMATION

The patient reported that on ___(date of accident)___ a light fixture fell onto her head from the ceiling as she bent over a display counter at a store. She does not know from what distance the fixture fell. She indicated that she did not lose consciousness. Her last recollection prior to being struck was of "enjoying looking at the watches." Her first memory following the injury was of thinking, "What happened?!" and being in pain and shock. She recalls "bleeding profusely" and feeling dazed and disoriented. She recollects that store employees ran over to her and placed her in a chair. She remembers seeing the light fixture on the floor (she described it as large and esti-

---

FIGURE 5.1. Sample report of a noncredible patient.

mated that it weighed 50–100 pounds). Store personnel located her mother, who had been shopping with the patient in the store, and the patient recalls being comforted by her mother. She remembers holding her cell phone and getting blood on it, and recalls being scared and tearful. Emergency medical service (EMS) personnel were summoned, and they bandaged the patient and asked her whether she wanted to be transported to a hospital. She was taken to _____ Medical Center, where she remembers undergoing a brain computed tomography (CT) scan. She indicated that she "waited for hours" to be sutured. She was given pain medication and kept until approximately 11:00 P.M. or midnight (she believes that the accident occurred at approximately 4:00 or 5:00 P.M.).

EMS records from ___(date of accident)___ indicate that a light fixture fell approximately 10 feet onto the patient's head but that she was not rendered unconscious. She was described as able to ambulate, and as alert and oriented with no weakness or dizziness; Glasgow Coma Scale (GCS) score was 15. Medical records show that the brain CT scan obtained on the day of the accident was normal.

Current physical symptoms that the patient attributes to this accident include the following:
1. "Tingling," "shooting" nerve pain on the top of her head where she was struck. She rates the typical level of pain as an 8–9 on a 10-point severity scale. She indicated that she experiences the pain three to four times per week up to daily, and that each episode lasts for approximately 5–10 minutes.
2. Headaches located on her "whole head," which at times occur daily and can last 1–2 hours. She rates the typical level of pain as a 9. She treats the headaches with Vicodin if she is not working, and with Tylenol if she is at work. She is not aware of any triggers for the headache pain.
3. Numbness in her hands, especially in the right hand, which she experiences daily and which lasts 1–15 minutes. She is aware of no triggers for the numbness.
4. Neck pain ("the worst"), which occurs daily and which she rates as a 10 on a 10-point scale. The pain lasts for several hours or until she takes Vicodin, and cold weather intensifies the pain. She also uses steroids to treat the pain, and reported that she is awaiting surgery to cauterize the nerves, but that the procedure was delayed because her blood pressure is elevated. She indicated that she has received pain management from Dr. _____ for 6 months.
5. Right-shoulder pain, which she rates as an 8–9 and which occurs two to three times per week, lasting for several hours. Treatment has included physical therapy for 2–3 months, which has helped "a little."
6. Dropping objects out of her right hand.

When questioned as to current cognitive symptoms that she believes are related to the store accident, the patient reported that she "can't remember things" and that she has to "write everything down." She provided the example that someone called for her boss, and the boss asked her who it was but she could not recall, even though the call had just occurred. The patient reported that she has to do things two to three times because she makes mistakes; for example, when giving information to coworkers she double- and triple-checks her work, whereas she did not need to do this prior to the store accident.

Regarding current psychological symptoms that she attributes to the store accident, the patient indicated that she feels "sad." When asked whether she is depressed, she responded affirmatively, and rated her depression as a 9–10 on a 10-point severity scale. She reported that she had experienced suicidal ideation, most recently 1 year ago. She also described social withdrawal; she indicated that before the accident she would see her mother on a daily basis and visit friends, but that she no longer socializes much and "wants to stay in bed." She further described herself as experiencing "a lot of anxiety," which she rates as typically an 8 on a 10-point scale. She initially stated that there were no triggers for her anxiety, but then indicated that she now becomes "panic-stricken" by elevators and flagpoles, and that she is always "looking up" in stores (worried that something will hit her). The patient reported that she no longer shops at _____ stores because she feels "nervous." She indicated that she was placed on Prozac 2 weeks prior to this exam. She reported that it was recommended earlier that she take antidepressants, but she declined because she was concerned about side effects. However, she indicated that she was told that the medication would also help with pain, so she agreed to take it. Regarding sleep, the patient reported that she finds it difficult to fall asleep, and that she at times awakens after 2–3 hours; she remains awake for 2 hours and then returns to sleep. She estimates that she sleeps 5–6 hours a night on average. She has not received any treatment for her sleep difficulties. The patient described her appetite as "fair" and reported that she gained 20–30 pounds after the accident due to less exercise. She indicated that the week before this exam she began treatment with a pain psychologist.

The patient denied any history of seizures, brain infections, stroke, diabetes, thyroid disorder, cardiac abnormalities, risk for HIV, hospitalizations or surgeries aside from a caesarian section, exposure to toxins, developmental abnormalities, alcohol or drug abuse, use of medications or substances by the patient's mother while pregnant with her, or significant psychological symptoms/treatment prior to the store accident. She denied any history of head injury with loss of consciousness. Medical records indicate that before the store accident, the patient was also struck in the head with a cleaning instrument in June of that year and sustained a contusion, but she was able to return to work the following day. The patient reported that the only headaches she experienced prior to the store accident were related to her menstrual period, and that she has gone through menopause and thus has no current menstrual-related headaches. She stated that she was born prematurely (at 7 months) and weighed 4 pounds, but that she experienced no complications related to this. The patient believes that she may have sleep apnea, although she has not been formally evaluated. She was diagnosed with hypertension 2–3 years ago, for which she takes Cozaar and a diuretic, but she reported that her condition is still not controlled. When queried as to respiratory problems, the patient indicated that 1 year ago she was thought to have possible congestive heart failure that might cause breathing problems. Her current medications are Cozaar, Prozac, a diuretic, Neurontin, and Vicodin (≤ 1 per day; she last took Vicodin the night before this exam). She denied a significant family psychiatric history, and denied experiencing any physical, sexual, or emotional abuse in childhood. She also denied experiencing any major life stressors within the past 5 years aside from the store accident.

The patient was raised by her biological mother and stepfather, and she speaks only English. She completed high school and 2 years of college; she indicated that she was a B–C student in high school. She denied any history of learning disability or attention-deficit/hyperactivity disorder. She is a certified medical technician and has worked in the field "on and off" for 30 years. She returned to work 10 weeks after the store accident, but was placed on disability after 3 weeks due to back pain and headaches; she remains off work.

The patient has three brothers, ages 59, 53, and 45. All completed Associate of Arts (AA) degrees and are described as in good health. One is employed at a local junior college; another worked in a personnel department but was laid off; and the third is unemployed. The patient's mother completed 2 years of college; she is a retired licensed vocational nurse and worked for a medical center for over 40 years. She currently suffers from heart problems. The patient reported that she has no information about her biological father. The patient has two children; her 22-year-old son completed an AA degree and works as a manager, and the 29-year-old daughter graduated from high school and works part-time. Both children as described as in good health, although she indicated that her daughter had learning difficulties, and medical records characterize her as having high-functioning autism.

The patient reported that she resides with her daughter. When queried about a typical day, the patient indicated that she arises between 6:00 and 7:00 A.M. and eats a bowl of cereal. She stated that she will then stay in her room/bed unless she needs something from a store. She reported that once per week she has an appointment with her pain doctor, and she has other sporadic medical appointments. Regarding cooking duties, the patient reported that she does some cooking for herself (e.g., cooking things in a rice cooker or microwave). She does her own grocery shopping and handles her own finances. Regarding housecleaning, the patient indicated that her daughter helps her; the daughter vacuums, dusts, cleans the stove, and takes the trash out. When queried about hobbies, the patient reported that she shops with her mother at the store chain where she was injured. When asked whether she socializes, the patient commented that currently she does not often socialize, but that a friend visits once in a while. She stated that she was last in a romantic relationship 10 years ago.

PREVIOUS TESTING

The patient underwent neuropsychological testing on _____ (10 months after the accident), with Dr. G and Dr. H. The patient was noted to have lowered intellectual skills as well as losses in several cognitive domains. She was diagnosed with cognitive disorder not otherwise specified (NOS) due to head injury, posttraumatic stress disorder (PTSD), and major depressive disorder.

The patient underwent psychiatric evaluation with Dr. J on _____ (18 months after the accident). Results of objective personality testing suggested that the patient "may have reported more psychological symptoms than objectively exist." She was diagnosed with major depression, generalized anxiety disorder, and PTSD.

BEHAVIORAL OBSERVATIONS

Ms. RG is a 57-year-old, right-handed, divorced, African American female who arrived on time and unaccompanied to the appointment. The patient was observed to be heavy-set and of short height; she was well groomed and attractively attired. She wore reading glasses. Speech characteristics were unremarkable, and thought processes were well organized and relevant. The patient was very pleasant, and social skills were intact. She became tearful at one point during the interview; mood was otherwise euthymic, and she was observed to be energetic and animated and to chuckle occasionally. No pain behaviors (grimacing, repositioning, massaging body areas, etc.) were observed. No signs of significant memory impairment were apparent during spontaneous behavior; after the interview, the patient reported that she needed coffee, went to three separate restaurants in the complex in search of coffee, and was able to find her way back to the office.

As detailed in the body of this report, various aspects of the patient's test responses indicated that she was in fact not performing to true capability on the neurocognitive tasks and was feigning deficits. Thus the test battery was abbreviated, because standard cognitive test scores would not have been accurate.

TESTS ADMINISTERED

Wechsler Adult Intelligence Scale–III (WAIS-III; Vocabulary, Digit Span, Digit Symbol, and Picture Completion subtests)
Rey Auditory Verbal Learning Test (RAVLT)
Rey–Osterrieth Complex Figure
Finger Tapping Test
Finger Agnosia Test
b Test
Rey Word Recognition Test
Rey 15-Item Memorization Test plus recognition trial
Dot Counting Test
Warrington Recognition Memory Test—Words
Minnesota Multiphasic Personality Inventory–2–Restructured Form (MMPI-2–RF)
Morel Emotional Numbing Test (MENT)
Modified Somatic Perception Questionnaire (MSPQ)

TEST RESULTS

Cognitive Symptom Validity

The patient failed four of five tests used to assess for symptom validity/response bias in the testing procedures. Specifically, she scored below cutoffs on the Rey Word Recognition Test (total = 5; combination score = 7; Nitch et al., 2006) and on the Rey 15-Item Memorization Test plus recognition trial (14; Boone, Salazar, et al., 2002), and beyond cutoffs on the b Test (E-score = 191; Boone, Lu, & Herzberg, 2002a) and the Dot Counting Test (5 errors; Boone, Lu, & Herzberg, 2002b). In contrast, she passed the Warrington Recognition Memory Test—Words (total correct = 43; 175 seconds; M. S. Kim et al., 2011).

Examination of performance on standard cognitive tests sensitive to feigned performance revealed failed indicators on six of seven tests. Specifically, the patient fell beyond cutoffs on the Finger Agnosia Test (4 errors; Trueblood & Schmidt, 1993), WAIS-III Digit Symbol recognition (−15; N. Kim et al., 2010), RO Figure Equation (29.5; Lu et al., 2003), RAVLT indicators (equation = 8, Boone et al., 2005; RO/RAVLT discriminant function = −1.228, Sherman et al., 2002), the Finger Tapping Test (dominant = 17.7; Arnold et al., 2005), and WAIS-III Picture Completion (age-corrected scaled score [ACSS] = 4; Most Discrepant Index = 1; Solomon et al., 2010). In contrast, she passed symptom validity indicators associated with WAIS-III Digit Span (ACSS = 9; reliable digit span [RDS] = 8; 3-digit time = 1.5 seconds; Babikian et al., 2006).

Research indicates that use of a criterion of failure on two symptom validity indicators best discriminates between credible and noncredible individuals (Larrabee, 2003c; Meyers & Volbrecht, 2003; Victor et al., 2009). The patient failed indicators from 10 of 12 separate tests. Thus the evidence indicates that she was not performing to true capability and was attempting to portray herself as more impaired than is actually the case. As a result, the following test scores should be considered underestimates of her true ability.

Attention and Information-Processing Speed

The patient scored within the average range on a test of basic attention (WAIS-III Digit Span). She achieved a forward span of 6 and a backward span of 4, for an overall performance at the 37th percentile for her age. The patient passed symptom validity indicators associated with this task, suggesting that she was likely performing to true capability.

In contrast, performance on a measure of mental speed was impaired (WAIS-III Digit Symbol = 2nd percentile for age), although as discussed above, she failed a symptom validity indicator associated with this test (Digit Symbol recognition), as well as other symptom validity tests evaluating processing speed (b Test). These failures indicate that she was not performing to true potential in this area.

Visual–Spatial Ability

Scores on measures of visual-perceptual/visual–spatial skills were within the impaired range, but the patient failed symptom validity measures associated with these abilities, indicating that she was not performing to true capability. Specifically, the patient scored in the impaired range in alertness to visual detail (WAIS-III Picture Completion = 2nd percentile for age), but as noted above, she failed a symptom validity indicator associated with this task. Similarly, the patient scored in the impaired range in pencil-and-paper copy of a complex line drawing (RO Figure copy = 20.5/36), but as discussed above, she also failed a symptom validity indicator derived from this task.

Language Function

As noted earlier, the patient's spontaneous speech was unremarkable, and no difficulties were observed in comprehension of task instructions. Vocabulary range was in the average range (WAIS-III Vocabulary = 50th percentile for age).

Learning and Memory

On the RAVLT, the patient learned 7 words by the 5th learning trial, an impaired score (2nd percentile for age as per meta-norms; Mitrushina, Boone, Razani, & D'Elia, 2005). Following an interference task, she recalled 4 words, also an impaired performance (2nd percentile for age as per meta-norms; Mitrushina et al., 2005). Following a 30-minute delay, she recalled 2 words, again an impaired performance (< 1st percentile for age/gender; Geffen, O'Hanlon, Clark, & Geffen, 1990). She recognized 6 words with no false positive errors. Of note, as discussed earlier, she failed symptom validity indicators derived from the RAVLT, as well as another verbal memory symptom validity measure (Rey Word Recognition Test). These failures indicate that she was not performing to true capability in this area.

The patient's 3-minute delayed recall of the RO Figure was within the low average range (14/36; 21st percentile for age/education; Boone, Lesser, Hill-Gutierrez, Berman, & D'Elia, 1993). As described above, she failed symptom validity indicators associated with this task (RO/RAVLT discriminant function; RO Figure Equation), as well as other symptom validity measures associated with visual memory (Rey 15-Item Memorization Test plus recognition trial, WAIS-III Digit Symbol recognition). These failures indicate that she was not performing to true ability in this skill.

Motor Function

The patient reported a strong right-hand preference. Results of motor dexterity testing revealed impaired performance with the right hand and low average performance with the left hand (Tapping: right = 17.7, < 1st percentile for age/gender; left = 36.3, 11th percentile for age/gender; Trahan, Patterson, Quintana, & Biron, 1987). However, as noted above, the patient failed a symptom validity indicator associated with this task, indicating that she was not performing to true ability.

Personality Function

MMPI-2–RF. Scores on validity scales suggested noncredible overreport of both psychiatric and physical/cognitive symptoms, not explained by failure to comprehend test items or by random responding (VRIN-r = 48*T*, TRIN-r = 57*T*, F-r = 88*T*, Fp-r = 59*T*, Fs = 58*T*, FBS-r = 86*T*, RBS = 92*T*, L-r = 52*T*, K-r = 42*T*).

A significant elevation was present on one of three Higher-Order scales (Emotional/Internalizing Dysfunction = 89*T*). Examination of Restructured Clinical scales (with item overlap and generalized demoralization removed) revealed a significant elevation on the Somatic Complaints scale (RC1 = 81T), consistent with physical symptom overreport. The patient also obtained significant elevations on scales measuring depression (RCd = 85*T*, RC2 = 99*T*), but she exceeded cutoffs identified for feigned depression on RCd (Henry et al., 2009). A significant, mild elevation was present on an anxiety scale (RC7 = 70*T*). Significant elevations were present on all somatic/cognitive scales (Malaise = 75*T*, GI Complaints = 72*T*, Head Pain Complaints = 78*T*, Neurological Complaints = 75*T*, Cognitive Complaints = 86*T*), again consistent with physical and cognitive symptom overreport (e.g., research shows that patients with true cognitive dysfunction do not have elevated scores on the Cognitive Complaints scale; Gervais, Ben-Porath, & Wygant, 2009).

The following narrative is provided by the test publisher:

> The test taker generated a larger than average number of infrequent responses to the MMPI-2–RF items. This level of infrequent responding may occur in individuals with genuine psychological difficulties who report credible symptoms. However, for individuals with no history or current corroborating evidence of dysfunction it likely indicates over-reporting. She also provided an unusual combination of responses that is associated with noncredible reporting of somatic and/or cognitive symptoms. This combination of responses may occur in individuals with substantial medical problems who report credible symptoms, but it could also reflect exaggeration. . . . In addition, she provided an unusual combination of responses that are associated with noncredible memory complaints. This combination of responses may occur in individuals with significant emotional dysfunction, but it could also reflect exaggeration. . . . (MMPI-2–RF Interpretive Report, 2011).

MSPQ. The patient scored at cutoffs on a measure assessing for overreport of pain complaints (raw = 14; Larrabee, 2003d).

MENT. The patient scored atypically on the MENT (7 errors; > 2 *SD*s beyond credible means for patients with PTSD), which suggests that she was likely feigning symptoms of PTSD.

SUMMARY AND CONCLUSIONS

Cognitive Function

Evidence emerged during the testing that the patient was not performing to true capability on the cognitive tasks, and was portraying herself as more cognitively impaired than is actually the case. This occurred despite the fact that before the evaluation began, the patient was specifically informed that it was important that she perform with her best effort on the cognitive tests, and that if she did not, it would make her profile more difficult to interpret.

Specifically, the patient performed atypically and in a noncredible manner on 10 of 12 measures used to detect suboptimal symptom validity and response bias. Research indicates that use of a criterion of failure on 2 symptom validity indicators best discriminates between credible and noncredible subjects (Larrabee, 2003c; Meyers & Volbrecht, 2003; Victor et al., 2009). To place her performance in context, individuals with IQ scores in the extremely low range, indicating mental retardation (i.e., FSIQ 60–69), typically fail 44% of symptom validity indicators; the patient failed 10 of 12 indicators (83%). Thus she performed worse than individuals with mental retardation, but she was able to work as a medical technician after the accident, handles her own finances, and drives. Available evidence shows that acute (Etherton et al., 2005a, 2005b) and chronic (Iverson et al., 2007) pain and depression (Goldberg et al., 2007) do not lead to symptom validity test failure and would not account for her failed performances.

The following graphs reproduce the patient's performances on a selection of the symptom validity indicators, and shows that she was performing like noncredible individuals and not like credible patients.

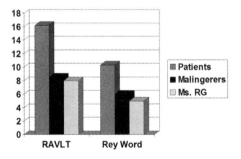
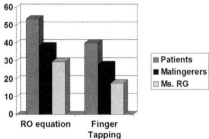

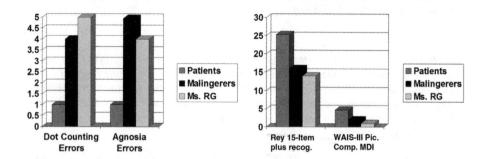

The patient performed within the average range on tests of language and attention. She scored in the low average range in visual memory, and in the impaired range on measures of verbal memory, processing speed, finger dexterity, and visual-perceptual/visual–spatial skills, but she failed symptom validity indicators measuring veracity of performance in these latter areas. Specifically, she failed indicators assessing for response bias in verbal memory (Rey Word Recognition Test, RAVLT equation, RO/RAVLT discriminant function), visual memory (WAIS-III Digit Symbol recognition, RO equation, Rey 15-Item Memorization Test plus recognition trial), processing speed (b Test, WAIS-III Digit Symbol recognition), motor dexterity (Finger Tapping Test), and visual-perceptual/visual–spatial skills (WAIS-III Picture Completion, RO equation; b Test; Dot Counting Test). The pattern of symptom validity test performance indicates that the patient was targeting verbal and visual memory tests, processing speed, motor dexterity, and visual-perceptual/visual–spatial skills on which to fabricate symptoms, and thus these scores cannot be accepted as valid.

In addition, the patient does not appear to have provided medical history to this examiner in an entirely forthright manner. For example, on current exam the examiner was told by the patient that her sleep difficulties were related to the store accident, but treatment records after the accident indicate that the patient's sleep was interrupted by her asthma and that she was not feeling well due to her asthma (no other medical conditions were cited as causing her to feel poorly). She did not even report to this examiner that she had asthma, even when specifically queried about respiratory problems.

Furthermore, the patient is described as the primary caretaker for her daughter with high-functioning autism and is able to conduct activities of daily living independently (including handling her own finances and driving), which she could not do if she had significantly impaired cognitive abilities. For example, her very low visual-perceptual/visual–spatial scores, if accurate, would be likely to preclude driving, and might necessitate that she be reported to the Department of Motor Vehicles for removal of her license. The low cognitive scores obtained on the current exam were also at variance with observations as to how the patient actually functions. For example, Finger Tapping Test scores were extremely low, yet the patient used her fingers entirely normally on all other tasks and in spontaneous movements (e.g., using a pen). Of further note, work evaluations from _____ Hospital show no deficits in her postacci-dent work skills, which included handling needles and drawing blood—tasks that she would probably not be able to execute if she had true impairments in finger dexterity. Moreover, the patient showed almost no ability to learn new verbal information on the current exam, yet she was able to relate to this examiner what was apparently told her 9 months earlier during her previous neuropsychological evaluation regarding the use of techniques to detect faking (see below). She was also able to provide a fairly detailed account of the store accident and of her postaccident symptoms and function, which would not be likely if she had significant memory impairment.

The patient would not have any current cognitive sequelae related to the store accident. No loss of consciousness, a GCS score of 15, no retrograde amnesia or anterograde amnesia, and normal brain CT imaging would indicate that if the patient sustained a traumatic brain injury (TBI), it was at most mild (mTBI). Research, including a review (Carroll et al., 2004) and six meta-analyses (133 studies, $n = 1,463$ mTBI), Belanger, Curtiss, Demery, Lebowitz, & Vanderploeg, 2005; 21 studies, $n = 790$ mTBI, Belanger & Vanderploeg, 2005; 8 studies, $n = 314$ mTBI, Binder, Rohling, & Larrabee, 1997; 17 studies, $n = 634$ mTBI, Frencham, Fox, & Maybery, 2005; 25 studies, $n = 2,828$, Rohling et al., 2011; 39 studies, $n = 1,716$ mTBI, Schretlen & Shapiro, 2003), shows that patients who experience mTBI have returned to baseline by weeks to months after injury. A recent book summarizing current research on mTBI and published under the auspices of the American Academy of Clinical Neuropsychology (the membership organization for board-certified neuropsychologists) has concluded that there is "no indication of permanent impairment on neuropsychological testing by three months postinjury" (McCrea, 2008). The only significant predictors of chronic symptoms after mTBI are litigation status and preexisting psychiatric history (Kashluba, Paniak, & Casey, 2008).

The patient meets criteria for probable malingered neurocognitive dysfunction (Slick et al., 1997) and definite noncredible cognitive performance (Boone, 2007b), and would also be classified as malingering/noncredible according to established research crite-ria (see Greiffenstein, Baker, & Gola, 1994; Greve, Bianchini, Love, Brennan, & Heinly, 2006; Solomon et al., 2010).

On evaluation 9 months prior to current exam, the patient is described as performing in a credible manner on cognitive testing, but examination of actual test data shows that of two symptom validity tests administered, the patient scored atypically on some scores from one (the Word Memory Test) and clearly fell below cutoffs for credible performance on the Finger Tapping test. The patient spontaneously commented to this examiner that at the previous evaluation, "they said they could tell if I was faking. They re-iterated that because some people don't do their best." This comment raises concerns about what the patient was told regarding symptom validity tests during that exam. Research has shown that if patients are informed that measures of response bias are present in a test battery, and if they are intent on faking, they in fact continue to fake but do so in a more careful and subtle manner (Gervais et al., 2001; Gunstad & Suhr, 2001; Youngjohn et al., 1999; Suhr & Gunstad, 2000). Thus the instructions and information given to the patient on the previous exam may have in fact sabotaged the ability of those examiners to detect feigning in this patient.

Furthermore, the previous examiners do not appear to have considered other, more likely etiologies for the patient's lowered scores, if in fact some of those scores are accurate. Specifically, she has poorly controlled hypertension, possible sleep apnea, and likely congestive heart failure, all of which would be expected to be associated with at least mild cognitive losses. She also reported poor performance in math in school, and in fact scored poorly on measures of math skill on the previous exam, but poor math skills were not considered in the interpretation of other test scores that rely on math skills (e.g., Auditory Consonant Trigrams). Finally, no adjustment for cultural factors appears to have been made; for example, the patient is described as showing word retrieval difficulties on the Boston Naming Test, when in fact she scored well within the expected range for her ethnic/cultural group (Boone et al., 2007).

Psychological Function

Results of objective personality testing suggested noncredible overreport of psychiatric symptoms, including depression and PTSD, as well as physical/cognitive symptoms. Although elevations on psychiatric symptom overreport scales can occur in individuals with genuine psychological difficulties, these individuals would display gross evidence of psychiatric disturbance not demonstrated by this patient. On exam she was animated and energetic with euthymic mood, including chuckling, and she is independent in activities of daily living, including caring for her daughter with autism. Of note, her elevation on the general overreport scale was even higher than the average for female psychiatric inpatients, who arguably have psychiatric dysfunction so disabling that they cannot function independently. The patient had not received any psychiatric treatment until a few weeks ago, and she clearly does not require inpatient care; thus her elevation on the overreport scale is not plausible. Whereas the patient claims current high levels of depression and anxiety, which she attributes to the store accident, a recent meta-analysis of the relationship between mTBI and psychiatric symptoms (depression, anxiety, psychosocial disability, reduced coping), concluded that "mTBI may have a very small to no measurable effect on psychological and psychosocial symptom reporting" (Panayiotou et al., 2010). Finally, although the patient initially reported in the interview that she no longer shops at the store chain where she was injured, she indicates in a listing of her typical daily activities that she shops with her mother at the chain. This would tend to argue against any substantial PTSD symptoms, such as avoiding the trauma context.

Although the level of elevation on the physical/cognitive symptom overreport validity scale obtained by the patient can occur in individuals with substantial medical problems, such individuals would show gross evidence of physical dysfunction not exhibited by this patient. She ambulated normally, and did not show signs of any physical discomfort or lack of stamina during the several-hour exam. Furthermore, her elevation on the physical/cognitive symptom overreport scales were markedly higher than that found in female candidates for bariatric and spinal cord surgery or stimulators, who arguably have multiple actual physical symptoms and pronounced pain. It is relevant to note that patients with mTBI do not show an increased rate of headache relative to controls by 3 months postaccident (Mickeviciene et al., 2004), raising questions regarding the veracity of the patient's headache report.

On previous testing 9 months earlier, the patient was described as showing evidence of depression and PTSD on objective testing. However, the Detailed Assessment of Posttraumatic Stress (DAPS) was used to document symptoms of PTSD, and the DPAS is not appropriate in a forensic setting, because there is no peer-reviewed empirical research documenting that the validity scales do in fact adequately detect the presence of feigning. Furthermore, on that exam the patient obtained a score of 27 on the MMPI-2 FBS scale, which suggests overreport of physical/cognitive symptoms and depression (Greiffenstein et al., 2007; Crawford et al., 2006). Similarly, on exam one month after current testing, results of objective personality testing revealed that the patient "may have reported more psychological symptoms than objectively exist."

In summary and conclusion, the patient responded in a noncredible manner on cognitive testing and in her report of physical/pain, cognitive, and psychiatric complaints, including depression and PTSD. This pattern of responding indicates that her claims of dysfunction in these areas cannot be accepted as accurate.

Postscript: After surveillance videotapes documenting normal motoric function were obtained on the patient, the brain injury component of her lawsuit was dropped.

6

Seven Common Flaws in Forensic Neuropsychological Reports

In the role of expert witness in forensic cases, I have had the opportunity to read many neuropsychological reports, particularly reports by plaintiff-retained experts. Seven types of flaws are frequently encountered; these are summarized in Table 6.1 and discussed in detail in this chapter.

FAILURE TO ASSESS APPROPRIATELY FOR NEGATIVE RESPONSE BIAS

Administering No, Not Enough, or Ineffective Measures

Current practice standards state plainly that formal measures of response bias are to be interspersed *throughout* a neuropsychological exam,

---

TABLE 6.1. Flaws in Reports

- Failure to assess appropriately for response bias
- Use of inappropriate tests or norms
- Failure to draw conclusions consistent with published research
- Failure to consider all possible etiologies
- Overinterpretation of lowered scores
- Claims that low cognitive scores document brain injury
- Misinterpretation of the MMPI-2/MMPI-2–RF

---

particularly in those instances in which a test taker has a motive to feign impairments (NAN—Bush et al., 2005), and that both *embedded* and *free-standing* measures are to be employed (AACN—Heilbronner et al., 2009).

Despite the fact that the assessment of response bias has been one of the most prominent topics in clinical neuropsychology for the past 15 years, I still occasionally encounter neuropsychological reports in a forensic setting in which neither dedicated nor embedded SVTs have been employed. It can be argued that such reports clearly fail to conform to published practice guidelines.

More common are reports that fail to assess adequately for response bias, in that only one or two SVTs have been administered and/or SVTs are used that have low sensitivity in the detection of response bias. As discussed on pages 32–40, it is now recommended (1) that symptom validity be evaluated continuously throughout a neuropsychological evaluation, because negative response bias is not static; and (2) that symptom validity should be assessed in various cognitive domains, given that test takers may decide to feign in some skill areas and not others (Boone, 2009). I frequently encounter reports in which the TOMM and the Rey 15-Item Memorization Test are administered, and if passing performances are obtained, it is determined that the test taker has performed to true capability. However, it can be argued that these two measures are assessing response bias on visual memory tasks, and do not necessarily provide data regarding adequacy of effort as applied to other skill areas. Furthermore, both the Rey 15-Item Test and the TOMM are relatively insensitive, with approximately 50% sensitivity at published cutoffs (< 9 for the former and < 45 on Trial 2 of the latter; Boone, Salazar, et al., 2002; Greve et al., 2008). Passing performances cannot be used to rule out response bias if half of noncredible individuals pass these tests (see p. 32) for further discussion of these issues).

Discounting Detected Response Bias

Some reports indicate that a patient has failed SVTs, but then the neuropsychological examiner will "explain away" the failures as due to pain, medications for pain or other conditions, depression/stress/anxiety, fatigue, attentional lapses, and the like (singly or in combination). But as discussed on pages 64–66, research shows that these variables do not lead to SVT failure.

In order to make an effective case that such factors (singly or in combination) have caused the person to fail SVTs, it would have to be argued that these conditions caused the person to have cognitive ability comparable to that found in the patient groups who truly do fail SVTs at a high rate despite performing to true capability—namely, patients with very low intellectual function and/or dementia. However, if pain, medications, psychiatric symptoms, fatigue, and so on caused extremely low mental function, the affected people would lose the ability to drive, to care for themselves, or to perform other ADLs. As demonstrated in the sample report in Figure 5.1, the following may be an effective way to address this issue in a neuropsychological report:

> To place the patient's performance in context, individuals with IQ scores in the extremely low range, indicating mental retardation, fail approximately 44% of symptom validity indicators administered despite performing to true capability (Dean, Victor, et al., 2008); the patient failed 91%. Thus she performed worse than individuals with mental retardation but she [works, drives, parents, handles the family finances, etc.]. The patient's low cognitive scores, if accurate, would in fact require that she [leave her job, be reported to the Department of Motor Vehicles for removal of her driver's license, etc.].

Also, obviously, if such factors were to affect SVT performance, they would also contaminate standard cognitive test results, which therefore could not be used as indicative of the sequelae of any frank brain injury.

Some reports will also attempt to dismiss any detected response bias by pointing to SVTs that were passed or to intact performance on some standard cognitive tasks—for example, "So this is not a profile of someone who looks as if she's not trying hard. If anything, it's the opposite. She does very, very well on many measures." However, cutoff points are set to protect credible patients, at the sacrifice of detecting noncredible patients; thus failed scores are more informative than passing scores. Also, as discussed earlier (pp. 36–37), the typical noncredible patient is not underperforming on every task. Furthermore, passing performances do not "override" failed SVTs; as discussed on pages 50–51, although it is not unusual for a credible patient to fail a single SVT out of several administered (with cutoffs set to $\geq 90\%$ to $< 100\%$ specificity), only 5% fail two, 1.5% fail three, and none fail four (Victor et al., 2009; see also Chafetz, 2011a; Larrabee, 2003c; Meyers & Volbrecht, 2003; Sollman et al., 2010). Thus, three or four SVT failures, which are virtually specific to noncredible patients, are not "canceled out" by passed SVTs.

Iverson (2006) has listed 11 "ethical concerns" regarding symptom validity assessment that are useful guidelines in evaluating opposing neuropsychological reports:

1. Failing to use well-researched SVTs.
2. Using SVTs only for defense cases.
3. Using more or fewer SVTs, systematically, depending on whether you were retained by the defendant or plaintiff.

4. Using different SVTs, depending on which side retains you.
5. Using SVTs differently, depending on which side retains you.
6, Warning or prompting patients immediately before administration of an SVT.
7. Interpreting SVTs differently, systematically, depending on which side retains you (e.g., "cry for help" if plaintiff-retained, malingering if defense-retained).
8. Assuming that someone who passes an SVT gave full effort during the evaluation.
9. Interpreting SVT failure, in isolation, as malingering.
10. Inappropriately interpreting SVT failure as a "cry for help."
11. Failing to make competent, informed, and up-to-date use of tests (or relying just on published test manuals).

The following deposition testimony from a plaintiff neuropsychologist illustrates advocacy in the selection of SVTs:

DEFENSE COUNSEL: Why didn't you give the Test of Memory Malingering in this case?

PLAINTIFF NEUROPSYCHOLOGICAL EXPERT: On the plaintiff side, I generally don't give a long number of tests of malingering. I usually give just a few, often just a couple, and it depends whether I think there's any reason to believe that the patient that I'm seeing is malingering. . . .

A surveillance videotape in this case actually demonstrated that the patient was feigning the cognitive and motor dysfunction he exhibited on neuropsychological exam. Specifically, despite grossly impaired Finger Tapping Test scores and a reproduction of the RO Figure that consisted of details drawn in a disconnected jumble on the page, surveillance showed this patient driving a car in a very able manner and using his fingers normally to retrieve a cell phone and keys from his pockets. This plaintiff neuropsychologist apparently did not appreciate that the role of an expert is not to function as an advocate for one side or the other, but rather to present objective and accurate neuropsychological information to the court.

USE OF INAPPROPRIATE TESTS OR NORMS

Use of Obsolete, Experimental, or Poorly Normed and Validated Tests

As discussed on page 18, it is important to administer tests in common usage for which there are appropriate normative data. At times I have been accused in depositions of unethical behavior for having used "obsolete" versions, but as discussed on pages 16–18, tests are determined to be obsolete by research showing that they are in fact obsolete. Tests such as the WAIS-III have much more validation research than newer versions, and it can be argued that because of this research base, they should be used in preference over newer versions.

Use of Valid Tests That Are Inappropriate for the Context

Because new tests and test batteries are published with increasing frequency, it is important to ensure not only that they have appropriate normative data, but that they have been validated for the purpose for which they are used in forensic settings. For example, many clinicians rapidly incorporated the D-KEFS into their test batteries for use in forensic TBI cases, even though at this writing, a search of PubMed reveals only two publications regarding the D-KEFS in individuals with TBI. Similarly, a frequent occurrence is to see the Conners CPT–II used to evaluate patients claiming TBI, with abnormal results used to buttress a conclusion that a plaintiff has a trauma-induced attentional disorder. However, a perusal of peer-reviewed literature at this writing shows no publications in which this instrument has been studied or validated in a sample with TBI.

FAILURE TO DRAW CONCLUSIONS CONSISTENT WITH PUBLISHED RESEARCH

The third common flaw in neuropsychological reports is a failure to draw conclusions that are in keeping with the published research. The most ubiquitous example is this: Many neuropsychological reports conclude that observed cognitive abnormalities are due to long-term effects of mTBI, but as detailed on pages 227–228, several meta-analyses of the mTBI literature have concluded that no cognitive abnormalities are detected within days to months after a concussion, leading a major review of the literature on mTBI to conclude that there is "no indication of permanent impairment on neuropsychological testing by three months postinjury" (McCrea, 2008, p. 177). Furthermore, as discussed on pages 228–231, publications purporting to document chronic cognitive abnormalities in mTBI are methodologically flawed.

Even when presented with current research and conclusions regarding outcome in mTBI, some opposing experts will make the following type of comment during testimony:

"I know there are people who believe that the research literature shows that patients with mild traumatic brain injury should recover within 6

months. I have come across this many, many times. I know the studies that are used to support that. I believe there are at least as many
studies and more that show that this is just simply not the case, and
there's a certain percentage of patients—I would guess 10%, but possibly more—who really don't recover, neither quickly nor ever. I think
these cases are very well documented. I've seen hundreds of such cases,
so it's not like I've seen a couple."

This testimony shows that the expert is not familiar with the current literature (interestingly, the expert does not provide any actual citations in
support of his/her conclusions). Moreover, the final statement, in which the
expert claims to have seen "hundreds of such cases," does not in fact provide
support for his/her position. If neuropsychologists do not avail themselves
of new knowledge, then such knowledge cannot inform and correct their
clinical practice. For instance, 25 years ago many mental health professionals cultivated entire practices of patients with dissociative identity disorder
(formerly called multiple personality disorder). Each patient they diagnosed
and treated provided confirmation that the condition existed, in a self-
perpetuating "closed loop." However, in hindsight we realize that claimed
multiple personalities were the creations of patients with probable borderline personality disorder, who provided therapists with what the patients
thought they wanted to hear and with what would garner attention for
the patients (see Nathan, 2011; see also Aldridge-Morris, 1989; McHugh,
1993; Merskey, 1992; Simpson, 1988; Spanos, 1994; Spanos, Weekes, &
Bertrand, 1985). Without the corrective function of subsequent empirical
research showing the dubious underpinnings of this claimed condition, we
might still be training students to provide services to such patients.

As evidence-based practitioners, we must draw conclusions consistent
with the preponderance of data provided by empirical research. A scientist
in the modern age cannot conclude that the earth is flat, given the incontrovertible scientific evidence that it is round; likewise, a neuropsychologist
should not conclude that mTBI is the cause of chronic cognitive impairments if current research does not support this conclusion.

FAILURE TO CONSIDER ALL POSSIBLE ETIOLOGIES

In many neuropsychological reports can be found examples of "prema-
ture foreclosure." For example, suppose that a neuropsychologist has been
informed by a referring attorney that a patient struck his/her head in a
motor vehicle accident, and then, if cognitive abnormalities are detected,
the psychologist concludes that the injury caused the lowered scores. However, as discussed on pages 227–228, research indicates that there are no

long-term cognitive deficits associated with a head injury in which loss of consciousness is < 30 minutes, anterograde amnesia is < 24 hours, no brain imaging abnormalities are found, and GCS is 13–15.

Dikmen and Levin (1993) have stated this problem well:

> A common mistake in clinical practice is automatically to attribute the cause of the difficulties observed in patients seen long after the injury to the head injury. [They note that preexisting condition such as] learning disabilities, psychiatric problems, neurological disorders (e.g., epilepsy), and particularly previous head injuries and alcohol abuse are prevalent in the population with head injury [and that] these conditions in themselves are known to be associated with neuropsychological and psychosocial problems. (p. 35)

Similarly, Greiffenstein and Baker (2003) have found that low premorbid grade point average is associated with impaired-range neuropsychological scores in nonmalingering postconcussive litigants. They conclude that "marginal premorbid achievement may be a risk factor for late developing postconcussion syndrome and litigation" (p. 561).

As shown in Figure 2.1 and discussed on pages 178–191, many psychiatric, neurological, medical, and developmental conditions (as well as linguistic/cultural differences) typically have a larger impact on cognitive scores than mTBI has.

The following case illustrates the confounding impact of learning disability on cognitive test performance in an individual litigating in the context of TBI.

> This patient was a 37-year-old, Caucasian, left-handed male with 16 years of education. He was employed as a bartender while attempting to start his own business. He was involved in a pedestrian-versus-auto accident 1 year prior to evaluation. At the scene, his GCS score was 10, but it had improved to 15 upon his arrival at the emergency room. Although neurological exam was normal, brain imaging showed a right frontal subdural hematoma. The patient's last recollection prior to being struck (assessing for retrograde amnesia) was of paying the bill in a restaurant where he had eaten (he was struck while crossing the street in front of the restaurant less than 5 minutes after paying the bill). His first recollection following the accident (assessing for anterograde amnesia) was of awakening in the emergency room (about 1 hour after accident). Given these injury characteristics, he was judged to have a TBI at the mild end of moderate brain injury.
>
> Claimed cognitive symptoms from the injury included decreased reading comprehension, poor memory, and losses in multitasking. The patient passed symptom validity indicators from five of five tests (the Finger Tapping Test, WAIS-IV Digit Span indicators, RO Figure equation, RAVLT variables, Rey Word Recognition Test), suggesting that he

was performing to true capability on the cognitive tasks. Neuropsychological scores were normal (average or higher). However, his WAIS-IV VCI was less than his Perceptual Reasoning Index (PRI) (102 vs. 113); Stroop A (rapid word reading) was at the lower end of average (28th percentile); and academic skills were average, but performance was below expectation for his 16 years of education (WRAT4 Spelling = 42nd percentile, 12.7 grade equivalent; Arithmetic = 34th percentile for age, 9.8 grade equivalent; Word Reading = 34th percentile for age, 11.9 grade equivalent; Sentence Comprehension = 42nd percentile for age, 12.7 grade equivalent, but the patient was noted to have pronounced difficulty when asked to read the sentences aloud). Memory scores were also average or higher, with the exception of a borderline score in recall of words after interference (3rd percentile), and a score at the lower end of average in delayed free recall of the list (27th percentile). Thus, in summary, the patient's cognitive profile was essentially normal, with these exceptions: one borderline score in word list recall; visual skills > verbal skills; visual memory > verbal memory; and PRI > VCI. Also, scores on tests of academic skills (arithmetic, reading, and spelling) were lower than would be expected for education completed, and the patient was noted to struggle when reading aloud.

The patient's previous medical and psychiatric history was unremarkable; there was no evidence of significant depression or anxiety on the MMPI-2–RF (RC2 and RC7 were not elevated); and he was prescribed no medications. However, he had been diagnosed with "dyslexia" requiring resource room placement throughout middle and high school. Although he had completed a college education, his degree was in a visual field (fine arts).

The following questions should be raised in such a case:

- *Were the lowered scores related to TBI?* Not likely. Scores that might be expected to be low in TBI were normal (e.g., processing speed; Dikmen, Machamer, Winn, & Temkin, 1995), whereas scores on verbal/language skills, normally generally well preserved in brain injury (Dikmen et al., 1995), were relatively lowered. Moreover, the imaging abnormality was in the right hemisphere (the "nonlanguage" hemisphere), whereas the patient's lowered scores were primarily language-related.
- *Are the lowered scores related to normal variability?* Not likely. The patient's scores were not scattered, but rather showed a "left-hemisphere" pattern.
- *Were the lowered scores related to a preexisting learning disability?* The cognitive profile suggested this, as did the patient's history of special education. As discussed on pages 180–181, adults with histories of childhood language-based learning disability show declines in naming speed, verbal learning and recall, word generation, rapid word reading, and vocabulary; their VIQ is also lower than their PIQ.

The opposing neuropsychologist tried to argue that the left-handedness pointed to atypical hemispheric specialization (i.e., language skills in the right hemisphere), and that therefore the imaging abnormalities would be consistent with the patient's cognitive profile. However, in most left-handers, language is primarily subserved by the left hemisphere (Knecht et al., 2000). Furthermore, the patient's premorbid history showed that he was poor in verbal skills and had strengths in visual skills, which was also true after the injury. Thus there was no evidence for any change in the pattern of cognitive skills from before to after the accident.

OVERINTERPRETATION OF LOWERED SCORES

Failure to Consider Normal Variability

As discussed on pages 174–178, substantial intraindividual variability in a battery of neuropsychological scores is common in normal adults.

Particularly problematic are the numerous CVLT-II and D-KEFS scores. Unfortunately, although the publishers of these tests have provided norms for individual scores, they have been slow to disseminate information regarding how many lowered scores are found in normal populations— data that are critically needed. As Binder et al. (2009) have stated, "for the developers of test batteries, the obvious implication of the studies reviewed here is that data on the extent of normal variability, the base rates of low scores, and the presence of large discrepancy scores should be provided to test users in the test manual and scoring software at the time of publication" (p. 13) In fact, Donders (2006) reported that for the CVLT-II, only discrepancies between scores of at least 1 or 1.5 z-score points should be considered unusual; however, one in three subjects in the standardization sample obtained discrepancies this large, indicating that such differences cannot be interpreted in isolation.

I find in reviewing reports that many neuropsychologists "overtest" (i.e., administer an excessive number of tests to address the referral question) and conclude that any lowered score is evidence of abnormality, with no consideration of normal variability. In these situations, it can be useful to produce a frequency count of the various scores from the battery; such an endeavor will often show the large majority of scores to be within the average range, a few above average, and a few below average. This visual demonstration will serve to illustrate to the jury that the plaintiff's overall cognitive function is normal, and that the lowered scores are isolated anomalies.

A related issue is the determination of premorbid level of function from isolated higher test scores documented on current testing. As discussed on pages 174–178, there is abundant literature showing that significant scatter across IQ subtests is the norm rather than the exception in "normal" individuals. As such, higher scores cannot automatically be assumed to represent evidence of an overall high premorbid level of function.

Incorrectly Assuming That A Patient's Functioning Was at Least Average before the Injury

On occasion I see a report in which the neuropsychologist has assumed that the test taker's functioning was average before the injury in question, and that any scores below average indicate a loss. However, 24% of the population have low average IQs or below, and these individuals are not protected from injury.

Although some published measures are available for estimating premorbid level of function, as discussed on pages 166–174, they underestimate IQ in higher-intelligence individuals and overestimate IQ in those with lower intelligence; they also have large confidence intervals. Their clinical use is thus highly problematic.

Referring to Low Average Scores (9th–24th Percentile) as "Impairments"

As discussed on pages 164–165, 16% of the "normal" population in fact obtains scores in the low average range, and thus it is questionable to refer to scores in this range as "impaired." The field of clinical neuropsychology has not reached agreement on a rubric for labeling percentile ranks (Guilmette et al., 2008), but in this vacuum it is preferable to use IQ-derived labels, so that a common interpretive algorithm is employed across tests:

- Impaired = ≤2nd percentile
- Borderline impaired = 3rd–8th percentile
- Low average = 9th–24th percentile
- Average = 25th–74th percentile
- High average = 75th–90th percentile
- Superior = 91st–97th percentile
- Very superior = ≥98th percentile

Low average scores, even if it can be argued that they are below expectation for a particular patient, are not "impairments" per se.

Incorrectly Assuming That Individuals of Above-Average Intelligence Will Score Above Average on Other Neurocognitive Tests

The reader may have encountered the following types of statements in some medical–legal neuropsychological reports and testimony:

> PLAINTIFF NEUROPSYCHOLOGICAL EXPERT: The patient, in his performance on the Wisconsin Card Sorting Test with me, had two failures to maintain set. That was below expectation and in the mildly impaired range. In addition, his overall performance on the WCST was only average in range. And the fact that he scored just in the average range on the WCST is inconsistent, actually, with this person's very high intelligence. . . . We would expect him to perform above average, more consistent with his intelligence level. On the FAS, the patient scored at one standard deviation below the mean on my initial testing with him. And that's quite dramatically inconsistent with this patient's overall verbal protocol, where his WAIS-III Vocabulary subtest is two standard deviations above that. On the Boston Naming Test, his standard score is 109. And while that is slightly above the mean, which is 100, it is lower than the superior-range verbal scores . . . it's right in line with a one-standard-deviation drop, even though it's slightly above the mean.

> DEFENSE COUNSEL: What is your explanation for that?

> PLAINTIFF NEUROPSYCHOLOGICAL EXPERT: That he suffered a frontal lobe injury.

(Note: The patient in fact sustained no loss of consciousness, showed no brain imaging abnormalities, and did not even present for medical treatment on the day of injury, but instead went car racing, successfully, at speeds well in excess of 100 mph.)

As discussed on pages 177–178, literature shows that healthy individuals of above-average intelligence do not obtain uniformly high scores across a neuropsychological battery. Furthermore, some tests have a "ceiling" on high performance (i.e., very skewed distributions, which virtually preclude scores above high average). The Boston Naming Test, RAVLT Trial 5 recall, RO Figure copy, and categories on the WCST fall in this category, but even for tests like Trails A and Stroop Word Reading and Color Naming, there is a ceiling in terms of how fast one can physically say words or draw lines. For example, full credit for copy of the RO Figure does not result in a percentile above average in any age group (meta-norms from Mitrushina et al., 2005). Similarly, even if a 30- to 34-year-old recalls all 15 words on Trial 5 of the RAVLT, performance is only high average (meta-norms from

Mitrushina et al., 2005). I believe the fastest score I have ever recorded for Trails A is 16 seconds, which for a person ages 16–19 would be high average (meta-norms from Mitrushina et al., 2005). Likewise, I am not sure I have ever seen a score faster than 35 seconds on the word-reading section of the Comalli version of the Stroop task, but this score would only fall at the 86th percentile for persons in the 50–59 age group (Boone, Miller, Lesser. Hill, & D'Elia, 1990). A standard score of 109 on the Boston Naming Test would correspond to a raw score above 57 out of 60 (in fact, an excellent performance); to refer to it as a "one-standard-deviation drop" from other verbal scores is misleading.

CLAIMING THAT LOW COGNITIVE SCORES DOCUMENT BRAIN INJURY

Some clinicians reason that if a patient with mTBI is still showing cognitive abnormalities on a long-term basis, this must prove that the initial injury was more severe than a mild injury. Such reasoning often leads to the following type of statement in their reports: "The patient shows low memory and executive scores on testing (3 years after the accident), which suggests that the original brain injury was more than mild."

But, as discussed on page 240, this line of reasoning "tends to confuse severity with outcome or independent variables with dependent variables" (Dikmen & Levin, 1993, p. 32). Determination of the severity of TBI is based on characteristics at the time of the injury, not on cognitive testing results remote from the injury. To illustrate, has the reader ever read a TBI study in which severity was determined by cognitive scores months/years after the injury? Rather, TBI severity is based on the algorithm reproduced on page 227.

Furthermore, a person can have documented significant brain injury, yet can recover with completely normal cognitive function. It is not the injury per se that is the variable of interest when determining damages in a lawsuit, but rather whether there are permanent, verifiable losses in function resulting from that injury. Many individuals sustain significant TBI, but appear to recover completely as evidenced by subsequent normal cognitive testing, although they may continue to show permanent imaging changes. If cognitive function is normal, the imaging abnormalities are a "red herring" in terms of lawsuit damages.

MISINTERPRETATION OF THE MMPI-2/MMPI-2–RF

Several assertions about scores on the MMPI-2/MMPI-2–RF repeatedly appear in neuropsychological and psychodiagnostic reports, but these need to be carefully examined for their empirical underpinnings (or lack there of). They are listed in Table 6.2.

Myth 1: A Normal MMPI-2 F Score Rules Out Malingering

At times one will encounter the following testimony from opposing experts regarding scores on the MMPI-2 F scale in neuropsychological assessments:

> DEFENSE COUNSEL: Did you find any evidence of overreporting of any of his physical or cognitive complaints or symptoms as a result of any of the tests or your examination of him?

> PLAINTIFF NEUROPSYCHOLOGICAL EXPERT: I found the opposite. I found evidence of underreporting. The F minus K index was 8 minus 20, which was minus 12, and indicates an underreporting or denial of psychological symptoms . . . and the L scale indicated the likelihood of a concerted effort on his part to present himself as an honest individual who would be above reproach, so to speak.

However, the MMPI-2 F scale is generally *not* elevated in head injury litigants found not to be credible on cognitive SVTs (Greiffenstein et al., 1995, 2002; Larrabee, 1998, 2003a, 2003b). The F scale captures feigned severe psychopathology (e.g., paranoid schizophrenia), but not "somatic misrepresentation" (Greiffenstein et al., 1995); it shares only one item in common with the Hypochondriasis and Hysteria clinical scales. Few personal injury litigants feign psychosis; thus F is of limited utility in this group.

The F-r scale on the MMPI-2–RF differs substantially from the F scale on the MMPI-2, in that it is a general overreporting scale rather than a severe mental illness overreporting indicator, and it does show elevations in

TABLE 6.2. MMPI-2/MMPI-2–RF: Myths or Facts?

1. A normal MMPI-2 F score rules out malingering of physical or memory complaints.
2. High F-family scale scores represent a "cry for help."
3. In personal injury litigants, elevations on the MMPI-2 Hypochondriasis and Hysteria clinical scales (or MMPI-2–RF) RC1 are consistent with expected concern over the injuries sustained in the accident.
4. The Hypochondriasis scale was not developed on medical/neurological patients and should not be used in this population.
5. The FBS/FBS-r scale misdiagnoses persons with actual disabilities as malingering.

the context of feigned cognitive symptom overreport (Wygant et al., 2009, 2011).

Myth 2: High F-Family Scores Represent a "Cry for Help"

Some neuropsychological and psychodiagnostic reports assert that high scores on the F family of validity scales do not reflect feigning/exaggeration of psychiatric symptoms, but rather a "cry for help"—specifically, an attempt by patients to ensure that their psychological distress is appreciated by the evaluating psychologist. No doubt the majority of clinical psychologists currently practicing recall being taught in graduate school about "cry for help" phenomena on the MMPI or MMPI-2.

"Cry for help" was coined to describe those patients who appeared to be feigning/exaggerating psychiatric symptoms on the MMPI or MMPI-2 in *the absence of any apparent secondary gain* (Berry et al., 1996). Dahlstrom, Welsh, and Dahlstrom (1972) noted that "this is particularly likely in a screening situation in which the patient comes to feel that unless he dramatizes his condition he will not be given appropriate attention" (p. 118).

But before psychologists can conclude that any "cry for help" is in fact present, firm empirical underpinnings for the claim need to be demonstrated. In fact, at this writing (November 2011), when the search terms "MMPI" and "cry for help" or "plea for help" were employed, only four relevant studies were identified.

Rogers, Sewell, and Ustad (1995) instructed 42 outpatients with chronic psychiatric disorders to complete the MMPI-2 under standard conditions, and then a second time while simulating the goal of immediate hospitalization for severe psychiatric problems. Rogers and colleagues found that patients completing the MMPI-2 under the simulating condition showed significantly higher scores on all overreporting scales (F, Fb, Fp, F minus K, Ds2).

Berry et al. (1996) asked clinic outpatients with mild to moderate psychiatric problems (anxiety, mood disorder, psychosis, adjustment disorder, personality disorder) who had taken the MMPI-2 upon intake to retake the test either with standard instructions ($n = 30$), or as if they had significant psychiatric symptoms but had been placed on a waiting list when they attempted to secure treatment ($n = 30$). Patients in this latter group were told that patients with more severe problems would move to the top of the waiting list, and they were instructed to complete the MMPI-2 in a manner that would enable them to receive treatment more quickly. Results showed that the simulators obtained elevated scores on all F scales as well as all clinical scales (excluding Masculinity–Femininity, which was not investigated), and their pattern was indistinguishable from that seen in frank malingerers. In both the Berry et al. (1996) and Rogers et al. (1995) studies, the Paranoia and Schizophrenia scales were the most commonly elevated in the simulating conditions.

The question arises as to why these studies observed a "malingering" profile. The astute reader will note that in fact, participants were instructed to malinger; specifically, they were instructed to feign symptoms deliberately in the service of obtaining an external goal, although in this case the external goal was treatment rather than compensation or other incentives. Thus the fact that they did not show a different pattern from malingerers is not surprising.

In the only study not employing simulators and in which there was no identified (or at least reported) motive to feign, Post and Gasparikova-Krasnec (1979) examined behavioral characteristics of 20 psychiatric inpatients who obtained MMPI F minus K scores >11 (referred to as a "plea for help"). These patients showed poorer impulse control and more "acting out" on the unit (sexual acting out, aggression, self-inflicted physical harm), met more requirements for seclusion, and caused more "feelings of frustration" in the staff. Thus it appears that the overreporters had the telltale signs of borderline personality disorder.

Greene (1988) initially raised concerns regarding the concept of "cry for help," because he noted that patients identified as overreporters on the MMPI were actually *less* likely to follow through with treatment than individuals not showing the "cry for help" pattern, and in fact typically only attended a single therapy session. That is, it can be questioned whether they were engaging in a "cry for help" when in fact they refused the proffered assistance.

The savvy reader will also note that in the original explanation of the "cry for help" pattern, the term was reserved for those individuals who appeared to be feigning psychiatric symptoms in the absence of obvious external incentives required for the diagnosis of malingering. Thus this interpretation of test performance was never intended for use with individuals who in fact have a *motive* to feign symptoms. Furthermore, when the concept was first articulated, there was much less understanding of the ubiquitousness of externally motivated symptom feigning. Before the 1990s, malingering was in fact thought to be rare (see, e.g., Binder, 1986), and it is likely that patients originally believed to be engaging in a "cry for help" in fact had external motives that were not appreciated.

In conclusion, there is little empirical evidence for a "cry for help" F-family pattern of elevations that is separate from frank malingering. Available evidence indicates that marked elevations on F-family scales are generally associated with deliberate, motivated feigning of symptoms, and that in cases when it is not, it appears to be related to borderline personality disorder.

Myth 3: Elevations on MMPI-2 Hypochondriasis and Hysteria and MMPI-2–RF RC1 Do Not Reflect Overreport in Injured Litigants

The following type of statement regarding the MMPI-2 is ubiquitous in medical–legal neuropsychological reports and testimony:

> Objective testing data revealed an individual who is experiencing . . . somatic or bodily preoccupation, not unlike many individuals with history of traumatic illnesses or injuries, consistent with sequelae of traumatic brain injury.

However, MMPI-2 reference sources indicate that patients with actual physical illness show only minor elevations on the Hypochondriasis scale:

> A person who is actually physically ill will obtain only moderate elevations (T score of 58 to 64) on Scale 1 [Hypochondriasis]. Such persons will endorse their legitimate physical complaints, but they will not endorse the entire gamut of vague physical complaints tapped by the scale. Scale 2 (Depression) is more likely to be elevated by actual physical illness than Scale 1. If a client with actual physical illness obtained a T score of 65 or higher on Scale 1, there are likely to be hypochondriacal features in addition to the physical condition, and the client is probably trying to manipulate or control significant others in the environment with the hypochondriacal complaints. (Greene, 1991, p. 137)

> Many clinicians assume that medical problems are necessarily very emotionally distressing to patients and that this distress will be reflected in highly deviant scores on the MMPI-2. It is important to develop some expectations concerning typical MMPI-2 scores and profiles produced by medical patients. Swenson, Pearson, and Osborne, (1973) reported summary MMPI data for approximately 25,000 males and 25,000 female patients at the Mayo Clinic. The mean profiles for both male and female patients fell within the normal limits. . . . T scores on scales 1, 2, and 3 [Hypochondriasis, Depression, and Hysteria] were near 50. Apparently, the medical problems of these patients were not psychologically distressing enough to lead to grossly elevated scores on the MMPI scales. . . . We expect that MMPI-2 profiles of medical patients will be within normal limits with scores on scales 1, 2, and 3 between 55 and 60 and scores on the rest of the clinical scales near 50. . . . symptoms studied have included low back pain, sexual impotence, neurologic complaints, and others. In general, the research indicated that patients with symptoms that were exclusively or primarily psychological in origin tended to score higher on scales 1, 2, and 3 than patients with similar symptoms that were clearly organic in origin. Particularly common among groups of patients with symptoms of psychological origin was the 13/31 two-point code type. When this code type was found, and scales 1 and 3 were elevated above $T = 65$ and were considerably higher than scale 2, the likelihood of functional origin increased. (Graham, 2000, pp. 231, 233)

In a study reporting MMPI data for a sample of patients with mixed chronic neurological disorders (diagnoses were confirmed by neurological exam and by brain imaging/EEG; Cripe, Maxwell, & Hill, 1995), the mean Hypochondriasis T-score was 65, and the mean Hysteria T-score was 66, confirming that markedly elevated scores are not typical in this population (on the MMPI, a T-score of ≥70 is considered significant). Similarly, MMPI-2 data obtained by Dearth et al. (2005) on patients with moderate to severe TBI (mean of 14.5 days of coma, neurosurgical intervention in 29%) documented means of only 65T and 62.5T, respectively, on the Hypochondriasis and Hysteria scales (whereas patients with moderate to severe TBI who were instructed to feign work disability secondary to brain injury obtained mean scores on the two scales of 80.7T and 74.7T, respectively). Comparable data have been provided by Miller and Donders (2001), who reported mean MMPI-2 T-scores of 61 for the Hypochondriasis and Hysteria scales in patients with moderate to severe TBI (vs. mean T-scores of 69 in non-compensation-seeking patients with mTBI and mean T-scores of 78–79 in compensation seekers with mTBI). Finally, Larrabee (2003a) compared MMPI-2 protocols of probable malingerers with those of patients with spinal cord injury and showed that the former obtained mean T-scores of 82 on the Hypochondriasis and Hysteria scales, in contrast to mean scores of 66.0 and 60.8, respectively, in the latter group. In fact, available evidence suggests that the "1–3 codetype" (highest scores on the two scales in question) predates the injury in persistent post-concussion syndrome (Greiffenstein & Baker, 2001).

On the MMPI-2–RF interpretive report provided by Pearson Assessments and the University of Minnesota Press, patients' scores can be plotted against those of a cohort awaiting bariatric surgery. These patients arguably have multiple, significant medical problems, yet, as a group, they do not show elevations on RC1.

Myth 4: The Hypochondriasis Scale Is Not Appropriate for Medical Patients

In some testimony, the following type of assertion will appear:

> "For me it's not unusual to find elevated somatic complaints on the MMPI-2, which is, after all, a test designed to assess psychiatric patients, not pain patients. And the patients I see who have a variety of physical symptoms tend to have elevations to some degree, more or less, on the Hypochondriasis and Hysteria scales."

In fact, the Hypochondriasis scale was developed with four groups (see Greene, 1991): healthy individuals; individuals diagnosed as having hypochondriasis by treating therapists; psychiatric patients; and true medical patients. The final version of the scale differentiated the hypochondriacal group from all others. The Hypochondriasis scale was the first clinical scale developed, indicating that differentiation of actual medical patients from hypochondriacal patients was of high priority to the MMPI creators. A "Hypochondriasis" scale that failed to distinguish actual medical patients from those with hypochondriasis would be of little use.

Myth 5: The FBS/FBS-r Scale Misidentifies Credible Patients as Malingerers

The FBS scale is a frequent target of attack by plaintiff-oriented neuro-psychologists, and it is routinely omitted from their reports, despite the fact that it was specifically developed in a personal injury litigation set-ting (Lees-Haley et al., 1991) and was found to have such strong empirical underpinnings that the publisher of the MMPI-2/MMPI-2–RF added it as one of the formal validity scales. The following type of statement is often encountered: "There is quite a bit of controversy in the field over the FBS."

The genesis of the FBS scale is discussed on page 112 (see also Greiffen-stein et al., 2007). FBS does not have a high false positive rate; at the rec-ommended raw score cutoff of ≥ 28, specificity is 98.8% across patients with severe TBI, psychiatric disorders, medical/neurological illness, substance abuse, brain disease, and epilepsy (Greiffenstein et al., 2007). To illustrate, in a sample of men awaiting organ transplants, the mean FBS score was 15.3, and a cutoff of 26 was associated with 90+% specificity (Iverson, Henrichs, Barton, & Allen, 2002b). In a group of patients with moder-ate to severe brain injury, the mean FBS score was 16.1, and specificity was 96% with a cutoff of 23 (Millis, Putnam, & Adams, 1995; see also Dearth et al., 2005, showing a mean score of 16.8 in a comparable popula-tion, although it rose to 23.1 in patients with moderate to severe TBI who were instructed to feign brain-injury-related work disability). In a sample of patients with documented neurological disease, none obtained an FBS score of >20 (Woltersdorf, 2005). Raw scores above 30 on FBS never or rarely produce false positive errors, and have a 99–100% probability of "indicating promotion of suffering" (Greiffenstein et al., 2007). Studies that report high false positive rates have not excluded participants with motive to feign (Larrabee, 2003a; see Greiffenstein et al., 2007, for a com-plete discussion).

CONCLUSIONS: WHAT TO CHECK FOR IN A NEUROPSYCHOLOGICAL REPORT

In summary, the following list provides guidance concerning important ele-ments to check for in a neuropsychological report:

- Were data obtained on several measures of response bias?
- Were appropriate tests with adequate normative data employed?
- Is the observed cognitive profile consistent with published literature for the claimed condition?
- Have all plausible causes for the cognitive abnormalities been considered?
- Have cognitive scores been interpreted in light of evidence about the patient's premorbid functioning, and has normal variability in test scores been considered?
- Have raw scores been correctly interpreted (in terms of "impaired," "low average," etc., labels)?
- Have personality test results been correctly interpreted?

7

The Special Problem of Mild Traumatic Brain Injury in the Forensic Neuropsychological Evaluation

Various criteria for identifying mild traumatic brain injury (mTBI) are summarized in McCrea (2008). The most commonly used (Arciniegas, Anderson, Topkoff, & McAllister, 2005) would be those of the American Congress of Rehabilitation Medicine (2003), which specify that loss of consciousness must be less than 30 minutes in duration, that posttraumatic amnesia must not exceed 24 hours, and that the GCS score must be ≥ 13 within 30 minutes after injury.

Approximately 75% of TBI cases involve mTBI (National Center for Injury Prevention and Control, 2003), and patients with mTBI are far and away the most common types of litigants evaluated in forensic neuropsychological practice. Yet, as discussed below, research now provides incontrovertible evidence that there are no long-term cognitive abnormalities in mTBI. Thus neuropsychologists are faced with the interesting conundrum that the type of litigant diagnosis most frequently evaluated in a forensic neuropsychological setting is one without neuropsychological loss.

NEUROPSYCHOLOGICAL OUTCOME IN mTBI

Reviews of the literature on neuropsychological function in mTBI as noted in Figure 5.1 (see Carroll et al., 2004, 120 studies; Dikmen et al., 2009,

33 studies), including 6 meta-analyses (133 studies, n = 1,463, Belanger et al., 2005; 21 studies, n = 790, Belanger & Vanderploeg, 2005, 8 studies, Binder et al., 1997; 17 studies, n = 634, Frencham et al., 2005; 25 studies, n = 2,828, Rohling et al., 2011; 39 studies, n = 1,716, Schretlen & Shapiro, 2003) show that patients who experience mild brain trauma have returned to baseline by weeks to months after injury. In a recent book summarizing the research on mTBI (McCrea, 2008), published under the auspices of the AACN (the membership organization for board-certified neuropsychologists), it is concluded that there is "no indication of permanent impairment on neuropsychological testing by three months postinjury" (p. 117).

Recent criticisms of these meta-analyses have appeared (Iverson, 2010; Pertab, James, & Bigler, 2009), but when methodological issues raised by these publications were addressed, the finding of no chronic mTBI effect on cognition was confirmed (Rohling et al., 2011). Rohling et al. (2012) examined the claim that a meta-analysis might obscure cognitive impairments in some patients with mTBI, but they could not produce evidence of such a subgroup in examining several possible distributions. They note that given their published mTBI effect size of −0.07 (Rohling et al., 2011), "for an impaired subgroup to exist, the level of impairment would have to be just under a 10th of a standard deviation, equivalent to a WMS-IV Index score value of 1 point" (p. 197).

Often individual studies have been cited as providing evidence of chronic cognitive abnormalities in mTBI, but they have later been found to be problematic methodologically. For example, Leininger, Gramling, Farrell, Kreutzer, and Peck (1990) described continuing cognitive deficits in the context of mild TBI, but 59–83% of their sample were pursuing claims for compensation, and no tests to detect and exclude patients who may have been malingering were administered. The authors reported that those pursuing litigation did not significant differ from those not litigating on most neuropsychological measures, but given the small sample size in the non-litigating group (n = 14), power was probably inadequate to detect group differences. No conclusions can be drawn regarding actual cognitive ability in mTBI from a sample that includes a substantial majority with motivation to be symptomatic. Many studies have shown that the effects of mTBI are very small in comparison to the effects of response bias on neurocognitive measures; the latter accounts for 20.3–33.6% of cognitive test score variance (Nelson et al., 2010), and for approximately five times more variance in neuropsychological test scores than does TBI severity (Rohling & Demakis, 2010). When response bias is controlled for in studies of mTBI, neuropsychological performance is normal (Nelson et al., 2010).

A study from Scotland (Thornhill et al., 2000) involving hundreds of patients with mTBI purported to document "moderate or severe disability" as commonly occurring after such injury. However, no objective testing was conducted; determination of disability was based on patient self-report. Furthermore, significant predictors of long-term disability were "preexisting physical limitations, and a history of brain illness" (p. 1633)—in other words, factors that were not related to the injury and would have been disabling in their own right. Finally, no information was provided as to whether patients were attempting to obtain compensation for their injuries.

Vanderploeg and colleagues (Vanderploeg, Curtiss, & Belanger, 2005; Vanderploeg, Curtiss, Luis, & Salazar, 2007) reported on a Vietnam veteran sample with either (1) no motor vehicle accident or head injury since discharge (*n* = 3,214), (2) motor vehicle accident but no mTBI (*n* = 539), and (3) motor vehicle accident and mTBI (*n* = 254). Groups were matched for premorbid cognitive ability, and comparison on 15 neuropsychological scores showed no group differences. However, the group with mTBI performed worse in proactive interference (increased) on the CVLT-II and continuation rate (reduced) on the Paced Auditory Serial Addition Test (PASAT), leading the authors to conclude that this group had mild attention problems. However, contained in a subsequent publication (Vanderploeg et al., 2007) is information that the group with mTBI was atypical, in that it had higher rates of hypertension, peripheral vascular disease, and preinjury psychiatric conditions. In particular, this group had two to three times the rate of antisocial personality disorder, as well as approximately twice the rates of substance abuse, major depression, anxiety disorder, and combat-related PTSD, as in the other groups. The veterans with self-reported mTBI had twice the rate of postconcussion symptoms, but once preinjury psychiatric factors were controlled for, these symptoms did not differ across groups (with the exception of more cognitive complaints and irritability in the group with mTBI).

Some authors have argued that even individuals with "nonimpact brain injury" (i.e., whiplash) show chronic cognitive dysfunction, particularly in executive skills (Henry, Gross, Herndon, & Furst, 2000). However, these conclusions were based on a sample composed of 97% litigants, one-third of whom were not administered any measures of response bias, while the remaining two-thirds were administered an insensitive measure (the Rey 15-Item Memorization Test; see Boone, Salazar, et al., 2002). Moreover, low average scores were incorrectly described as "mildly impaired." Of note, 97% of the sample complained of problems in attention and concentration (interestingly, the same percentage as were in litigation).

Some studies have excluded mTBI patients with failed SVTs, but have not excluded participants with motive to feign; the researchers have apparently assumed that inclusion of symptom validity checks will adequately screen out participants not performing to true capability (e.g., Cicerone & Azulay, 2002). However, no SVTs have 100% sensitivity, meaning that at least some noncredible individuals will remain undetected by the measures and inappropriately retained in analyses. Various studies in fact show that even when participants who fail SVTs are excluded, mTBI subjects in litigation still underperform relative to patients with moderate to severe TBI (e.g., Curtis et al., 2009; Greve et al., 2003; Heinly et al., 2005)—a nonsensical finding, and one indicating that noncredible individuals with mTBI were undetected by the SVTs administered.

Other studies have excluded potential participants based on motivation to feign and/or SVT failures, but have recruited through advertisement posters inviting persons "with mTBI" to participate (e.g., Sterr, Herron, Hayward, & Montaldi, 2006). A related methodological problem is recruitment from existing mTBI samples when only a subset agrees to participate (e.g., Konrad et al., 2010). Individuals who agree to participate in a study of mTBI may be those with stronger identification with the diagnosis.

This type of methodology is contaminated by selection bias. That is, only individuals who perceive they are symptomatic will self-identify as "having mTBI," and some individuals without motive to feign will still underperform on cognitive testing because they believe that they are dysfunctional. Specifically, Suhr and Gunstad (2005) documented that individuals who were told that their mTBI was the reason for invitation to be study participants underperformed on tests of attention/working memory, psychomotor speed, and memory tasks as compared to individuals with histories of mTBI who were provided "neutral" information regarding the study (see the additional discussion of "diagnosis threat" below).

As an example of the potential impact of "diagnosis threat," Geary, Kraus, Pliskin, and Little (2010) reported that patients with remote mTBI ($\geq$6 months; n = 40) underperformed relative to controls without TBI (n = 35) on Trial 1 of the CVLT-II, but did not differ on the remaining 10 scores. The sample with mTBI had been screened for compensation seeking and passed SVTs, and those with significant preaccident psychiatric history, substance abuse, or other neurological/medical conditions that could affect cognition were excluded. The authors argued that the results suggest the presence of "subtle cognitive deficits that reflect diminished initial acquisition" (p. 506), as well as decreased proactive interference (because groups did not differ on recall of List B; interestingly, Vanderploeg et al., 2005, found *increased* proactive interference in their sample!). However, subjects were recruited through advertisements seeking "individuals who had ever sustained a closed head injury, concussion, brain injury, or traumatic brain injury" (p. 507), raising the possibility of selection bias. In this vein, it is interesting that the group difference occurred on the very first sample of cognitive function. Furthermore, if the group with mTBI truly had a deficit in initial acquisition, the groups should have differed on List B, but they did not. Finally, although exclusion criteria appeared to be adequate, it was not specifically indicated whether participants with histories of ADHD were excluded; such a diagnosis would be likely to have a different impact on initial learning.

The Konrad et al. (2010) study illustrates an additional methodological problem—namely, comparison of patient groups against "super-normal" persons. Individuals who volunteer for participation in research studies tend to be of above-average intelligence (e.g., IQ mean = high average; Palmer et al., 1998). Careful examination of the mean scores obtained in the Konrad et al. (2010) study shows that the performance of the group with mTBI was not particularly low; rather, the scores of the control group were above average (e.g., Trails A mean = 19.48 seconds, 75th percentile for age; Trails B = 46.48 seconds, 75th percentile for age; RAVLT recall after interference mean = 13.85, 77th percentile), which would account for the significant group differences.

Dikmen and Levin (1993) conclude that studies cited as documenting long-term cognitive symptoms in mTBI "were flawed by inclusion of patients with preexisting conditions (e.g., previous head injury) and failure to use appropriate controls to correct for these conditions," and they suggest that "subsequent controlled studies have indicated time-limited neuropsychological impairments that disappear by 1 to 3 months postinjury" (p. 35). Dikmen, Machamer, and Temkin (2001) note that the impact of demographic factors is typically more pronounced than any mTBI effect, and as discussed on pages 26 and 178–185, mTBI effects are less than those associated with depression, learning disability, ADHD, or substance abuse. Greiffenstein and Baker (2003) documented that in nonmalingering individuals claiming chronic postconcussive symptoms, a developmental origin for low cognitive scores was suggested, given that low grades in high school predicted poor cognitive performance. Belanger et al. (2005) documented that the effect sizes of clinical studies of mTBI are larger than those of nonclinical studies; this finding further supports the assertion that "non-TBI" factors are driving the findings of a relationship between TBI and reported symptoms.

THE "MYTHIC" 10–15% WHO DO NOT RECOVER

In many reports and depositions, plaintiff experts opine that although most patients with mTBI completely recover from their brain injuries, a small percentage—typically cited as 10–15%—do not recover. However, interestingly, experts can rarely provide a reference for this mythic "10–15%."

In fact, Alexander (1995) published a review of mTBI in the journal *Neurology*, in which he stated that "at 1 year after injury, 10 to 15% of mild TBI patients have not recovered" (p. 1256) and for which he provided two references (Rutherford, Merrett, & McDonald, 1978; McLean,

Temkin, Dikmen, & Wyler, 1983). However, examination of these publications shows that they do not support Alexander's conclusion.

Rutherford et al. (1978) did report that of 131 patients with mild concussion, 14.5% "still had symptoms after 1 year." However, they go on to state: "Of the 19 patients who had symptoms at 1 year, 8 were involved in law suits and 6 had been suspected of malingering 6 weeks after their accident. Five of these patients were both involved in law suits and suspected of malingering" (p. 225). Furthermore, the authors indicate that it was recorded "whether it was known that the patient was making a legal claim for compensation," but this statement suggests the possibility that in some cases compensation seeking was present but not known to the examiners. Samples that include individuals with motives to feign/exaggerate symptoms cannot be used to estimate the prevalence of true cognitive symptoms.

In the Rutherford et al. (1978) study, patients were asked to rate themselves on 16 symptoms, including two cognitive categories: loss of concentration and loss of memory. Of note, only 3.1% ($n = 4$) reported loss of concentration, and 3.8% ($n = 5$) reported loss of memory. Thus it would not be true that 10–15% reported continuing cognitive symptoms; <4% did. Moreover, the presence of symptoms was based on patient self-report, not objective testing.

Thus, to summarize, the Rutherford et al. (1978) study cannot be used as proof that 10–15% of patients with mTBI have chronic cognitive dysfunction from their injuries, for these reasons: (1) In this small sample ($n = 19$), almost half were involved in lawsuits and/or thought to be malingering; (2) noncognitive symptoms were included in the symptom tabulation (<4% actually claimed continuing cognitive dysfunction); and (3) no objective cognitive testing was performed to corroborate self-report of cognitive loss.

In the second study cited by Alexander (1995), McLean et al. (1983, p. 361) reported on a very small sample ($n = 20$) with "mostly mild" TBI but with "a few cases" of moderately severe head injury, and concluded that compared to controls, the patients showed "significant neuropsychological difficulties at 3 days, but not at 1 month postinjury," although the patients did endorse more postconcussional symptoms at 1 month. Thus, although a subset of patients with "mostly" mTBI may *report* more symptoms at 1 month, this report is not corroborated by objective test results.

What is hard to fathom is that even if these two publications had provided solid evidence for continuing cognitive dysfunction on a chronic basis in in a subset of patients with mTBI, the conclusion would have been based on a combined total of <40 symptomatic individuals!

Subsequent publications have cited the same two studies in support of the assertion that 15% of patients with mTBI continue to show long-term symptoms 1 year after injury (see Ghaffar, McCullagh, Ouchterlony,

& Feinstein, 2006; Guerrero, Thurman, & Snieziek, 2000). Of particular concern, a fact sheet about mTBI published by the Centers for Disease Control and Prevention (2006) for physicians again parrots the assertion that "up to 15% of patients diagnosed with MTBI may have experienced persistent disabling symptoms" (p. 3). As support for this conclusion, the fact sheet cites two references: the Alexander (1995) article, and a second article (Kushner, 1998) that provides no new data but instead again references the Alexander (1995) article. The moral of this story: Read the supporting literature cited as references for statements in publications.

Occasionally other studies are cited as purporting to document long-term cognitive compromise in a subset of patients with mTBI, but these are also problematic methodologically. For example, Wrightson and Gronwall (1981) reported that 20% ($n = 13$) of their non-compensation-seeking sample of patients with mTBI were still symptomatic at 90 days, but only half of these were reporting cognitive problems, and symptoms were assessed by interview but not psychometric testing. At 2 years, a subset of the original 13 ($n = 8$) were able to be contacted; half ($n = 4$) still reported memory problems, but 2 of these attributed the deficits to advancing age. Thus this sample involved very small n's; the authors did not provide actual testing data to confirm the presence of cognitive abnormalities; and the reported symptoms may have been the result of non-TBI-related factors.

Ponsford et al. (2000) found that patients with mTBI reported more concentration difficulties at 3 months than trauma controls did, but there were no actual significant group differences on neuropsychological tests. Comparison of those patients with mTBI reporting symptoms (24%) as compared to those who did not, failed to reveal any differences on neuropsychological testing, with the exception of more PASAT errors in the reporters. However, available information suggested that these 20 were atypical and/or were compensation-seeking. For example, two had sustained intervening concussions; one showed elements of a somatoform disorder (i.e., reported chronic fatigue syndrome); one had a previous significant TBI; one had a history of three previous concussions and alcohol abuse; one had stress in the household, due to a stepbrother's having been struck by a car; two were receiving workers' compensation, and the "majority were showing significant levels of psychopathology" (p. 576). In addition, within a week of the concussion, the sample had been given a booklet containing information about common symptoms of mTBI, which may have primed them to be sensitive and overvigilant to such symptoms. Furthermore, of the entire sample with mTBI, 13% had histories of prior learning problems; 39% had a previous history of head injury; 29% had a premorbid history of neurological or psychiatric problems; and the participants averaged a low level of education (11.4 years). Thus this sample was at very high risk for cognitive abnormalities even before the mTBI.

In summary, the minority of patients with mTBI who continue to report long-term cognitive abnormalities associated with the injury are atypical, and non-TBI-related factors appear to account for chronic symptoms.

DETERMINATION OF LOSS OF CONSCIOUSNESS

At times opposing counsel and plaintiff neuropsychological experts will argue that the plaintiff's apparently not losing of consciousness at the scene cannot be verified:

> DEFENSE COUNSEL: Did you find in your review of the medical records any evidence that it was reported that Mr. B did not lose consciousness following this incident?
>
> PLAINTIFF NEUROPSYCHOLOGICAL EXPERT: Yes.
>
> DEFENSE COUNSEL: And did you give any weight to that in terms of your ultimate opinions and conclusions with respect to brain injury?
>
> PLAINTIFF NEUROPSYCHOLOGICAL EXPERT: No. I think that the absolute loss of consciousness is something that one will never be able to know for sure, since a loss of consciousness can be quite brief, and an outside observer, without a mechanical device, would not really be able to tell, or without sophisticated examination would not be able to tell. So we would really not know the answer to that. A person can suffer some very significant brain damage without appreciable loss of consciousness.

But what is not appreciated is that one criterion for mTBI is loss of consciousness of < 30 minutes, and in patients with documented mTBI neuropsychological function is normalized within days or weeks (see discussion above). Thus, whether or not the patient briefly lost consciousness is not at issue, but rather whether any loss of consciousness exceeded 30 minutes.

DETERMINATION OF ANTEROGRADE AND RETROGRADE AMNESIA

Some neuropsychological experts opine that if a patient has *any* "patchy" recall following an injury, this is evidence of posttraumatic or anterograde amnesia. However, no person recalls a complete, uninterrupted sequence of memories for any event, but rather the most salient portions. (As evidence, the reader should attempt to recall the exact sequences of events for the hour ending 4 hours ago.)

PLAINTIFF COUNSEL: When you interviewed her, she told you that she recalled only fragments of the collision?

DEFENSE NEUROPSYCHOLOGICAL EXPERT: Well, actually, in questioning her, she has very good recall of events, and I think that there is a misunderstanding that in the course of a collision, it's normal to remember every single second of the sequence. And that's not true. For someone to remember key parts of major events would be entirely normal. I wouldn't expect anyone to remember every single aspect of any event, collision-related or otherwise.

PLAINTIFF COUNSEL: What about not being able to account for about a 5-minute period of time? Would that be, in itself, something unusual under this type of stress?

DEFENSE NEUROPSYCHOLOGICAL EXPERT: I don't see any 5-minute period of time that's missing in the narrative she provided. She recollects that during the collision everything became dark as the windshield "crashed onto me." She also remembered that the top of her car flew off and she became cold. And she also remembers being struck a second time and remembers seeing the bumper of the truck "being right next to me." After her vehicle stopped moving, she recollects taking off her seat belt and retrieving her cell phone to call 911. She then recalls that a man told her he had already contacted emergency personnel. The patient remembers seeing the driver of the truck pacing back and forth in front of her car, "begging me to be all right." She then recalls police officers and paramedics arriving. So she seems to have detailed, essentially continuous memories.

At times patients will appear to have intact postaccident recall, but once they reach the emergency department, their memories cease, and this information is used to argue for anterograde amnesia. However, if a person is laying down memories shortly after an injury, this provides evidence that the brain structures involved in memory encoding and consolidation were in fact not significantly damaged, and these brain areas would not subsequently become dysfunctional unless there is frank neurological deterioration (e.g., a developing intracranial hematoma). Examiners fail to consider that many patients are sedated once they arrive at the emergency room, so that their orthopedic and other injuries can be better managed, and this medication would account for an inability to consolidate memories once in the hospital. Furthermore, Rimel, Giordani, Barth, Boll, and Jane (1981) reported that 35% of their sample of patients with TBI were intoxicated at the time of admission, which also could contribute to apparent posttraumatic amnesia. Finally, as with any self-reported information from individuals in compensation-seeking settings, the examiner needs to consider whether the information is in fact accurate. For example, one plaintiff's neuropsychological expert opined:

> "His statement concerning his poor memory for about at least a week following the injury is one indication of that severity of that injury, making it clearly more severe rather than less severe, since posttraumatic amnesia is implied for over 1 week following the injury."

In this testimony, the expert attempted to argue that a head injury from an assault was "more severe," based on the patient's report of lengthy postinjury memory loss. However, this report is not plausible, given that immediately after the assault (which involved no loss of consciousness), the patient did not seek medical attention and actually drove directly to a venue where he raced cars at speeds of over 120 mph (without crashing)—behavior that would not have been possible if the patient had sustained a significant brain injury associated with lengthy anterograde amnesia.

On occasion a patient will be examined who claims extensive retrograde amnesia (loss of recall for events preceding the injury) in association with mTBI, or retrograde amnesia equal to the length of anterograde amnesia. However, the available research would suggest that this is not plausible. In a consecutive sample of 119 patients with mTBI who were seen at hospital emergency departments, retrograde amnesia was either not present or very brief; it was only present if there was also anterograde amnesia; and the ratio of duration of anterograde to retrograde amnesia was 300:1 (Paniak, MacDonald, Toller-Lobe, Durand, & Nagy, 1998).

THE CONCERN WITH PATIENT SELF-REPORT OF POSTCONCUSSION SYMPTOMS

The problem with relying on patient self-report of symptoms is illustrated by literature showing that putative "postconcussion" symptoms (e.g., headache, dizziness, memory loss, poor concentration, anxiety, depression, irritability, sleep disorder, fatigue, noise sensitivity) are actually ubiquitous in noninjured populations (Fox, Lees-Haley, Earnest, & Dolezal-Wood, 1995; Garden & Sullivan, 2010; Gouvier, Uddo-Crane, & Brown, 1988; Iverson & Lange, 2003; McLean, Dikmen, & Temkin, 1993; Wang, Chan, & Deng, 2006) and in patients with back pain (Gasquoine, 2000) and injuries not involving the central nervous system (Lees-Haley, Fox, &

Courtney, 2001). In fact, such symptoms occur with the same frequency in head-injured individuals as in non-head-injured controls (Davis, 2002; Hanna-Pladdy, Berry, Bennett, Phillips, & Gouvier, 2001; Gouvier, Cubic, Jones, Brantley, & Cutlip, 1992).

Meares et al. (2011) found that when patients with mTBI were compared to trauma controls, mTBI was not associated with postconcussive symptoms; rather, preinjury depression/anxiety, pain, and acute posttraumatic stress were the predictors of continuing symptoms (see also Machulda, Bergquist, Ito, & Chew, 1998). Luis, Vanderploeg, and Curtiss (2003) noted that early-life psychiatric problems (including anxiety and depression), reduced social support, and lower intelligence were the most salient predictors of postconcussion syndrome. Likewise, Stulemeijer, Vos, Bleijenberg, and van der Werf (2007) observed that cognitive complaints after mTBI were related to lower educational level, personality traits, emotional distress, and poorer physical function, but not to injury characteristics, and Hanna-Pladdy et al. (2001) noted that severity of postconcussive symptoms varied with daily stress levels. Kirsch et al. (2010) identified 6% (14 cases) of their sample who were outliers in terms of postconcussion symptom report, and of these, 43% were in some stage of litigation (compared to 13% of the nonoutlier group). Additional predictors of outlier status were elevated somatic symptoms in the emergency department (blurred vision, headache, light sensitivity); prior head injury; and preinjury disability, history of substance use, and unemployment. Kirsch et al. conclude that "preinjury physical and mental health status, rather than head injury severity, are predictive of postconcussion syndrome and fatigue at 12 months" (p. 39). Many authors have found that depressive symptoms have a much more substantial relationship with postconcussive symptoms than does mTBI (Sawchyn, Brulot, & Strauss, 2000; Suhr & Gunstad, 2002a; Trahan, Ross, & Trahan, 2001). Fenton, McClelland, Montgomery, MacFlynn, and Rutherford (1993) reported that "social adversity" prior to injury was associated with emergence and maintainance of the postconcussive syndrome, while Whittaker, Kemp, and House (2008) observed that those patients with mTBI "who believe that their symptoms have serious negative consequences on their lives and will continue to do so, are at heightened risk of experiencing significant enduring post-concussional symptoms" (p. 644).

Other authors note that increased postconcussion symptom report is higher in patients receiving sick leave for mTBI (Ingebrigtsen, Waterloo, Marup-Jensen, Attner, & Romner, 1998). Moreover, Lange, Iverson, Brooks, and Rennison (2010), as well as Tsanadis et al. (2008), found significantly higher postconcussive symptom report in patients with mTBI who failed SVTs; and Lange, Iverson, et al. (2010) suggest that the findings "highlight the importance of considering the influence of poor effort, in conjunction with a growing list of factors than can influence, maintain, and/or mimic the persistent postconcussion symdrome" (p. 961).

Finally, a large literature (e.g., Armistead-Jehle, Gervais, & Green, 2012; Stulemeijer et al., 2007; Wang, 2001; Wang et al., 2006) shows little relationship between subjective report of memory and other postconcussion problems on the one hand, and objective measurement of cognitive function on the other. In fact, the most ubiquitous memory complaint in individuals reporting long-term cognitive deficits associated with mTBI (i.e., "I go into a room and forget why I went there"), is a normal phenomenon. Memory is disrupted as we move through doorways because the change requires an update in our model of the environment, "which can slow processing and allow for more errors to occur" (p. 1155; Radvansky & Copeland, 2006).

NEUROIMAGING AND NEUROPATHOLOGY IN mTBI

A review of the literature on neuroimaging is beyond the scope of this book, and the interested reader is referred to the summary provided by McCrea (2008). Of note, he concludes that available literature suggests that brain computed tomography (CT) and magnetic resonance imaging (MRI) data "have limited utility in identifying or predicting delayed recovery or persistent problems after MTBI" (p. 64).

Some have argued that with advances in neuroimaging (e.g., functional MRI, magnetic resonance spectroscopy, magnetic transfer imaging and magnetic source imaging, diffusion tensor imaging [DTI], positron emission tomography [PET], single-photon-emission computed tomography [SPECT]), we now may be able to identify subtle structural and functional abnormalities associated with mTBI. However, as summarized by McCrea (2008), even findings obtained via these newer techniques generally do not correlate with long-term cognitive function (see also Lee et al., 2008). Although some medical practitioners will obtain PET and/or SPECT imaging on plaintiffs in an attempt to document injury, Granacher (2008) argues that these techniques do not meet *Daubert v. Merrell Dow Pharmaceuticals, Inc.* (1993) standards for introduction of scientific evidence at trial, due to unknown error rates. In particular, he notes that "comorbidities, medications, substance abuse, pre-existing psychiatric illness, prior head trauma, and even mental activity can generate false positives in either SPECT or PET neuroimaging, which cannot be distinguished from those produced by mild TBI" (p. 327). Granacher (2008) concludes that "use of SPECT and PET as evidence of mild TBI, without structural neuroimaging clinical correlation, cannot be supported in a legal forum" (p. 327). Similarly, Wortzel, Kraus, Filley, Anderson, and Arciniegas (2011), in examining whether research on the role of DTI in demonstrating white matter injury in mTBI meets *Daubert* testimony admissibility standards, suggested that "expert testimony regarding DTI findings will seldom be appropriate in legal proceedings focused on mTBI" (p. 511).

Bigler (2004) described a case of a 47-year-old male who sustained an mTBI and showed normal brain imaging, but subsequently died 7 months later of an unrelated cardiac event. Brain autopsy showed macrophages in the perivascular space and white matter, particularly in the frontal lobe. The patient reported difficulties performing in his job as an appraiser upon his postinjury return to work, and neuropsychological testing was conducted, although the Bigler (2004) report did not specify how soon after the injury the testing was completed. The patient obtained high average IQ scores (FSIQ = 116, VIQ = 115, PIQ = 115), and he scored within the average range or higher on at least 44 separate tests/subtests, although three other scores were described as below expectation (37th percentile on WAIS-R Digit Symbol, 5 of 15 words on Trial 1 of the RAVLT, and a score of 13 on 15-minute delay of the RO Figure). However, the patient also scored at the 37th percentile on WAIS-R Picture Completion, and scored in the average range on two WAIS-R verbal subtests (Vocabulary = 63rd percentile, Comprehension = 50th percentile); thus it is unclear why Digit Symbol was judged to be low. It was noted that the patient was probably going to pursue litigation, but he passed several embedded SVTs (Warrington Recognition Memory Test—Words, Finger Tapping Test, Digit Span indicators, Finger Agnosia Test errors, RAVLT recognition, Trails A, and Hooper Visual Organization Test), and therefore it was unlikely that he was engaging in negative response bias. The most likely explanation for the three isolated, questionably mildly lowered scores would be normal variability. That is, neurologically intact individuals of average to above-average intellectual function do not in fact obtain uniformly average to above-average neuropsychological scores (see pp. 177–178) .

In a compensation-seeking setting, what is at issue is functional outcome, not "injury" per se. The original studies reporting no long-term cognitive loss in patients with TBI and normal brain imaging used standard brain CT (e.g., Mataro et al., 2001); whether those patients had more "subtle" injury is unknown, but arguably irrelevant, because if standard brain CT was normal, there was no long-term cognitive loss. Furthermore, while mild head injury may result in microscopic changes to brain tissue (as suggested by Bigler, 2004), if there are no associated cognitive abnormalities, this information has little bearing. The analogy would be that if one fractures a leg, complete recovery of function may in fact be achieved, despite the fact that evidence of the fracture will remain on x-rays for the rest of the person's life. Finally, it should also be kept in mind that a sizable percentage of "normal" individuals in fact are found to have imaging abnormalities;

for example, Katzman, Dagher, and Patronas (1999) reported an 18% rate of brain MRI abnormalities in 1,000 uninjured volunteers.

PERSISTENT COGNITIVE ABNORMALITIES USED AS EVIDENCE OF MORE SEVERE BRAIN INJURY

Some clinicians reason that if a patient with mTBI is still showing cognitive abnormalities on a long-term basis, this must prove that the initial injury was more severe than a mild injury. But as Dikmen and Levin (1993) note, this line of reasoning "tends to confuse severity with outcome or independent variables with dependent variables" (p. 32). Determination of TBI severity is based on injury characteristics at the time of the injury, not on cognitive testing results remote from the injury. Readers who have read peer-reviewed studies on outcome in brain injury will note that patients are assigned to mild versus moderate/severe groupings according to injury parameters (e.g., loss of consciousness, imaging findings, GCS scores), not cognitive findings.

DOES INTOXICATION AT THE TIME OF INJURY LEAD TO WORSE COGNITIVE OUTCOME?

The prevalence of intoxication at the time of injury in mTBI has been reported as approximately 50% (Lange, Iverson, & Franzen, 2007). On occasion, opposing neuropsychological experts have argued that because a plaintiff was intoxicated at the time of the injury, this magnified the extent of the injury and led to a worse outcome than expected for mTBI. However, Lange et al. (2007) showed that prevalence of preinjury alcohol abuse exceeded 40% in their sample with mTBI, and that this, rather than day-of-injury intoxication, has a stronger impact on neuropsychological testing obtained 7 days after injury. The question arises as to whether a history of pre-TBI alcohol abuse contributes to worse outcome after TBI (e.g., a so-called "eggshell plaintiff"), but Dikmen, Donovan, Loberg, and Temkin (1993) did not find a greater effect of head injury in subjects with more severe preinjury alcohol problems.

WHAT ABOUT THE IMPACT OF OLDER AGE ON RECOVERY IN mTBI?

The question arises as to whether the excellent prognosis for mTBI also applies to an older population. Although older individuals would appear to be at risk for more complicated recovery from mTBI, given cumulative insults to the brain over the lifetime, researchers have not been able to detect cognitive deficits in patients with mTBI age 50 and older relative to age-matched controls (Goldstein & Levin, 2001; Goldstein, Levin, Goldman, Clark, & Altonen, 2001). Moreover, in the subacute stage, older patients do not show worse cognitive function than younger patients (Stapert, Houx, de Kruijk, Ponds, & Jolles, 2006). Mazzucchi et al. (1992) reported a less positive outcome in older individuals with TBI (including a subset with mTBI), but 80% of their sample were receiving disability compensation, raising questions regarding symptom validity in their sample.

WHAT ABOUT mTBI IN CHILDREN/ADOLESCENTS?

Satz et al. (1997), in a review of mTBI studies in children and adolescents from 1970 to 1995, noted that 13 studies reported adverse findings, 18 found no effect, and 9 were indeterminate. However, it was indicated that the more methodologically sound studies generally showed no effect, and that some of the less sound studies described transitory abnormalities in the early postinjury period. These findings led the authors to conclude that "at the present time, cautious acceptance of the null hypothesis is recommended" (p. 107). In a subsequent meta-analysis of 28 studies (1988 to 2007; Babikian & Asarnow, 2009), it was noted that the data showed "few, if any, impairments in the neurocognitive domains reviewed at any time point, including postacute outcomes" (p. 293); that effect sizes were generally small (generally between 0.2 and 0.3); and that lower postaccident scores probably reflected preaccident neurocognitive and behavioral abnormalities. In particular, they noted that the children who experienced TBI had higher rates of preinjury ADHD/behavioral problems (13–22%; Bloom et al., 2001; Max et al., 1998) and learning difficulties (up to 50%; Dicker, 1992). More recently, Babikian et al. (2011), reporting on the results of a longitudinal study, observed lowered scores in pediatric patients with mTBI in the domains of memory, psychomotor processing speed, and language—but the same abnormalities were observed in groups with injury other than head injury, suggesting a "general injury effect." They conclude that "when controlling for pre-injury factors, there is no evidence of long-term neurocognitive impairment in this group relative to another injury control group" (p. 886).

WHAT ABOUT THE IMPACT
OF REPEATED CONCUSSION?

Some neuropsychologists have the belief that while a single concussion may not result in permanent cognitive sequelae, more than one in a person's lifetime does. That is, while the mTBI associated with the accident in question may not have resulted in cognitive problems in a person with no history of TBI, the fact that the plaintiff had a previous concussion rendered him/her an "eggshell plaintiff" who was predisposed to chronic cognitive problems from any subsequent mTBI.

But what does the literature say in regard to the effects of multiple concussion? Most investigations have found no relationship between number of concussions and cognitive test performance (Collie, McCrory, & Makdissi, 2006; Guskiewicz, Marshall, Broglio, Cantu, & Kirkendall, 2002; Iverson, Brooks, Lovell, & Collins, 2006; Pellman, Lovell, Viano, Casson, & Tucker, 2004). Bijur, Haslum, and Golding (1996), in analyzing the effect of multiple mTBIs in children, found that increasing numbers of head injuries were significantly related to lower scores on measures of general intelligence, reading, and math; however, the same negative impact on cognition was found for numbers of non-brain-injury traumas, leading the authors to conclude that "cognitive deficits associated with multiple mild head injury are due to social and personal factors related to multiple injuries and not to specific damage to the head" (p. 143). This study highlighted the importance of using trauma controls in examining the impact of mTBI on cognitive function, and also identified the role of social factors in lowered cognitive function in children with multiple injuries, including lower SES. Belanger, Spiegel, and Vanderploeg (2010), in a recent meta-analysis of the literature comparing the effects of one self-reported TBI versus more than one, found that the "overall effect of multiple mTBI on neuropsychological functioning was minimal (d = .06) and not significant" (p. 262). In specific cognitive domains, poorer performance with multiple TBIs was found on measures of delayed memory and executive functioning, although effect sizes were small (d's = 0.16 and 0.24, respectively) and "their clinical significance is unclear" (p. 4).

IS THERE INCREASED RISK FOR DEMENTIA AFTER mTBI?

Some neuropsychological experts assert that while mTBI may not result in significant cognitive problems immediately, the patient is placed at higher risk for developing dementia in the future. However, although some literature suggests that there may be a small increased risk of dementia in patients sustaining moderate to severe TBI—especially in individuals who sustain their head injury after age 70 and who have relatives with onset of Alzheimer's disease prior to age 70 (Mayeux et al., 1993)—there is no evidence of increased risk in isolated mTBI events (Mehta et al., 1999; Plassman et al., 2000).

But how does this mesh with recent mass media reports describing increased rates of dementia in National Football League players? Although there do not appear to be neuropsychological abnormalities associated with concussion in current players (Pellman et al., 2004), recurrent concussion may be associated with increased rates of mild cognitive impairment in retired players (Guskiewicz et al., 2005); also, while Alzheimer's disease was not associated with recurrent concussion in this population, onset of Alzheimer's disease was earlier than in the general male U.S. population. It should be noted that football players are repeatedly struck in the head, even if not repeatedly rendered unconscious. Thus it is possible that hundreds of repeated blows to the head, with the vast majority not resulting in loss of consciousness, cause cumulative subclinical injury that predisposes players to future mild cognitive impairment and earlier onset of dementia. However, these findings would not apply to a patient who may have had one or two concussions prior to the accident at issue.

IS THERE ANOSAGNOSIA IN mTBI?

On occasion I have encountered cases in which the plaintiff did not claim any chronic, long-term cognitive problems after an mTBI, but testing by the plaintiff's neuropsychological expert detected abnormalities. The neuropsychologist then opined that the patient did in fact have accident-related cognitive problems, and that the brain injury caused the patient to be unaware of, and to lack insight regarding, the cognitive dysfunction (i.e., anosagnosia). It is true that experienced neuropsychologists will have encountered anosagnosia in many patients with severe brain disorders (e.g., severe brain injury, dementias) who claim no or minimal cognitive dysfunction, despite the necessity of confinement to residential facilities for their cognitive disorders. However, a perusal of the research literature shows no accounts of anosagnosia in patients with mTBI.

ARE THERE LONG-TERM PSYCHIATRIC SYMPTOMS AFTER mTBI?

Some experts in litigated mTBI cases claim that long-term psychiatric difficulties in plaintiffs are due to the injury, and some even allege that neuropsychological abnormalities caused acutely by the brain injury are then maintained over time by the psychiatric disorders. Thus they back away from blaming the concussion itself as the cause of the permanent cognitive changes, but still maintain that it is the indirect cause, because it provoked the psychiatric condition that is perpetuating the cognitive disorder.

An initial review of the literature suggested a 35% prevalence of depression after mTBI (Busch & Alpern, 1998). More recently, Panayiotou et al. (2010) investigated this issue through a meta-analysis of available research: 11 studies were suitable for inclusion and represented a total of 352 patients with mTBI and 765 controls. The categories of psychological symptoms included depression, anxiety, psychosocial disability, and poor coping. Effect sizes were smaller when studies were weighted, indicating that unweighted effect sizes were unduly influenced by studies with small n's and highly variable findings. When the most appropriate weighting technique (inverse variance) was used, effect sizes ranged from -0.28 to 0.26, and did not significantly differ from zero ($p = .76$). Panayiotou et al. indicate that "effect sizes found in the current study are considered meaningless; indicating that only 7.7–21.3% of mTBI patients obtained scores not obtained by the control groups" (pp. 467–468), and they concluded that "mTBI may have a very small to no measurable effect on psychological and psychosocial symptom reporting" (p. 468).

On occasion some neuropsychological experts will acknowledge that a litigant has a somatoform disorder that is provoking nonphysiological symptom report in mTBI, but then will opine that the injury triggered the somatoform disorder. However, in a very interesting study, Greiffenstein and Baker (2001) were able to compare pre- and postaccident MMPI-2 profiles in compensation seekers with persistent postconcussion syndrome. They found no increase in global psychopathology (defined as the mean T-score for eight clinical scales); in fact, only 1 subject showed an increase, while the remaining 22 showed significantly *lower* postaccident means. In particular, postinjury declines were noted on the mania and antisocial scales, and there was no significant change on the "neurotic triad" (the Hypochondriasis, Depression, and Hysteria scales were elevated above 65T in 88% of the preinjury protocols vs. 90% of postinjury profiles). The authors conclude from these data that "pre-existing somatoform psychopathology is of a very high base rate in persons likely to pursue disability claims following minor head and cervical trauma" (p. 165).

In fact, the available literature suggests that psychiatric symptom endorsement in mTBI is driven by litigation status and/or preexisting psychiatric condition. Youngjohn, Davis, and Wolf (1997) reported that litigating patients with mTBI scored significantly higher on the MMPI-2 Hypochondriasis, Depression, Hysteria, Psychasthenia, Schizophrenia, and Somatic Complaints scales than patients with severe TBI (although the authors acknowledge that lack of insight into deficits could have led the severely injured patients to underreport psychiatric symptoms). Likewise, Berry et al. (1995) observed that litigants with TBI scored significantly higher than non-litigating patients with TBI on the MMPI-2 Hypochondriasis, Depression,

Hysteria, Psychasthenia, Schizophrenia, and Social Introversion scales. Furthermore, Ghaffar et al. (2006) reported that patients endorsing depression and psychosocial difficulties after mTBI had preinjury psychiatric histories.

Based on these findings, the most appropriate conclusion in a forensic neuropsychological report would be that an mTBI is not the likely cause of any long-term psychiatric symptoms.

RELATIONSHIP BETWEEN CLAIMED
PTSD AND mTBI SYMPTOMS

Lippa, Pastorek, Benge, and Thornton (2010) noted that PTSD accounted for a substantial amount of postconcussive symptom report (46.6%) in veterans, but they did not control for compensation-seeking status, mood disorder, or substance abuse. They suggest that "the combination of mTBI and posttraumatic stress symptoms may be producing this unusually large amount of [postconcussive] symptom report so long after the injury," but they state that "other factors, such as the availability of financial compensation for residual effects of mTBI, may also contribute to persistent symptom report" (p. 863).

In fact, Demakis, Gervais, and Rohling (2008), in examining a large sample of medical–legal claimants with claimed symptoms of PTSD ($n = 301$), observed that after screening for cognitive symptom validity and genuine reporting of psychological symptoms, severity of PTSD symptoms was not significantly associated with cognitive scores.

Greiffenstein and Baker (2008) examined a large sample of compensation seekers with persistent postconcussion syndrome ($n = 799$), of whom 95 were reporting both brief anterograde amnesia but also reexperiencing of the event, and an additional 228 were describing subsyndromal signs of PTSD (e.g., avoidance and autonomic hyperarousal in the absence of reexperiencing symptoms). The highest SVT failure rates were observed in the group with both mTBI and full PTSD; 52–69% failed a cognitive SVT (WAIS-III Digit Span RDS, TOMM) and 25–40% failed a motor SVT (Finger Tapping Test, Grip Strength Test), while 88% exceeded cutoffs on the MMPI-2 FBS. In the group with subsyndromal PTSD and mTBI, 44–61% failed a cognitive SVT, 22–36% failed a motor SVT, and 75% exceeded FBS cutoffs. For comparison, in the group with mTBI but without reported symptoms of PTSD, 31–45% failed a cognitive SVT, 17–27% failed a motor SVT, and 56% exceeded FBS cutoffs. These findings led the authors to conclude that "the more complex the post-traumatic presentation after mild neurological injury, the stronger the association with response bias. Late-appearing dual diagnosis is a litigation phenomenon so intertwined with secondary gain as to be a byproduct of it" (p. 565).

ARE THERE LONG-TERM PHYSICAL SYMPTOMS ASSOCIATED WITH mTBI?

The question arises as to whether mTBI is associated with chronic physical symptoms, such as anosmia, headache, pain, fatigue, and light or sound sensitivity. Green, Rohling, Iverson, and Gervais (2003; see also Green & Iverson, 2001) observed that when patients with mTBI who failed cognitive SVTs were removed from the sample, no patients with GCS of 13–15, normal brain imaging, and no posttraumatic amnesia had evidence of anosmia; these patients showed smell test scores comparable to those of orthopedic controls. Furthermore, patients who failed SVTs were five times as likely to obtain impaired smell test scores as patients who passed SVTs, indicating that abnormalities in smell perception reported by patients with mTBI are likely to be noncredible.

Regarding fatigue, available data indicate that at 12 months after injury, mean measures of vitality in individuals with histories of mTBI are comparable to population means (de Leon et al., 2009); poor medical health, mental illness, unmarried marital status, and litigation status were significant predictors of fatigue at 1 year.

Stovner, Schrader, Mickeviciene, Surklene, and Sand (2008) found that headache after mTBI in individuals living in a society without injury litigation (Lithuania) occurred at the same frequency as in patients with minor orthopedic trauma not involving the head, and that concussed individuals appeared to underreport the preinjury presence of headache. The authors also noted that pretraumatic headache was a predictor of posttraumatic headache, leading them to conclude that "headache occurring 3 months or more after concussion is not caused by the head or brain injury" (p. 112). In a companion publication, Mickeviciene et al. (2004) noted that Lithuanian patients with mTBI did not show an increased rate of headache relative to controls by 3 months after injury.

A recent meta-analysis of the prevalence of chronic pain associated with TBI, which included samples not screened for presence of motive to feign symptoms, showed paradoxically that rates of chronic pain were higher in samples with mTBI (75%) than in patients with moderate (32%) or severe (29%) TBI (Nampiaparampil, 2008). Given that there is no plausible explanation for chronic pain to be more prevalent in mTBI than in moderate/severe TBI, these data suggest that approximately 40% of pain reports of chronic pain in mTBI are without merit—interestingly, the same "magical number" posited by Larrabee et al. (2009) as the rate of feigned cognitive symptoms in mTBI.

Some authors have reported increased light and sound sensitivity in patients with mTBI who claimed postconcussional symptoms, but the samples were very small and were not screened for compensation-seeking status (Bohnen, Twijnstra, Wijnen, & Jolles, 1991). Of note, it has been reported (Bengtzen, Woodward, Lynn, Newman, & Biousse, 2008) that 80% of patients who wore sunglasses when presenting for neuro-ophthalmological exam were determined to have nonorganic visual loss; that nearly half of patients with nonorganic visual loss in fact wore sunglasses to the exam; and that 96% of patients who wore sunglasses and were diagnosed with nonorganic visual loss either were compensation-seeking or had a "highly positive review of systems" (i.e., endorsement of many symptoms). The authors conclude that "the 'sunglasses sign' in a patient without an obvious ophthalmic reason to wear sunglasses is highly suggestive of nonorganic visual loss" (p. 218).

PROCESSES AND DISORDERS ACCOUNTING FOR LONG-TERM SYMPTOM REPORT IN mTBI

The literature reviewed above indicates that there are no permanent cognitive abnormalities associated with mTBI. Estimates suggest that approximately 40% of litigants with mTBI are malingering (Larrabee, 2003c; Mittenberg et al., 2002). Who, then, are the remaining 60% who litigate for nonexistent symptoms? Two different sets of factors may account for this 60%: common psychological processes (i.e., misattribution and self-fulfilling prophecy) and preexisting/current psychiatric disorders.

Common Psychological Processes

Some psychological processes common to all individuals may predispose patients to long-term report of symptoms in mTBI—namely, misattribution ("good old days" bias) and self-fulfilling prophecy ("diagnosis threat").

Misattribution ("Good Old Days" Bias)

In an interesting series of studies, Mittenberg and colleagues (Mittenberg, DiGiulo, Perrin, & Bass, 1992; Ferguson, Mittenberg, Barone, & Schneider, 1999) reported that athletes with a history of concussion rated themselves high on postconcussive symptoms after the concussion, but when asked to rate their preinjury level of such symptoms, they endorsed a low level. However, ratings after concussion were comparable to those of athletes without histories of concussion, suggesting that the concussed athletes were "misremembering" how they functioned pre-injury, and were misattributing normal cognitive "slip-ups" and transient physical symptoms to the injury. Gunstad and Suhr (2004) showed that this same phenomenon occurs in non-compensation-seeking headache sufferers and nonathletes with head injury.

In a similar study, Davis (2002) obtained symptom ratings from post-concussion patients and non-brain-injured trauma patients regarding function before injury and at 1 week and 3 months afterward, as well as from controls. Both trauma groups endorsed fewer preinjury symptoms than reported by normal controls, suggesting that misattribution is not specific to mTBI, and patient symptom ratings at 1 week after injury did not differ from control ratings. At 3 months after injury the patients with mTBI endorsed fewer preinjury symptoms than they had at 1 week, suggesting that they "now attributed more of their current somatic symptoms to their mild TBI than they did 1 week after their injury" (p. 617). Furthermore, these patients reported more memory symptoms at 3 months than they had at 1 week, suggesting "increasingly more memory symptoms as [an] individual recovers" (p. 617).

In contrast, Hilsabeck, Gouvier, and Boulter (1998) observed that misattribution was more prominent in nonlitigant patients with head injuries than in nonlitigants with back injuries or controls. Specifically, they found that that head-injured patients reported worse function after injury as compared to patients with back injuries and controls, and that the head-injured patients also appeared to overestimate the amount of change from pre- to postinjury, as evidenced by reporting fewer preinjury symptoms than either the back-injured patients or the controls.

More recently, Iverson, Lange, Brooks, and Rennison (2010) examined postconcussion symptom report in a sample of patients with mTBI who were deemed fully disabled and were receiving workers' compensation benefits; these patients endorsed fewer preinjury symptoms than did controls, and of particular note, those who failed symptom validity testing reported fewer symptoms than those passing an SVT.

Apparently the experience of being in an accident and possibly injured renders the victim "hypervigilant" to any signs of dysfunction, and primes him/her to notice cognitive "malfunctions" that are in fact ubiquitous in the noninjured population (e.g., transient episodes of becoming lost when driving, temporarily "forgetting" one's Social Security number) and to attribute them incorrectly to the injury. Data from Iverson et al. (2010) indicate that this phenomenon is exacerbated in compensation-seeking settings, in which both nonconscious (misattribution) and conscious (malingering) factors serve to drive down preinjury symptom report.

Self-Fulfilling Prophecy ("Diagnosis Threat")

In another relevant study, college students with a history of concussion were administered a battery of cognitive tests, and half of the students were told ahead of time that individuals with a history of concussion perform poorly on the tests (Suhr & Gunstad, 2002b). In fact, the group provided with this information scored more poorly on the measures of memory and IQ (but not measures of attention and processing speed) than the students who did not receive this information, suggesting that postconcussion patients who believe that there are deficits associated with this condition tend to produce lowered scores in a "self-fulfilling prophecy." In a follow-up study (Suhr & Gunstad, 2005), the "diagnosis threat" group scored more poorly than the nonprimed group on measures of memory, psychomotor speed, and attention/working memory, but not on executive tasks and on an SVT; furthermore, performance in this group was not predicted by depression or anxiety. More recently, Ozen and Fernandes (2011) found that the effect of "diagnosis threat" was primarily confined to self-report of attention and memory complaints, rather than linked with actual underperformance on neuropsychological measures, although only measures of attention and processing speed were administered. Iverson et al. (2007) reported that diagnosis threat was associated with a much larger effect size on cognitive functioning than was mTBI (d's = −0.45 vs. −0.12), and that its influence was equal to that associated with litigation (d = 0.48) and depression (d = −0.49).

Cultures may differ in expectations of symptoms after mTBI. Ferrari et al. (2001) observed that Lithuanians had a low rate of expectation of chronic symptoms after mTBI as compared to Canadians, whereas expectations of acute symptoms were comparable across the two cultures.

Preexisting and Current Psychiatric Disorders

Many studies have found strong relationships between persistent postconcussive symptom report and psychiatric symptoms/emotional distress (Belanger, Kretzmer, Vanderploeg, & French, 2010; Benge, Pastorek, & Thornton, 2009; Gasquoine, 2000; Karzmark, Hall, & Englander, 1995; McCauley, Boake, Levin, Contant, & Song, 2001; Mooney & Speed, 2001; Ponsford et al., 2000). Patients with current depression and anxiety report levels of postaccident cognitive dysfunction that are not corroborated on cognitive screening measures, and current depression is associated with report of increasingly severe postconcussion symptoms over time (Fann, Katon, Uomotor, & Esselman, 1995). Kashluba et al. (2008) documented that predictors of long-term symptoms after mTBI were preexisting psychiatric history and litigation status; injury severity was not a prediction.

The finding that 10–15% of persons who have sustained mTBI may still *report* continuing postconcussive symptoms (see pp. 231–233) is of interest, given that 10% of general medical patients (Löwe et al., 2008) and 30% of neurological clinical patients (Jackson et al., 2006) are thought to have somatoform orientations. Such an orientation is not protective against mTBI, so it would be expected that these patients would be present in the same proportions in samples with mTBI as in medical or neurological samples.

I recently published a case of a litigant with mTBI who held a fixed belief in cognitive dysfunction despite normal neuropsychological scores, which I suggested represented "cognitive hypochondriasis" (Boone, 2009). Similarly, Greiffenstein (2000) has conceptualized late postconcussion syndrome in some individuals as "learned illness behavior." Whittaker, Kemp, and House (2007) observed that "following a mild head injury, symptomatic patients who believe that their symptoms have serious negative consequences on their lives and will continue to do so, are at heightened risk of experiencing significant enduring post-concussional symptoms"(p. 644).

In my experience, many patients use chronic mTBI symptoms to solve life problems that they were experiencing at the time of the accident and that they had otherwise been unable to remedy. For the vast majority of these patients, I find that the pressing stressor in their lives is their work situation; the majority are unhappy in their jobs. The continuing symptoms allow them either to leave a problematic job or to obtain accommodations to make the job more palatable. Of interest, Rimel et al. (1981), in comparing patients with mTBI who were employed versus not employed 3 months after the accident, found that the latter reported more stress in the year preceeding the accident.

Persistent postconcussive symptoms can also "solve" other psychosocial stressors. For example, marked, chronic symptoms can be used to keep a patient's maturing children tied to the home and prevent them from separating and starting their own lives; to excuse the patient from the responsibilities of single parenthood; or to keep a spouse from leaving and distract him/her from a conflictual marital situation. Klonoff and Lamb (1998) documented that significant preaccident stressors were predictors of chronic postconcussive symptom report. In particular, some data link chronic postconcussion symptoms to the number of adverse life events in the year preceeding the accident, leading to the conclusion that "the emergence and persistence of the postconcussional syndrome are associated with social adversity before the accident" (Fenton et al., 1993, p. 493).

Moore and Donders (2004) suggest that "individuals with longstanding emotional difficulties tend to be more likely to make reattribution errors, associated with under-estimation of their pre-morbid problems and selective augmentation of cognitive and somatic symptoms due to the perception of dysfunction as the result of physical trauma being more socially acceptable" (p. 980).

CONCLUSIONS

In conclusion, research does not support the view that long-term cognitive abnormalities are caused by mTBI in all or even a small subset of patients. Rather, chronic symptom report and underperformance on cognitive measures are driven by other factors. In my experience, litigants with mTBI fall into one or more of the following three categories:

1. Malingerers who feign cognitive symptoms in the service of enhancing damage awards.
2. Individuals with somatoform orientations or other psychiatric disorders who perceive that they have acquired symptoms related to the injury, but who in fact have experienced no change in function.
3. Individuals with actual cognitive abnormalities that are due to other etiologies but are misattributed to the mTBI.

8

Testimony

*Protecting Your Data
and Conclusions from Attack*

In the forensic practice of clinical neuropsychology, generating an accurate report grounded in the published literature is the first step—but, as a neuropsychologist expert witness, you must also be able to defend the report from attack by opposing experts and counsel. In this chapter, I cover many of the common methods used in attempts to discredit testifying neuropsychologists and to override their conclusions.

YOUR QUALIFICATIONS AND PRACTICE VERSUS THOSE OF OPPOSING EXPERTS

Board Certification

The opposing counsel may claim that his/her neuropsychologist is more qualified than you are. Board certification is desirable in this situation, because it provides evidence that peers have deemed your work product competent and that you have an adequate body of knowledge (as evidenced by passing a comprehensive written exam) about the practice of neuropsychology. If the opposing neuropsychologist is not board-certified, it can be reasonably argued that there is no evidence of that neuropsychologist's competence (i.e., qualified peers have not deemed the neuropsychologist's work product competent), and thus the neuropsychologist may be conducting exams and interpreting test scores in an idiosyncratic manner that is out of compliance with the rest of the field.

Some opposing experts may present themselves as board-certified in neuropsychology or other areas of psychology, but on examination it may be discovered that they hold "vanity board" credentials rather than true board certification. This can be checked by searching the claimed certification on the Internet. If the "board certification" requires only submission of a curriculum vitae and a check, it is not true certification. To expose this problem, a psychologist, Dr. Steve K. D. Eichel, submitted fabricated applications on behalf of his cat (Dr. Zoe D. Katze), and the cat was subsequently granted numerous professional certifications (Eichel, 2011). The only recognized boards granting board certification in neuropsychology are the American Board of Clinical Neuropsychology, which operates under the auspices of the APA's American Board of Professional Psychology, the American Board of Professional Neuropsychology, and the American Board of Pediatric Neuropsychology.

Pitting an MD Degree against a PhD Degree

Opposing counsel may also attempt to claim that because you hold a doctorate in psychology rather than medicine, you are testifying outside your area of expertise in a case involving brain injury: "Doctor, you're not a physician? You're not qualified to diagnose brain injury, are you?"

An appropriate response to this question might be this:

> "No, I am not a physician. My area of expertise is in objectively measuring cognitive dysfunction. What is at issue here is not brain damage per se, but whether the patient has any loss in cognitive function from alleged brain injury. Only a neuropsychologist can accurately diagnose cognitive dysfunction through comprehensive, objective, and psychometrically valid testing."

With this statement, you are appropriately educating the jury that your conclusions as a neuropsychologist are the most important opinions in such a case, because they directly speak to any residual loss of function in cognition. Many individuals suffer severe TBI, but subsequently appear to recover from a cognitive standpoint, as documented by normal test results on neuropsychological exam (e.g., a third of patients with severe TBI have been found to achieve good recovery; Levin, Grossman, Rose, & Teasdale, 1979). Thus the magnitude of the initial injury is less important than residual function.

Questioning may also take the form of pitting your conclusions against those of a physician:

PLAINTIFF COUNSEL: You know who Dr. X is?

DEFENSE NEUROPSYCHOLOGICAL EXPERT: Yes, I do.

PLAINTIFF COUNSEL: Is he considered to be a competent neurologist?

DEFENSE NEUROPSYCHOLOGICAL EXPERT: I find I disagree with his conclusions routinely.

PLAINTIFF COUNSEL: Do you think he's in a better position to diagnose brain injury than you would be?

DEFENSE NEUROPSYCHOLOGICAL EXPERT: I would say no.

PLAINTIFF COUNSEL: What makes you better at diagnosing brain injury than Dr. X?

DEFENSE NEUROPSYCHOLOGICAL EXPERT: Well, he seems to rely routinely on the patient's self-report rather than established diagnostic algorithms. He diagnoses brain injury when there is no objective evidence for it.

PLAINTIFF COUNSEL: Is there anything from your testing that would rule in or rule out a brain injury?

DEFENSE NEUROPSYCHOLOGICAL EXPERT: Not my testing, but information from the medical records.

PLAINTIFF COUNSEL: If Dr. X believes that my client sustained a brain injury because of this accident, is he wrong?

DEFENSE NEUROPSYCHOLOGICAL EXPERT: I would disagree with him.

PLAINTIFF COUNSEL: Does that make him wrong?

DEFENSE NEUROPSYCHOLOGICAL EXPERT: We have different opinions. When I look at he published algorithms for determining the presence of a traumatic brain injury, the plaintiff's characteristics at the time at the time of the accident do not match those for traumatic brain injury.

PLAINTIFF COUNSEL: What doesn't match?

DEFENSE NEUROPSYCHOLOGICAL EXPERT: She wasn't rendered unconscious. She seems to have laid down memories consistently from before to after the collision. She had no brain imaging abnormalities. Her Glasgow Coma Scale score was 15.

Opinions about Opposing Experts

At times attorneys will ask for your opinions about opposing experts. I am not sure what the intent of such questioning is, but if you have negative perceptions of the opposing neuropsychologist, perhaps the attorneys want to imply that your disagreements with the opposing experts are driven by personal animosity rather than objective findings. Alternatively, if they can get you to say positive things about the opposing expert, this may undercut any differences of opinion you have with that expert's conclusions (e.g., if that expert is such a good neuropsychologist, why are you disagreeing with him/her?). If you provide negative assessments of an opposing expert, limit your criticisms to objective data, not personal attacks:

PLAINTIFF COUNSEL: Do you have any criticisms of Dr. Z [opposing neuropsychologist]?

DEFENSE NEUROPSYCHOLOGICAL EXPERT: Yes, I do.

PLAINTIFF COUNSEL: What are those criticisms, if you would, please?

DEFENSE NEUROPSYCHOLOGICAL EXPERT: He's not board-certified, which means that colleagues in the field have not judged his work product to be competent.

PLAINTIFF COUNSEL: You're not saying that his work is incompetent, though, are you?

DEFENSE NEUROPSYCHOLOGICAL EXPERT: Well, I think that when someone draws conclusions that are at variance with the published literature, I don't know if "incompetent" is the correct term, but it is at least inaccurate.

PLAINTIFF COUNSEL: Can't professionals disagree?

DEFENSE NEUROPSYCHOLOGICAL EXPERT: Professionals can disagree, but within constraints. For example, the research literature shows that Alzheimer's disease and vascular dementia may result in similar cognitive deficits. Thus it is reasonable that two neuropsychologists might disagree as to whether a patient has vascular dementia versus Alzheimer's disease. On the other hand, the preponderance of the available literature indicates that there are no long-term cognitive abnormalities associated with mild traumatic brain injury. Thus, for Dr. Z to conclude that the plaintiff's cognitive abnormalities are due to the mild traumatic brain injury is not reasonable, because his conclusions are inconsistent with the published literature.

"Bet You Haven't Seen This Before!"

An opposing attorney may also attempt to dismiss your expertise by characterizing his/her client as so unusual and unique that your knowledge does not apply to this patient. The message to the jury is that you do not have relevant experience to comment on this patient:

PLAINTIFF COUNSEL: How many near-drowning patients who have been in a coma for 3 weeks have you tested before?

DEFENSE NEUROPSYCHOLOGICAL EXPERT: None. Fortunately, near-drownings are relatively unusual; no neuropsychologist I know has had the opportunity to test very many of these individuals. However, the results of objective cognitive testing can be used to show whether or not this individual has significant impairment from this condition."

Here you are attempting to convey that while you have not seen this precise condition, the results of your testing are useful and relevant in describing this patient's cognitive function. Obviously, if there are other neuropsychologists locally available who have seen the condition at issue many times, then this will be a liability for you when you are testifying.

In a variation on this theme, an opposing attorney may ask:

"How many patients with moderate traumatic brain injury have you evaluated? How many were struck by a car? How many had coup-contre-coup left parietal and right frontal injury? How many were left-handed?"

Here, a relatively common condition that most neuropsychologists have encountered many times is whittled down to a situation that is highly unique, so that most neuropsychologists will not have tested a patient with these exact characteristics. Again, the goal is to have you admit that you have no expertise in the plaintiff's precise condition. In this situation, the attorney who retained you needs to follow up with questions illuminating that there are infinite constellations of patient characteristics, and even though you have not seen this exact one before, your knowledge is still relevant. For example, he or she may ask:

"Doctor, all patients are unique, right? You are board-certified, right? When you became board-certified, did you have to demonstrate expertise in every type of patient with moderate traumatic brain injury? Has any neuropsychologist ever evaluated every type of patient with moderate traumatic brain injury?"

The Neuroanatomy Exam

Some attorneys will take the tack of quizzing you regarding your knowledge of neuroanatomy. The hope is that if you fail to answer the questions correctly, juries will assume that you have substandard knowledge and are not qualified to testify. For example, you may be asked a string of questions like this one: "What is a neuron? How long are neurons? Some are a foot long—where are those located? What is a mirror neuron?" And so forth.

The goal here is to pull you away from your area of expertise. Although you may be able to answer initial questions, the plan is to keep asking more obtuse questions until you are repeatedly answering, "I don't know," and/or you provide answers that are incorrect. The message the attorney is trying to convey to the jury is that you "don't know" anything and/or that your knowledge is faulty, so why should they listen to you?

The schematic illustrated in Figure 8.1 may characterize most neuropsychologists' knowledge bases. They know a tremendous amount about neuropsychology, but most have less knowledge about the intricacies of brain imaging, neuropathology, medications, and so on. As long as questions remain within your area of expertise—namely, neuropsychology and clinical psychology—you are not likely to answer with many "I don't know" or wrong answers. But if an attorney can prod you into answering questions in the other areas, the chances of your providing incorrect information will rise dramatically. And if your answers are shown to the jury to be wrong, this is a difficult position from which to recover. In other words, the attorney does not even have to attack you on your neuropsychological conclusions; he/she can simply discredit you through your answers in other content areas. I can remember on one occasion watching a physician testifying incorrectly about IQ tests, and it did not play well to the jury.

You might try to respond as follows to such a line of questioning:

DEFENSE NEUROPSYCHOLOGICAL EXPERT: I was not retained to provide expert opinions regarding neurons. My expertise is in cognitive testing, and I am here to provide accurate and verifiable information regarding the plaintiff's cognitive skills. I defer questions regarding neurons to other experts.

PLAINTIFF COUNSEL: Are you telling us you don't know what a neuron is?

DEFENSE NEUROPSYCHOLOGICAL EXPERT: I know what a neuron is, but I am deferring all questions regarding neurons to other experts.

PLAINTIFF COUNSEL: You don't think it is relevant whether my client has damaged neurons?

DEFENSE NEUROPSYCHOLOGICAL EXPERT: I am here to provide testimony regarding cognitive functioning. I am deferring all questions regarding neurons to other experts.

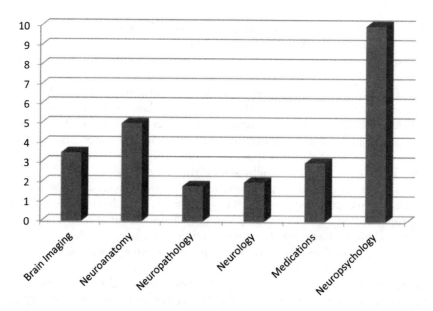

FIGURE 8.1. Schematic of the extent of most neuropsychologists' knowledge bases.

Some attorneys are very persistent, anticipating that at some point you will give up and start providing answers. Keep giving the same answer.

Appeal to a "Higher Power"

Occasionally an attorney will quote from published resources in the field that contradict your conclusions, in an attempt to undercut your opinions. That is, he or she will attempt to argue that a "more important" neuropsychologist disagrees with your conclusions:

> PLAINTIFF COUNSEL: You're familiar with Dr. Muriel Lezak?
>
> DEFENSE NEUROPSYCHOLOGICAL EXPERT: Yes.
>
> PLAINTIF COUNSEL: In your opinion, is Dr. Lezak considered to be the foremost authority in neuropsychological assessment?
>
> DEFENSE NEUROPSYCHOLOGICAL EXPERT: No, although she has made a considerable contribution to the field.
>
> PLAINTIFF COUNSEL: On page 171, Dr. Lezak recognized that with mild traumatic brain injury you can have things like attention deficits, correct?
>
> DEFENSE NEUROPSYCHOLOGICAL EXPERT: Yes. I agree with much that

she says in her book; however, this statement is not consistent with current empirical knowledge.

Deviation from the "50–50" Plaintiff–Defense Retention Rate

A very common situation in depositions and trial testimony is for an expert witness to be questioned regarding the percentage of cases for which he or she is retained by plaintiff versus defendant, with the assumption that if the retention rate is skewed toward one or the other side, the expert is "biased." However, most litigated cases in which neuropsychologists are retained involve claimed TBI, and of those, 80% are cases alleging mTBI. As discussed on pages 227–234, current research overwhelmingly shows that no chronic cognitive losses are associated with this condition. Because of these data, several years ago I began declining to be retained for plaintiffs in cases of mTBI, which de facto makes me primarily a defense expert. Neuropsychologists need to be committed to providing conclusions that are consistent with the published literature, and this stance may skew their retention rate from the idealized "50–50."

At times, attorneys will accuse the neuropsychological expert as adopting a role as "advocate" for the side that retained him or her:

> PLAINTIFF COUNSEL: By the way, do you consider yourself an advocate for [the defendant]?
>
> DEFENSE NEUROPSYCHOLOGICAL EXPERT: No.
>
> PLAINTIFF COUNSEL: I assume you would like the [X Law Firm] to hire you again in the future?
>
> DEFENSE NEUROPSYCHOLOGICAL EXPERT: I am kept very busy not working for [X Law Firm].
>
> PLAINTIFF COUNSEL: So nothing about the opinions that you've expressed so far in this matter has anything to do with the possibility of getting hired by the [X Law Firm] in the future?
>
> DEFENSE NEUROPSYCHOLOGICAL EXPERT: My commitment is to the integrity of the data, what the data show, what the objective literature shows.

In a similar vein:

> PLAINTIFF COUNSEL: In terms of outlining my client's deposition, did you look at and mark those pages that assist you in the position that you're taking to support your opinion, or did you highlight things in a fair and impartial manner?

DEFENSE NEUROPSYCHOLOGICAL EXPERT: I marked things I thought were relevant, symptoms she is reporting, and so forth.

YOUR EXAMINATION

Claimed Adversarial Nature of the Defense Neuropsychological Exam

On a few occasions, I have had some plaintiffs and their attorneys and/or experts claim that measures of response bias were failed during my examinations because I was "mean" to examinees, clearly did not like them, or was in some other way unprofessional in my deportment, which caused them to be uninterested in the test results and to just "mark down anything." Curiously, such claims have never emerged until after a plaintiff's team received a copy of my report in which I detailed numerous SVT failures, and the plaintiff then had to account for the test results. (If I was so unpleasant, why did not the plaintiff report the behavior immediately to his/her attorney upon completion of the exam?)

The following deposition testimony by the opposing plaintiff neuropsychologist pertained to my exam of a patient litigating in the context of a claimed head injury from a fall 2½ years earlier. Medical records suggested equivocal mTBI (no loss of consciousness, alert and oriented with GCS score of 15, brief retrograde/anterograde amnesia, normal brain CT). On neuropsychological exam, the plaintiff failed 8 of 11 SVTs and answered the last 196 MMPI-2–RF items false.

DEFENSE COUNSEL: You believe she took an adversarial position? Why?

PLAINTIFF NEUROPSYCHOLOGICAL EXPERT: She was basically trying to impeach as opposed to trying to be a true clinician and find out what the real problem is. She did, I think, correctly point out some lower scores that she obtained, compared to [previous testing]. And that's a little worrisome. Why should she get lower scores? My feeling about this is that I don't know the answer. But my suspicion is that she lost this guy early on in the assessment, and by the time she got to the end of the assessment, you know, he probably had both middle fingers out onto the table, because he then marked all these MMPI items false . . . and I know he did that because he was sick of the whole process. He didn't do that to malinger. That would be an extraordinarily dumb way to malinger.

Obviously it is very important to be pleasant, professional, and courteous to all patients at all times during an exam. If you strictly adhere to this policy as an examiner, then whether or not a patient fails SVTs and defaults to a false response bias on the MMPI-2–RF is determined by patient, not examiner, variables.

Some neuropsychology experts opine that SVT failures occur more often on defense neuropsychological evaluations, which they attribute to an "adversarial" process in which plaintiffs do not expect to be listened to or treated courteously by defense examiners. However, the available research does not support this contention. Meyers, Reinsch-Boothby, Miller, Rohling, and Axelrod (2011) found no significant difference in rate of SVT failure between plaintiff-referred (n = 42) and defense-referred (n = 53) patients who were administered the same neuropsychological battery: 12.5% of plaintiff-referred versus 15.9% of defense-referred test takers failed at least 2 SVTs, and plaintiff-referred and defense-referred patients did not differ in mean number of SVTs failed (1.12 vs. 1.16). Furthermore, there was no significant difference in neuropsychological and psychological test results in plaintiff-referred versus defense-referred exams in which SVTs were passed, or in those exams in which SVTs were failed. Likewise, the FBS score on the MMPI-2 was not significantly different across plaintiff-referred and defense-referred exams; these data are comparable to that observed by Greiffenstein et al. (2010). Interestingly, Fox, Gerson, and Lees-Haley (1995) reported that plaintiff-referred examinees actually exhibited more exaggeration on the MMPI-2 validity scores.

Acceptance of Patient Self-Report

Questioning in deposition and cross-examination may take the form of pressuring you as the defense neuropsychologist to explain why patient self-report cannot be relied upon:

> PLAINTIFF COUNSEL: Are you saying that you do not believe that my client is a reliable historian in reporting how she functions—for example, in trying to follow a recipe at home now versus how she did before the accident? Is that correct?

> DEFENSE NEUROPSYCHOLOGICAL EXPERT: I absolutely believe that she is telling the truth as she sees it, but there are various psychological processes that cause people to misremember how they functioned before an accident and to inflate their preaccident abilities.

> PLAINTIFF COUNSEL: So if she tells you that before the accident, when she's doing her free reading, she could put a book down and come

back to it a week later and remember where she left off, but now she has to reread that, would you discount that? Or would you put any significance to that self-report?

DEFENSE NEUROPSYCHOLOGICAL EXPERT: Obviously I would attach significance to that report. However, many times people are not particularly accurate about remembering how they were before an accident. There's a large literature explaining why that could be, and that's also why we have to rely on test scores. If we could simply rely on someone's report regarding how they changed after the accident, we wouldn't need to test them. So I'm certainly not saying she's a liar; it is her perspective, but an individual's perspective on how he or she has changed is not always accurate.

Information from Collaterals

A common attack by plaintiff attorneys is to criticize the defense neuropsychologist for not interviewing family members and friends regarding the examinee. As discussed in chapters 2, 3, and 4, a neuropsychologist can use cognitive SVTs and psychological test results to determine whether a test taker is being forthright in providing data, but the examiner has no such measures to apply to information provided by friends and family about the patient. Because I do not know whether the latter information is accurate, I would in most circumstances prefer not to collect it. If a plaintiff's attorney challenges me on this, here is how I usually respond:

PLAINTIFF COUNSEL: Doctor, you didn't bother to talk to this man's wife or coworkers to hear how they—people who see him every day—say he has changed?

DEFENSE NEUROPSYCHOLOGICAL EXPERT: What friends and family members have to say may have relevance, but I have no way of verifying that what they say is accurate and truthful. As a result, I must rely on my objective cognitive test results. If the patient's score on memory testing is at the 75th percentile, but yet the family says he has memory problems, do I alter the percentile on the test? No. If we could rely on friends and family to quantify the extent of cognitive dysfunction, we would not need objective testing.

Choice of Test and Test Version

Perhaps you continue to administer the WAIS-III or WMS-III in your neuropsychological exam, despite the fact that fourth editions have recently been published. A major reason for continuing to use the WAIS-III and WMS-III is the very large research base on these two instruments. Another reason, relevant to the goal of continuous measurement of response bias, is that both the WAIS-III and WMS-III have validated embedded symptom validity indicators (Picture Completion Most Discrepant Index, Solomon et al., 2010; Digit Symbol recognition, N. Kim et al., 2010; Digit Span variables, Babikian & Boone, 2007; Logical Memory Symptom validity Index, Bortnik et al., 2010; WAIS-III Indexes, Curtis et al., 2009; etc.), whereas minimal data are available regarding embedded SVTs for the WAIS-IV and WMS-IV. Finally, as discussed on pages 16–18, recent publications have noted that tests do not become obsolete simply because new versions are published.

However, if you have given the WAIS-III or WMS-III, you might hear the following question:

PLAINTIFF COUNSEL: When you tested her, you went ahead and gave her a third-edition test when fourth-edition tests were available. Correct?

DEFENSE NEUROPSYCHOLOGICAL EXPERT: Yes, I did.

PLAINTIFF COUNSEL: Is it considered to be appropriate and ethical to give older version of tests when new versions are available?

DEFENSE NEUROPSYCHOLOGICAL EXPERT: Well, yes, if you can demonstrate that the test is valid. There are recent practice recommendations in the field indicating that you do not have to switch to a newer version of a test unless it can be demonstrated that the earlier version is in some way invalid.

Choice of Normative Data Employed

For many standard neuropsychological tests, there are alternative normative data sets available to clinicians for use in interpreting patient test scores. As described in Mitrushina et al. (2005), a neuropsychologist attempts to employ normative data that best match a test taker on demographic data and geographic location, and gives preference to more recent normative data because of potential cohort effects (i.e., differing age cohorts may have had varying educational and life experiences that affect test performance). However, alternative test administration formats have been published for some tests, and the neuropsychologist must make sure that the norms selected in fact match the specific test administration used with the patient. In the example below, the patient was administered the Finger Tapping Test in three trials alternating between hands; this administration matches testing procedures employed in the normative data provided by Trahan et al. (1987). Like the neuropsychologist in this example, you should be able to provide justification for the particular norms selected for a given patient.

> PLAINTIFF COUNSEL: You use outdated norms, don't you?
>
> DEFENSE NEUROPSYCHOLOGICAL EXPERT: No.
>
> PLAINTIFF COUNSEL: You're using norms that are from 1987 when in fact there are norms that have been published in 2004?
>
> DEFENSE NEUROPSYCHOLOGICAL EXPERT: Which test are you talking about?
>
> PLAINTIFF COUNSEL: In the Finger Tapping Test, you used norms from 1987 that are well over 20 years old. Yet there are the 2004 revised comprehensive norms by Heaton. Why don't you use those?
>
> DEFENSE NEUROPSYCHOLOGICAL EXPERT: Because I don't administer the test in the same way Heaton does. You have to use norms that match the way you administer the tests.

YOUR CONCLUSIONS

Documentation of Response Bias on Cognitive Testing

Plaintiff attorneys may complain that a particular expert diagnoses malingering or the presence of response bias excessively, but if the rate of detection matches that expected in the published literature for the clinician's setting, then this criticism has no merit. In the survey published by Mittenberg et al. (2002), experienced neuropsychologists reported that they estimated that approximately 29% of litigants, and nearly 40% of those seeking compensation for mTBI, are feigning their symptoms. Similarly, Larrabee (2003c), in summarizing 11 studies on mTBI, concluded that the rate of feigned symptoms was 40%. More recently, he and his colleagues have posited that the "magical number" of 40% ± 10 is the rate of feigned cognitive symptoms across compensation-seeking settings (Larrabee et al., 2009).

Given these findings, an expert whose rates of detection of feigned symptoms does not match published rates is the one who should be held to explain his/her clinical practice. Appropriate questions for such an expert might be these:

> "How often and in what percentage of litigants do you identify suspect effort? What is the published rate of faking of cognitive symptoms in compensation-seeking settings? It is 40%; why does your rate of detection of faked cognitive symptoms in litigants not match the published base rate?"

At times opposing experts have argued that a patient cannot be diagnosed as malingering because the patient "does not meet DSM-IV criteria for malingering." However, DSM-IV was published by the American Psychiatric Association in 1994, long before the vast majority of literature on detection of feigned symptoms appeared. (DSM-IV-TR [American Psychiatric Association, 2000] only updates the text of DSM-IV, not the actual diagnostic criteria). Furthermore, DSM is a manual developed primarily by psychiatrists for use in all mental health disciplines, and it would not be an appropriate resource for practice in regard to psychological testing conducted by a psychologist; psychologists should rely on published practice guidelines in the field of psychology regarding identification of malingering via psychometric instruments.

The most common attack on SVT data is to "explain away" test failures as due to non-effort-related factors (fatigue, pain, psychological distress, medications, etc.). Although these explanations might initially seem plausible, as discussed on pages 64–66, the empirical literature does not provide evidence that these conditions are associated with SVT failure. To make the case that SVT failures are due to these conditions, one would have to argue that the claimed confounds have caused the test taker to become cognitively comparable to the groups of individuals who in fact fail the tests despite best performing to true capability—namely, patients with very low IQ (Dean et al., 2008) and with dementia/amnestic disorder (Dean, Victor, et al., 2009). I do not believe that anyone contends that depression, anxiety, fatigue, psychological distress, PTSD, medications, and/or pain, singly or in combination, will cause an individual to function at the level of someone with mental retardation or dementia.

DEFENSE NEUROPSYCHOLOGICAL EXPERT: On cognitive testing, she passed 8 out of 10 indicators of response bias. On the previous neuropsychological exam, she failed 2 symptom validity indicators. This suggests that on the cognitive testing, most of the time she may have been performing to true capability, but part of the time—perhaps 20% of the time—she was not.

PLAINTIFF COUNSEL: Sometimes that 20%—you have to think about other factors that may have caused a fluctuation; correct?

DEFENSE NEUROPSYCHOLOGICAL EXPERT: Such as?

PLAINTIFF COUNSEL: Such as a person who was in pain and also suffering from PTSD and having some type of depression all at one time.

DEFENSE NEUROPSYCHOLOGICAL EXPERT: That's not true, because the literature shows that these conditions do not cause individuals to fail symptom validity tests.

> PLAINTIFF COUNSEL: Not depression or pain or PTSD alone. I'm very careful. I'm saying chronic pain with depression with PTSD. Is it your testimony that those combined effects on a person will cause no fluctuation during examination?
>
> DEFENSE NEUROPSYCHOLOGICAL EXPERT: I would say, that with no evidence to support that statement, the answer would be no.
>
> PLAINTIFF COUNSEL: You are saying that these factors would not cause a person to lose attention, momentary attention, during the exam?
>
> DEFENSE NEUROPSYCHOLOGICAL EXPERT: Well, these tests are not measuring momentary attention. They are measuring response bias, which is the disposition to present oneself as more cognitively impaired than is actually the case. A momentary lapse in attention will not cause a person to fail a symptom validity test.

Similarly:

> PLAINTIFF COUNSEL: We don't know whether it's a brain injury, faking, medication, pain, anxiety, or depression causing the failed scores on the symptom validity tests, right?
>
> DEFENSE NEUROPSYCHOLOGICAL EXPERT: Yes, we do. Research shows that mild brain injury, pain, and depression/psychological distress do not cause failures on symptom validity tests.

The argument that fatigue has interfered with SVT performance can be rebutted if the MMPI-2–RF is administered at the conclusion of the exam and a normal VRIN-r score is obtained:

> PLAINTIFF COUNSEL: Did you track any fatigue effects that could have affected her performance on symptom validity tests?
>
> DEFENSE NEUROPSYCHOLOGICAL EXPERT: Well, I am present, administering the tests, watching her. At no point did she appear unduly fatigued. And at the end of the cognitive testing she completed the MMPI-2–RF, and data from its validity scales show that she was more careful and self-consistent in completing the test than asymptomatic individuals.

Relatedly, some plaintiff's attorneys may opine that neuropsychological test batteries are lengthy, and that patients with actual brain dysfunction or depression "may have difficulty staying on task and may end up frustrated and simply randomly responding toward the end of the 16 hours" (Sims, 2007, p. 2), and thereby inadvertently fail SVTs. It would be a rare neuropsychological evaluation that would take 16 hours, and even if it did, such an evaluation would be conducted over more than 1 day with breaks. It is the responsibility of the examiner to monitor a patient's behavior, and if the patient does not appear able to respond appropriately to task instructions due to fatigue, all testing should be discontinued. Furthermore, if responding was random toward the end of the exam, all scores (including those on standard neurocognitive measures) would not be valid, not just the scores on the SVTs.

On occasion some opposing neuropsychologists have characterized multiple SVT failures as a "cry for help," apparently importing language that has often been used to describe high F scores on the MMPI-2. However, as discussed on pages 221–222, "cry for help" interpretations do not have adequate empirical support for the MMPI-2, let alone for SVTs.

Attacks on SVTs also include inaccurate claims regarding how they were validated: ". . . what 'malingering' tests were normed on individuals who have just undergone 16 hours of testing in the first place?" (Sims, 2007, p. 2), and "no malingering test was normed on individuals forced to be examined by a doctor he or she did not trust because of a relationship with the defendant" (Sims, 2007, p. 2). Similar complaints involve claims that "brain-injury plaintiffs" were not included in tests' normative samples (Sims, 2007). However, most SVTs have in fact been validated on data obtained from actual neuropsychological exams of credible and noncredible patients, many of which were conducted in the context of litigation (see numerous publications from the labs of Greve, Bianchini, Greiffenstein, Meyers, and Larrabee, as well as my own). It is also claimed that SVT validation studies do not report either how many participants were on pain medication, or whether the participants were experiencing the same level of pain and physical problems as any given patient undergoing clinical evaluation (Sims, 2007). But, in fact, most SVT validation studies have included credible patients with moderate to severe TBI, some of whom were still in rehab (see, e.g., Boone, Lu, & Herzberg, 2002a, 2002b). It would be a rare rehab sample that was not experiencing physical problems associated with moderate to severe TBI, including pain and use of pain medications.

Some attorneys and neuropsychological experts attempt to argue that measures of response bias cannot be used in a clinical setting because they have not been validated on actual malingerers. It is true that while some SVTs have been developed with simulators (volunteers instructed to fake for the purposes of research), the majority have been validated with "real-world" known groups of credible and noncredible patients. When you are using measures of response bias, it is important to be knowledgeable about how they were validated, so that you can successfully rebut the following type of inaccurate testimony:

"They're based on a—in my mind—a totally inadequate database with not malingerers who have been identified and trapped and sent to prison, but imitation malingerers who are either volunteers or paid volunteers who pretend to be malingerers for the purpose of this study. So when Dr. Boone puts a table in her report and shows malingerers here, those are not malingerers. Those are pretend malingerers that she, like the others, have incorporated in their studies."

Attacks on SVTs also include the claim that SVT cutoffs require "impossibly high scores" to pass. The example provided is often that of the TOMM (which traditionally has set cutoffs at < 90% correct), and the contention is made that that "no school would 'flunk' a student who tests at 89 percent" (Sims, 2007, p. 2). However, it must be kept in mind that SVTs are very easy but only appear difficult, whereas academic tests are in fact difficult because they are designed to measure whether students have learned course content. SVT cutoffs are typically set to allow ≤10% of credible patients to fail, but in the case of the TOMM, cutoffs have actually been set to nearly 100% specificity (virtually no patients fall below the cutoffs). The appropriateness of any test cutoff cannot be critiqued without information regarding how credible patients with brain injury perform on the measure.

As shown in the first interchange below, some opposing neuropsychologists claim that because a patient performed well on some standard tests, or portions of tests, negative response bias has been ruled out. However, as discussed on pages 33–40, response bias is typically not static across an exam; most noncredible individuals are "picking and choosing" on which tests to perform poorly, because they are intuiting that they will not appear credible if they perform poorly on every measure.

> DEFENSE COUNSEL: This is a pretty easy one to fake, isn't it? I mean, somebody reads you a list of 15 words, and you wait a little bit and you give them back the words. Wouldn't you agree, as a clinician, this is a pretty easy one that someone can dump?
>
> PLAINTIFF NEUROPSYCHOLOGICAL EXPERT: They could. But if they were going to do that, you'd expect much poorer performances across all the trials, not just on two. And if someone was intentionally trying to do poorly on this particular measure, ordinarily they'd also do much worse than that.
>
> DEFENSE COUNSEL: OK. Everything else, all the other testing, she was average or high average or I think she had superior on a couple of them, didn't she?
>
> PLAINTIFF NEUROPSYCHOLOGICAL EXPERT: Yes. She did well across so many areas of the assessment. And she did well in the areas where

people who are trying to dump the test, so to speak, or do poorly would actually do much more poorly than she did. So this is not a profile of someone who looks like they're not trying hard. If anything, it's the opposite. She does very, very well in many measures.

The following are potential responses to this line of questioning.

Example 1

PLAINTIFF COUNSEL: If you set out to fake tests, how would someone who's not sophisticated in this process make those selections? In other words, how do you explain that he's 95th percentile over here, or that he's doing a bang-up job on all these tests, and then these are real low?

DEFENSE NEUROPSYCHOLOGICAL EXPERT: There is research in which people have been asked to fake brain injury symptoms, and then they are asked what strategies they used. The most common strategy is to pretend that you are very poor in memory—for example, that you can't remember what people say to you—which translates into doing poorly on tests in which you're asked to repeat back what the examiner says to you. So it would in fact be common that someone faking brain injury symptoms would aim to do poorly on memory tests and in fact do well in other areas.

Example 2

PLAINTIFF COUNSEL: You say the plaintiff failed these effort measures, but she scored high on a memorization test. That's not consistent with a person who is trying to deceive about their memory, is it?

DEFENSE NEUROPSYCHOLOGICAL EXPERT: No, that's not true. Research we have done shows that only 16% of noncredible patients fail every symptom validity test administered. It is much more common to be selective, because I think that most people who are faking realize it's not going to look believable if they do poorly on every task. The typical malingerer picks and chooses, during the exam, which tests to underperform on. It's a rare malingerer who does poorly on every symptom validity test administered.

Some attorneys and opposing experts will emphasize the SVTs that were passed to argue against the presence of negative response bias. For instance, a plaintiff's attorney may ask: "You claim that my client failed four symptom validity indicators, but he also passed six. Why are you ignoring the six he passed? Or the plaintiff's neurospcyhological expert may say:

> "In his performance with me, he scored extremely high on the Finger Tapping Test. Dr. Boone had a publication with another doctor indicating that low performance on this test could be a sign of inadequate effort. So this would be one more example of his performance showing that adequate effort was produced.

SVT cutoffs are set to protect patients at the expense of failing to detect noncredible individuals, so they err on the side of underdiagnosing response bias. No SVT has perfect sensitivity; if an SVT has 65% sensitivity, it detects 65% of noncredible patients, but fails to detect 35%. Also, as noted earlier, most noncredible individuals do not perform poorly on every test administered, because they realize that it may not be believable to do so. Furthermore, as discussed on pages 50–51, the study by Victor et al. (2009) showed that while a single SVT failure is not unusual in credible patients, only 5% fail two tests, 1.5% fail three tests, and zero fail four. Other studies have also found an almost perfect specificity with failure on two tests (Larrabee, 2003c; Meyers & Volbrecht, 2003). Thus, for these various reasons, failing scores are more informative than passing scores. To place passed SVTs in context, David Hartman (personal communication, 2010) provides the analogy that "if there are 10 banks and a robber only robs 4, does that make him not a bank robber?"

Some neuropsychological clinicians hold the view that response bias is not a viable construct, and that SVTs do not in fact "measure anything" because they are not measuring discrete cognitive skills per se. A plaintiff's neuropsychologist opined:

> "The problem with the malingering tests is that they don't measure anything. So it becomes wholly subjective. I think they're not tests in the legitimate sense of the word, because they don't measure anything. You've not gotten a measure of anything, and you're saying that if the person does this or that, they must be malingering. It bewilders me."

However, as discussed on pages 25–26, response bias/malingering has a much greater effect on cognitive scores than virtually any other condition except mental retardation. Thus SVTs are clearly measuring "something."

Another tack in circumventing the results of SVTs is to dismiss the results of one exam as "invalid," and instead to rely on the results of another exam (in which adequate SVTs were not given, available embedded indicators were not interpreted, etc.). In this case, the plaintiff's neuropsychologist may say:

> "It is true that the patient was not performing to true ability on Dr. Boone's exam, which means that those results are invalid and should be discarded. But she passed two symptom validity tests on my exam, so we can rely on those results."

There is a misunderstanding that when SVTs are failed, the results of these exams are "not valid." However, SVT failure in fact documents, in a very valid manner, that a patient is not performing to true capability; in this context results from all exams must be carefully scrutinized for response bias. Arguably, the *conclusions* from the exam with failed SVTs are much more "valid" (documenting response bias) than those from the other exam (purportedly documenting neurocognitive dysfunction) but with inadequate SVT analysis.

In a similar vein, on some occasions an opposing attorney will argue that in the context of SVT failure: "Well, you don't know one way or the other if my client has deficits?" In other words, the attorney is leaving the door open that deficits may still in fact be present. However, in making the claim for damages, it is incumbent on the plaintiff to provide objective, verifiable evidence of cognitive dysfunction. A test taker who fails multiple SVTs has not done this.

Some neuropsychologists take the position that even if a plaintiff fails SVTs, we should attempt to maneuver around the obstacles the patient has thrown in our path and attempt to discern the presence of any true cognitive abnormalities. However, there are serious problems with this approach. First, there is no verified method to do this effectively. That is, do we add points to test scores; if so, how much, and across which tests? Rely on the patient's or others' reports of the patient's deficits, which may have very limited reliability?

Second, if as a field we wish to reduce malingering, this approach will only encourage it. If patients feign and are detected, but still receive the monetary award they would have received if they had not feigned, we have given them an incentive to feign. That is, if they feign successfully they will receive a much larger award than they are truly entitled to, but if they are detected, the "worst" that will happen is that they receive the award they would have received in the absence of feigning. We should take the position that if a test taker fails multiple SVTs and has no condition that would account for such failures (e.g., mental retardation, dementia), then cognitive deficits have not been objectively documented by the plaintiff, and that there can be no compensable damages until he/she does so.

When several SVTs are failed, an attorney may ask whether any of the data are usable:

PLAINTIFF COUNSEL: Is it your view, in light of the three or four failed symptom validity tests, that the entire testing is invalidated?

DEFENSE NEUROPSYCHOLOGICAL EXPERT: Well, he obtained average to high average scores in all areas except one, so those are usable, although he may actually be higher in these areas. The only low scores on exam were on the verbal memory tests, ranging from low average to impaired. However, these cannot be relied upon, because the symptom validity tests he failed all involved verbal memory.

Yet another approach to undercutting your testimony regarding SVT failures may be to contrast your conclusions with those of treating professionals and friends/family who "know the patient better than you do."

PLAINTIFF COUNSEL: Did you or did you not review any records of any writing of any kind where a doctor, any nurse, any physician, any surgeon, any psychologist, psychiatrist or neuropsychiatrist, if there was ever such a person that examined her, ever questioned her credibility?

DEFENSE NEUROPSYCHOLOGICAL EXPERT: No, I didn't. But they examined and treated her in a clinical context and assumed that she was reporting symptoms truthfully. They had no objective test data regarding whether she was reporting symptoms accurately. I did have this information. If we could rely on interview and standard exams regarding credibility of symptoms, we would not have had to develop symptom validity measures.

PLAINTIFF COUNSEL: Did you ever talk to any of her friends, family members, or anyone else that know her, such as coworkers, regarding whether she is the type of person that would fake an injury or overexaggerate symptoms?

DEFENSE NEUROPSYCHOLOGICAL EXPERT: No. If we could rely on this information, we would not have needed to develop objective measures to check for feigning.

Similarly, at times one will read deposition testimony provided by other professionals who attempt to "pull rank." For instance, a plaintiff neurosurgeon expert may opine:

"What I will say about this is that malingering is a powerful word, and it's a very negative word. And to use it in a patient who has part of their brain missing [brain imaging showed some encephalomalacia] . . . seems overly critical of the patient, and I think it's inappropriate, especially given this doctor's really limited capacity in the field of medicine. This is a neuropsychologist."

This expert does not appear to be aware that malingering and documented brain injury are not mutually exclusive; in the Mittenberg et al. (2002) survey, experienced neuropsychologists estimated that 9% of litigants with moderate to severe TBI were malingering, and others have provided case reports of patients with severe TBI who were documented to be feigning (Boone & Lu, 2003; Bianchini, Greve, & Love, 2003). We neuropsychologists have produced more research on detection of feigned cognitive presentations than members of any other profession, and as such we are the preeminent practitioners in this area.

At times plaintiff attorneys will attempt to force you as the defense neuropsychological expert to use inflammatory language in describing the test performance of a plaintiff, apparently to lead you into providing opinions that the courts have determined are the sole purview of the jury— namely, judgment as to whether the plaintiff is lying:

> PLAINTIFF COUNSEL: Are you saying my client is a liar?
>
> DEFENSE NEUROPSYCHOLOGICAL EXPERT: That is not a particularly useful term in my field. The test results indicate that the person was not performing to her true capability on the testing, and that, as a result, test results do not reflect her true level of function.

Or, in a similar vein:

> PLAINTIFF COUNSEL: Is malingering just a fancy name for lying?
>
> DEFENSE NEUROPSYCHOLOGICAL EXPERT: Malingering means conscious, deliberate faking of symptoms for an external goal. Malingering is a diagnostic category in the DSM; liar is not.

Functional Significance of Low Cognitive Scores

There is often confusion as to the functional significance of impaired scores on neuropsychological testing, with the assumption that low scores correlate with very low functioning in ADLs. However, particularly when test score distributions have small standard deviations, "impaired" scores can be obtained that do not in fact reflect "impairment" in ADLs. For example, on the Comalli version of the Stroop word-reading task, a normal time score is approximately 40 seconds, and a score of 55 seconds would fall within the impaired range for a younger adult, although a person scoring at this level could still have intact reading skills in most real-world activities. Thus a distinction should be made between "psychometric" impairment and "functional" impairment:

> PLAINTIFF COUNSEL: My client scored at the 1st percentile on delayed verbal recall. Would that not be a profound deficit?
>
> DEFENSE NEUROPSYCHOLOGICAL EXPERT: I'm uncomfortable with the term "profound." She scored at the first percentile, which means that 99 out of 100 normal individuals in her age range would score better than she does. However, there is not a one-to-one relationship between a test scores and how functional a person is in daily life. You can have individuals who score at the 1st percentile who are relatively functional, and others who are not. Within the 1st percentile, there can in fact be a range of skills—some may have Alzheimer's disease and have no ability to learn. Certainly this patient is not in that category. She is attending a high-caliber college and is obtaining passing grades, albeit with some tutoring help.

Challenges to Opinions on mTBI

The following is a typical line of questioning regarding conclusions in claimed cases of mTBI:

> PLAINTIFF COUNSEL: Do you have an opinion as to whether or not Mr. L has any residual effects of a traumatic brain injury, at least as of the time you saw him early last year?
>
> DEFENSE NEUROPSYCHOLOGICAL EXPERT: Yes.
>
> PLAINTIFF COUNSEL: And what is your opinion?
>
> DEFENSE NEUROPSYCHOLOGICAL EXPERT: That he does not.
>
> PLAINTIFF COUNSEL: And the basis for that opinion is what, if you can summarize it for us?
>
> DEFENSE NEUROPSYCHOLOGICAL EXPERT: There is accumulating research—six meta-analyses of the literature. A meta-analysis involves taking all of the available studies in a given area and collapsing them for an ultimate conclusion. There have been six meta-analytic studies to date of the literature on mild traumatic brain injury or mTBI, and all of them are showing no long-term consequences of a cognitive nature. They involved dozens and dozens of studies, and thousands of patients in the aggregate. So the research is now very clear that there are no long-term cognitive

consequences from this type of injury. And this book [expert holds up a copy McCrea, 2008] came out in 2008. It is published under the auspices of the American Academy of Clinical Neuropsychology, which is the membership organization for board-certified neuropsychologists. It reviews the literature on cognitive function in mTBI, and on page 117 the concluding statement is "No indication of permanent impairment on neuropsychological testing by 3 months post-injury."

PLAINTIFF COUNSEL: And does your clinical experience tell you differently?

DEFENSE NEUROPSYCHOLOGICAL EXPERT: No, not at all. Actually, before these publications starting appearing, it was my growing clinical sense that this was the case, because in every patient who was claiming long-term problems from mTBI, there were either issues regarding symptom validity, or the MMPI suggested that the person was hypochondriacal, or the person had true cognitive problems but there were much more plausible reasons for those than the mTBI.

PLAINTIFF COUNSEL: Isn't it true that a subset, albeit small—about 10–15%—of patients with mTBI do not recover and do in fact show permanent cognitive problems?

DEFENSE NEUROPSYCHOLOGICAL EXPERT: No. That belief came from very flawed, older studies in which no consideration was given regarding motive to maintain symptoms. For example, litigants were not excluded, and the studies were based on patient self-report of symptoms, not actual testing of cognitive skills.

PLAINTIFF COUNSEL: Are there any contrary studies or articles that conclude differently that you've seen?

DEFENSE NEUROPSYCHOLOGICAL EXPERT: I'm sure there are, but when you look at large meta-analyses in which all of the studies in a given area have been collapsed for an ultimate conclusion, all of them indicate that there are no long-term consequences from a mTBI.

PLAINTIFF COUNSEL: Are there studies that disagree with your position in this case?

DEFENSE NEUROPSYCHOLOGICAL EXPERT: Not my position. The field as a whole is taking the position that there is no long-term cognitive consequence from mTBI.

PLAINTIFF COUNSEL: Are you saying that *all* patients with mTBI recover? Every single one?

DEFENSE NEUROPSYCHOLOGICAL EXPERT: I have seen some very elderly individuals who seemed to have a problematic recovery from apparent mTBI, and I tested an individual with a previous severe TBI who seemed to have a problematic recovery from a subsequent mTBI. Aside from these possible examples, when individuals come in with the presenting diagnosis of mTBI and cognitive problems are detected, in my experience there is always a more plausible etiology or explanation for the lowered scores, such as preexisting learning disability or ADHD, baseline low premorbid cognitive function, concurrent chronic medical illnesses, or use of large amounts of pain medication.

PLAINTIFF COUNSEL: I believe you also reported that his family had mentioned—he told you that his family had mentioned that he seemed more irritable and temperamental after the accident. Did you find that information informative as to whether or not there was a TBI here?

DEFENSE NEUROPSYCHOLOGICAL EXPERT: When research has evaluated patients with postconcussive complaints and normal individuals who have not had concussions, the two groups show the same amount of symptoms. So it is not true that irritability, anger, mood changes, and so forth are signals of mTBI. They are common in the normal population, and they are common in medical populations that have not had a head injury. So you can't conclude, "He's angry and irritable; ergo, he had a TBI."

PLAINTIFF COUNSEL: Do you recall reading that Dr. X [neurologist] and Dr. Y [psychiatrist] or any other treaters diagnosed the patient with a concussion?

DEFENSE NEUROPSYCHOLOGICAL EXPERT: I do believe they did, but their diagnoses were apparently based on patient report of symptoms months or years after the accident. The diagnosis of mTBI/concussion is made from injury characteristics at the time of the injury, not the patient's report of symptoms later in time.

PLAINTIFF COUNSEL: A case of mTBI can be missed by an emergency room, doctor, can it ?

DEFENSE NEUROPSYCHOLOGICAL EXPERT: It is possible that an emergency room doctor may not provide a diagnosis of mTBI, but the various mTBI criteria are placed in records by numerous personnel—emergency medical technicians, physicians, nurses. I have rarely seen records that did not have information regarding loss of consciousness, whether the patient had amnesia for the accident,

Glasgow Coma Scale score, brain imaging. With that information, the diagnosis can easily be made after the fact.

PLAINTIFF COUNSEL: So do you disagree with Dr. N's conclusion that he suffered mTBI?

DEFENSE NEUROPSYCHOLOGICAL EXPERT: Yes, I do.

PLAINTIFF COUNSEL: Do you believe that Dr. N is qualified to make that diagnosis?

DEFENSE NEUROPSYCHOLOGICAL EXPERT: Yes, Dr. N is qualified, but he's not using established diagnostic algorithms. He is apparently using the patient's complaints of cognitive problems as evidence that the patient had mTBI, and that would not be the criteria. The determination of mTBI is based on parameters at the time of the injury, not what the patient reports years later.

PLAINTIFF COUNSEL: So you don't believe that Mr. L's reports of his condition years after the accident informs a diagnosis of whether he suffered a brain injury?

DEFENSE NEUROPSYCHOLOGICAL EXPERT: That's correct.

PLAINTIFF COUNSEL: In other words, his current symptoms are irrelevant to a determination of whether he suffered mTBI?

DEFENSE NEUROPSYCHOLOGICAL EXPERT: That's correct.

PLAINTIFF COUNSEL: Is it your belief that my client does not have mTBI because the emergency room doctor did not find one?

DEFENSE NEUROPSYCHOLOGICAL EXPERT: No. The reason why I don't think he had mTBI is that no criteria for mTBI were positive. He didn't lose consciousness. He didn't have anterograde or retrograde amnesia. He had normal brain imaging. His Glasgow Coma Scale score was 15. He was alert and oriented in the hospital. He was neurologically normal. So there was no evidence at all of any brain dysfunction.

Conclusions Regarding the MMPI-2/MMPI-2–RF

Attacks on the MMPI-2/MMPI-2–RF can take several forms.

Test Results Were Contaminated by Patient Distractibility or Pain

The plaintiff's counsel may argue that the MMPI-2/MMPI-2–RF results cannot be accepted as valid, because (1) the plaintiff was distracted by other people entering the waiting room, and this contaminated the results; (2) the patient was in pain, and this contaminated the results. Fortunately, you have a very effective defense against such an argument—namely, VRIN/VRIN-r. VRIN/VRIN-r is a validity scale that measures whether a patient responded consistently to similar items. A normal VRIN/VRIN-r score indicates that the patient answered MMPI-2/MMPI-2–RF items in a very self-consistent manner, which can only occur if the patient was not unduly distracted by others or by pain. So what could be your response?

> "While the patient may have looked up when others entered the room, or been in pain, the normal VRIN [or VRIN-r] score shows that the patient was able to return to task and answer questions in a careful, self-consistent manner. Because administration of the MMPI-2 [or MMPI-2–RF] involves reading statements and providing true–false answers, periodic minor distractions do not invalidate administration."

In other words, the MMPI-2 and MMPI-2–RF are not continuous performance tests. Rather, completing them is analogous to the ubiquitous filling out of medical questionnaires in a medical office waiting room prior to being seen by a physician: It is understood that waiting rooms have distractions in the form of patients coming and going, and patients filling out the forms may be experiencing uncomfortable symptoms, but no one raises concerns about the impact of distractibility or pain on the data provided in these forms.

> PLAINTIFF COUNSEL: Do you go out of your way to make the area where they take the test quiet and where there's no distractions or anything that would interfere with their focus?
>
> DEFENSE NEUROPSYCHOLOGICAL EXPERT: It's incredibly quiet there. It's like a tomb.
>
> PLAINTIFF COUNSEL: Is that important?
>
> DEFENSE NEUROPSYCHOLOGICAL EXPERT: Well, obviously, you want them to be able to attend to the test. And when you look at the scores, it shows that she was very much able to attend and concentrate, she was able to be highly consistent—more so than most patients in completing this test.
>
> PLAINTIFF COUNSEL: Does that indicate a good effort on her part?
>
> DEFENSE NEUROPSYCHOLOGICAL EXPERT: It means she was very careful when she completed the test.

Similarly:

PLAINTIFF COUNSEL: Can pain interfere with test taking?

DEFENSE NEUROPSYCHOLOGICAL EXPERT: Well, the literature shows that it does not cause failure on symptom validity/malingering tests. On the MMPI-2–RF, she was more consistent and careful than the typical person taking the test. So if she was in pain, it did not interfere with her ability to take the test.

Responses to Individual Test Items Contradict Overall Scale Results

The plaintiff's attorney may argue:

> "You claim that my client obtained a score of X on the Y scale indicating Z, but when we look at my client's answers to these particular items on the scale—for example, she's having headaches, and she marks that she is having headaches—how does this reflect overreport?"

Individual items on an inventory are not psychometric instruments; they only represent self-report, with no correction for under- or overreport. When the focus is on items, the instrument is no longer an "objective test." So what could be your response?

> "The MMPI-2 [or MMPI-2–RF] is a psychometric instrument that was developed for interpretation of scales, not individual items. Although the patient did endorse individual items that by themselves could be consistent with a true medical disorder, the large numbers of symptoms endorsed, as well as the unusual combination of items—reflected in the elevated scores on the Hypochondriasis scale, Somatic Complaints scale, FBS [or FBS-r], and/or Fs scale—are rarely found in patients with true medical illness. Patients with bona fide medical illness endorse the actual symptoms associated with their illness, but not the wide range of symptoms found on these scales."

You could make the analogy that when patients with bona fide medical problems complete symptom checklists at a medical office, they typically endorse 5 or 10 symptoms (from a list of 50 or so) that correspond to the problems they are experiencing related to their condition. However, if they endorse 40 out of 50 symptoms, this would be implausible for virtually any condition or combination of conditions. It is not the content of the individual items that is implausible, but rather the total numbers and/or the combinations of items endorsed.

A Physician's Medical Diagnosis Trumps
MMPI-2/MMPI-2–RF Results

The plaintiff's attorney may also argue:

> "My client has been diagnosed by Dr. A with medical condition B. You opine that my client's report of physical symptoms is not credible, but you are not a physician and you do not diagnose medical conditions, correct?" (in other words, "Who cares what the MMPI-2 or MMPI-2–RF says?")

Do not assume that because a physician uses a technique, it is more valid or accurate than psychological test results. For example, in regard to the "trigger point exam" used by physicians to document fibromyalgia, research has shown that "the methodological quality of the majority of studies for the purpose of establishing trigger point reproducibility is generally poor" (Myburgh, Larsen, & Hartvigsen, 2008, p. 1169). As discussed in chapter 4 and on pages 223–225, marked elevations on physical and cognitive symptom report scales on the MMPI-2 or MMPI-2–RF have not been found to occur in patients with bona fide medical conditions who are accurately reporting their symptoms. Thus, when high elevations are obtained, "something else is going on" regarding the patient's report of symptoms. Stick by your guns: You have strong data regarding alternative diagnoses to those of the physician. So what could be your response?

> "The results of objective personality testing show that the patient was endorsing physical symptoms in a nonplausible manner, according to test cutoffs set to allow few false positive errors. The pattern of scores matches that found in malingerers and/or patients with somatoform orientations, and does not match that observed in true medical patients.
>
> "In contrast, the physician relied on patient self-report and/or _____ exam [e.g., trigger points], which has been shown to be easily faked." (Or "There are no data regarding how malingerers or patients with somatoform orientations perform on this measure," or "the validity and reliability of the technique have not been demonstrated," etc.)
>
> "Thus, the personality test results are more accurate, objective, and compelling; have known error rates [important for forensic testimony]; and better account for the 'symptoms' noted by the physician."

The following exchange provides a further illustration:

PLAINTIFF COUNSEL: Did you know that he has a 5-millimeter herniated disc that's impinging on nerves in his cervical spine?

DEFENSE NEUROPSYCHOLOGICAL EXPERT: He responded to the MMPI-2–RF in a way that people exaggerating their physical symptoms respond to it, and not the way credible medical patients respond.

PLAINTIFF COUNSEL: OK. So your belief is that, even though there's an MRI that documents his impingement of the nerve in his neck, and he has got radiculopathy that's also verified by an electromyogram, he is exaggerating his pain from that?

DEFENSE NEUROPSYCHOLOGICAL EXPERT: He is exaggerating his physical symptoms. There's not a one-to-one relationship between imaging and symptoms. You can have very abnormal imaging and have no symptoms, and people can report symptoms and have no imaging abnormalities. But the MMPI-2–RF clearly indicates that the patient is vastly overreporting his physical symptoms in a noncredible manner not seen in credible medical patients.

The Patient Is Unique (No One in the Normative Sample Had This Test Taker's Characteristics)

The plaintiff's lawyer may contend:

"My client is a spouse of someone who has become disabled because of the accident. How many subjects in the MMPI-2 standardization sample were spouses of patients with spinal cord injury? The MMPI-2 was not developed on spouses of patients with spinal cord injury; it was developed on psychiatric patients. Would not you agree that the findings do not apply to her?"

The argument is that unless the MMPI-2/MMPI-2–RF comparison group *exactly* matches the test taker, *any* findings from these inventories are nonapplicable and irrelevant. So what could be your response?

"All patients are unique, and it would not be possible to have groups representing every type of psychological stressor. Your client's personality test results show that she has no more psychiatric symptoms than typical persons in the general population." (Or " ... she was reporting psychological distress in a nonplausible manner—her profile matched that of malingerers and not that of credible depressed individuals.")

The Results Are a Computer's Impersonal "Read" Regarding the Test Taker

The plaintiff's attorney may take this tack:

> "The MMPI-2 is actuarial and scored by a computer; as such, it provides only a 'statistical guess' as to the characteristics of my client. It is not 100% accurate, and the results may not reflect my client's characteristics at all."

So what could be your response?

> "Virtually all diagnostic tests are actuarially based; the goal of the psychological tests is to provide objective data with a low error rate regarding likely characteristics of the patient."

The following testimony also illustrates this issue:

DEFENSE NEUROPSYCHOLOGICAL EXPERT: He had elevations on scales addressing overreported psychiatric symptoms and overreported physical symptoms.

PLAINTIFF COUNSEL: So we don't know that he's actually overreporting symptoms; we know that he scores in a manner that's consistent with others who do overreport symptoms. Is that right?

DEFENSE NEUROPSYCHOLOGICAL EXPERT: Well, I think the conclusion would be, you are overreporting symptoms if you're scoring like people who overreport. What the test is saying is that the number of symptoms he's reporting vastly exceeds what is expected for people with true medical and psychiatric conditions.

PLAINTIFF COUNSEL: Really? So we can draw that kind of hard conclusion from the taking of a true–false questionnaire?

DEFENSE NEUROPSYCHOLOGICAL EXPERT: He's working full-time. He's living independently. He's not in an inpatient in a psychiatric unit. So the extent of psychiatric symptoms he is reporting is not corroborated by how functional he is in his daily life. Thus the conclusion that he is overreporting symptoms is supported by external information.

PLAINTIFF COUNSEL: So we can't draw that conclusion simply from what the test scores say; we have to look at the clinical picture. Is that right?

DEFENSE NEUROPSYCHOLOGICAL EXPERT: That would be true.

The Inventory Is Biased against Ethnic Minorities

Consider this exchange:

> PLAINTIFF COUNSEL: By the way, is the MMPI-2–RF biased against African Americans?

> DEFENSE NEUROPSYCHOLOGICAL EXPERT: Well, it is true that in any given study there might be slight differences detected between African Americans and European Americans, but when you take all of the studies together, the two groups are really performing comparably.

> PLAINTIFF COUNSEL: He was also elevated on the Cynicism and Ideas of Persecution scales, and those elevations, if accurate, suggest that he views others as out to harm him—that he views individuals as exploiting opportunities for their own gain. Does that mean he would be more likely not to trust someone like you?

> DEFENSE NEUROPSYCHOLOGICAL EXPERT: That's possible.

> PLAINTIFF COUNSEL: And think that maybe you're out to hurt him?

> DEFENSE NEUROPSYCHOLOGICAL EXPERT: That's possible.

> PLAINTIFF COUNSEL: Would that tend to affect his performance on symptom validity tests?

> DEFENSE NEUROPSYCHOLOGICAL EXPERT: I don't think it would have produced this performance, because he scored incredibly well on many standard tests—the 95th and 96th percentiles. And across exams, he only underperformed on the verbal memory domain and symptom validity tests associated with that domain. So if it was a true wariness, it would not explain his selective underperformance on the testing.

The interested reader is referred to a meta-analysis of MMPI and MMPI-2 data involving over 1,500 African Americans, 500 Latino Americans, and over 4,000 European Americans, which indicated that "none of the aggregate effect sizes suggest substantive differences from either a statistical or clinical perspective. The MMPI and MMPI-2 apparently do not unfairly portray African Americans and Latinos as pathological" (Hall, Nagayama, Bansal, & Lopez, 1999, p. 186).

The FBS/FBS-r Is Deemed Questionable

Several objections may be raised to the FBS-FBS-r. First, a plaintiff's attorney may argue that it is highly controversial:

PLAINTIFF COUNSEL: In fact, the Fake Bad Scale or FBS has been excluded from testimony all over the country, hasn't it?

DEFENSE NEUROPSYCHOLOGIST EXPERT: No. It has been excluded in a few cases, based on incomplete information provided to the judges. It has been used in thousands of cases nationwide.

PLAINTIFF COUNSEL: The FBS has garnered significant criticism from psychologists, correct?

DEFENSE NEUROPSYCHOLOGICAL EXPERT: No. Dozens of studies have supported its use, and the research underpinning was so strong that the publishers of the MMPI-2 decided to include it in the scoring program. Recent meta-analyses have confirmed support for its use in forensic settings.

PLAINTIFF COUNSEL: Isn't it true that the APA—that is, the American Psychological Association—has asked for an investigation on the FBS?

DEFENSE NEUROPSYCHOLOGICAL EXPERT: No. In August 2007, an APA committee on disabilities issued a letter indicating that the APA was not taking a stand against the FBS.

Be prepared to address publications that have been critical of the scale; as discussed on page 225, research showing excessive false positive rates for the FBS was methodologically flawed.

Second, the plaintiff's neuropsychologist may use lack of elevations on other MMPI-2/MMPI-2–RF scales and other tests to explain away FBS/FBS-r elevations:

"On the other hand, he did not endorse any items on the Fs scale, which consists of somatic types of items that are not typically endorsed in individuals with real medical problems. In combination, these scales indicate that his FBS elevation may reflect some degree of true medical difficulty, as opposed to exaggeration of medical problems."

Or,

"The Personality Assessment Inventory's Somatic Complaints scale ($T = 69$) was only subclinically elevated, with subclinical elevations on all three subscales: Conversion ($T = 66$), Somatization ($T = 65$), and Health Concerns ($T = 69$). Overall, this indicates 'some concerns about physical functioning and health matter in general,' but is not elevated to the degree that confirms suspicions from the MMPI-2–RF that he might be exaggerating somatic complaints. . . . The MMPI-2–RF indicates that individuals with such pervasive somatic complaints are 'likely to be prone to developing physical symptoms in response to stress.' However, the score on the Personality Assessment Inventory's Anxiety Physiological subscale ($T = 58$) was in the average range, indicating that he is not likely to develop significant somatic complaints as a result of feeling anxious."

There is no research showing that when Fs is not elevated, FBS-r elevations reflect genuine medical problems. Indeed, samples of individuals with very serious medical problems (e.g., candidates for bariatric surgery or spinal surgery in the MMPI-2–RF technical manual) do not produce significant elevations on FBS-r.

Perusal of research databases also shows that the MMPI-2 and MMPI-2–RF have substantially more research regarding somatization than other psychological test inventories, including the PAI. Therefore, the practice of "overriding" the former instruments' results when they do not match findings from other inventories is not supported.

Finally, the plaintiff's attorney may resort to examining individual item content:

"Out of the 33 items she got on FBS, if we took away the 22 which we know to be truthful answers, we would be left with 11 possible responses. Is there any research ever that's been published to suggest that a score of 11 on the FBS suggests symptom magnification?"

You might respond:

"Again, it is not the individual item content that is relevant, but rather how many symptoms she is reporting—just as endorsing 33 out of 43 symptoms on a medical history symptom checklist would not be plausible."

Basing Conclusions on Record Review without Exam

On occasion, a neuropsychologist may be asked to testify on the basis of a record review rather than an examination of a plaintiff. There is a misunderstanding that to do so would be contrary to the APA ethics code (APA, 2010). However, what the code actually states is this:

9.01 Bases for Assessments

(a) Psychologists base the opinions contained in their recommendations, reports, and diagnostic or evaluative statements, including forensic testimony, on information and techniques sufficient to substantiate their findings. (See also Standard 2.04, Bases for Scientific and Professional Judgments.)

(b) Except as noted in 9.01c, psychologists provide opinions of the psychological characteristics of individuals only after they have conducted an examination of the individuals adequate to support their statements or conclusions. When, despite reasonable efforts, such an examination is not practical, psychologists document the efforts they made and the result of those efforts, clarify the probable impact of their limited information on the reliability and validity of their opinions, and appropriately limit the nature and extent of their conclusions or recommendations. (See also Standards 2.01, Boundaries of Competence, and 9.06, Interpreting Assessment Results.)

(c) When psychologists conduct a record review or provide consultation or supervision and an individual examination is not warranted or necessary for the opinion, psychologists explain this and the sources of information on which they based their conclusions and recommendations.

The following types of questions may be encountered:

PLAINTIFF COUNSEL: Do you believe you have conducted your forensic evaluation of my client in a thorough manner?

DEFENSE NEUROPSYCHOLOGICAL EXPERT: I have not conducted an evaluation of her. I was asked to read the records, and I'm providing my opinions based on those records.

PLAINTIFF COUNSEL: You have rendered opinions, right?

DEFENSE NEUROPSYCHOLOGICAL EXPERT: Based on the material and records provided to me.

PLAINTIFF COUNSEL: To the extent that you evaluated those records, do you believe you've done your forensic evaluation of her in a thorough manner?

DEFENSE NEUROPSYCHOLOGICAL EXPERT: I have not evaluated her. I have been provided records. I'm rendering opinions based on those records. And, obviously, having not seen the patient and only having records, I am somewhat limited in what I can say. But the opinions I'm providing today are certainly reasonable, given the records I was given.

PLAINTIFF COUNSEL: Doesn't at least one of the organizations you belong to require its members to conduct legal evaluations in a thorough manner and personally examine the injured person, if at all possible?

DEFENSE NEUROPSYCHOLOGICAL EXPERT: The ethical guidelines for psychologists indicate that you can provide opinions based on the records.

PLAINTIFF COUNSEL: Would you agree that, based on your limited access to the records that are available on my client, the nature and extent of your conclusions should be appropriately limited?

DEFENSE NEUROPSYCHOLOGICAL EXPERT: That's true.

PLAINTIFF COUNSEL: And don't those ethical standards require that if you're basing a forensic opinion as a psychologist only on reading and reviewing records, you need to indicate that there's a definite limit to the medical probability of your opinion?

DEFENSE NEUROPSYCHOLOGICAL EXPERT: I don't think I would agree that there is a limited medical probability to my opinions, but certainly there are limitations to just reading records. So you have to indicate that your opinion is based on a record review and not on seeing the patient.

MAINTAINING TEST SECURITY IN THE TESTIMONY PROCESS

Threats to test security are frequently encountered in testifying. For example, plaintiff counsel may ask, "What is the b Test?" The neuropsychologist should craft a response that does not describe the test paradigm. An appropriate response in this instance might be the following:

"The b Test is a measure to check for credibility of test performances. On this test, individuals who are not performing to true capability tend to perform very differently from patients exerting adequate effort. If a patient falls beyond test cutoffs, one could make the case that the patient resembles the population of noncredible individuals and not the population of credible patients."

At times you may be asked to show test stimuli:

PLAINTIFF COUNSEL: What is the RO Complex Figure?

DEFENSE NEUROPSYCHOLOGICAL EXPERT: It is a complicated design that you ask the patient to copy with paper and pen.

PLAINTIFF COUNSEL: Do you have a specimen that we can show to the video camera, so that we can see what the stimulus was that was presented to Ms. C?

DEFENSE NEUROPSYCHOLOGICAL EXPERT: I would be uncomfortable with that, because these are protected tests. If the tests are disseminated within the general public, then they will lose their ability to measure the cognitive skills they were developed to test. Test results are only accurate if the test taker is naïve to the testing process. It would be a violation of American Psychological Association ethical standards for me to show this. Test materials can only be shared between licensed psychologists who are ethically bound to protect the tests.

Most attorneys are respectful of this position, realizing that our tests are, in the words of one attorney, "the centerpiece of our profession." However, at times attorneys continue to argue for exposure:

PLAINTIFF COUNSEL: OK. Let's talk about each of these tests. The Rey Word Recognition Test—what does that entail?

Defense Neuropsychological expert: Well, I'm not comfortable saying that, again for test protection reasons. If I describe the test in a deposition, which is a public record, then anyone in the future can read the description of the test and figure out how to pass it.

PLAINTIFF COUNSEL: Well, can't we find out what this test is about, the Rey Word Recognition Test?

DEFENSE NEUROPSYCHOLOGICAL EXPERT: All I can tell you is that it is to measure symptom validity. But I will not describe what I have the person do on that test.

PLAINTIFF COUNSEL: You understand this is our opportunity to find out what you are going to be able to testify about at trial. This is some sort of secret test that you can't describe?

DEFENSE NEUROPSYCHOLOGICAL EXPERT: If I completely describe the test format—what I ask the person to do, what the test stimuli are—anyone reading this in the future could pass the test. So, again, the ethics code for psychologists indicates that we have to maintain test security. We cannot disclose protected test information to nonpsychologists.

PLAINTIFF COUNSEL: So is it your understanding that you can withhold this test, your opinion that Mr. Z was faking it, you can get away with not telling us what you did? That you can form your opinion without giving me the basis of the opinion, and you think that this is something that you will be able to testify about at trial?

DEFENSE NEUROPSYCHOLOGIST: Well, again, if you have a licensed psychologist look through my data, that psychologist can see if I scored the tests correctly and that the patient did in fact fall below cutoffs. So that psychologist can independently verify whether or not the test data are correct.

An occasional attorney will attempt to attach raw testing records as an appendix to a deposition:

PLAINTIFF COUNSEL: We will attach your entire file as an appendix to the deposition.

DEFENSE NEUROPSYCHOLOGICAL EXPERT: Because the raw test data sheets show protected test information, the procedure is that the licensed psychological experts retained by defense and plaintiff directly exchange copies of the raw test data sheets from the exams.

Some attorneys press for attachment of the raw test data sheets by offering a protective order in which it is specified that only individuals directly involved in the case can view the materials, and that the appendix is to be returned to the psychologist or destroyed at the conclusion of the case. However, judges have acknowledged that protective orders cannot be effectively policed, so if at all possible, you should insist on conveyance of the records to the opposing licensed psychological expert and not allow them to be inserted in an appendix. It may also be useful to point out to attorneys intent on appending the data as an exhibit that if the litigation had to do with the bar exam, it is unlikely that the test would be attached as an appendix to a deposition. The same vigilant protections that an attorney extends to critical measurement instruments in the field of law should be provided to those in clinical psychology and neuropsychology.

At times an attorney will agree to have raw data forwarded to his/her expert, but will request that the data be forwarded to a nonpsychologist:

PLAINTIFF COUNSEL: OK, I will give you the address of Dr. Y [a psychiatrist] so you can forward the raw test data sheets to her.

DEFENSE NEUROPSYCHOLOGICAL EXPERT: Psychiatrists are not ethically bound to protect psychological tests. I cannot release the raw test data sheets to Dr. Y.

CLOSING COMMENTS

I recall that when I first began testifying, much of my energy while I was on the stand was focused on trying not to let my knees knock together under the table. Once I had finished with my testimony, I would be so exhausted from the depletion of adrenalin that I wondered whether I could drive home safely. Thankfully those experiences become less frequent, but testifying can still remain anxiety-provoking. It is helpful to keep in mind that psychological testimony grounded in accurate test results is critical for juries and the larger society, and that if your testimony is based on empirical research, the field of neuropsychology and clinical psychology is standing behind you.

References

Aguerrevere, L. E., Greve, K. W., Bianchini, K. J., & Meyers, J. E. (2008). Detecting malingering in traumatic brain injury and chronic pain with an abbreviated version of the Meyers Index for the MMPI-2. *Archives of Clinical Neuropsychology, 23,* 831–838.

Aguerrevere, L. E., Greve, K. W., Bianchini, K. J., & Ord, J. S. (2011). Classification accuracy of the Millon Clinical Multiaxial Inventory–III Modifier Indices in the detection of malingering in traumatic brain injury. *Journal of Clinical and Experimental Neuropsychology, 33,* 497–504.

Albert, S., Fox, H. M., & Kahn, M. W. (1980). Faking psychosis on the Rorschach: Can expert judges detect malingering? *Journal of Personality Assessment, 44,* 115–119.

Aldridge-Morris, R. (1989). *Multiple personality: An exercise in deception.* Hove, UK: Psychology Press.

Alexander, M. P. (1995). Mild traumatic brain injury: Pathophysiology, natural history, and clinical management. *Neurology, 45,* 1253–1260.

Alfano, K., & Boone, K. B. (2007). The use of effort tests in the context of actual versus feigned attention-deficit/hyperactivity disorder and learning disability. In K. B. Boone (Ed.), *Assessment of feigned cognitive impairment: A neuropsychological perspective* (pp. 366–383). New York: Guilford Press.

Allen, L., Conder, R. L., Green, P., & Cox, D. R. (1997). *CARB '97 manual for the computerized assessment of response bias.* Durham, NC: CogShell.

Alwes, Y. R., Clark, J. A., Berry, D. T., & Granacher, R. P. (2008). Screening for feigning in a civil forensic setting. *Journal of Clinical and Experimental Neuropsychology, 30,* 133–140.

American Academy of Clinical Neuropsychology (AACN). (2001). Policy statement on the presence of third party observers in neuropsychological assessments. *The Clinical Neuropsychologist, 15,* 433–439.

American Academy of Clinical Neuropsychology (AACN). (2007). American Academy of Clinical Neuropsychology (AACN) practice guidelines for neuropsychological assessment and consultation. *The Clinical Neuropsychologist, 21,* 209–231.

American Congress of Rehabilitation Medicine. (1993). Definition of mild traumatic brain injury. *Journal of Head Trauma Rehabilitation, 8,* 6–87.

American Psychiatric Association. (1994). *Diagnostic and statistical manual of mental disorders* (4th ed.). Washington DC: Author.

American Psychiatric Association. (2000). *Diagnostic and statistical manual of mental disorders* (4th ed., text rev.). Washington, DC: Author.

American Psychological Association (APA). (2010). *Ethical principles of psychologists and code of conduct (2010) ammendments.* Retrieved from *www.apa. org/ethics/code/index.aspx.*

American Psychology–Law Society. (2011). *Specialty guidelines for forensic psychology.* Washington, DC: Author.

Ancelin, M., L., le Roquefeuil, G., Ledesert, B., Ritchie, K., Bonnel, F., & Chaminal, J. (2001). Exposure to anaesthetic agents, cognitive functioning and depressive symptomatology in the elderly. *British Journal of Psychiatry, 178,* 360–366.

Anderson-Hanley, C., Sherman, M. L., Riggs, R., Agocha, V. B., & Compas, B. E. (2003). Neuropsychological effects of treatments for adults with cancer: A meta-analysis and review of the literature. *Journal of the International Neuorpsychological Society, 9,* 967–982.

Arciniegas, D. B., Anderson, C. A., Topkoff, J. L., & McAllister, T. W. (2005). Mild traumatic brain injury: A neuropsychiatric approach to diagnosis, evaluation, and treatment. *Neuropsychiatric Disease and Treatment, 1,* 311–327.

Ardila, A., & Rosselli, M. (1989). Neuropsychological assessment in illiterates: Visuospatial and memory abilities. *Brain and Cognition, 11,* 147–166.

Ardolf, B. R., Denney, R. L., & Houston, C. M. (2007). Base rates of negative responses bias and malingered neurocognitive dysfunction among criminal defendants referred for neuropsychological evaluation. *The Clinical Neuropsychologist, 21,* 899–916.

Armistead-Jehle, P., Gervais, R. O., & Green, P. (2012). Memory Complaints Inventory results as a function of symptom validity test performance. *Archives of Clinical Neuropsychology, 27*(1), 101–113.

Arnold, G., & Boone, K. B. (2007). Use of motor and sensory tests as effort measures. In K. B. Boone (Ed.), *Assessment of feigned cognitive impairment: A neuropsychological perspective* (pp. 178–209). New York: Guilford Press.

Arnold, G., Boone, K. B., Lu, P., Dean, A., Wen, J., Nitch, S., et al. (2005). Sensitivity and specificity of Finger Tapping Test scores for the detection of suspect effort. *The Clinical Neuropsychologist, 19,* 105–120.

Artiola i Fortuny, L., & Mullaney, H. A. (1998). Assessing patients whose language you do not know: Can the absurd be ethical? *The Clinical Neuropsychologist, 12,* 113–126.

Arts, B.., Jabben, N., Krabbendam, L., & van Os, J. (2007). Meta-analyses of cognitive functioning in euthymic bipolar patients and their first-degree relatives. *Psychological Medicine, 38,* 771–785.

Axelrod, B. N. (2002). Validity of the Wechsler Abbreviated Scale of Intelligence and other very short forms of estimating intellectual functioning. *Assessment, 9,* 17–23.

Axelrod, B. N., & Schutte, C. (2010). Analysis of the dementia profile on The Medical Symptom Validity Test. *The Clinical Neuropsychologist, 24,* 873–881.

Axelrod, B. N., Vanderploeg, R. D., & Rawlings, D. B. (1999). WAIS-R prediction equations in patients with traumatic brain injury. *Journal of Clinical and Experimental Neuropsychology, 21,* 368–374.

Axelrod, B. N., Vanderploeg, R. D., & Schinka, J. A. (1999). Comparing methods for estimating premorbid intellectual functioning. *Archives of Clinical Neuropsychology, 14,* 341–346.

Babikian, T., & Asarnow, R. (2009). Neurocognitive outcomes and recovery after pediatric TBI: Meta-analytic review of the literature. *Neuropsychology, 23,* 283–296.

Babikian, T., & Boone, K. B. (2007). Intelligence tests as measures of effort. In K. B. Boone (Ed.), *Assessment of feigned cognitive impairment: A neuropsychological perspective* (pp. 103–127). New York: Guilford Press.

Babikian, T., Boone, K. B., Lu, p., & Arnold, G. (2006). Sensitivity and specificity of various Digit Span scores in the detection of suspect effort. *The Clinical Neuropsychologist, 20,* 145–159.

Babikian, T., Satz, P., Zaucha, K., Light, R., Lewis, R. S., & Asarnow, R. (2011). The UCLA Longitudinal study of neurocognitive outcomes following mild pediatric traumatic brain injury, *Journal of the International Neuropsychological Society, 17,* 886–895.

Back, C., Boone, K. B., Edwards, C., Parks, C., Burgoyne, K., & Silver, B. (1996). The performance of schizophrenics on three cognitive tests of malingering: Rey 15-Item Memory Test, Rey Dot Counting, and Hiscock Forced-Choice method. *Assessment, 3,* 449–457.

Backhaus, S. L., Fichtenberg, N. L., & Hanks, R. A. (2004). Detection of suboptimal performance using a floor-effect strategy in patients with traumatic brain injury. *The Clinical Neuropsychologist, 18,* 591–603.

Baddeley, A. D., & Warrington, E. K. (1970). Amnesia and the distinction between long- and short-term memory. *Journal of Verbal Learning and Verbal Behavior, 9,* 176–189.

Bagby, R. M., Gillis, J. R., Toner, B. B., & Goldberg, J. (1991). Detecting fake-good and fake-bad responding on the Millon Clinical Multiaxial Inventory–II. *Psychological Assessment: A Journal of Consulting and Clinical Psychology, 3,* 496–498.

Bagby, R. M., Marshall, M. B., & Bacchiochi, J. R. (2005). The validity and clinical utility of the MMPI-2 Malingering Depression Scale. *Journal of Personality Assessment, 85,* 304–311.

Bagby, R. M., Nicholson, R. A., Bacchiochi, J.R., Ryder, A. G., & Bury, A. S. (2002). The predictive capacity of the MMPI-2 and PAI validity scales and indexes to detect coached and uncoached feigning. *Journal of Personality Assessment, 78,* 69–86.

Ball, J. D., Hart, R. P., Stutts, M. L., Turf, E., & Barth, J. T. (2007). Comparative utility of Barona formulae, WTAR demographic algorithms, and WRAT-3 Reading for estimating premorbid ability in a diverse research sample. *The Clinical Neuropsychologist, 21,* 422–433.

Barona, A., & Chastain, R. L. (1986). An improved estimate of premorbid IQ for blacks and whites on the WAIS-R. *International Journal of Clinical Neuropsychology, 8,* 169–173.

Barona, A., Reynolds, C. R., & Chastain, R. (1984). A demographically based index of premorbid intelligence for the WAIS-R. *Journal of Consulting and Clinical Psychology, 52,* 885–887.

Basso, M. R., & Bornstein, R A. (1999). Relative memory deficits in recurrent first-episode major depression on a word-list learning task. *Neuropsychology, 13,* 557–563,

Basso, M.R., Bornstein, R. A., Roper, B. L., & McCoy, V. (2000). Limited accuracy of premorbid intelligence estimators: A demonstration of regression to the mean. *The Clinical Neuropsychologist, 14,* 325–340.

Bate, A. J., Mathias, J. L., & Crawford, J. R. (2001). The covert orienting of visual attention following severe traumatic brain injury. *Journal of Clinical and Experimental Neuropsychology, 23,* 386–398.

Bauer, L., & McCaffrey, R. J. (2006). Coverage of the Test of Memory Malingering, Victoria Symptom Validity Test, and Word Memory Test on the Internet: Is test security threatened? *Archives of Clinical Neuropsychology, 21,* 121–126.

Beaber, R. J., Marston, A., Michelli, J., & Millis, M. J. (1985). A brief test for measuring malingering in schizophrenic individuals. *American Journal of Psychiatry, 142,* 1478–1481.

Bearden, C. E., Hoffman, K. M., & Cannon, T. D. (2001). The neuropsychology and neuroanatomy of bipolar affective disorder: A critical review. *Bipolar Disorders, 3,* 106–150.

Beebe, D. W., Groesz, L., Wells, C., Nichols, A., & McGee, K. (2003). The neuropsychological effects of obstructive sleep apnea: A meta-analysis of norm-referenced and case-controlled data. *Sleep, 26,* 298–307.

Beery, D. T. R., Carpenter, G. S., Campbell, D. A., Schmitt, F. A., Helton, K., & Lipke-Molby, T. (1994). The New Adult Reading Tests–Revised: Accuracy in estimating WAIS-R IQ scores obtained 3.5 years earlier from normal older persons. *Archives of Clinical Neuropsychology, 9,* 239–250.

Belanger, H. G., Curtiss, G., Demery, J. A., Lebowitz, B. K., & Vanderploeg, R. D. (2005). Factors moderating neuropsychological outcomes following mild traumatic brain injury: A meta-analysis. *Journal of the International Neuropsychological Society, 11,* 215–227

Belanger, H.G., Kretzmer, T., Vanderploeg, R.D., & French, L. M. (2010). Symptom complaints following combat-related traumatic brain injury: Relationship to traumatic brain injury severity and posttraumatic stress disorder. *Journal of the International Neuropsychological Society, 16,* 194–199.

Belanger, H.G., Spiegel, E., & Vanderploeg, R. D. (2010). Neuropsychological performance following a history of multiple self-reported concussions: A meta-analysis. *Journal of the International Neuropsychological Society, 16,* 262–267.

Belanger, H. G., & Vanderploeg, R. D. (2005). The neuropsychological impact of sports-related concussion: A meta-analysis. *Journal of the International Neuropsychological Society, 11,* 345–357.

Benge, J. F., Pastorek, N. J., & Thornton, G. M. (2009). Postconcussive symptoms in OEF-OIF veterans: Factor structure and impact of posttraumatic stress. *Rehabilitation Psychology, 54,* 270–278.

Bengtzen, R., Woodward, M., Lynn, M.J., Newman, N.J., & Biousse, V. (2008). The sunglasses sign" predicts nonorganic visual loss in neuroophthalmologic practice. *Neurology, 70,* 218–221.

Ben-Porath, Y. S., Graham, J., & Tellegen, A. (2009). *The MMPI-2 Symptom Validity (FBS) scale: Development, research findings, and interpretive recommendations.* Minneapolis: University of Minnesota Press.

Ben-Porath, Y. S., & Tellegen, A. (2008). *The Minnesota Multiphasic Personality Inventory–2 Restructured Form: Manual for administration, scoring, and interpretation.* Minneapolis: University of Minnesota Press.

Bernard, L. C., Houston, W., & Natoli, L. (1993). Malingering on neuropsychological memory tests: Potential objective indicators. *Journal of Clinical Psychology, 49,* 45–53.

Bernard, L. C., McGrath, M. J., & Houston, W. (1996). The differential effects of simulating malingering, closed head injury, and other CNS pathology on the Wisconsin Card Sorting Test: Support for the "pattern of performance" hypothesis. *Archives of Clinical Neuropsychology, 11,* 231–245.

Berry, D. T. R., Adams, J. J., Clark, C. D., Thacker, S. R., Burger, T. L., Wetter, M. W., et al. (1996). Detection of a cry for help on the MMPI-2: An analog investigation. *Journal of Personality Assessment, 67,* 26–36.

Berry, D. T. R., Carpenter, G. S., Campbell, D. A., Schmitt, F. A., Helton, K., & Lipke-Molby, T. (1994). The New Adult Reading Test–Revised: Accuracy in estimating WAIS-R IQ scores obtained 3.5 years earlier from normal older persons. *Archives of Clinical Neuropsychology, 9,* 239–250.

Berry, D. T. R., Wetter, M. W., Baer, R. A., Youngjohn, J. R., Gass, C. S., Lamb, D. G., et al. (1995). Overreporting of closed-head injury symptoms on the MMPI-2. *Psychological Assessment, 7,* 517–523.

Bianchini, K. J., Greve, K. W., & Love, J. M. (2003). Definite malingered neurocognitive dysfunction in moderate/severe traumatic brain injury. *The Clinical Neuropsychologist, 17,* 574–580.

Bigler, E. D. (2004). Neuropsychological results and neuropathological findings at autopsy in a case of mild traumatic brain injury. *Journal of the International Neuropsychological Society, 10,* 794–806.

Bijur, P. E., Haslum, M., & Golding, J. (1996). Cognitive outcomes of multiple mild head injuries in children. *Journal of Developmental and Behavioral Pediatrics, 17,* 143–148.

Binder, L. M. (1986). Persisting symptoms after mild head injury: A review of the postconcussive syndrome. *Journal of Clinical and Experimental Neuropsychology, 8,* 323–346.

Binder, L. M. (1993). Assessment of malingering after mild head trauma with the Portland Digit Recognition Test. *Journal of Clinical and Experimental Neuropsychology, 15,* 170–182.

Binder, L. M., & Binder, A. I.. (2011). Relative subtest scatter in the WAIS-IV standardization sample. *The Clinical Neuropsychologist, 25,* 62–71.

Binder, L. M., Iverson, G. L., & Brooks, B. L. (2009). To err is human: "Abnormal" neuropsychological scores and variability are common in healthy adults. *Archives of Clinical Neuropsychology, 24,* 31–46.

Binder, L. M., Kelly, M. P., Villanueva, M.R., & Winslow, M. M. (2003). Motivation and neuropsychological test performance following mild head injury. *Journal of Clinical and Experimental Neuropsychology, 25,* 420–430.

Binder, L. M., Rohling, M. L., & Larrabee, G. J. (1997). A review of mild head trauma: Part I. Meta-analytic review of neuropsychological studies. *Journal of Clinical and Experimental Neuropsychology, 19,* 421–431.

Binder, L. M., & Johnson-Greene, D. (1995). Observer effects on neuropsychological performance: A case report. *The Clinical Neuropsychologist, 9,* 74–78.

Binder, L. M., & Willis, S. C. (1991). Assessment of motivation after financially compensable minor head trauma. *Psychological Assessment, 3,* 175–181.

Birns, J., Morris, R., Donaldson, N., & Kalra, L. (2006). The effects of blood pressure reduction on cognitive function: A review of effects based on pooled data from clinical trials. *Journal of Hypertension, 24,* 1907–1914.

Black, W. F. (1986). Digit repetition in brain-damaged adults: Clinical and theoretical implications. *Journal of Clinical Psychology, 42,* 770–782.

Blair, J. R., & Spreen, O. (1989). Predicting premorbid IQ: A revision of the National Adult Reading Test. *Clinical Neuropsychologist, 3,* 129–136.

Bloom, D. R., Levin, H. S., Ewing-Cobbs, L., Saunders, A. E., Song, J., Fletcher, J. M., et al. (2001). Lifetime and novel psychiatric disorders after pediatric traumatic brain injury. *Journal of the American Academy of Child and Adolescent Psychiatry, 40,* 572–579.

Boccaccini, M. T., & Brodsky, S. L. (1999). Diagnostic test usage by forensic psychologists in emotional injury cases. *Professional Psychology: Research and Practice, 30,* 253–259.

Boccaccini, M. T., Murrie, D. C., & Duncan, S. A. (2006). Screening for malingering in a criminal forensic sample with the Personality Assessment Inventory. *Psychological Assessment, 18,* 415–423.

Boekamp, J. R., Strauss, M. E., & Adams, N. (1995). Estimating premorbid intelligence in African-American and white elderly veterans using the American version of the National Adult Reading Test. *Journal of Clinical and Experimental Neuropsychology, 17,* 645–653.

Bohnen, N., Twijnstra, A., Wijnen, G., & Jolles, J. (1991). Tolerance for light and sound of patients with persistent post-concussional symptoms 6 months after mild head injury. *Journal of Neurology, 238,* 443–446.

Boone, K. B. (Ed.). (2007a). *Assessment of feigned cognitive impairment: A neuropsychological perspective.* New York: Guilford Press.

Boone, K. B. (2007b). A reconsideration of the Slick et al. (1999) criteria for malingered neurocognitive dysfunction. In K. B. Boone (Ed.), *Assessment of feigned cognitive impairment: A neuropsychological perspective* (pp. 29–49). New York: Guilford Press.

Boone, K. B. (2009). The need for continuous and comprehensive sampling of effort/response bias during neuropsychological examinations. *The Clinical Neuropsychologist, 23,* 729–741.

Boone, K. B., Lesser, I. M., Hill-Gutierrez, E., Berman, N. G., & D'Elia, L. F. (1993). Rey–Osterrieth Complex Figure performance in healthy, older adults: Relationship to age, education, sex, and IQ. *The Clinical Neuropsychologist, 7,* 22–28.

Boone, K. B., Lesser, I. M., Miller, B. L., Wohl, M., Berman, N., Lee, A., et al. (1995). Cognitive functioning in older depressed outpatients: Relationship of presence and severity of depression to neuropsychological scores. *Neuropsychology, 9,* 390–398.

Boone, K. B., & Lu, P. (2003). Noncredible cognitive performance in the context of severe brain injury. *The Clinical Neuropsychologist, 17,* 244–254.

Boone, K. B., & Lu, P. H. (2007). Non-forced-choice effort measures. In G. J. Larrabee (Ed.), *Assessment of malingered neuropsychological deficits* (pp. 27–43). New York: Oxford University Press.

Boone, K. B., Lu, P., Back, C., King, C., Lee, A., Philpott, L., et al. (2002). Sensitivity and specificity of the Rey Dot Counting Test in patients with suspect effort and various clinical samples. *Archives of Clinical Neuropsychology, 17,* 625–642.

Boone, K. B., Lu, P., & Herzberg, D. (2002a). *b Test manual.* Los Angeles: Western Psychological Services.

Boone, K. B., Lu, P., & Herzberg, D. (2002b). *Dot Counting Test manual.* Los Angeles: Western Psychological Services.

Boone, K. B., Lu, P., Sherman, D., Palmer, B., Back, C., Shamieh, E., Warner-Chacon, K., et al. (2000). Validation of a new technique to detect malingering of cognitive symptoms: The b Test. *Archives of Clinical Neuropsychology, 15,* 227–241.

Boone, K. B., Lu, P., & Wen, J. (2005). Comparisons of various RAVLT scores in the detection of noncredible memory performance. *Archives of Clinical Neuropsychology, 20,* 301–219.

Boone, K. B, Miller, B., Lesser, I., Hill, E., & D'Elia, L. (1990). Performance on frontal lobe tests in healthy older individuals. *Developmental Neuropsychology, 6,* 215–223.

Boone, K. B., Miller, B. L., Lesser, I. M., Mehringer, C. M., Hill-Gutierrez, E., Goldberg, M. A., et al. (1992). Neuropsychological correlates of white-matter lesions in healthy elderly subjects: A threshold effect. *Archives of Neurology, 49,* 549–554.

Boone, K. B., Salazar, X., Lu, P., Warner-Chacon, K., & Razani, J. (2002). The Rey 15-Item recognition trial: A technique to enhance sensitivity of the Rey 15-Item Memorization Test. *Journal of Clinical and Experimental Neuropsychology, 24,* 561–573.

Boone, K. B., Savodnik, I., Ghaffarian, S., Lee, A., Freeman, D., & Berman, N. G. (1995). Rey 15-Item Memorization and Dot Counting scores in a stress" claim worker's compensation population: Relationship to personality (MCMI) scores. *Journal of Clinical Psychology, 51*, 457–463.

Boone, K. B., Swerdloff, R. S., Miller, B. L., Geschwind, D. H., Razani, J., Lee, A., et al. (2001). Neuropsychological profiles of adults with Klinefelter Syndrome. *Journal of the International Neuropsychological Society, 7*, 446–456.

Boone, K. B., Wen, J., Razani, J., & Ponton, M. (2007). The association between ethnicity and neuropsychological scores in a large patient population. *Archives of Clinical Neuropsychology, 22*, 355–365.

Bortnik, K. E., Boone, K. B., Marion, S. D., Amano, S., Cottingham, M., Ziegler, E., et al. (2010). Examination of various WMS-III Logical Memory scores in the assessment of response bias. *The Clinical Neuropsychologist, 24*, 344–357.

Bortnik, K. E., Boone, K. B., Marion, S. D., Amano, S., Ziegler, E., Victor, T. L., et al. (2010). Examination of various WMS-III Logical Memory scores in the assessment of response bias. *The Clinical Neuropsychologist, 24*, 344–357.

Brand, B. L., McNary, S. W., Loewenstein, R. J., Kolos, A. C., & Barr, S. R. (2006). Assessment of genuine and simulated dissociative identity disorder on the Structured Interview of Reported Symptoms. *Journal of Trauma Dissociation, 7*, 63–85.

Brands, A. M. A., Biessels, G. J., de Haan, E. H. F., Kappelle, L. J., & Kessels, R. P. C. (2005). The effects of Type 1 diabetes on cognitive performance. *Diabetes Care, 28*, 726–735.

Brems, C., & Johnson, M. E. (1991). Subtle–obvious scales of the MMPI: Indicators of profile validity in a psychiatric population. *Journal of Personality Assessment, 56*, 536–544.

Briere, J. (1995). *Trauma Symptom Inventory: Professional manual.* Odessa, FL: Psychological Assessment Resources.

Briere, J. (2001). *Detailed Assessment of Posttraumatic Stress (DAPS): Professional manual.* Odessa, FL: Psychological Assessment Resources.

Briere, J. (2011). *Trauma Symptom Inventory–2: Professional manual.* Lutz, FL: Psychological Assessment Resources.

Bright, P., Jaldow, E., & Kopelman, M. D. (2002). The National Adult Reading Test as a measure of premorbid intelligence: A comparison with estimates derived from demographic variables. *Journal of the International Neuropsychological Society, 8*, 847–854.

Brooks, B. L., Holdnack, J. A., & Iverson, G. L. (2010). Advanced clinical interpretation of the WAIS-IV and WMS-IV: Prevalence of low scores varies by level of intelligence and years of education. *Assessment, 18*, 156–167.

Brooks, B. L., Iverson, G. L., & White, T. (2007). Substantial risk of "Accidental MCI" in healthy older adults: Base rates of low memory scores in neuropsychological assessment. *Journal of the International Neuropsychological Society, 13*, 490–500.

Busch, C. R., & Alpern, H. P. (1998). Depression after mild traumatic brain injury: A review of current research. *Neuropsychology Review, 8*, 95–108.

Bush, S. S. (2010). Determining Whether Or When To Adopt New Versions Of

Psychological And Neuropsychological Tests: Ethical and professional considerations. *The Clinical Neuropsychologist, 24*, 7–16.

Bush, S. S., Ruff, R. M., Troster, A. I., Barth, J. T., Koffler, S. P., Pliskin, N. H., et al. (2005). Symptom validity assessment: Practice issues and medical necessity: NAN Policy & Planning Committee. *Archives of Clinical Neuropsychology, 20*, 419–426.

Butcher, J. N., Dahlstrom, W. G., Graham, J. R., Tellegen, A., & Kaemmer, B. (1989). *Manual for the restandardized Minnesota Multiphasic Personality Inventory: MMPI-2. An interpretive and administrative guide.* Minneapolis: University of Minnesota Press.

Butcher, J. N., Graham, J. R., Ben-Porath, Y. S., Tellegen, A., Dahlstrom,W. G., & Kaemmer, B. (2001). *MMPI-2: Manual for administration, scoring and interpretation* (rev. ed.). Minneapolis: University of Minnesota Press.

Caldwell, A. B. (1997). MMPI-2 data research field for clinical patients. Unpublished raw data.

Carmody, D. P., & Crossman, A. M. (2005). Youth deception: Malingering traumatic stress. *Journal of Forensic Psychiatry and Psychology, 16*, 477–493.

Carmody, D. P., & Crossman, A. M. (2011). Artful liars: Malingering on the Draw-A-Person task. *Open Criminology Journal, 4*, 1–9.

Carpenter v. Superior Court of Alameda County (Yamaha Motor Corporation), Cal. App. 4th (2006).

Carroll, S., Abrahamse, A., & Vaiana, M. (1995). *The costs of excess medical claims for automobile personal injuries.* Santa Monica, CA: Rand.

Carroll, L. J., Cassidy, J. D., Peloso, P. M., Borg, J., von Holst, H., Holm, L., et al. (2004). Prognosis for mild traumatic brain injury: Results of the WHO Collaborating Centre Task Force on Mild Traumatic Brain Injury. *Journal of Rehabilitation Medicine, 43*(Suppl.), 84–105.

Castro-Caldas, A., Reis, A., & Guerreiro, M. (1997). Neuropsychological aspects of illiteracy. *Neuropsychological Rehabilitation, 7*, 327–338.

Centers for Disease Control and Prevention. (2006). *Heads up: Facts for physicians about mild traumatic brain injury.* Atlanta, GA: Author.

Chafetz, M. (2011a). Reducing the probability of false positives in malingering detection of social security disability claimants. *The Clinical Neuropsychologist, 25*, 1239–1252.

Chafetz, M. (2011b). The Psychological Consultative Examination for Social Security disability. *Psychological Injury and Law, 4*(3–4), 235–244.

Chafetz, M., Prenthowski, E., & Rao, A. (2011). To work or not to work: Motivation (not low IQ) determines SVT findings. *Archives of Clinical Neuropsychology, 26*, 306–313.

Chuk, S. (2009). Note; It's (not) bad, it's (not) bad, you know it: The growing acceptance of the "Fake Bad Scale." *Villanova Law Review, 54*, 479.

Cicerone, K. D., & Azulay, J. (2002). Diagnostic utility of attention measures in postconcussion syndrome. *The Clinical Neuropsychologist, 16*, 280–289.

Cohen, J. B. (1990). Misuse of computer software to detect faking on the Rorschach: A reply to Kahn, Fox, and Rhode. *Journal of Personality Assessment, 54*, 58–62.

Collie, A., McCrory, P., & Makdissi, M. (2006). Does history of concussion affect current cognitive status? *British Journal of Sports Medicine, 40,* 550–551.

Constantinou, M., Ashendorf, L., & McCaffrey, R. J. (2002). When the third party observer of a neuropsychological evaluation is an audio-recorder. *The Clinical Neuropsychologist, 16,* 407–412.

Constantinou, M., Ashendorf, L., & McCaffrey, R. J. (2005). Effects of a third party observer during neuropsychological assessment: When the observer is a video camera. *Journal of Forensic Neuropsychology, 4,* 39–48.

Cornblatt, B. A., Lenzenweger, M. F., & Erlenmeyer-Kimling, L. (1989). The continuous performance test, identical pairs version: II. Contrasting attentional profiles in schizophrenic and depressed patients. *Psychiatry Research, 29,* 65–85.

Correa, A. A., Rogers, R., & Hoersting, R. (2010). Validation of the Spanish SIRS with monolingual Hispanic outpatients. *Journal of Personality Assessment, 92,* 458–464.

Cottingham, M. E., & Boone, K. B. (2010). Non-credible language deficits following mild traumatic brain injury. *The Clinical Neuropsychologist, 24,* 1006–1025.

Craig, R. J. (1999). Testimony based on the Millon Clinical Multiaxial Inventory: Review, commentary, and guidelines. *Journal of Personality Assessment, 73,* 290–304.

Cramer, R. J., & Brodsky, S. L. (2007). Undue influence or ensuring rights: Attorney presence during forensic psychology evaluations. *Ethics and Behavior, 17,* 51–60.

Crawford, J. R., Deary, I. J., Starr, J., & Whalley, L. J. (2001). The NART as an index of prior intellectual functioning: A retrospective validity study covering a 66-year interval. *Psychological Medicine, 31,* 451–458.

Crawford, E. F., Greene, R. L., Dupart, T. M., Bongar, B., & Childs, H. (2006). MMPI-2 assessment of malingered emotional distress related to a workplace injury: A mixed group validation. *Journal of Personality Assessment, 86,* 217–221.

Crawford, J. R., Parker, D. M., & Besson, J. A. (1988). Estimation of premorbid intelligence in organic conditions. *British Journal of Psychiatry, 153,* 178–181.

Crawford, J. R., Parker, D. M., Stewart, L .E., Besson, J. A. O., & DeLacey, G. (1989). Prediction of WAIS IQ with the National Adult Reading Test: Cross-validation and extension. *British Journal of Clinical Psychology, 28,* 267–273.

Cripe, L. I., Maxwell, J. K., & Hill, E. (1995). Multivariate discriminant function analyses of neurologic, pain, and psychiatric patients with the MMPI. *Journal of Clinical Psychology, 51,* 258–268.

Curiel, A. (2012). *A re-examination of the Meyers and Volbrecht Motor Equation for the identification of suspect effort.* Unpublished doctoral dissertation, Pepperdine University, Malibu, CA.

Curtis, K. L., Greve, K. W., & Bianchini, K. J. (2009). The Wechsler Adult Intelligence Scale-III and malingering in traumatic brain injury: Classification accuracy in known groups. *Assessment, 16,* 401–414.

Curtis, K. L., Greve, K. W., Brasseux, R., & Bianchini, K. J. (2010). Criterion groups validation of the Seashore Rhythm Test and Speech Sounds Perception Test for the detection of malingering in traumatic brain injury. *The Clinical Neuropsychologist, 24,* 882–897.

Curtis, K. L., Thompsom, L. K., Greve, K. W., & Bianchini, K. J. (2008). Verbal fluency indicators of malingering in traumatic brain injury: Classification accuracy in known groups. *The Clinical Neuropsychologist, 22,* 930–945.

Dahlstrom, W. G., Welsh, G. S., & Dahlstrom, L. E. (1972). *An MMPI handbook.* Minneapolis: University of Minnesota Press.

Dandachi-FitzGerald, B., Ponds, R. W. H. M., Peters, M. U. V., & Merckelbach, H. (2011). Cognitive underperformance and symptom over-reporting in a mixed psychiatric sample. *The Clinical Neuropsychologist, 25,* 812–828.

Daubert, S. D., & Metzler, A. E. (2000). The detection of fake-bad and fake-good responding on the Millon Clinical Multiaxial Inventory III. *Psychological Assessment, 12,* 18–24.

Daubert v. Merrell Dow Pharmaceuticals, Inc., 509 U.S. 579 (1993).

Davis, C. H. (2002). Self-perception in mild traumatic brain injury. *American Journal of Physical Medicine and Rehabilitation, 81,* 609–618.

Dean, A. C., Victor, T. L., Boone, K. B., & Arnold, G. (2008). The relationship of IQ to effort test performance." *The Clinical Neuropsychologist, 22,* 705–722.

Dean, A. C., Victor, T., Boone, K. B., Philpott, L., & Hess, R. (2009). Dementia and effort test performance. *The Clinical Neuropsychologist, 23,* 133–152.

Dearth, D. S., Berry, D. T. R., Vickery, C. D., Vagnini, V. L., Baser, R. E., Orey, S. A., et al. (2005). Detection of feigned head injury symptoms on the MMPI-2 in head injured patients and community controls. *Archives of Clinical Neuropsychology, 20,* 95–110.

DeClue, G. (2011). Harry Potter and the structured interview of reported symptoms?" *Open Access Journal of Forensic Psychology, 3,* 1–18.

de Leon, M. B., Kirsch, N. L., Maio, R. F., Tan-Schriner, C. U., Millis, S. R., Frederiksen, S., et al. (2009). Baseline predictors of fatigue 1 year after mild head injury. *Archives of Physical Medicine and Rehabilitation, 90,* 956–965.

Demakis, G. J., Gervais, R. O., & Rohling, M L. (2008). The effect of failure on cognitive and psychological symptom validity tests in litigants with symptoms of post-traumatic stress disorder. *The Clinical Neuropsychologist, 22,* 879–895.

Diaz-Asper, C. M., Schretlen, D. J., & Pearlson, G. D. (2004). How well does IQ predict neuropsychological test performance in normal adults? *Journal of the International Neuropsychological Society, 10,* 82–90.

Dicker, B. G. (1992). Profile of those at risk for minor head injury, *Journal of Head Trauma Rehabilitation, 7,* 83–91.

Dikmen, S. S., Donovan, D. M., Loberg, T., Machamer, J. E., & Temkin, N. R. (1993). Alcohol use and its effects on neuropsychological outcome in head injury. *Neuropsychology, 7,* 296–305.

Dikmen, S. S., & Levin, H. S. (1993). Methodological issues in the study of mild head injury. *Journal of Head Trauma Rehabilitation, 8,* 30–37.

Dikmen, S. S., Machamer, J. E., Winn, H. R., & Temkin, N. R. (1995).

Neuropsychological outcome at 1–year post head injury. *Neuropsychology, 1*, 80–90.

Dikmen, S., Machamer, J., & Temkin, N. (2001). Mild head injury: Facts and artifacts. *Journal of Clinical and Experimental Neuropsychology, 23*, 729–738.

Dionysus, K. E., Denney, R. L., & Halfaker, D. A. (2011). Detecting negative response bias with the Fake Bad Scale, Response Bias Scale, and Henry–Heilbronner Index of the Minnesota Multiphasic Personality Inventory–2. *Archives of Clinical Neuropsychology, 26*, 81–88.

Dodd, J. W., Getov, S. V., & Jones, P. W. (2010). Cognitive function in COPD. *European Respiratory Journal, 35*, 913–922.

Donders, J. (2006). Performance discrepancies on the California Verbal Learning Test—Second Edition (CVLT-II) in the standardization sample. *Psychological Assessment, 18*, 458–463.

Donders, J., & Strong, C. A. H. (2011). Embedded effort indicators on the California Verbal Learning Test—Second Edition (CVLT–II): An attempted cross-validation. *The Clinical Neuropsychologist, 25*, 173–184.

Duff, K. (2010). Predicting premorbid memory functioning in older adults. *Applied Neuropsychology, 17*, 278–282.

Duff, K., Chelune, G. J., & Dennett, K. (2011). Predicting estimates of premorbid memory functioning: Validation in a dementia sample. *Archives of Clinical Neuropsychology, 26*, 701–705.

Duff, K., & Fisher, J. M. (2005). Ethical dilemmas with third party observers. *Journal of Forensic Neuropsychology, 4*, 65–82.

Eastvold, A. D., Belanger, H. G., & Vanderploeg, R. D. (2012). Does a third party observer affect neuropsychological test performance?: It depends. *The Clinical Neuropsychologist, 26*, 520–541.

Edens, J. F., Cruise, K. R., & Buffington-Vollum, J. K. (2001). Forensic and correctional applications of the Personality Assessment Inventory. *Behavioral Sciences and the Law, 19*, 519–543.

Edens, J. F., Otto, R. K., & Dwyer, T. J. (1998). Susceptibility of the Trauma Symptom Inventory to malingering. *Journal of Personality Assessment, 71*, 379–392.

Edens, J. F., Otto, R. K., & Dwyer, T. (1999). Utility of the Structured Inventory of Malingered Symptomatology in identifying persons motivated to malinger psychopathology. *Journal of the American Academy of Psychiatry and the Law, 27*, 387–396.

Edens, J. F., Poythress, N. G., & Watkins-Clay, M. M. (2007). Detection of malingering in psychiatric unit and general population prison inmates: A comparison of the PAI, SIMS, and SIRS. *Journal of Personality Assessment, 88*, 33–42.

Efendov, A. A., Sellbom, M., & Bagby, R. M. (2008). The utility and comparative incremental validity of the MMPI-2 and Trauma Symptom Inventory validity scales in the detection of feigned PTSD. *Psychological Assessment, 20*, 317–326.

Eichel, S. K. D. (2011). *Credentialing: It may not be the cat's meow*. Retrieved May 15, 2012, from *DrEichel.com*.

Ekman, P., & Friesen, W. V. (1976). *Pictures of facial affect.* Palo Alto, CA: Consulting Psychologists Press.

Elhai, J. D., Gray, M. J., Naifeh, J. A., Butcher, J. J., Davis, J. L., Falsetti, S. A., et al. (2005). Utility of the Trauma Symptom Inventory's atypical response scale in detecting malingered posttraumatic stress disorder. *Assessment, 12,* 210–219.

Ersche, K. D., & Sahakian, B. (2007). The neuropsychology of amphetamine and opiate dependence: Implications for treatment. *Neuropsychology Review, 17,* 317–336.

Essig, S. M., Mittenberg, W., Petersen, R. S., Strauman, S., & Cooper, J. T. (2001). Practices in forensic neuropsychology: Perspectives of neuropsychologists and trial attorneys. *Archives of Clinical Neuropsychology, 16,* 271–291.

Etherton, J. L., Bianchini, K. J., Ciota, M. A., & Greve, K. W. (2005). Reliable Digit Span is unaffected by laboratory-induced pain: Implications for clinical use. *Assessment, 12,* 101–106.

Etherton, J. L., Bianchini, K. J., Greve, K. W., & Ciota, M. A. (2005). Test of Memory Malingering Performance is unaffected by laboratory-induced pain: Implications for clinical use. *Archives of Clinical Neuropsychology, 20,* 375–384.

Etherton, J. L., Bianchini, K. J., Heinly, M. T., & Greve, K. W. (2006). Pain, malingering, and performance on the WAIS-III Processing Speed Index. *Journal of Clinical and Experimental Neuropsychology, 28,* 1218–1237.

Etminian, M., Gill, S., & Samii, A. (2003). The role of lipid-lowering drugs in cognitive function: A meta-analysis of observational studies. *Pharmacotherapy, 23,* 726–730.

Exner, J. (1974). *The Rorschach: A comprehensive system.* New York: Wiley.

Exner, J. (1985). *Systematic interpretation of the Rorschach protocol utilizing the Comprehensive system.* Minneapolis, MN: National Computer Systems.

Fann, J. R., Katon, W. J., Uomoto, J. M., & Esselman, P. C. (1995). Psychiatric disorders and functional disability in outpatients with traumatic brain injuries. *American Journal of Psychiatry, 152,* 1493–1499.

Fann, J. R., Uomoto, J. M., & Katon, W. J. (2001). Cognitive improvement with treatment of depression following mild traumatic brain injury. *Psychosomatics: Journal of Consultation Liaison Psychiatry, 42,* 48–54.

Faust, D., Hart, K. J., & Guilmette, T. J. (1988). Pediatric malingering: The capacity of children to fake believable deficits on neuropsychological testing. *Journal of Consulting and Clinical Psychology, 56,* 578–582.

Faust, D., Hart, K. J., Guilmette, T. J., & Arkes, H. R. (1988). Neuropsychologists' capacity to detect adolescent malingerers. *Professional Psychology: Research and Practice, 19,* 508–515.

Felton, R. H., Naylor, C. E., & Wood, F. B. (1990). Neuropsychological profile of adult dyslexics. *Brain and Language, 39,* 485–497.

Fenton, G., McClelland, R., Montgomery, A., MacFlynn, G., & Rutherford, W. (1993). The postconcussional syndrome: Social antecedents and psychological sequelae. *British Journal of Psychiatry, 162,* 493–497.

Ferguson, R. J., Mittenberg, W., Barone, D. F., & Schneider, F. (1999).

Postconcussion syndrome following sports-related head injury: Expectation as etiology. *Neuropsychology, 13,* 582–589.

Ferrari, R., Obelieniene, D., Russell, A., Darlington, P., Gervais, R., & Green, P. (2001). Symptom expectation after minor head injury: A comparative study between Canada and Lithuania. *Clinical Neurology and Neurosurgery, 103,* 184–190.

Fox, D. D. (2011). Symptom Validity Test failure indicates invalidity of neuropsychological tests. *The Clinical Neuropsychologist, 25,* 488–495.

Fox, D. D., Gerson, A., & Lees-Haley, P. R. (1995). Interrelationship of MMPI-2 validity scales in personal injury claims. *Journal of Clinical Psychology, 51,* 42–47.

Fox, D. D., Lees-Haley, P. R., Earnest, K., & Dolezal-Wood, S. (1995). Base rates of postconcussive symptoms in health maintenance organization patients and controls. *Neuropsychology, 9,* 606–611.

Franzen, M. D., Burgess, E. J., & Smith-Seemiller, L. (1997). Methods of estimating premorbid functioning. *Archives of Clinical Neuropsychology, 12,* 711–738.

Frederick, R. I. (1997). *Validity Indicator Profile manual.* Minneapolis, MN: National Computer Systems.

Freeman, J., Godfrey, H. P. D., Harris, J. K. J., & Partridge, F. M. (2001). Uitility of a demographic equation in detecting impaired NART performance after TBI. *British Journal of Clinical Psychology, 40,* 221–224.

Frencham, K. A. R., Fox, A. M., & Maybery, M. T. (2005). Neuropsychological studies of mild traumatic brain injury: A meta-analytic review of research since 1995. *Journal of Clinical and Experimental Neuropsychology, 27,* 334–351.

Frueh, B. C., & Kinder, B. N. (1994). The susceptibility of the Rorschach Inkblot Test to malingering of combat-related PTSD. *Journal of Personality Assessment, 62,* 280–298.

Ganellen, R. J., Wasyliw, O. E., Haywood, T. W., & Grossman, L. S. (1996). Can psychosis be malingered on the Rorschach?: An empirical study. *Journal of Personality Assessment, 66,* 65–80.

Garden, N., & Sullivan, K. A. (2010). An examination of the base rates of postconcussion symptoms: The influence of demographics and depression. *Applied Neuropsychology, 17,* 1–7.

Gasquoine, P. G. (2000). Postconcussional symptoms in chronic back pain. *Applied Neuropsychology, 7,* 83–89.

Gasquoine, P. G. (2009). Race-norming of neuropsychological tests. *Neuropsychology Review, 19,* 250–262.

Gasquoine, P. G. (2011). Cognitive impairment in common, noncentral nervous system medical conditions of adults and the elderly. *Journal of Clinical and Experimental Neuropsychology, 33,* 486–496.

Gaven, B. E., Lynch, J. K., & McCaffrey, R. J. (2005). Third party observers: The effect size is greater than you might think. *Journal of Forensic Neuropsychology, 4,* 49–64.

Geary, E. K., Kraus, M. F., Pliskin, N. H., & Little, D. M. (2010). Verbal learning differences in chronic mild traumatic brain injury, *Journal of the International Neuropsychological Society, 16,* 506–516.

Geffen, G., O'Hanlon, A. P., Clark, C. R., & Geffen, L. B. (1990). Performance measures for 16 to 86-year-old males and females on the Auditory Verbal Learning Test. *The Clinical Neuropsychologist, 4,* 45–63.

Geraerts, E., Kozaric-Kovacic, D., Merchelbach, H., Peraica, T., Jelicic, M., & Candel, I. (2009). Detecting deception of war-related posttraumatic stress disorder. *Journal of Forensic Psychiatry and Psychology, 20,* 278–285.

Gervais, R. O., Ben-Porath, Y. S., & Wygant, D. B. (2009). Empirical correlates and interpretation of the MMPI-2-RF Cognitive Complaints (COG) scale. *The Clinical Neuropsychologist, 23,* 996–1015.

Gervais, R. O., Ben-Porath, Y. S., Wygant, D. B., & Green, P. (2007). Development and validation of a Response Bias Scale (RBS) for the MMPI-2. *Assessment, 14,* 196–208.

Gervais, R. O., Ben-Porath, Y. S., Wygant, D. B., & Green, P. (2008). Differential sensitivity of the Response Bias Scale (RBS) and MMPI-2 validity scales to memory complaints. *The Clinical Neuropsychologist, 22,* 1061–1079.

Gervais, R. O., Ben-Porath, Y. S., Wygant, D. B., & Sellbom, M. (2010). Incremental validity of the MMPI-2-RF over-reporting scales and RBS in assessing the veracity of memory complaints. *Archives of Clinical Neuropsychology, 25,* 274–284.

Gervais, R O., Green, P., Allen, L. M., & Iverson, G. L. (2001). Effects of coaching on symptom validity testing in chronic pain patients presenting for disability assessments. *Journal of Forensic Neuropsychology, 2,* 1–19.

Gervais, R. O., Rohling, M. L., Green, P., & Ford, W. (2004). A comparison of WMT, CARB, and TOMM failure rates in non-head injury disability claimants. *Archives of Clinical Neuropsychology, 19,* 475–487.

Gervais, R. O., Wygant, D. B., Sellbom, M., & Ben-Porath, Y. S. (2011). Associations between symptom validity test failure and scores on the MMPI-2-RF validity and substantive scales. *Journal of Personality Assessment, 93,* 508–517.

Ghaffar, O., McCullagh, S., Ouchterlony, D., & Feinstein, A. (2006). Randomized treatment trial in mild traumatic brain injury. *Journal of Psychosomatic Research, 61,* 153–160.

Giger, P., Merten, T., Merckelbach, H., & Oswald, M. (2010). Detection of feigned crime-related amnesia: A multi-method approach. *Journal of Forensic Psychology Practice, 10,* 440–463.

Gillis, J. R., Rogers, R., & Bagby, R. M. (1991). Validity of the M Test: Simulation-design and natural-group approaches. *Journal of Personality Assessment, 57,* 130–140.

Gladsjo, J. A., Heaton, R. K., Palmer, B. W., Taylor, M. J., & Jeste, D. V. (1999). Use of oral reading to estimate premorbid intellectual and neuropsychological functioning. *Journal of the International Neuropsychological Society, 5,* 247–254.

Glassmire, D. M., Bierley, R. Z., Wisniewski, A. M., Greene, R. L., Kennedy, J. E., & Date, E. (2003). Using the WMS-III Faces Subtest to detect malingered memory impairment. *Journal of Clinical and Experimental Neuropsychology, 25,* 465–481.

Goldberg, H. E., Back-Madruga, C., & Boone, K. B. (2007). The impact of psychiatric disorders on cognitive symptom validity test scores. In K. B. Boone (Ed.), *Assessment of feigned cognitive impairment: A neuropsychological perspective* (pp. 281–309). New York: Guilford Press.

Goldberg, J. Q., & Miller, H. R. (1986). Performance of psychiatric inpatients and intellectually deficient individuals on a task that assesses the validity of memory complaints. *Journal of Clinical Psychology, 42,* 792–795.

Goldstein, F. C., & Levin, H. S. (2001). Cognitive outcome after mild and moderate traumatic brain injury in older adults. *Journal of Clinical and Experimental Neuropsychology, 23,* 739–753.

Goldstein, F. C., Levin, H. S., Goldman, W. P., Clark, A. N., & Altonen, T. K. (2001). Cognitive and neurobehavioral functioning after mild versus moderate traumatic brain injury in older adults. *Journal of the International Neuropsychological Society, 7,* 373–383.

Golfland Entertainment Centers, Inc., vs. Superior Court of San Joaquin County, No. CO43143. (May 13, 2003).

Gonzalez, R. (2007). Acute and non-acute effects of cannabis on brain functioning and neuropsychological performance. *Neuropsychology Review, 17,* 347–362.

Gonzalez, R., Vassileva, J., & Scott, J. C. (2009). Neuropsychological consequences of drug abuse. In I. Grant & K. M. Adams (Eds.), *Neuropsychological assessment of neuropsychiatric and neuromedical disorders* (pp. 455–479). New York: Oxford University Press.

Goodenough, F. (1926). *Measurement of intelligence by drawings.* New York: World Book.

Gouvier, W. D., Cubic, B., Jones, G., Brantley, P., & Cutlip, Q. (1992). Postconcussive symptoms and daily stress in normal and head-injured college populations. *Archives of Clinical Neuropsychology, 7,* 193–211.

Gouvier, W. D., Uddo-Crane, M., & Brown, L. M. (1988). Base rates of postconcussional symptoms. *Archives of Clinical Neuropsychology, 3,* 273–278.

Graham, J. R. (2000). *MMPI-2: Assessing personality and psychopathology.* New York: Oxford University Press.

Granacher, R. P. (2008). Commentary: Applications of functional neuroimaging to civil litigation of mild traumatic brain injury. *Journal of the American Academy of Psychiatry and the Law Online, 36,* 323–28.

Grant, I., Gonzalez, R., Carey, C. L., Natarajan, L., & Wolfson, T. (2003). Nonacute (residual) neurocognitive effects of cannabis use: A meta-analytic study. *Journal of the International Neuropsychological Society, 9,* 679–689.

Graue, L. O., Berry, D. T. R., Clark, J. A., Sollman, M. J., Cardi, M., Hopkins, J., et al. (2007). Identification of feigned mental retardation using the new generation of malingering detection instruments: Preliminary findings. *The Clinical Neuropsychologist, 21,* 929–942.

Gray, M. J., Elhai, J. D., & Briere, J. (2010). Evaluation of the Atypical Response scale of the Trauma Symptom Inventory–2 in detecting simulated posttraumatic stress disorder. *Journal of Anxiety Disorders, 24,* 447–451.

Green, D., & Rosenfeld, B. (2011). Evaluating the gold standard: A review and meta-analysis of the Structured Interview of Reported Symptoms. *Psychological Assessment, 23*, 95–107.

Green, D., Rosenfeld, B., Dole, T., Pivovarova, E., & Zapt, P. A. (2008). Validation of an abbreviated version of the Structured Interview of Reported Symptoms in outpatient psychiatric and community settings. *Law and Human Behavior, 32*, 177–186.

Green, P. (2003). *Green's Word Memory Test for Windows: User's manual*. Edmonton, Canada: Green's.

Green, P. (2004). *Green's Medical Symptom Validity Test (MSVT) for Microsoft Windows. User's manual*. Edmonton, Canada: Green's.

Green, P. (2008). *Green's Non-Verbal Medical Symptom ValidityTest (NV-MSVT) for Microsoft Windows. User's Manual 1.0*. Edmonton, Canada: Green's.

Green, P., & Iverson, P. L. (2001). Effects of injury severity and cognitive exaggeration on olfactory deficits in head injury compensation claims. *NeuroRehabilitation, 16*, 237–243.

Green, P., Rohling, M. L., Iverson, G. L., & Gervais, R. O. (2003). Relationships between olfactory discrimination and head injury severity. *Brain Injury, 17*, 479–496.

Green, P., Rohling, M. L., Lees-Haley, & Allen, L. M. (2001). Effort has a greater effect on test scores than severe brain injury in compensation claimant. *Brain Injury, 15*, 1045–1060.

Greenberg, G. D., Rodriguez, N.M., & Sesta, J. J. (1994). Revised scoring, reliability, and validity investigations of Piaget's Bicycle Drawing Test. *Assessment, 1*, 89–102.

Greene, R. (1988). The relative efficacy of F-K and the obvious and subtle scales to detect overreporting of psychopathology on the MMPI. *Journal of Clinical Psychology, 44*, 152–159.

Greene, R. L. (1991). *MMPI-2/MMPI: An interpretive manual*. Needham Heights, MA: Allyn & Bacon.

Greene, R. L. (2000). *The MMPI-2: An interpretive manual* (2nd ed.). Needham Heights, MA: Allyn & Bacon.

Gregoire, J., Coalson, D. L., & Zhu, J. (2011). Analysis of WAIS-IV Index score scatter using significant deviation from the mean Index Scores. *Assessment, 18*, 168–177.

Greiffenstein, M. F. (2000). Late post-concussion syndrome as learned illness behavior: Proposal for a multifactorial model. Brain Injury Source, 4, 26–27.

Greiffenstein, M. F. (2009). Clinical myths of forensic neuropsychology. *The Clinical Neuropsychologist, 23*, 286–296.

Greiffenstein, M. F., & Baker, W. J. (2001). Comparison of premorbid and postinjury MMPI-2 profiles in late postconcussion claimants. *The Clinical Neuropsychologist, 15*, 162–170.

Greiffenstein, M. F., & Baker, W. J. (2003). Premorbid clues?: Preinjury scholastic performance and present neuropsychological functioning in late postconcussion syndrome. *The Clinical Neuropsychologist, 17*, 561–573.

Greiffenstein, M. F., & Baker, W. J. (2008). Validity testing in dually diagnosed post-traumatic stress disorder and mild closed head injury. *The Clinical Neuropsychologist, 22,* 565–82.

Greiffenstein, M. F., Baker, W. J., & Gola, T. (1994). Validation of malingered amnesia measures with a large clinical sample. *Psychological Assessment, 6,* 218–224.

Greiffenstein, M. F., Baker, W. J., Gola, T., Donders, J., & Miller, L. (2002). The Fake Bad Scale in atypical and severe closed head injury litigants. *Journal of Clinical Psychology, 58,* 1591–1600.

Greiffenstein, M. F., Baker, W. J., Tsushima, W. T., Boone, K., & Fox, D. D. (2010). MMPI-2 validity scores in defense- versus plaintiff-selected examinations: A repeated measures study of examiner effects. *The Clinical Neuropsychologist, 24,* 305–314.

Greiffenstein, M. F., Fox, D., & Lees-Haley, P. R. (2007). The MMPI-2 Fake Bad Scale in detection of noncredible brain injury claims. In K. B. Boone (Ed.), *Assessment of feigned cognitive impairment: A neuropsychological perspective* (pp. 210–235). New York: Guilford Press.

Greiffenstein, M. F., Gola, T., & Baker, W. J. (1995). MMPI-2 validity scales versus domain specific measures in detection of factitious traumatic brain injury. *The Clinical Neuropsychologist, 9,* 230–240.

Greve, K. W., & Bianchini, K. J. (2007). Detection of cognitive malingering with tests of executive function. In G. J. Larabee (Ed.), *Assessment of malingered neuropsychological deficits* (pp. 171–225). New York: Oxford University Press.

Greve, K. W., Bianchini, K. J., Black, F. W., Heinly, M. T., Love, J. M., Swift, D. A., et al. (2006). The prevalence of cognitive malingering in persons reporting exposure to occupational and environmental substances. *NeuroToxicology, 27,* 940–950.

Greve, K. W., Bianchini, K. J., Mathias, C. W., Houston, R. J., & Crouch, J. A. (2003). Detecting malingered performance on the Wechsler Adult Intelligence Scale: Validation of Mittenberg's approach in traumatic brain injury. *Archives of Clinical Neuropsychology, 18,* 245–260.

Greve, K. W., Heinly, M. T., Bianchini, K. J., & Love, J. M. (2009). Malingering detection with the Wisconsin Card Sorting Test in mild traumatic brain injury. *The Clinical Neuropsychologist, 23,* 343–362.

Greve, K. W., Ord, J. S., Bianchini, K. J., & Curtis, K. L. (2009). Prevalence of Malingering in Patients With Chronic Pain Referred for Psychologic Evaluation in a Medico-Legal Context. *Archives of Physical Medicine and Rehabilitation, 90,* 1117–1126.

Greve, K. W., Ord, J. S., Curtis, K. L., Bianchini, K. J., & Brennan, A. (2008). Detecting malingering in traumatic brain injury and chronic pain: A comparison of three forced choice symptom validity tests. *The Clinical Neuropsychologist, 22,* 896–918.

Griffin, S. L., Mindt, M. R., Rankin, E. J., Ritchie, A. J., & Scott, J. G. (2002). Estimating premorbid intelligence: Comparison of traditional and contemporary methods across the intelligence continuum. *Archives of Clinical Neuropsychology, 17,* 497–507.

Grober, E., & Sliwinski, M. (1991). Development and validation of a model for estimating premorbid verbal intelligence in the elderly. *Journal of Clinical and Experimental Neuropsychology, 13,* 933–949.

Grove, W. M. (2001). Bias and error rates for premorbid IQ estimators: Comment on Veiel and Koopman (2001). *Psychological Assessment, 13,* 396–398.

Gruber, S. A., Silveri, M. M., & Yurgelun-Todd, D.A. (2007). Neuropsychological consequences of opiate use. *Neuropsychology Review, 17,* 299–315.

Guerrero, J. L., Thurman, D. J., & Sniezek, J. E. (2000). Emergency department visits associated with traumatic brain injury: United States, 1995–1996. *Brain Injury, 14,* 181–186.

Guilmette, T. J., Hagan, L. D., & Giuliano, A. J. (2008). Assigning qualitative descriptions to test scores in neuropsychology: Forensic implications. *The Clinical Neuropsychologist, 22,* 122–139.

Gunning-Dixon, F. M., & Raz, N. (2000). The cognitive correlates of white matter abnormalities in normal aging: A quantitative review. *Neuropsychology, 14,* 224–232.

Gunstad, J., & Suhr, J. A. (2001). Efficacy of the full and abbreviated forms of the Portland Digit Recognition Test: Vulnerability to coaching. *The Clinical Neuropsychologist, 15,* 397–404.

Gunstad, J., & Suhr, J. A. (2004). Cognitive factors in postconcussion syndrome symptom report. *Archives of Clinical Neuropsychology, 19,* 391–405.

Guriel, J., & Fremouw, W. (2003). Assessing malingered posttraumatic stress disorder: A critical review. *Clinical Psychology Review, 23,* 881–904.

Guriel, J., Yanez, Y. T., Fremouw, W., Shreve-Neiger, A., Ware, L., Filcheck, H., et al. (2004). Impact of coaching on malingered posttraumatic stress symptoms on the M-FAST and the TSI. *Journal of Forensic Psychology Practice, 4,* 37–56.

Guriel-Tennant, J., & Fremouw, W. (2006). Impact of trauma history and coaching on malingering of posttraumatic stress disorder using the PAI, TSI, and M-FAST. *Journal of Forensic Psychiatry and Psychology, 17,* 577–592.

Guskiewicz, K. M., Marshall, S. W., Broglio, S. P., Cantu, R. C., & Kirkendall, D. T. (2002). No evidence of impaired neurocognitive performance in collegiate soccer players. *American Journal of Sports Medicine, 30,* 157–162.

Guy, L. S., Kwartner, P. P., & Miller, H. A. (2006). Investigating the M-FAST: Psychometric properties and utility to detect diagnostic specific malingering. *Behavioral Sciences and the Law, 24,* 687–702.

Guy, L. S., & Miller, H. A. (2004). Screening for malingered psychopathology in a correctional setting: Utility of the Miller Forensic Assessment of Symptoms Test (M-FAST). *Criminal Justice and Behavior, 31,* 695–716.

Haggerty, K. A., Frazier, T. W., Busch, R. M., & Naugle, R. I. (2007). Relationship among Victoria Symptom Validity Test indices and Personality Assessment Inventory validity scales in a large clinical sample. *The Clinical Neuropsychologist, 20,* 917–928.

Hall, G., Nagayama, C., Bansal, A., & Lopez, I. R. (1999). Ethnicity and psychopathology: A meta-analytic review of 31 years of comparative MMPI/MMPI-2 research. *Psychological Assessment, 11,* 186–197.

Hankins, G. C., Barnard, G. W., & Robbins, L. (1993). The validity of the M Test in a residential forensic facility. *Bulletin of the American Academy of Psychiatry and the Law, 21,* 111–121.

Hanna-Pladdy, B., Beery, Z. M., Bennett, T., Phillips, H. L., & Gouvier, W. D. (2001). Stress as a diagnostic challenge for postconcussive symptoms: Sequelae of mild traumatic brain injury or physiological stress response. *The Clinical Neuropsychologist, 15,* 289–304.

Harp, J. P., Jasinski, L.J., Shandera-Ochsner, A. L., Mason, L. H., & Berry, D. T. R. (2011). Detection of malingered ADHD using the MMPI-2-RF. *Psychological Injury and Law, 4,* 32–43.

Harris, J. G., Tulsky, D. S., & Schultheis, M. T. (2003). Assessment of the non-native English-speaker: Assimilating history and research findings to guide clinical practice. In D. S. Tulsky, D. H. Saklofske, G. J. Chelune, R. K. Heaton, R. J. Ivnik, R. Bornstein, et al. (Eds.), *Clinical interpretation of the WAIS-III and WMS-III* (pp. 343–391). San Diego, CA: Academic Press.

Hawes, S. W., & Boccaccini, M. T. (2009). Detection of overreporting of psychopathology on the Personality Assessment Inventory: A meta-analytic review. *Psychological Assessment, 21,* 112–124.

Hawkins, K. A., & Tulsky, D. S. (2001). The influence of IQ stratification on WAIS-III/WMS-III FSIQ-general memory index discrepancy base-rates in the standardization sample. *Journal of the International Neuropsychological Society, 7,* 875–880.

Hayes, J. S., Hale, D. B., & Gouvier, W. D. (1997). Do tests predict malingering in defendants with mental retardation? *Journal of Psychology, 13,* 575–576.

Hayes, J. S., Hale, D. B., & Gouvier, W. D. (1998). Malingering detection in a mentally retarded forensic population. *Applied Neuropsycholoogy, 5,* 33–36.

Heaton, R., Miller, W., Taylor, M., & Grant, I. (2004). *Revised comprehensive norms for an expanded Halstead–Reitan Battery: Demographically adjusted neuropsychological norms for African American and Caucasian adults.* Lutz, FL: Psychological Assessment Resources.

Heaton, R. K., Smith, H. H., Jr., Lehman, R. A. W., & Vogt, A. T. (1978). Prospects for faking believable deficits on neuropsychological testing. *Journal of Consulting and Clinical Psychology, 46,* 892–900.

Heilbronner, R. L., Sweet, J. J., Attix, D. K., Krull, K. R., Henry, G. K., & Hart, R. P. (2010). Official position of the American Academy of Clinical Neuropsychology on serial neuropsychological assessment: The utility and challenges of repeat test administrations in clinical and forensic contexts. *The Clinical Neuropsychologist, 24,* 1267–1278.

Heilbronner, R. L., Sweet, J. J., Morgan, J. E., Larrabee, G., Millis, S., and Conference Participants. (2009). American Academy of Clinical Neuropsychology Consensus Conference Statement on the neuropsychological assessment of effort, response bias, and malingering. *The Clinical Neuropsychologist, 23,* 1093–129.

Heinly, M. T., Greve, K. W., Bianchini, K. J., Love, J. M., & Brennan, A. (2005). WAIS Digit Span-based indicators of malingered neurocognitive dysfunction. *Assessment, 12,* 429–444.

Heinze, M., & Purisch, A. (2001). Beneath the mask: Use of psychological tests to detect and subtype malingering in criminal defendants. *Journal of Forensic Psychology Practice, 1,* 23–52.

Henry, G. K. (2005). Probable malingering and performance on the Test of Variables of Attention. *The Clinical Neuropsychologist, 19,* 121–129.

Henry, G. K., & Enders, C. (2007). Probable malingering and performance on the Continuous Visual Memory Test. *Applied Neuropsychology: Adult, 14,* 267–274.

Henry, G. K., Gross, H. S., Herndon, C. A., & Furst, C. J. (2000). Nonimpact brain injury: Neuropsychological and behavioral correlates with consideration of physiological findings. *Applied Neuropsychology, 7,* 65–75.

Henry, G. K., Heilbronner, R. L., Mittenberg, W., & Enders, C. (2006). The Henry–Heilbronner Index: A 15-item empirically derived MMPI-2 subscale for identifying probable malingering in personal injury litigants and disability claimants. *The Clinical Neuropsychologist, 20,* 786–797.

Henry, G. K., Heilbronner, R. L., Mittenberg, W., Enders, C., & Domboski, K. (2009). Comparison of the MMPI-2 Restructured Demoralization scale, Depression scale, and Malingered Mood Disorder scale in identifying noncredible symptom reporting in personal injury litigants and disability claimants. *The Clinical Neuropsychologist, 23,* 153–166.

Henry, G. K., Heilbronner, R. L., Mittenberg, W., Enders, C., & Roberts, D. M. (2008). Empirical derivation of a new MMPI-2 scale for identifying probable malingering in personal injury litigants and disability claimants: The 15-Item Malingered Mood Disorder Scale (MMDS). *The Clinical Neuropsychologist, 22,* 158–168.

Henry, G. K., Heilbronner, R. L., Mittenberg, W., Enders, C., & Stanczak, S. R. (2008). Comparison of the Lees-Haley Fake Bad Scale, Henry–Heilbronner Index, and Restructured Clinical Scale 1 in identifying noncredible symptom reporting. *The Clinical Neuropsychologist, 22,* 919–929.

Henry, G. K., Heilbronner, R. L., Mittenberg, W., Enders, C., Stevens, A., & Dux, M. (2011). Noncredible performance in individuals with external incentives: Empirical derivation and cross-validation of the Psychosocial Distress Scale (PDS). *Applied Neuropsychology, 18,* 47–53.

Hilsabeck, R. C., Gouvier, W. D., & Bolter, J. F. (1998). Reconstructive memory bias in recall of neuropsychological symptomatology. *Journal of Clinical and Experimental Neuropsychology, 20,* 328–338.

Hopwood, C. J., Morey, L. C., Rogers, R., & Sewell, K. (2007). Malingering on the Personality Assessment Inventory: Identification of specific feigned disorders. *Journal of Personality Assessment, 88,* 43–48.

Horwitz, J. E., & McCaffrey, R. J. (2006). A review of Internet sites regarding independent medical examinations: Implications for clinical neuropsychological practitioners. *Applied Neuropsychology, 13,* 175–179.

Howe, L. L., & Loring, D. W. (2009). Classification accuracy and predictive ability of the Medical Symptom Validity Test's dementia profile and general memory impairment profile. *The Clinical Neuropsychologist, 23,* 329–342.

Hoyt, R. D. (2009, Fall). Is the Fake Bad scale here to stay? *Mass Torts, 8*(1), 14–15, 23.

Hurley, K. E., & Deal, W. P. (2006). Assessment instruments measuring malingering used with individuals who have mental retardation: Potential problems and issues. *Mental Retardation, 44,* 112–119.

Iezzi, T., Duckworth, M., Vuong, L. N., Archibald, Y. M., & Klinck, A. (2004). Predictors of neurocognitive performance in chronic pain patients. *International Journal of Behavioral Medicine, 11,* 56–61.

Ingebrigtsen, T., Waterloo, K.., Marup-Jensen, S., Attner, E., & Romner, B. (1998). Quantification of post-concussion symptoms 3 months after minor head injury in 100 consecutive patients. *Journal of Neurology, 245,* 609–612.

Iverson, G. (2001). Can malingering be identified with the Judgment of Line Orientation Test? *Applied Neuropsychology, 8,* 167–173.

Iverson, G. L. (2006). Ethical issues associated with the assessment of exaggeration, poor effort, and malingering. *Applied Neuropsychology, 13,* 77–90.

Iverson, G. L. (2010). Mild traumatic brain injury meta-analyses can obscure individual differences. *Brain Injury, 24,* 1246–1255.

Iverson, G. L., Henrichs, T. S., Barton, E. A., & Allen, S. (2002b). Specificity of the MMPI-2 Fake Bad Scale as a marker for personal injury malingering. *Psychological Reports, 90,* 131–136.

Iverson, G. L., & Lange, R. T. (2003). Examination of postconcussion like symptoms in a healthy sample. *Applied Neuropsychiatry, 10,* 137–144.

Iverson, G. L., Lange, R. T., Brooks, B.L., & Rennison, V. L. A. (2010). "Good old days" bias following mild traumatic brain injury. *The Clinical Neuropsychologist, 24,* 17–37.

Iverson, G. L., Lange, R. T., Green, P., & Franzen, M. D. (2002a). Detecting exaggeration and malingering with the Trail Making Test. *The Clinical Neuropsychologist, 16,* 398–406.

Iverson, G. L., Lange, G. L., & Rose, A. (2007). Post-concussive disorder. In N. D. Zasler, D. I. Katz, & R. D. Zafonte (Eds.), *Brain injury medicine: Principles and practice* (pp. 373–403). New York: Demos Medical.

Ivnik, R. J., Smith, G. E., Malec, J. F., Petersen, R. C., & Tangalos, E. G. (1995). Long-term stability and intercorrelations of cognitive abilities in older persons. *Psychological Assessment, 7,* 155–161.

Jackson, J., Fiddler, M., Kapur, N., Wells, A., Tomenson, B., & Creed, F. (2006). Number of bodily symptoms predicts outcome more accurately than health anxiety in patients attending neurology, cardiology, and gastroenterology clinics. *Journal of Psychosomatic Research, 60,* 357–363.

Jackson, R. L., Rogers, R., & Sewell, K. W. (2005). Forensic applications of the Miller Forensic Assessment of Symptoms Test (MFAST): Screening for feigned disorders in competency to stand trial evaluations. *Law and Human Behavior, 29,* 199–210.

Jansen, C. E., Miaskowski, C., Dodd, M., Dowling, G., & Kramer, J. (2005). A meta-analysis of studies of the effects of cancer chemotherapy on various domains of cognitive function. *Cancer, 104,* 2222–2233.

Jastak, J., & Jastak, S. (1978). *Wide Range Achievement Test—Revised.* Wilmington, DE: Jastak Associates.

Jelicic, M., Ceunen, E., Peters, M. J. V., & Merckelbach, H. (2011). Detecting coached feigning using the Test of Memory Malingering (TOMM) and the

Structured Inventory of Malingered Symptomatology (SIMS). *Journal of Clinical Psychology, 67*, 850—855.

Jelicic, M., Hessels, A., & Merckelbach, H. (2006). Detection of feigned psychosis with the Structured Inventory of Malingered Symptomatology (SIMS): A study of coached and uncoached simulators. *Journal of Psychopathology and Behavioral Assessment, 28*, 19–22.

Jelicic, M., Merckelbach, H., Candel, I., & Geraerts, E. (2007). Detection of feigned cognitive dysfunction using special malinger tests: A simulation study in naïve and coached malingerers. *International Journal of Neuroscience, 117*, 1185–1192.

Jelicic, M., Peters, M. J. V., Leckie, V., & Merckelbach, H. (2007). Basic knowledge of psychopathology does not undermine the efficacy of the Structured Inventory of Malingered Symptomatology (SIMS) to detect feigned psychosis. *Netherlands Journal of Psychology, 63*, 107–110.

Johnstone, B., Callahan, C. D., Kapila, C. J., & Bouman, D. E. (1996). The comparability of the WRAT-R reading test and NAART as estimates of premorbid intelligence in neurologically impaired patients. *Archives of Clinical Neuropsychology, 11*, 513–519.

Johnstone, B., & Wilhelm, K. L. (1996). The longitudinal stability of the WRAT-R Reading subtest: Is it an appropriate estimate of premorbid intelligence? *Journal of the International Neuropsychological Society, 2*, 282–285.

Johnstone, L., & Cooke, D. J. (2003). Feigned intellectual deficits on the Wechsler Adult Intelligence Scale—Revised. *British Journal of Clinical Psychology, 42*, 303–318.

Jones, A., & Ingram, M. V. (2011). A comparison of selected MMP-2 and MMPI-2-RF validity scales in assessing effort on cognitive tests in a military sample. *The Clinical Neuropsychologist, 25*, 1207–1227.

Jovanovski, D., Erb, S., & Zakzanis, K. K. (2005). Neurocognitive deficits in cocaine users: A quantitative review of the evidence. *Journal of Clinical and Experimental Neuropsychology, 27*, 189–204.

Kahn, M. W., Fox, H., & Rhode, R. (1988). Detecting faking on the Rorschach: Computer versus expert clinical judgment. *Journal of Personality Assessment, 52*, 516–523.

Kalechstein, A. D., De La Garza, R., Mahoney, J. J., Fantegrossi, W. E., & Newton, T. F. (2007). MDMA use and neurocognition: A meta-analytic review. *Psychopharmacology, 189*, 531–537.

Kareken, D. A., Gur, R. C., & Saykin, A. J. (1995). Reading on the Wide Range Achievement Test—Revised and parental education as predictors of IQ: Comparison with the Barona formula. *Archives of Clinical Neuropsychology, 10*, 147–157.

Karzmark, P., Hall, K., & Englander, J. (1995). Late-onset post-concussive symptoms after mild brain injury: The role of premorbid, injury related, environmental, and personality factors. *Brain Injury, 9*, 21–26.

Kashluba, S., Paniak, C., & Casey, J. E. (2008). Persistent symptoms associated with factors identified by the WHO Task Force on Mild Traumatic Brain Injury. *The Clinical Neuropsychologist, 22*, 195–208.

Katzman, G. L., Dagher, A. P., & Patronas, N. J. (1999). Incidental findings on brain magnetic resonance imaging from 1000 asymptomatic volunteers. *Journal of the American Medical Association, 282*, 36–39.

Kehrer, C. A., Sanchez, P. N., Habif, U., Rosenbaum, J. G., & Townes, B. D. (2000). Effects of a significant-other observer on neuropsychological test performance. *The Clinical Neuropsychologist, 14*, 67–71.

Keiski, M. A., Shore, D. L., & Hamilton, J. M. (2007). The role of depression in verbal memory following traumatic brain injury. *The Clinical Neuropsychologist, 21*, 744–761.

Kim, M. S., Boone, K. B., Victor, T., Marion, S. D., Amano, S., Cottingham, M. E., et al. (2010). The Warrington Recognition Memory Test for Words as a measure of response bias: Total score and response time cutoffs developed on "real world" credible and noncredible subjects. *Archives of Clinical Neuropsychology, 25*(1), 60–70.

Kim, N., Boone, K. B., Victor, T., Lu, P., Keatinge, C., & Mitchell, C. (2010). Sensitivity and specificity of a Digit Symbol recognition trial in the identification of response bias. *Archives of Clinical Neuropsychology, 25*, 420–428.

King, J., & Sullivan, K. (2009). Deterring malingered psychopathology: The effect of warning simulating malingerers. *Behavioral Sciences and the Law, 27*, 35–49.

Kinsbourne, M., Rufo, D. T., Gamzu, E., Palmer, R. L., & Berliner, A. K. (1991). Neuropsychological deficits in adults with dyslexia. *Developmental Medicine and Child Neurology, 33*, 763–775.

Kirsch, N. L., de Leon, M. B., Maio, R. F., Millis, S. R., Tan-Schriner, C. U., & Frederiksen, S. (2010). Characteristics of a mild head injury subgroup with extreme, persisting distress on the Rivermead Postconcussion Symptoms Questionnaire. *Archives of Physical Medicine and Rehabilitation, 91*, 35–42.

Klonoff, P. S., & Lamb, D. G. (1998). Mild head injury, significant impairment on neuropsychological test scores, and psychiatric disability. *The Clinical Neuropsychologist, 12*, 31–42.

Knecht, S., Dräger, B., Deppe, M., Bobe, L, Lohmann, H., Flöel, A., et al. (2000). Handedness and hemispheric language dominance in healthy humans. *Brain, 123*, 2512–2518.

Konrad, C., Geburek, A. J., Risk, F., Blumenroth, H., Fischer, B., Husstedt, I., et al. (2011, September 22). Long-term cognitive and emotional consequences of mild traumatic brain injury. *Psychological Medicine, 41*, 1197–1211.

Krull, K. R., Scott, J. G., & Sherer, M. (1995). Estimation of premorbid intelligence from combined performance and demographic variables. *The Clinical Neuropsychologist, 9*, 83–88.

Kucharski, L. T., Toomey, J. P., Fila, K., & Duncan, S. (2007). Detection of malingering of psychiatric disorder with the Personality Assessment Inventory: An investigation of criminal defendants. *Journal of Personality Assessment, 88*, 25–32.

Kushner, D. (1998). Mild traumatic brain injury: Toward understanding manifestations and treatment. *Archives of Internal Medicine, 158*, 1617–1624.

Lally, S. J. (2003). What tests are acceptable for use in forensic evaluations?: A survey of experts. *Professional Psychology: Research and Practice, 34*, 491–498.

Lange, R. T., Iverson, G. L., Brooks, B. L., & Rennison, V. L. A. (2010). Influence of poor effort on self-reported symptoms and neurocognitive test performance following mild traumatic brain injury. *Journal of Clinical and Experimental Neuropsychology, 32,* 961–972.

Lange, R. T., Iverson, G. L., & Franzen, M. D. (2007). Short-term neuropsychological outcome following uncomplicated mild TBI: Effects of day-of-injury intoxication and pre-injury alcohol abuse. *Neuropsychology, 21,* 590–598.

Lange, R. T., Sullivan, K. A., & Scott, C. (2010). Comparison of MMPI-2 and PAI validity indicators to detect feigned depression and PTSD symptom reporting. *Psychiatry Research, 176,* 229–235.

Larrabee, G. L. (1998). Somatic malingering on the MMPI and MMPI-2 in personal injury litigants. *The Clinical Neuropsychologist, 12,* 179–188.

Larrabee, G. L. (2003a). Exaggerated MMPI-2 symptom report in personal injury litigants with malingered neurocognitive deficit. *Archives of Clinical Neuropsychology, 18,* 673–686.

Larrabee, G. L. (2003b). Detection of symptom exaggeration with the MMPI-2 in litigants with malingered neurocognitive dysfunction. *The Clinical Neuropsychologist, 17,* 54–68.

Larrabee, G. J. (2003c). Detection of malingering using atypical performance patterns on standard neuropsychological tests. *The Clinical Neuropsychologist, 17,* 410–425.

Larrabee, G. J. (2003d). Exaggerated pain report in litigants with malingered neurocognitive dysfunction. *The Clinical Neuropsychologist, 17,* 395–401.

Larrabee, G. J. (2004, February). *Identification of subtypes of malingered neurocognitive dysfunction.* Presented at the 32nd Annual Meeting of the International Neuropsychological Society, Baltimore, MD.

Larrabee, G. J. (Ed.). (2007). *Assessment of malingered neuropsychological deficits.* New York: Oxford University Press.

Larrabee, G. J. (2008a). Aggregation across multiple indicators improves the detection of malingering: Relationship to likelihood ratios. *The Clinical Neuropsychologist, 22,* 666–679.

Larrabee, G. J. (2008b). Flexible vs. fixed batteries in forensic neuropsychological assessment: Reply to Bigler and Hom. *Archives of Clinical Neuropsychology, 23,* 763–776.

Larrabee, G. J. (2009). Malingering Scales for the Continuous Recognition Memory Test and the Continuous Visual Memory Test. *The Clinical Neuropsychologist, 23,* 167–180.

Larrabee, G. J., Millis, S. R., & Meyers, J. E. (2008). Sensitivity to brain dysfunction of the Halstead–Reitan versus an ability-focused neuropsychological battery. *The Clinical Neuropsychologist, 22,* 813–825.

Larrabee, G. J., Millis, S. R., & Meyers, J. E. (2009). 40 plus or minus 10, a new magical number: Reply to Russell. *The Clinical Neuropsychologist, 23,* 841–849.

Laws, K. R., & Kokkalis, J. (2007). Ecstasy (MDMA) and memory function: A meta-analytic update. *Human Psychopharmacology: Clinical and Experimental, 22,* 381–388.

Lee, H., Wintermark, M., Gean, A. D., Ghajar, J., Manley, G. T., & Mukherjee, P. (2008). Focal lesions in acute mild traumatic brain injury and neurocognitive outcome: CT versus 3T MRI. *Journal of Neurotrauma, 25,* 1049–1056.

Lees-Haley, P. R. (1992). Efficacy of MMPI-2 validity scales and MCMI-II modifier scales for detecting spurious PTSD claims: F, F-K, Fake Bad Scale, Ego Strength, Subtle–Obvious subscales, DIS, and DEB. *Journal of Clinical Psychology, 48,* 681–688.

Lees-Haley, P. R., English, L. T., & Glenn, W. J. (1991). A Fake Bad Scale on the MMPI-2 for personal injury claimants. *Psychological Reports, 68,* 203–210.

Lees-Haley, P. R., Fox, D. D., & Courtney, J. C. (2001). A comparison of complaints by mild brain injury claimants and other claimants describing subjective experiences immediately following their injury. *Archives of Clinical Neuropsychology, 16,* 689–695.

Lees-Haley, P. R., Smith, H. H., Williams, C. W., & Dunn, J. T. (1995). Forensic neuropsychological test usage: An empirical study. *Archives of Clinical Neuropsychology, 11,* 45–51.

Lees-Haley, P. R., Williams, C. W., Zasler, N. D., Marguilies, S., English, L. T., & Stevens, K. B. (1997). Response bias in plaintiff's histories. *Brain Injury, 11,* 791–800.

Leininger, B. E., Gramling, S. E., Farrell, A. D., Kreutzer, J. S., & Peck, E. A. (1990). Neuropsychological deficits in symptomatic minor head injury patients after concussion and mild concussion. *Journal of Neurology, Neurosurgery and Psychiatry, 53,* 293–296.

Levin, H., Grossman, R. G., Rose, J. E., & Teasdale, G. (1979). Long-term neuropsychological outcome of closed head injury. *Journal of Neurosurgery, 50,* 412–422.

Lewis, J. S., Simcox, A. M., & Berry, D. T. (2002). Screening for feigned psychiatric symptoms in a forensic sample by using the MMPI-2 and the Structured Inventory of Malingered Symptomatology. *Psychological Assessment, 14,* 170–176.

Lezak, M. D., Howieson, D. B., & Loring, D. W. (2004). *Neuropsychological assessment* (4th ed.). New York: Oxford University Press.

Lilienfeld, S. O., Wood, J. M., & Garb, H. N. (2000). 'The scientific status of projective techniques. *Psychological Science in the Public Interest, 1,* 27–66.

Lindstrom, W., Coleman, C., Thomassin, K., Southall, C. M., & Lindstrom, J. H. (2011). Simulated dyslexia in postsecondary students: Description and detection using embedded validity indicators. *The Clinical Neuropsychologist, 25,* 302–322.

Lippa, S. M., Pastorek, N. J., Benge, J. F., & Thornton, G. M. (2010). Postconcussive symptoms after blast and nonblast-related mild traumatic brain injuries in Afghanistan and Iraq war veterans. *Journal of the International Neuropsychological Society, 16,* 856–866.

Loring, D. W., & Bauer, R. M. (2010). Testing the limits: Cautions and concerns regarding the new Wechsler IQ and Memory Scales. *Neurology, 74,* 685–690.

Loring, D. W., Lee, G. P., & Meador, K. J. (2005). Victoria Symptom Validity Test performance in non-litigating epilepsy surgery candidates. *Journal of Clinical and Experimental Neuropsychology, 27,* 610–617.

Löwe, B., Spitzer, R. L., Williams, J. B. W., Mussell, M., Schellberg, D., & Kroenke, K. (2008). Depression, anxiety and somatization in primary care: Syndrome overlap and functional impairment. *General Hospital Psychiatry, 30,* 191–199.

Lu, P. H., Boone, K. B., Cozolino, L., & Mitchell, C. (2003). Effectiveness of the Rey–Osterrieth Complex Figure Test and the Meyers and Meyers recognition trial in the detection of suspect effort. *The Clinical Neuropsychologist, 17,* 426–440.

Lu, P. H., Boone, K. B., Jimenez, N., & Razani, J. (2004). Failure to inhibit the reading response on the Stroop Test: A pathognomonic indicator of suspect effort. *Journal of Clinical and Experimental Neuropsychology, 26,* 180–189.

Luis, C. A., Vanderploeg, R. D., & Curtiss, G. (2003). Predictors of postconcussion symptom complex in community dwelling male veterans. *Journal of the International Neuropsychological Society, 9,* 1001–1015.

Lynch, J. K. (2005). Effect of a third party observer on neuropsychological test performance. *Journal of Forensic Neuropsychology, 4,* 17–25.

Machulda, M. M., Bergquist, T. F., Ito, V., & Chew, S. (1998). Relationship between stress, coping, and postconcussion symptoms in a healthy adult population. *Archives of Clinical Neuropsychology, 13,* 415–424.

Manly, J. J., Miller, S. W., Heaton, R. K., Byrd, D., Reilly, J., Velasquez, R. J., et al. (1998). The effect of African-American acculturation on neuropsychological test performance in normal and HIV-positive individuals. *Journal of the International Neuropsychological Society, 4,* 291–302.

Manly, J. J., Byrd, D. A., Touradji, P., & Stern, Y. (2004). Acculturation, reading level, and neuropsychological test performance among African American elders. *Applied Neuropsychology, 11,* 37–46.

Manly, J. J., Jacobs, D. M., Sano, M., Bell, K., Merchant, C. A., Small, S. A., et al. (1999). Effect of literacy on neuropsychological test performance in nondemented, education-matched elders. *Journal of the International Neuropsychological Society, 5,* 191–202.

Manly, J. J., Jacobs, D. M., Touradji, P., Small, S. A., & Stern, Y. (2002). Reading level attenuates differences in neuropsychological test performance between African American and white elders. *Journal of the International Neuropsychological Society, 8,* 341–348.

Mapou, R. L. (2008). *Adult learning disabilities and ADHD.* New York: Oxford University Press.

Marcopulos, B. A., McLain, C. A., & Guiliano, A. J. (1997). Cognitive impairment or inadequate norms?: A study of healthy, rural, older adults with limited education. *The Clinical Neuropsychologist, 11,* 111–131.

Marion, B. E., Sellbom, M., & Bagby, R. M. (2011). The detection of feigned psychiatric disorders using the MMPI-2-RF overreporting validity scales: An analog investigation. *Psychological Injury and Law, 4,* 1–12.

Marshall, P., & Happe, M. (2007). The performance of individuals with mental retardation on cognitive tests assessing effort and motivation. *The Clinical Neuropsychologist, 21*, 826–840.

Mataro, M., Poca, M. A., Sahuquillo, J., Pedraza, S., Ariza, M., Amoros, S., et al. (2001). Neuropsychological outcome in relation to the traumatic coma data bank classification of computed tomography imaging. *Journal of Neurotrauma, 18*, 869–879.

Mathias, C. W., Greve, K. W., Bianchini, K. J., Houston, R. J., & Crouch, J. A. (2002). Detecting malingered neurocognitive dysfunction using the reliable digit span in traumatic brain injury. *Assessment, 9*, 301–308.

Mathias, J. L., Bowden, S., Bigler, E. D., & Rosenfeld, J. V. (2007). Is performance on the Wechsler test of adult reading affected by traumatic brain injury? *British Journal of Clinical Psychology, 46*, 457–466.

Max, J. E., Koele, S. L., Smith, W. L., Jr., Sato, Y., Lindgren, S. D., Robin, D. A., et al. (1998). Psychiatric disorders in children and adolescents after severe traumatic brain injury: A controlled study. *Journal of the American Academy of Child and Adolescent Psychiatry, 37*, 832–840.

Mayeux, R., Ottman, R., Tang, M., Noboa-Bauza, L., Marder, K., Gurland, B., et al. (1993). Genetic susceptibility and head injury as risk factors for Alzheimer's disease among community-dwelling elderly persons and their first-degree relatives. *Annals of Neurology, 33*, 494–501.

Mazzucchi, A., Cattelani, R., Missale, G., Gugliotta, M., Brianti, R., & Parma, M. (1992). Head-injured subjects aged over 50 years: Correlations between variables of trauma and neuropsychological follow-up. *Journal of Neurology, 239*, 256–260.

McCaffrey, R. J. (2005). Some final thoughts and comments regarding the issues of third party observers. *Journal of Forensic Neuropsychology, 4*, 83–91.

McCaffrey, R. J., Fisher, J. M., Gold, B. A., & Lynch, J. K. (1996). Presence of third parties during neuropsychological evaluations: Who is evaluating whom? *The Clinical Neuropsychologist, 10*, 435–449.

McCaffrey, R. J., Lynch, J. K., & Yantz, C. (2005). Third party observers: Why all the fuss? *Journal of Forensic Neuropsychology, 4*, 1–15.

McCaffrey, R. J., O'Bryant, S. E., Ashendorf, L., & Fisher, J. M. (2003). Correlations among the TOMM, Rey-15, and MMPI-2 validity scales in a sample of TBI litigants. *Journal of Forensic Neuropsychology, 3*, 45–53.

McCauley, S. R., Boake, C., Levin, H. S., Contant, C. F., & Song, J. X. (2001). Postconcussional disorder following mild to moderate traumatic brain injury: Anxiety, depression, and social support as risk factors and comorbidities. *Journal of Clinical and Experimental Neuropsychology, 23*, 792–808.

McCrea, M. A. (2008). *Mild traumatic brain injury and postconcussion syndrome: The new evidence base for diagnosis and treatment.* New York: Oxford University Press.

McGurn, G., Starr, J. M., Topfer, J. A., Pattie, A., Whiteman, M. C., Lemmon, H. A., et al. (2004). Pronunciation of irregular words is preserved in dementia, validating premorbid IQ estimation. *Neurology, 62*, 1184–1186.

McHugh, P. R. (1993). Multiple personality disorder. *Harvard Mental Health Letter, 10*, 4.

McLean, A. M., Dikmen, S. S., & Temkin, N. R. (1993). Psychosocial recovery after head injury. *Archives of Physical Medicine and Rehabilitation, 74,* 1041–1046.

McLean, A., Temkin, N. R., Dikmen, S., & Wyler, A. R. (1983). The behavioral sequelae of head injury. *Journal of Clinical Neuropsychology, 5,* 361–376.

McSweeny, A. J., Becker, B. C., Naugle, R. I., Snow, W. G., Binder, L. M., & Thompson, L. L. (1998). Ethical issues related to the presence of third party observers in clinical neuropsychological evaluations. *The Clinical Neuropsychologist, 12,* 552–559.

Meares, S., Shore, E. A., Bryant, R. A., Taylor, A. J., Batchelor, J., Baguley, I. J., et al. (2011). The prospective course of postconcussion syndrome: The role of mild traumatic brain injury. *Neuropsychology, 25,* 454–465.

Mehta, K. M., Ott, A., Kalmijm, S., Slooter, A. J. C., van Duijn, C. M., Hofman, A., et al. (1999). Head trauma and risk of dementia and Alzheimer's disease. *Neurology, 53,* 1959–1962.

Meisner, S. (1988). Susceptibility of Rorschach distress correlates to malingering. *Journal of Personality Assessment, 52,* 564–571.

Merckelbach, H., & Smith, G. P. (2003). Diagnostic accuracy of the Structured Inventory of Malingered Symptomatology (SIMS) in detecting instructed malingering. *Archives of Clinical Neuropsychology, 18,* 145–152.

Merten, T., Bossink, L., & Schmand, B. (2007). On the limits of effort testing: Symptom validity tests and severity of neurocognitive symptoms in nonlitigant patients. *Journal of Clinical and Experimental Neuropsychology, 29,* 308–318.

Merten, T., Lorenz, R., & Schlatow, S. (2010). Posttraumatic stress disorder can easily be faked, but faking can be detected in most cases. *German Journal of Psychiatry, 13,* 140–149.

Merten, T., Thies, E., Schneider, K., & Stevens, A. (2009). Symptom validity testing in claimants with alleged posttraumatic stress disorder: Comparing the Morel Emotional Numbing Test, the Structured Inventory of Malingered Symptomatology, and the Word Memory Test. *Psychological Injury and Law, 2,* 284–293.

Merskey, H. (1992). The manufacture of personalities: The production of multiple personality disorder. *British Journal of Psychiatry, 160,* 327–340.

Messer, J. M., & Fremouw, W. J. (2007). Detecting malingered posttraumatic stress disorder using the Morel Emotional Numbing Test—Revised (Ment-R) and the Miller Forensic Assessment of Symptoms Test (M-Fast). *Journal of Forensic Psychology Practice, 7,* 33–57.

Meyers, J. E. (1995). *Rey Complex Figure Test and recognition trial: Professional manual.* Odessa, FL: Psychological Assessment Resources.

Meyers, J. E., & Diep, A. (2000). Assessment of malingering in chronic pain patients using neuropsychological tests. *Applied Neuropsychology, 7,* 133–139.

Meyers, J. E., Millis, S. R., & Volkert, K. (2002). A validity index for the MMPI-2. *Archives of Clinical Neuropsychology, 17,* 157–169.

Meyers, J. E., Morrison, A. L., & Miller, J. C. (2001). How low is too low, revisited: Sentence Repetition and AVLT-Recognition in the detection of malingering. *Applied Neuropsychology, 8,* 234–241.

Meyers, J. E., Reinsch-Boothby, L., Miller, R., Rohling, M., & Axelrod, B. (2011). Does the source of a forensic referral affect neuropsychological test performance on a standardized battery of tests? *The Clinical Neuropsychologist, 25,* 477–487.

Meyers, J. E., & Volbrecht, M. E. (2003). A validation of multiple malingering detection methods in a large clinical sample. *Archives of Clinical Neuropsychology, 18,* 261–276.

Meyers, J. E., Volbrecht, M., Axelrod, B. N., & Reinsch-Boothby, L. (2011). Embedded symptom validity test and overall neuropsychological test performance. *Archives of Clinical Neuropsychology, 26,* 8–15.

Mickeviciene, D., Schrader, H., Obelieniene, D., Surkiene, D., Kunickas, R., Stovner, L. J., et al. (2004). A controlled prospective inception cohort study on the post-concussion syndrome outside the medicolegal context. *European Journal of Neurology, 11,* 411–419.

Miller, H. A. (2001). *Miller Forensic Assessment of Symptoms Test.* Odessa, FL: Psychological Assessment Resources.

Miller, H. A. (2004). Examining the use of the M-FAST with criminal defendants incompetent to stand trial. *International Journal of Offender Therapy and Comparative Criminology, 48,* 268–280.

Miller, H. A. (2005). The Miller-Forensic Assessment of Symptoms Test (M-Fast): Test generalizability and utility across race, literacy, and clinical opinion. *Criminal Justice and Behavior, 32,* 591–611.

Miller, L. J., & Donders, J. (2001). Subjective symptomatology after traumatic head injury. *Brain Injury, 15,* 297–304.

Millis, S. A., Putnam, S. H., & Adams, K. M. (1995, March 19). *Neuropsychological malingering and the MMPI-2: Old and new indicators.* Paper presented at the 30th Annual Symposium on Recent Developments in the Use of the MMPI, MMPI-2, and MMPI-A, St. Petersburg Beach, FL.

Millon, T. (1994). *Millon Clinical Multiaxial Inventory–III.* Minneapolis, MN: National Computer Systems.

Mitrushina, M. N., Boone, K. B., Razani, J., & D'Elia, L. F. (2005). *Handbook of normative data for neuropsychological assessment* (2nd ed.). New York: Oxford University Press.

Mittenberg, W., Azrin, R., Millsaps, C., & Heilbronner, R. (1993). Identification of malingered head injury on the Wechsler Memory Scale—Revised. *Psychological Assessment, 5,* 34–40.

Mittenberg, W., DiGiulio, D., Perrin, S., & Bass, A. E. (1992). Symptoms following mild head-injury: Expectation as aetiology. *Journal of Neurology Neurosurgery, and Psychiatry, 55,* 200–204.

Mittenberg, W., Patton, C., Canyock, E. M., & Condit, D. C. (2002). Base rates of malingering and symptom exaggeration. *Journal of Clinical and Experimental Neuropsychology, 24,* 1094–1102.

Mittenberg, W., Rotholc, A., Russell, E., & Heilbronner, R. (1996). Identification of malingered head injury on the Halstead–Reitan battery. *Archives of Clinical Neuropsychology, 11,* 271–281.

Mittenberg W., Theroux, S., Aguila-Puentes, G., Bianchini, K., Greve, K., & Rayls,

K. (2001). Identification of malingered head injury on the Wechsler Adult Intelligence Scale—3rd Edition. *The Clinical Neuropsychologist, 15*, 440–445.

Mittenberg, W., Theroux-Fichera, S., Zielinski, R., & Heilbronner, R. L. (1995). Identification of malingered head injury on the Wechsler Adult Intelligence Scale—Revised. *Professional Psychology: Research and Practice, 26*, 491–498.

Mogge, N. L., Lepage, J. S., Bella, T., & Ragatz, L. (2010). The Negative Distortion scale: A new PAI validity scale. *Journal of Forensic Psychiatry and Psychology, 21*, 77–90.

Mooney, G., & Speed, J. (2001). The association between mild traumatic brain injury and psychiatric conditions. *Brain Injury, 15*, 865–877.

Moore, B. A., & Donders, J. (2004). Predictors of invalid neuropsychological test performance after traumatic brain injury. *Brain Injury, 18*, 975–984.

Morel, K. R. (1998a). Development and preliminary validation of a forced-choice test of response bias. *Journal of Personality Assessment, 70*, 299–314.

Morel, K. R. (1998b). *Morel Emotional Numbing Test for Posttraumatic Stress Disorder: Manual*. Cantonment, FL: Author.

Morel, K. R. (2008a). Comparison of the Morel Emotional Numbing Test for post-traumatic stress disorder to the Word Memory Test in neuropsychological evaluations. *The Clinical Neuropsychologist, 22*, 350–362.

Morel, K. R. (2008b). Development of a validity scale for posttraumatic stress disorder: Evidence from simulated malingerers and actual disability claimants. *Journal of Forensic Psychiatry and Psychology, 19*, 52–63.

Morel, K. R. (2010). *Morel Emotional Numbing Test for Posttraumatic Stress Disorder, Second Edition: Manual*. Cantonment, FL: Author.

Morel, K. R., & Shepherd, B. E. (2008). Meta-analysis of the Morel Emotional Numbing Test for PTSD: Comment on Singh, Avasthi, and Grover. *German Journal of Psychiatry, 11*, 128–131.

Morey, L. C. (1991). *The Personality Assessment Inventory: Professional manual*. Odessa, FL: Psychological Assessment Resources.

Morey, L. C. (1996). *An interpretative guide to the Personality Assessment Inventory*. Odessa, FL: Psychological Assessment Resources.

Morgan, C. D., Schoenberg, M. R., Dorr, D., & Burke, M. J. (2002). Overreport on the MCMI-III: Concurrent validation with the MMPI-2 using a psychiatric inpatient sample. *Journal of Personality Assessment, 78*, 288–300.

Morris, P. G., Wilson, J. T. L., Dunn, L. T., & Teasdale, G. M. (2005). Premorbid intelligence and brain injury. *British Journal of Clinical Psychology, 44*, 209–214.

Moss, A., Jones, C., Fokias, D., & Quinn, D. (2003). The mediating effects of effort upon the relationship between head injury severity and cognitive functioning. *Brain Injury, 17*, 377–387.

Mullen, K. L., & Edens, J. F. (2008). A case law survey of the Personality Assessment Inventory: Examining its role in civil and criminal trials. *Journal of Personality Assessment, 90*, 300–303.

Myburgh, C., Larsen, A. H., & Hartvigsen, J. (2008). A systematic, critical review of manual palpation for identifying myofascial trigger points: Evidence and clinical significance. *Archives of Physical Medicine and Rehabilitation, 89,* 1169–1176.

Naglieri, J. A. (1988). *DAP: Draw a Person: Quantitative Scoring System. The psychological corporation.* New York: Psychological Corporation.

Nampiaparampil, D. E. (2008). Prevalence of chronic pain after traumatic brain injury" *Journal of the American Medical Association, 300,* 711–719.

Nathan, D. (2011). *Sybil exposed.* New York: Free Press.

National Academy of Neuropsychology (NAN). (2000a). Test security: Official position statement of the National Academy of Neuropsychology. *Archives of Clinical Neuropsychology, 15,* 383–386.

National Academy of Neuropsychology (NAN). (2000b). Presence of third party observers during neuropsychological testing: Official statement of the National Academy of Neuropsychology. *Archives of Clinical Neuropsychology, 15,* 379–380.

National Academy of Neuropsychology (NAN). (2006). The use, education, training and supervision of neuropsychological test technicians (psychometrists) in clinical practice: Official statement of the National Academy of Neuropsychology. *Archives of Clinical Neuropsychology, 21,* 837–839.

National Center for Injury Prevention and Control. (2003). *Report to Congress on mild traumatic brain injury in the United States.* Atlanta, GA: Centers for Disease Control and Prevention.

Nelson, H. E. (1982). *National Adult Reading Test (NART): For the assessment of premorbid intelligence in patients with dementia: Test manual.* Windsor, UK: NFER–Nelson.

Nelson, H. E., & McKenna, P. (1975). The use of current reading ability in the assessment of dementia. *British Journal of Social and Clinicul Psychology, 14,259–267.*

Nelson, H. E., & Willison, J. R. (1991). *Revised National Adult Reading Test.* Windsor, Berkshire: NFER-Nelson Publishing Co.

Nelson, N. W., Boone, K., Dueck, A., Wagener, L., Lu, P., & Grills, C. (2003). Relationships between eight measures of suspect effort, *The Clinical Neuropsychologist, 17,* 263–272.

Nelson, N. W., Hoelzle, J. B., McGuire, K. A., Ferrier-Auerbach, A. G., Charlesworth, M. J., & Sponheim, S. R. (2010). Evaluation context impacts neuropsychological performance of OEF/OIF veterans with reported combat-related concussion. *Archives of Clinical Neuropsychology, 25,* 713–723.

Nelson, E. B., Sax, K. W., & Strakowski, S. M. (1998). Attentional performance in patients with psychotic and nonpsychotic major depression and schizophrenia. *American Journal of Psychiatry, 155,* 137–139.

Nelson, N. W., Sweet, J. J., Berry, D. T. R., Bryant, F. B., & Granacher, R P. (2007). Response validity in forensic neuropsychology: Exploratory factor analytic evidence of distinct cognitive and psychological constructs. *Journal of the International Neuropsychological Society, 13,* 440–449.

Netter, B. E., & Viglione, D. J. (1994). An empirical study of malingering schizophrenia on the Rorschach. *Journal of Personality Assessment, 62,* 45–57.

Nitch, S., Boone, K. B., Wen, J., Arnold, G., & Alfano, K. (2006). The utility of the Rey Word Recognition Test in the detection of suspect effort. *The Clinical Neuropsychologist, 20,* 873–887.

Nitrini, R.., Caramelli, P., Herrera, E., Porto, C. S., Charchat-Fichman, H., Carthery, M. T., et al. (2004). Performance of illiterate and literate nondemented elderly subjects in two tests of long-term memory. *Journal of the International Neuropsychological Society, 10,* 634–638.

Nye, E. C., Qualls, C., & Katzman, J. (2006). The Trauma Symptom Inventory: Factors associated with invalid profiles in a sample of combat veterans with post-traumatic stress disorder. *Military Medicine, 171,* 857–860.

O'Carroll, R., Walker, M., Dunan, J., Murray, C., Blackwood, D., Ebmeier, K. P., et al. (1992). Selecting controls for schizophrenia research studies: The use of the National Adult Reading Test (NART) is a measure is a measure of premorbid ability. *Schizophrenia Research, 8,* 137–141.

Ord, J. S., Boettcher, A. C., Greve, K. W., & Bianchini, K. J. (2010). Detection of malingering in mild traumatic brain injury with the Conners' Continuous Performance Test-II. *Journal of Clinical and Experimental Neuropsychology, 32,* 380–387.

Ord, J.S., Greve, K.W., Bianchini, K.J., & Aguerrevere, L.E. (2010). Executive dysfunction in traumatic brain injury: The effects of injury severity and effort on the Wisconsin Card Sorting Test. *Journal of Clinical and Experimental Neuropsychology, 32,* 132–140.

Orme, D. R., Johnstone, B., Hanks, R., & Novack, T. (2004). The WRAT-3 Reading subtest as a measure of premorbid intelligence among persons with brain injury. *Rehabilitation Psychology, 49,* 250–253.

Oscar-Berman, M., & Marinkovic, K. (2007). Alcohol: Effects on neurobehavioral functions and the brain. *Neuropsychology Review, 17,* 239–257.

Osimani, A., Alon, A., Berger, A., & Abarbanel, J. M. (1997). Use of the Stroop phenomenon as a diagnostic tool for malingering. *Journal of Neurology, Neurosurgery and Psychiatry, 62,* 617–621.

Osman, D. C., Plambeck, E., Klein, L., & Mano, Q. (2006). The Word Reading Test of Effort in adult learning disability: A simulation study. *The Clinical Neuropsychologist, 20,* 315–324.

Osmon, D. C., Smerz, J. M., Braun, M. M., & Plambeck, E. (2006). Processing abilities associated with math skills in adult learning disability. *Journal of Clinical and Experimental Neuropsychology, 28,* 84–95.

Ostrosky-Solis, F., Ardila, A., Rosselli, M., Lopez-Arango, G., & Uriel-Mendoza, V. (1998). Neuropsychological test performance in illiterate subjects. *Archives of Clinical Neuropsychology, 13,* 645–660.

Otto, M. W., Bruder, G. E., Fava, M., Delis, D. C., Quitkin, F. M., & Rosenbaum, J. F. (2004). Norms for depressed patients for the California Verbal Learning Test: Associations with depression severity and self-report of cognitive difficulties. *Archives of Clinical Neuropsychology, 9,* 81–88.

Ozen, L. J., & Fernandes, M. A. (2011). Effect of "diagnosis threat" on cognitive and affective functioning long after mild head injury. *Journal of the International Neuropsychological Society, 17,* 219–229.

Palmer, B. W., Boone, B. K., Lesser, I. M., & Wohl, M. A. (1998). Base rates of "impaired" neuropsychological test performance among healthy older adults. *Archives of Clinical Neuropsychology, 13*, 503–511.

Panayiotou, A., Jackson, M., & Crowe, S. F. (2010). A meta-analytic review of the emotional symptoms associated with mild traumatic brain injury. *Journal of Clinical and Experimental Neuropsychology, 32*, 463–473.

Paniak, C., MacDonald, J., Toller-Lobe, G., Durand, A., & Nagy, J. (1998). A preliminary normative profile of mild traumatic brain injury diagnostic criteria. *Journal of Clinical and Experimental Neuropsychology, 20*, 852–855.

Paolo, A. M., Ryan, J. J., Troster, A. I., & Hilmer, C. D. (1996). Utility of the Barona demographic equations to estimate premorbid intelligence: Information from the WAIS?R standardization sample. *Journal of Clinical Psychology, 52*, 335–343.

Peace, K. A., Porter, S., & Cook, B. (2010). Investigating differences in truthful and fabricated symptoms of traumatic stress over time. *Psychological Injury and Law, 3*, 118–129.

Pellman, E. J., Lovell, M.R., Viano, D.C., Casson, I. R., & Tucker, A. M. (2004). Concussion in professional football: Neuropsychological testing—Part 6. *Neurosurgery, 55*, 1290–1305.

Perry, G. G., & Kinder, B. N. (1990). The susceptibility of the Rorschach to malingering: A critical review. *Journal of Personality Assessment, 54*, 47–57.

Pertab, J. L., James, K. M., & Bigler, E. D. (2009). Limitations of mild traumatic brain injury meta-analyses. *Brain Injury, 23*, 498–508.

Piotrowski, C., & Belter, R. W. (1999). 'Internship training in psychological assessment: Has managed care had an impact? *Assessment, 6*, 381–389.

Plassman, B. L., Havlik, R. J., Steffens, D. C., Helms, M. J., Newman, T. N., Drosdick, D., et al. (2000). Documented head injury in early adulthood and risk of Alzheimer's disease and other dementias. *Neurology, 55*, 1158–1166.

Ponsford, J., Willmott, C. Rothwell, A., Cameron, P., Kelly, A., Nelms, R., et al. (2000). Factors influencing outcome following mild traumatic brain injury in adults. *Journal of the International Neuropsychological Society, 6*, 568–579.

Pope, K., Butcher, J. N., & Seelen, J. (2000). *The MMPI, MMPI-2, and MMPI-A in court* (2nd ed.). Washington, DC: American Psychological Association.

Porter, S., Peace, K. A., & Emmett, K. A. (2007). You protest too much, methinks: Investigating the features of truthful and fabricated reports of traumatic experiences. *Canadian Journal of Behavioural Science, 39*, 79–91.

Post, R., & Gasparikova-Krasnec, M. (1979). MMPI validity scales and behavioral disturbance in psychiatric inpatients. *Journal of Personality Assessment, 43*, 155–158.

Powell, B. D., Brossart, D. F., & Reynolds, C. R. (2003). Evaluation of the accuracy of two regression-based methods for estimating premorbid IQ. *Archives of Clinical Neuropsychology, 18*, 277–292.

Poythress, N. G., Edens, J. F., & Watkins, M. M. (2001). The relationship between psychopathic personality features and malingering symptoms of major mental illness. *Law and Human Behavior, 25*, 567–582.

Psychological Corporation (2009). *Wechsler Test of Adult Reading manual*. San Antonio, TX: .PsychCorp/Pearson.

Purdon, S. E., Purser, S. M., & Goddard, K. M. (2011). MMPI-2 Restructured Form over-reporting scales in first-episode psychosis. *The Clinical Neuropsychologist, 25*, 829–842.

Quraishi, S., & Frangou, S. (2002). Neuropsychology of bipolar disorder: A review. *Journal of Affective Disorders, 72*, 209–226.

Rabin, L. A., Barr, W. B., & Burton, L. A. (2005). Assessment practices of clinical neuropsychologists in the United States and Canada: A survey of INS, NAN, and APA Division 40 members. *Archives of Clinical Neuropsychology 20*, 33–65.

Radvansky, G. A., & Copeland, D. E. (2006). Walking through doorways causes forgetting: Situation models and experienced space. *Memory and Cognition, 34*, 1150–1156.

Ransby, M. J., & Swanson, H. L. (2003). Reading comprehension skills of young adults with childhood diagnoses of dyslexia. *Journal of Learning Disabilities, 36*, 538–555.

Rawling, P., & Brooks, N. (1990). Simulation Index: A method for detecting factitious errors on the WAIS-R and WMS. *Neuropsychology, 4*, 223–238.

Razani, J., Burciaga, J., Madore, M., & Wong, J. (2007). Effects of acculturation on tests of attention and information processing in an ethnically diverse group. *Archives of Clinical Neuropsychology, 22*, 333–341.

Razani, J., Murcia, G., Tabares, J., & Wong, J. (2006). The effects of culture on WASI test performance in ethnically diverse individuals. *The Clinical Neuropsychologist, 21*, 776–788.

Reedy, S. (2011). *A cross-validation of the Rey–Osterrieth Complex Figure Test and the Meyers and Meyers recognition trial in the detection of suspect effort*. Unpublished doctoral dissertation, Alliant International University, Los Angeles, CA.

Reese, C., Suhr, J., Larrabee, G., & Rasmussen, K. (2011). *Third party observation effects on credible and noncredible performance* Poster presented at the 39th Annual Meeting of the International Neuropsychological Society, Boston.

Reis, A., Guerreiro, M., & Petersson, K. M. (2003). A sociodemographic and neuropsychological characterization of an illiterate population. *Applied Neuropsychology, 10*, 191–204.

Reitan, R. M., & Wolfson, D. (1985). *The Halstead–Reitan neuropsychological test battery: Theory and clinical interpretation*. Tucson, AZ: Neuropsychology Press.

Resnick, P. J., West, S., & Payne, J. W. (2008). Malingering of posttraumatic disorders. In R. Rogers (Ed.), *Clinical assessment of malingering and deception* (3rd ed., pp. 109–127). New York: Guilford Press.

Richman, J., Green, P., Gervais, R., Flaro, L., Merten, T., Brockhaus, R., & Ranks, D. (2006). Objective tests of symptom magnification in independent medical examinations. *Journal of Occupational and Environmental Medicine, 48*, 303–311.

Riley, G. A., & Simmonds, L. V. (2003). How robust is performance on the national adult reading test following traumatic brain injury. *British Journal of Clinical Psychology, 42*, 319–328.

Rimel, R. W., Giordani, B., Barth, J. T., Boll, T. J., & Jane, J. A. (1981). Disability caused by mild traumatic brain injury, *Neurosurgery, 9, 221–228.*

Robinson, L. J., Thompson, J. M., Gallagher, P., Goswami, U., Young, A. H., Ferrier, I. N., et al. (2006). A meta-analysis of cognitive deficits in euthymic patients with bipolar disorder. *Journal of Affective Disorders, 93*, 105–115.

Rogers, R. (1992). *Structured Interview of Reported Symptoms (SIRS).* Odessa, FL: Psychological Assessment Resources.

Rogers, R. (1997). Researching dissimulation. In R. Rogers (Ed.), *Clinical assessment of malingering and deception* (2nd ed., pp. 398–426). New York: Guilford Press.

Rogers, R., Bagby, R. M., & Gillis, J. R. (1992). Improvements in the M Test as a screening measure for malingering. *Bulletin of the American Academy of Psychiatry and the Law, 20*, 101–104.

Rogers, R., Gillard, N. D., Berry, D. T. R., & Granacher, R. P. (2011). Effectiveness of the MMPI-2-RF validity scales for feigned mental disorders and cognitive impairment: A known-groups study. *Journal of Psychopathology and Behavioral Assessment, 33*, 355–367.

Rogers, R., Hinds, J. D., & Sewell, K. W. (1996). Feigning psychopathology among adolescent offenders: Validation of the SIRS, MMPI-A, and SIMS. *Journal of Personality Assessment, 67*, 244–257.

Rogers, R., Jackson, R. L., & Kaminski, P. L. (2005). Factitious psychological disorders: The overlooked response style in forensic evaluations. *Journal of Forensic Psychology Practice, 5*, 21–41.

Rogers, R., Payne, J. W., Berry, D. T., & Granacher, R. P. (2009). Use of the SIRS in compensation cases: An examination of its validity and generalizability. *Law and Human Behavior, 33*, 213–224.

Rogers, R., Salekin, R. T., & Sewell, K. W. (1999). Validation of the Millon Clinical Multiaxial Inventory for Axis II Disorders: Does it meet the Daubert standard? *Law and Human Behavior, 23*, 425–443.

Rogers, R., Sewell, K. W., Cruise, K. R., Wang, E. W., & Ustad, K. L. (1998). The PAI and feigning: A cautionary note on its use in forensic–correctional settings. *Assessment, 5*, 399–405.

Rogers, R., Sewell, K. W., & Gillard, N. D. (2010). *Structured Interview of Reported Symptoms, 2nd Edition (SIRS-2).* Lutz, FL: Psychological Assessment Resources.

Rogers, R., Sewell, K., Martin, M. A., & Vitacco, M. J. (2003). Detection of feigned mental disorders: A meta-analysis of the MMPI-2 and malingering. *Assessment, 10*, 160–177.

Rogers, R., Sewell, K., & Ustad, K. (1995). Feigning among chronic outpatients on the MMPI-2: A systematic examination of fake-bad indicators. *Assessment, 2*, 81–89.

Rogers, R., Ustad, K. L., & Salekin, R. T. (1998). Convergent validity of the

Personality Assessment Inventory: A study of emergency referrals in a correctional setting. *Assessment, 5*, 3–12.

Rogers, R., Vitacco, M. J., & Kurus, S. J. (2010). Assessment of malingering with repeat forensic evaluations: Patient variability and possible misclassification on the SIRS and other feigning measures. *Journal of the American Academy of Psychiatry and the Law, 38*, 109–114.

Rohling, M. L., Binder, L. M., Demakis, G. J., Larrabee, G. J., Ploetz, D. M., & Langhinrichsen-Rohling, J. (2011). A meta-analysis of neuropsychological outcome after mild traumatic mild injury: Re-analyses and reconsiderations of Binder et al. (1997), Frencham et al. (2005), and Pertab et al. (2009). *The Clinical Neuropsychologist, 25*, 608–623.

Rohling, M. L., & Demakis, G. J. (2010). Bowden, Shores, & Mathias (2006): Failure to replicate or just failure to notice? Does effort still account for more variance in neuropsychological test scores than TBI severity? *The Clinical Neuropsychologist, 24*, 119–36.

Rohling, M. L., Larrabee, G. J., & Millis, S. R. (2012). The "Miserable Minority" following mild traumatic brain injury: Who they are and do meta-analyses hide them? *The Clinical Neuropsychologist, 26*, 197–213.

Rohling, M. L., Meyers, J. E., & Millis, S. R. (2003). Neuropsychological impairment following traumatic brain injury: A dose–response analysis. *The Clinical Neuropsychologist, 17*, 289–302.

Root, J. G., Robbins, R. N., Chang, L., & van Gorp, W. (2006). Detection of inadequate effort on the California Verbal Learning Test—Second Edition: Forced choice recognition and critical item analysis. *Journal of the International Neuropsychological Society, 12*, 688–696.

Rorschach, H. (1921). *Psychodiagnostik*. Bern: Bircher.

Rosen, G. M., Sawchuk, C. N., Atkins, D. C., Brown, M., Price, J. R., & Lees-Haley, P. R. (2006). Risk of false positives when identifying malingered profiles using the Trauma Symptom Inventory. *Journal of Personality Assessment, 86*, 329–333.

Rosenfeld, B., Green, D., Pivovarova, E., Dole, T., & Zapf, P. (2010). What to do with contradictory data?: Approaches to the integration of multiple malingering measures. *International Journal of Forensic Mental Health, 9*, 63–73.

Rosenfeld, B., Sands, S. A., & van Gorp, W. G. (2000). Have we forgotten the base rate problem?: Methodological issues in the detection of distortion. *Archives of Clinical Neuropsychology, 15*, 349–359.

Rosenhan, D. L. (1973). On being sane in insane places. *Science, 179*, 250–258.

Ross, S. R., & Adams, K. M. (1999). Test review: One more test of malingering? *The Clinical Neuropsychologist, 13*, 112–116.

Ross, S. R., Putnam, S. H., Millis, S. R., Adams, K. M., & Krukowski, R. A. (2006). Detecting insufficient effort using the Seashore Rhythm and Speech Sounds Perception Test in head injury. *The Clinical Neuropsychologist, 20*, 798–815.

Rosselli, M., Ardila, A., & Rosas, P. (1990). Neuropsychological assessment in illiterates: II. Language and praxic abilities. *Brain and Cognition, 12*, 281–296.

Rourke, S. B., & Grant, I. (2009). The neurobehavioral correlates of alcoholism. In I. Grant & K. M. Adams (Eds.), *Neuropsychological assessment of neuropsychiatic and neuromedical disorders (pp.* 398–454). New York: Oxford University Press.

Rubenzer, S. (2010). Review of the Structured Inventory of Reported Symptoms–2 (SIRS-2). *Open Access Journal of Forensic Psychology, 2,* 273–286.

Rubinsky, E. W., & Brandt, J. (1986). Amnesia and criminal law: A clinical overview." *Behavioral Sciences and the Law, 4,* 27–46.

Ruiz, M. A., Drake, E. B., Glass, A., Marcotte, D., & van Gorp, W. G. (2002). Trying to beat the system: Misuse of the Internet to assist in avoiding the detection of psychological symptom dissimulation. *Professional Psychology: Research and Practice, 33,* 294–299.

Ruocco, A. C., Swirsky-Sacchetti, T., Chute, D. L., Mandel, S., Platek, S. M., & Zillmer, E. A. (2008). Distinguishing between neuropsychological malingering and exaggerated psychiatric symptoms in a neuropsychological setting. *The Clinical Neuropsychologist, 22,* 547–564.

Russell, A. J., Munro, J., Jones, P. B., Hayward, P., Hemsley, D. R., & Murray, R. M. (2000). The National Adult Reading Test as a measure of premorbid IQ in schizophrenia. *British Journal of Clinical Psychology, 39,* 297–305.

Russell, E. (2001). Toward an explanation of Dodrill's observation: High neuropsychological test performance does not accompany high IQs. *The Clinical Neuropsychologist, 15,* 423–428.

Russell, E. W. (2010). The "obsolescence" of assessment procedures. *Applied Neuropsychology, 17,* 60–67.

Russell, E. W., Russell, S. L., K, & Hill, B. D. (2005). The fundamental psychometric status of neuropsychological batteries. *Archives of Clinical Neuropsychology, 20,* 785–794.

Rutherford, W. H., Merrett, J. D., & McDonald, J. R. (1978). Symptoms at one year following concussion from minor head injuries. *Injury, 10,* 225–230.

Salazar, S., Lu, P. H., Wen, J., & Boone, K. (2007). The use of effort tests in ethnic minorities and in non-English speaking and English as a second language populations. In K. B. Boone (Ed.), *Assessment of feigned cognitive impairment: A neuropsychological perspective* (pp. 405–427). New York: Guilford Press.

Salekin, K. L., & Doane, B. M. (2009). Malingering intellectual disability: The value of available measures and methods. *Applied Neuropsychology, 16,* 105–113.

Satz, P., Zaucha, K., McCleary, C., Light, R., Asarnow, R., & Becker, D. (1997). Mild head injury in children and adolescents: A review of studies (1970–1995). *Psychological Bulletin, 122,* 107–131.

Sawchyn, J. M., Brulot, M. M., & Strauss, E. (2000). Note on the use of the Postconcussion Syndrome Checklist. *Archives of Clinical Neuropsychology, 15,* 1–8.

Schoechlin, C., & Engel, R. R. (2005). Neuropsychological performance in adult attention-deficit hyperactivitiy disorder: Meta-analysis of empirical data. *Archives of Clinical Neuropsychology, 20,* 727–744.

Schoenberg, M. R., Dorr, D., & Morgan, C. D. (2003). The ability of the Millon

Clinical Multiaxial Inventory—Third Edition to detect malingering. *Psychological Assessment, 15,* 198–204.

Schoenberg, M. R., Scott, J. G., Duff, K., & Adams, R. L. (2002). Estimation of WAIS-III intelligence from combined performance and demographic variables: Development of the OPIE-3. *The Clinical Neuropsychologist, 16,* 426–438.

Schretlen, D. J., Buffington, A. L. H., Meyer, S. M., & Pearlson, G. D. (2005). The use of word-reading to estimate "premorbid" ability in cognitive domains other than intelligence. *Journal of the International Neuropsychological Society, 11,* 784–787.

Schretlen, D. J., Munro, C. A., Anthony, J. C., & Pearlson, G. D. (2003). Examining the range of normal intraindividual variability in neuropsychological test performance. *Journal of the International Neuropsychological Society, 9,* 864–870.

Schretlen, D. J., Neal, J., & Lesikar, S. (2000). Screening for malingered mental illness. *American Journal of Forensic Psychology, 18,* 5–16.

Schretlen, D. J., & Shapiro, A. M. (2003). A quantitative review of the effects of traumatic brain injury on cognitive functioning. *International Review of Psychiatry, 15,* 341–349.

Schretlen, D. J., Testa, S. M., Winicki, J. M., Pearlson, G. D., & Gordon, B. (2008). Frequency and bases of abnormal performance by healthy adults on neuropsychological testing. *Journal of the International Neuropsychological Society, 14,* 436–445.

Schroeder, R. W., Baade, L. E., Peck, C. P., VonDran, E. J., Brockman, C. J., Webster, B. K., et al. (2012). Validation of MMPI-2-RF validity scales in criterion group neuropsychological samples. *The Clinical Neuropsychologist, 26,* 129–146.

Schroeder, R. W., & Marshall, P. S. (2010). Validation of the Sentence Repetition Test as a measure of suspect effort. *The Clinical Neuropsychologist, 24,* 326–343.

Schutte, C., Millis, S., Axelrod, B., & VanDyke, S. (2011). Derivation of a composite measure of embedded symptom validity indices. *The Clinical Neuropsychologist, 25,* 454–462.

Scott, J. C., Woods, S. P., Matt, G. E., Meyer, R. A., Heaton, R. K., Atkinson, J. H., et al. (2007). Neurocognitive effects of methamphetamine: A critical review and meta-analysis. *Neuropsychology Review, 17,* 275–298.

Seamons, D. T., Howell, R. J., Carlisle A. L., & Roe, A. V. (1981). Rorschach simulation of mental illness and normality by psychotic and nonpsychotic legal offenders. *Journal of Personality Assessment, 45,* 130–135.

Sellbom, M., & Bagby, R. M. (2008). Response styles on multiscale inventories. In R. Rogers (Ed.), *Clinical assessment of malingering and deception* (3rd ed., pp. 182–206). New York: Guilford Press.

Sellbom, M., & Bagby, R. M. (2010). Detection of overreported psychopathology with the MMPI-2-RF validity scales. *Psychological Assessment, 22,* 757–767.

Sellbom, M., Toomey, J. A., Wygant, D. B., Kucharski, L. T., & Duncan, S. (2010). Utility of the MMPI-2-RF (Restructured Form) validity scales in detecting malingering in a criminal forensic setting: A known-groups design. *Psychological Assessment, 22,* 22–31.

Selnes, O., A., & Gottesman, R. F. (2010). Neuropsychological outcomes after coronary artery bypass grafting. *Journal of the International Neuropsychological Society, 16,* 221–226.

Shandera, A. L., Berry, D. T. R., Clark, J. A., Schipper, L. J., Graue, L. O., & Harp, J. P. (2010). Detection of malingered mental retardation. *Psychological Assessment, 22,* 50–56.

Sharland, M. J., & Gfeller, J. D. (2007). A survey of neuropsychologists' beliefs and practices with respect to the assessment of effort. *Archives of Clinical Neuropsychology, 22,* 213–223.

Shaw, D. J., & Matthews, C. G. (1965). Differential MMPI performance of brain damaged versus pseudoneurologic groups. *Journal of Clinical Psychology, 21,* 405–408.

Sherman, D. S., Boone, K .B., Lu, P., & Razani, J. (2002). Re-examination of a Rey Auditory Verbal Learning Test/Rey Complex Figure discriminant function to detect suspect effort. *The Clinical Neuropsychologist, 16,* 242–250.

Silverberg, N.D., Hanks, R.A., Buchanan, L., Fichtenberg, N., & Millis, S.R. (2008). Detecting response bias with performance patterns on an expanded version of the controlled oral word association test. *The Clinical Neuropsychologist, 22,* 140–157.

Simon, M. J. (2007). Performance of mentally retarded forensic patients on the test of memory malingering. *Journal of Clinical Psychology, 63,* 339–344.

Simpson, M. A. (1988). Multiple personality disorder. *British Journal of Psychiatry, 155,* 565.

Sims, D. C. (2007, December). The myth of malingering: Is it the truth or a lie? *Plaintiff Magazine,* pp. 1–4.

Singh, J., Avasthi, A., & Grover, S. (2007). Malingering of psychiatric disorders: A review. *German Journal of Psychiatry, 10,* 126–132.

Singhal, A., Green, P., Ashaye, K., Shankar, K., & Gill, D. (2009). High specificity of the Medical Symptom Validity Test in patients with very severe memory impairment. *Archives of Clinical Neuropsychology, 24,* 721–728.

Slick, D., Hopp, G., Strauss, E., Hunter, M., & Pinch, D. (1994). Detecting dissimulation: Profiles of simulated malingerers, traumatic brain-injury patients, and normal controls on a revised version of Hiscock and Hiscock's forced-choice memory test. *Journal of Clinical and Experimental Neuropsychology, 16,* 472–481.

Slick, D. J., Hopp, G., Strauss, E., & Thompson, G. B. (1997). *VSVT: Victoria Symptom Validity Test, version 1.0, professional manual.* Odessa, FL: Psychological Assessment Resources.

Slick, D. J., Sherman, E. M. S., & Iverson, G. L. (1999). Diagnostic criteria for malingered neurocognitive dysfunction: Proposed standards for clinical practice and research. *The Clinical Neuropsychologist, 13,* 545–561.

Slick, D. J., Tan, J. E., Strauss, E., & Hultsch, D. F. (2004). Detecting malingering: A survey of experts' practices. *Archives of Clinical Neuropsychology, 19,* 465–473.

Smart, C. M., Nelson, N. W., Sweet, J. J., Bryant, F. B., Berry, D. T. R., Granacher, R. P., et al. (2008). Use of MMPI-2 to predict cognitive effort: A hierarchically optimal classification tree analysis. *Journal of the International Neuropsychological Society, 14*, 842–852.

Smith, G. P., & Borum, R. (1992). Detection of malingering in a forensic sample: A study of the M Test. *Journal of Psychiatry and the Law, 20*, 505–514.

Smith, G. P., Borum, R., & Schinka, J. A. (1993). Rule-Out and Rule-In scales for the M Test for malingering: A cross-validation. *Bulletin of the American Academy of Psychiatry and the Law, 21*, 107–110.

Smith, G. P., & Burger, G. K. (1997). Detection of malingering: Validation of the Structured Inventory of Malingered Symptomatology (SIMS). *Journal of the American Academy of Psychiatry and the Law, 25*, 183–189.

Smith, P. J., Blumenthal, J. A., Babyak, M. A., Hinderliter, A., & Sherwood, A. (2011). Association of vascular health and neurocognitive performance in overweight adults with high blood pressure. *Journal of Clinical and Experimental Neuropsychology, 33*, 559–566.

Smith, S. R., Gorske, T. T., Wiggins, C., & Little, J. A. (2010). Personality assessment use by clinical neuropsychologists. *International Journal of Testing, 10*, 6–20.

Sollman, M. J., Ranseen, J. D., & Berry, D. T. R. (2010). Detection of feigned ADHD in college students. *Psychological Assessment, 22*, 325–335.

Solomon, R. E., Boone, K. B., Miora, D., Skidmore, S., Cottingham, M., Victor, T., et al. (2010). Use of the WAIS-III Picture Completion subtest as an embedded measure of response bias. *The Clinical Neuropsychologist, 24*, 1243–1256.

Spanos, N. P. (1994). Multiple identity enactments and multiple personality disorder: A sociocognitive perspective. *Psychological Bulletin, 116*, 143–165.

Spanos, N. P., Weekes, J. R., & Bertrand, L. D. (1985). Multiple personality: A social psychological perspective. *Journal of Abnormal Psychology, 94*, 362–376.

Stapert, S., Houx, P., de Kruijk, J., Ponds, R., & Jolles, J. (2006). Neurocognitive fitness in the sub-acute stage after mild TBI: The effect of age. *Brain Injury, 20*, 161–165.

Stebbins, G. T., Wilson, R. S., Gilley, D. W., Bernard, B. A., & Fox, J. H. (1990). Use of the National Adult Reading Test to estimate premorbid IQ in dementia. *The Clinical Neuropsychologist, 4*, 18–24.

Steffan, J. S., Clopton, J. R., & Morgan, R. D. (2003). An MMPI-2 scale to detect malingered depression (Md scale). *Assessment, 10*, 382–392.

Sterr, A., Herron, K. A., Hayward, C., & Montaldi, D. (2006). Are mild head injuries as mild as we think?: Neurobehavioral concomitants of chronic postconcussion syndrome. *BMC Neurology, 6*, 7.

Stevens, A., Friedel, E., Mehren, G., & Merten, T. (2008). Malingering and uncooperativeness in psychiatric and psychological assessment: Prevalence and effects in a German sample of claimants. *Psychiatry Research, 157*, 191–200.

Storandt, M., Stone, K., & LaBarge, E. (1995). Deficits in reading performance in very mild dementia of the Alzheimer Type. *Neuropsychology, 9*, 174–176.

Stovner, L. J., Schrader, H., Mickeviciene, D., Surklene, D., & Sand, T. (2008). Headache after concussion. *European Journal of Neurology, 16,* 112–120.

Strasburger, L. H., Gutheil, T. G., & Brodsky, A. (1997). On wearing two hats: Role conflict in serving as both psychotherapist and expert witness. *American Journal of Psychiatry, 154,* 448–456.

Street, R. (1931). A Gestalt Completion Test: The study of a cross section of intellect. *Teachers College Record, 33,* 280–282.

Stulemeijer, M., Vos, P. E., Bleijenberg, G., & van der Werf, S. P. (2007). Cognitive complaints after mild traumatic brain injury: Things are not always what they seem. *Journal of Psychosomatic Research, 63,* 637–645.

Suhr, J. A., & Gunstad, J. (2000). The effects of coaching on the sensitivity and specificity of malingering measures. *Archives of Clinical Neuropsychology, 15,* 415–424.

Suhr, J., & Gunstad, J. (2002a). Postconcussive symptom report: The relative influence of head injury and depression. *Journal of Clinical and Experimental Neuropsychology, 24,* 981–993.

Suhr, J., & Gunstad, J. (2002b). "Diagnosis threat": The effect of negative expectations on cognitive performance in head injury, *Journal of Clinical and Experimental Neuropsychology, 24,* 448–457.

Suhr, J., & Gunstad, J. (2005). Further exploration of the effect of "diagnosis threat" on cognitive performance in individuals with mild head injury. *Journal of the International Neuropsychological Society, 11,* 23–29.

Suhr, J., Tranel, D., Wefel, J., & Barrash, J. (1997). Memory performance after head injury: Contributions of malingering, litigation status, psychological factors, and medication use. *Journal of Clinical and Experimental Neuropsychology, 19,* 500–514.

Sullivan, K., & King, J. (2010). Detecting faked psychopathology: A comparison of two tests to detect malingered psychopathology using a simulation design. *Psychiatry Research, 176,* 75–81.

Sumanti, M., Boone, K. B., Savodnik, I., & Gorsuch, R. (2006). Noncredible psychiatric and cognitive symptoms in a workers' compensation "stress claim" sample. *The Clinical Neuropsychologist, 20,* 754–765.

Sweet, J. J., Malina, A., & Ecklund-Johnson, E. (2006). Application of the new MMPI-2 Malingered Depression scale to individuals undergoing neuropsychological evaluation: Relative lack of relationship to secondary gain and failure on validity indices. *The Clinical Neuropsychologist, 20,* 541–551.

Sweet, J. J., Moberg, P. J., & Tovian, S. M. (1990). Evaluation of Wechsler Adult Intelligence Scale—Revised premorbid IQ formulas in clinical populations. *Psychological Assessment, 2,* 41–44.

Sweet, J. J., Nelson, N. W., & Moberg, P. J. (2006). The TCN/AACN 2005 "Salary Survey": Professional practices, beliefs, and incomes of U.S. neuropsychologists. *The Clinical Neuropsychologist, 20,* 325–364.

Sweet, J. J., Peck, E., Abramowitz, C., & Etzweiler, S. (2002). National Academy of Neuropsychology/Division 40 of the American Psychological Association practice survey of clinical neuropsychologists in the United States: Part

I. Practitioner and practice characteristics, professional activities and time requirements. *The Clinical Neuropsychologist, 16*, 109–127.

Swenson, W. M., Pearson, J. S., & Osborne, D. (1973). *An MMPI source book: Basic item, scale, and pattern data on 50,000 medical patients*. Minneapolis: University of Minnesota Press.

Tan, J. E., Slick, D. J., Strauss, E., & Hultsch, D. F. (2002). How'd they do it?: Malingering strategies on symptom validity tests. *The Clinical Neuropsychologist, 16*, 495–595.

Taylor, K. I., Salmon, D. P., Rice, V. A., Bondi, M. W., Hill, L. R., Ernesto, C. R., et al. (1996). Longitudinal examination of American National Adult Reading Rest (AMNART) performance in dementia of the Alzheimer type (DAT): Validation and correction based on degree of cognitive decline. *Journal of Clinical and Experimental Neuropsychology, 18*, 883–891.

Taylor, R. (1999). National Adult Reading Test performance in established dementia. *Archives of Gerontology and Geriatrics, 29*, 291–296.

Teichner, G., & Wagner, M. T. (2004). The Test of Memory Malingering (TOMM): Normative data from cognitively intact, cognitively impaired, and elderly patients with dementia. *Archives of Clinical Neuropsychology, 19*, 455–464.

Thomas, M. L., & Youngjohn, J. R. (2009). Let's not get hysterical: Comparing the MMPI-2 Validity, Clinical, and RC scales in TBI litigants tested for effort. *The Clinical Neuropsychologist, 23*, 1067–1084.

Thornhill, S., Teasdale, G. M., Murray, G. D., McEwen, J., Roy, C. W., & Penny, K. I. (2000). Disability in young people and adults one year after head injury: Prospective cohort study. *British Medical Journal, 320*, 1631–1635.

Tombaugh, T. N. (1996). *Test of Memory Malingering*. Toronto: Multi-Health Systems.

Torres, I. J., Boudreau, V. G., & Yatham, L. N. (2007). Neuropsychological functioning in euthymic bipolar disorder: A meta-analysis. *Acta Psychiatrica Scandinavica, 116*(Suppl, 434), 17–26.

Touradji, P., Manly, J. J., Jacobs, D. M., & Stern, Y. (2001). Neuropsychological test performance: A study of non-Hispanic white elderly. *Journal of Clinical and Experimental Neuropsychology, 23*, 643–649.

Trahan, D. E., Patterson, J., Quintana, J., & Biron, R. (1987). *The Finger Tapping Test: A reexamination of traditional hypotheses regarding normal adult performance*. Paper presented at the 15th Annual Meeting of the International Neuropsychological Society, Washington, DC.

Trahan, D. E., Ross, C. E., & Trahan, S. L. (2001). Relationship among postconcussional symptoms, depression, and anxiety in neurologically normal young adults and victims of mild brain injury. *Archives of Clinical Neuropsychology, 16*, 435–445.

Trueblood, W., & Schmidt, M. (1993). Malingering and other validity considerations in the neuropsychological evaluation of mild head injury. *Journal of Clinical and Experimental Neuropsychology, 15*, 578–590.

Tsanadis, J., Montoya, E., Hanks, R. A., Millis, S. R., Fichtenberg, N. L., & Axelrod, B. N. (2008). Brain injury severity, litigation status, and self-report of postconcussive symptoms. *The Clinical Neuropsychologist, 22*, 1080–1092.

Tsushima, W. T., Geling, O., & Fabrigas, J. (2011). Comparison of MMPI-2 validity scale scores of personal injury litigants and disability claimants. *The Clinical Neuropsychologist, 25*, 1403–1414.

Vagnini, V. L., Sollman, M. J., Berry, D. T. R., Granacher, R. P., Clark, J. A., Burton, R., et al. (2006). Known-groups cross-validation of the Letter Memory Test in a compensation-seeking mixed neurologic sample. *The Clinical Neuropsychologist, 20*, 289–304.

van Beilen, M., Griffioen, B. T., Gross, A., & Leenders, K. L. (2009). Psychological assessment of malingering in psychogenic neurological disorders and non-psychogenic neurological disorders: Relationship to psychopathology levels. *European Journal of Neurology, 16*, 1118–1123.

Vanderploeg, R. D., Curtiss, G., & Belander, H. G. (2005). Long-term neuropsychological outcomes following mild traumatic brain injury. *Journal of the International Neuropsychological Society, 11*, 228–236.

Vanderploeg, R. D., Curtiss, G., Luis, C. A., & Salazar, A. M. (2007). Long-term morbidities following self-reported mild traumatic brain injury. *Journal of Clinical and Experimental Neuropsychology, 29*, 585–598.

Vanderploeg, R. D., & Schinka, J. A. (1995). Predicting WAIS-R IQ premorbid ability: Combining subtest performance and demographic variable predictors. *Archives of Clinical Neuropsychology, 10*, 225–239.

Vanderploeg, R. D., Schinka, J. A., & Axelrod, B. N. (1996). Estimation of WAIS-R premorbid intelligence: Current ability and demographic data used in a best-performance fashion. *Psychological Assessment, 8*, 404–411.

Van Gorp, W. G., & Kalechstein, A. (2005). Threats to the validity of the interpretation and conveyance of forensic neuropsychological reports. *Journal of Forensic Neuropsychology, 4*, 67–77.

van Hout, M. S. E., Schmand, B., Wekking, E. M., & Deelman, B. G. (2006). Cognitive functioning in patients with suspected chronic toxic encephalopathy: Evidence for neuropsychological disturbances after controlling for insufficient effort. *Journal of Neurology, Neurosurgery and Psychiatry, 77*, 296–303.

Veazey, C. H., Wagner, A. L., Hays, J. R., & Miller, H. A. (2005). Validity of the Miller Forensic Assessment of Symptoms Test in psychiatric inpatients. *Psychological Reports, 96*, 771–774.

Veiel, H. O. F., & Koopman, R. F. (2001). The bias in regression-based indices of premorbid IQ. *Psychological Assessment, 13*, 356–368.

Verdelho A., Madureira, S., Ferro, J. M., Basile, A. M., Chabriat, H., Erkinjuntti, T., et al. (2007). Differential impact of cerebral white matter changes, diabetes, hypertension and stroke on cognitive performance among non-disabled elderly: The LADIS study. *Journal of Neurology, Neurosurergy, and Psychiatry, 78*, 1325–1330.

Vickery, C. D., Berry, D. T. R., Dearth, C. S., Vagnini, V. L., Baser, R. E., Cragar, D. E., et al.. (2004). Head injury and the ability to feign neuropsychological deficits. *Archives of Clinical Neuropsychology, 19*, 37–48.

Victor, T. L., & Boone, K. B. (2007). Identification of feigned mental retardation. In K. B. Boone (Ed.), *Assessment of feigned cognitive impairment: A neuropsychological perspective* (pp. 310"345). New York: Guilford Press.

Victor, T. L., Boone, K. B., Serpa, J. G., Buehler, J., & Ziegler, E. A. (2009). Interpreting the Meaning of Multiple Symptom Validity Test Failure. *The Clinical Neuropsychologist, 23,* 297–313.

Victor, T. L., Kulick, A. D., & Boone, K. B. (in press-a). Methods for assessment noncredible presentation in domains other than memory in cases of mild traumatic brain injury: Part I. Attention, processing speed, language and visuospatial/perceptual function. In D. A. Carone & S. S. Bush (Eds.), *Mild traumatic brain injury: Symptom validity assessment and malingering.* New York: Springer.

Victor, T. L., Kulick, A. D., & Boone, K. B. (in press-b). Methods for assessment noncredible presentation in domains other than memory in cases of mild traumatic brain injury: Part II. Motor/sensory function, executive function and test batteries. In D. A. Carone & S. S. Bush (Eds.), *Mild traumatic brain injury: Symptom validity assessment and malingering.* New York: Springer.

Vitacco, M. J., Rogers, R., Gabel, J., & Munizza, J. (2007). An evaluation of malingering screens with competency to stand trial patients: A known-groups comparison. *Law and Human Behavior, 31,* 249–260.

Waldstein, S. R., Ryan, C. M., Jennings, J. R., Muldoon, M. F., & Manuck, S. B. (1997). Self-reported levels of anxiety do not predict neuropsychological performance in healthy men. *Archives of Clinical Neuropsychology, 12,* 567–574.

Walker, A. J., Batchelor, J., & Shores, A. (2009). Effects of education and cultural background on performance on WAIS-III, WAIS-R, and WMS-R measures: Systematic review. *Australian Psychologist, 44,* 216–223.

Walker, A. J., Batchelor, J., Shores, E. A., & Jones, M. (2010). Effects of cultural background on WAIS-III and WMS-III performances after moderate-severe traumatic brain injury. *Australian Psychologist, 45,* 112–122.

Walters, G. L., & Clopton, J. R. (2000). Effect of symptom information and validity scale information on the malingering of depression on the MMPI-2. *Journal of Personality Assessment, 75,* 183–199.

Wang, E. W., Rogers, R., Giles, C. L., Diamond, P. M., Herrington-Wang, L. E., & Taylor, E. R. (1997). A pilot study of the Personality Assessment Inventory (PAI) in corrections: Assessment of malingering, suicide risk, and aggression in male inmates. *Behavioral Sciences and the Law, 15,* 469–482.

Wang, R. C. K. (2001). Base rate of post-concussion symptoms among normal people and its neuropsychological correlates. *Clinical Rehabilitation, 15,* 266–273.

Wang, Y., Chan, R. C. K., & Deng, Y. (2006). Examination of postconcussion-like symptoms in healthy university students: Relationships to subjective and objective neuropsychological function performance. *Archives of Clinical Neuropsychology, 21,* 339–347.

Watkins, C., Campbell, V., Nieberding, R., & Hallmark, R. (1995). Contemporary practice of psychological assessment by clinical psychologists. *Professional Psychology: Research and Practice, 26,* 54–60.

Watt, K. J., & O'Carroll, R. E. (1999). Evaluation methods for estimating premorbid intellectual ability in closed head injury. *Journal of Neurology, Neurosurgery, and Psychiatry, 66,* 474–479.

Wechsler, D. (2001). *Wechsler Test of Adult Reading: Manual*. San Antonio, TX: Psychological Corporation.

Weiss, R. A., Rosenfeld, B., & Farkas, M. R. (2011). The utility of the Structured Interview of Reported Symptoms in a sample of individuals with intellectual disabilities. *Assessment, 18*, 284–290.

Whiteside, D., Wald, D., & Busse, M. (2011). Classification accuracy of multiple visual spatial measures in the detection of suspect effort. *The Clinical Neuropsychologist, 25*, 287–301.

Whittaker, R., Kemp, S., & House, A. (2008). Illness perceptions and outcome in mild head injury: A longitudinal study. *Journal of Neurology, Neurosurgery and Psychiatry, 78*, 644–646.

Whiteside, D. M., Clinton, C., Diamonti, C., Stroemel, J., White, C., Zimberoff, A., et al. (2010). Relationship between suboptimal cognitive effort and the clinical scales of the Personality Inventory. *The Clinical Neuropsychologist, 24*, 315–325.

Whiteside, D. M., Dunbar-Mayer, P., & Waters, D. (2009). Relationship between TOMM performance and PAI validity scales in a mixed clinical scale. *The Clinical Neuropsychologist, 23*, 523–533.

Whitney, K. A., Davis, J. J., Shepard, P. H., & Herman, S. M. (2008). Utility of the Response Bias Scale (RBS) and other MMPI-2 validity scales in predicting TOMM performance. *Archives of Clinical Neuropsychology, 23*, 777–786.

Whittaker, R., Kemp, S., & House, A. (2007). Illness perceptions and outcome in mild head injury: A longitudinal study. *Journal of Neurology, Neurosurgery and Psychiatry, 78*, 644–646.

Widows, M. R., & Smith, G. P. (2005). *Structured Inventory of Malingered Symptomatology*. Odessa, FL: Psychological Assessment Resources.

Wiens, A. N., Bryan, J. E., & Crossen, J. R. (1993). Estimating WAIS-R FSIQ from the National Adult Reading Test-Revised in normal subjects. *The Clinical Neuropsychologist, 7*, 70–84.

Wierzbicki, M. (1997). Use of subtle and obvious scales to detect faking on the MCMI-II. *Journal of Clinical Psychology, 53*, 421–426.

Wiggins, E. C., & Brandt, J (1988). The detection of simulated amnesia. *Law and Human Behavior, 12*, 57–78.

Wilkinson, J. S. (1993). *Wide Range Achievement Test–3*. Wilmington, DE: Wide Range.

Williams, J. M. (1997). The prediction of premorbid memory ability. *Archives of Clinical Neuropsychology, 12*, 745–756.

Willshire, D., Kinsella, G., & Prior, M. (1991). Estimating WAIS-R IQ from the national adult reading test: A cross-validation. *Journal of Clinical and Experimental Neuropsychology, 13*, 204–216.

Wingo, A. P., Wingo, T. S., Harvey, P. D., & Baldessarini, R. J. (2009). Effects of lithium on cognitive performance: A meta-analysis. *Journal of Clinical Psychiatry, 70*, 1588–1597.

Wisdom, N. M., Callahan, J. L., & Shaw, T. G. (2010). Diagnostic utility of the Structured Inventory of Malingered Symptomatology to detect malingering in a forensic sample. *Archives of Clinical Neuropsychology, 25*, 118–125.

Wolfe, P. L., Millis, S. R., Hanks, R., Fichtenberg, N., Larrabee, G. J., & Sweet, J. J. (2010). Effort indicators within the California Verbal Learning Test–II (CVLT-II). *The Clinical Neuropsychologist, 24,* 153–168.

Woltersdorf, M. A. (2005, October). *FBS in clinical and forensic practice sample in Midwest.* Poster presented at the 25th Annual Conference of the National Academy of Neuropsychology, Tampa, FL.

Wortzel, H.S., Kraus, M. F., Filley, C. M., Anderson, C. A., & Arciniegas, D. B. (2011). Diffusion tensor imaging in mild traumatic brain injury litigation. *Journal of the American Academy of Psychiatry and the Law, 39,* 511–523.

Wrightson, P., & Gronwall, D. (1981). Time off work and symptoms after minor head injury. *Injury, 12,* 445–454.

Wrobel, N. H., & Wrobel, T. A. (1996). The problem of assessing brain damage in psychiatric samples: Use of personality variables in prediction of WAIS-R scores. *Archives of Clinical Neuropsychology, 11,* 625–635.

Wygant, D. B., Anderson, J., Sellbom, M., Rapier, J., Allgeier, L, & Granacher, R. (2011). Association of the MMPI-2 Restructured Form (MMPI-2-RF) validity scales with structured malingering criteria. *Psychological Injury and Law, 4,* 13–23.

Wygant, D. B., Ben-Porath, Y. S., Arbisi, P. A., Berry, D. T. R., Freeman, D. B., et al. (2009). Examination of the MMPI-2 Restructured Form (MMPI-2-RF) validity scales in civil forensic settings: Findings from simulation and known group designs. *Archives of Clinical Neuropsychology, 24,* 671–680.

Wygant, D. B., Sellbom, M., Gervais, R. O., Ben-Porath, Y. S., Stafford, K. P., Freeman, D. B., et al. (2010). Further validation of the MMPI-2 and MMPI-2-RF Response Bias Scale: Findings from disability and criminal forensic settings. *Psychological Assessment, 22,* 745–756.

Yantz, C., & McCaffrey, R. J. (2005). Effects of a supervisor's observation on memory test performance of the examinee: Third party observer effect confirmed. *Journal of Forensic Neuropsychology, 4,* 27–38.

Youngjohn, J. R., Davis, D., & Wolf, I. (1997). Head injury and the MMPI-2: Paradoxical severity effects and the influence of litigation, *Psychological Assessment, 9,* 177–184.

Youngjohn, J. R., Lees-Haley, P., & Binder, L. M. (1999). Comment: Warning malingerers produces more sophisticated malingering. *Archives of Clinical Neuropsychology, 14,* 511–515.

Youngjohn, J. R., Wershba, R., Stevenson, M., Sturgeon, J., & Thomas, M. L. (2011). Independent validation of the MMPI-2-RF Somatic/Cognitive and Validity scales in TBI litigants tested for effort. *The Clinical Neuropsychologist, 25,* 463–476.

Yucel, B. E., Pantelis, C., & Berk, M. (2011). Meta-analytic review of neurocognition in bipolar II disorder. *Acta Psychiatrica Scandinavica, 123,* 165–174.

Zakzanis, K. K., Campbell, Z., & Jovanovski, D. (2007). The neuropsychology of ecstasy (MDMA) use: A quantative review. *Human Psychopharmacology: Clinical and Experimental, 22,* 427–435.

Zakzanis, K. K., & Jeffay, E. (2011). Neurocognitive variability in high-functioning individuals: Implications for the practice of clinical neuropsychology. *Psychological Reports, 108,* 290–300.

Ziegler, E. A., Boone, K. B., Victor, T. L., & Zeller, M. (2008a). *The specificity of digit span effort indicators in patients with poor math abilities.* Poster presented at the 6th Annual Conference American Academy of Clinical Neuropsychology, Boston.

Ziegler, E. A., Boone, K. B., Victor, T. L., & Zeller, M. (2008b). *The specificity of the Dot Counting Test in patients with poor math abilities.* Poster presented at the 6th Annual Conference American Academy of Clinical Neuropsychology, Boston.

Index

Page numbers in *italic* refer to figures or tables.